COMMUNICATING HOPE
and RESILIENCE
ACROSS *the* LIFESPAN

LIFESPAN COMMUNICATION

Children, Families, and Aging

Thomas J. Socha
GENERAL EDITOR

Vol. 4

The Lifespan Communication series
is part of the Peter Lang Media and Communication list.
Every volume is peer reviewed and meets
the highest quality standards for content and production.

PETER LANG
New York • Bern • Frankfurt • Berlin
Brussels • Vienna • Oxford • Warsaw

COMMUNICATING HOPE *and* RESILIENCE ACROSS *the* LIFESPAN

EDITED BY *Gary A. Beck*
AND *Thomas J. Socha*

PETER LANG
New York • Bern • Frankfurt • Berlin
Brussels • Vienna • Oxford • Warsaw

Library of Congress Cataloging-in-Publication Data

Communicating hope and resilience across the lifespan /
edited by Gary A. Beck, Thomas J. Socha.
pages cm. — (Lifespan communication: children, families, and aging; vol. 4)
Includes bibliographical references and indexes.
1. Communication in families. 2. Hope. 3. Resilience (Personality trait).
I. Beck, Gary A. II. Socha, Thomas J.
HQ734.C6417   306.87—dc23   2014048947
ISBN 978-1-4331-2493-8 (hardcover)
ISBN 978-1-4331-2492-1 (paperback)
ISBN 978-1-4539-1520-2 (e-book)
ISSN 2166-6466 (print)
ISSN 2166-6474 (online)

Bibliographic information published by **Die Deutsche Nationalbibliothek**.
Die Deutsche Nationalbibliothek lists this publication in the "Deutsche
Nationalbibliografie"; detailed bibliographic data are available
on the Internet at http://dnb.d-nb.de/.

On the cover: *Sphagnum flexuosum* is mainly a northern hemisphere moss,
featuring a complex cell structure that allows it to retain water and air for survival
in a variety of weather conditions. The ability to demonstrate resilience in drier
or wetter conditions makes this moss a valuable part of its surrounding ecosystem.
Demonstrating hope and promise throughout its lifespan, sphagnum moss
also serves a variety of healing, fertilizing, and sanitizing purposes.
(http://www.theplantencyclopedia.org/wiki/Sphagnum)

© 2015 Peter Lang Publishing, Inc., New York
29 Broadway, 18th floor, New York, NY 10006
www.peterlang.com

All rights reserved.
Reprint or reproduction, even partially, in all forms such as microfilm,
xerography, microfiche, microcard, and offset strictly prohibited.

Contents

Series Editor's Preface vii
Acknowledgments ix
Foreword xi
    Anita Vangelisti

Chapter One. Embracing the Insights of "Murphy":
    New Frontiers of Communication, Hope, and Resilience
    Across the Lifespan 1
      Gary A. Beck and Thomas J. Socha

Section I: Contributing Processes

Chapter Two. On Being (and Becoming) Mindful:
    One Pathway to Greater Resilience 15
      Valerie Manusov and Jacquelyn Harvey-Knowles

Chapter Three. "We Could Sure Use a Laugh":
    Building Hope and Resilience Through Humorous Communication 34
      Rachel L. DiCioccio

Chapter Four. Fostering Hope in a Hurtful World:
    The Role of Communication in Promoting Hope
    and Resilience in the Face of Difficult Experiences 53
      Rachel M. McLaren and Joshua Pederson

Chapter Five. Unfolding the Transgression Scene:
    From Distress to Hope and Resilience 75
      Sandra Metts and Bryan Asbury

Section II: Contexts

Chapter Six. (Re)Envisioning Hope & Resilience
    in U.S. and Norwegian Prisons 97
      Brittany L. Peterson and Tim P. McKenna-Buchanan

Chapter Seven. Employment Transitions in the Aftermath
of Economic Collapse: Emerging and Older Adults 119
    Gary A. Beck, Ashley M. Poole, and Lisa M. Ponche

Chapter Eight. Resilience, Work, and Family
Communication Across the Lifespan 138
    Patrice M. Buzzanell and Suchitra Shenoy-Packer

Chapter Nine. Fear of the Unknown, Hope for the Unseen:
Resilience of Child Soldiers in Uganda, East Africa 156
    Erik W. Green

Chapter Ten. When All Seems Lost:
Building Hope Through Communication After Natural Disasters 176
    Andy J. Merolla

Chapter Eleven. The State of Cancer Care Communication
Across the Lifespan: The Role of Resilience, Hope,
and Decision-making 195
    Lisa Sparks, Veronica Hefner, and Amy H. Rogeness

Section III: Imparting Hope and Resilience

Chapter Twelve. Life's "War Stories": Accounts of Resilience and Hope 219
    Thomas J. Socha and Alfredo Torres

Chapter Thirteen. Fostering Civic Resilience and Hope
Through Communication Activism Education 235
    David L. Palmer and Lawrence R. Frey

About the Editors and Contributors 259
Authors Index 261
Subject Index 277

Series Editor's Preface

This latest volume in the *Lifespan Communication: Children, Families, and Aging* series focuses on a highly significant topic that faces everyone across the lifespan—using messages to manage life's myriad adversities. From serious illness, to natual disasters, to wars, and more, humans turn to communication as a major source of strength to help us to bounce back and to keep on growing and thriving. Dr. Gary Beck, a leading communication resilience researcher, has assembled a stellar group of communication scholars who collectively begin to shed light on communication pathways to resilience and hope.

Like all of the volumes in the *Lifespan Communication* series, I sincerely desire this volume to spur much discussion, motivate research, and inspire teachers and educators to create communication lessons and applications with an eye to using communication as a source of lifespan empowerment.

–Thomas J. Socha

Acknowledgments

There are many people that I recognize as important contributors to my own resilience process and sources of hope: My wife Tori, family, and my close collegues who I am lucky to consider true friends. In particular, my co-editor Tom Socha has been an endless advocate for strength-based communication practices cast across the lifespan, and his encouraging dialogue and provocative questions helped fuel many of the important contributions this volume strives to emphasize within the field. I would also like to acknowledge Anita Vangelisti for her ongoing mentorship, thoughtful feedback, and enduring patience with a young scholar throughout the development and exploration of this subject area. Finally, a special thanks to all of the chapter contributors for going above and beyond, and especially those who reached out with additional curiousities and ideas for future projects as we continue to explore these promising areas of research.

–GAB

First, the lion's share of accolades for this volume go to Dr. Gary Beck. He is an incredibly bright, rising communication star who cares deeply that his work matters not just to advancing the scholarly literature, but more importantly that it can help all who need a communication boost. He is exceedingly hardworking and always willing to go the extra distance; a pure joy to count as my colleague and friend. Second, my thanks to the many authors who answered Gary Beck's clarion call for research on this most important and essential front of positive lifespan communication. It is further testament to Gary Beck's key leadership on this topic that many of those whose work appears in this volume are counted among the who's who of the communication field. Finally, I want to thank Mary Savigar and all of the good folks at Peter Lang International Publishers for supporting this volume as well as the *Lifespan Communication: Children, Families, and Aging* book series.

–TJS

• FOREWORD •

Communication, Hope, and Resilience: Challenges and Promises

Anita L. Vangelisti
University of Texas at Austin

What enables some people to endure, and even thrive, as they walk through difficult or traumatic experiences while others stumble and fall? This question has been asked by theorists, practitioners, and laypeople. It has generated volumes of research, spawned therapeutic programs, and plagued those who manage to flourish while they watch their friends, neighbors, or siblings languish. On the surface, the answer is easy: Some people are more resilient and more hopeful than others. Dig a little deeper, though, and the answer becomes quite complex.

Conceptualizing Hope and Resilience

Hope and resilience are not easy concepts to master. As evidenced by the chapters that make up *Communicating Hope and Resilience Across the Lifespan*, they can be conceived in a number of different ways. The majority of the literature on hope and resilience examines the concepts at the level of *individuals*. In other words, most research looks at hope and resilience as traits or qualities that people possess—either temporarily or on an ongoing basis. Snyder's (2000) hope theory is a case in point. Snyder defines hope as individuals' belief that they can find pathways to achieve their goals and that they have the motivation to use those pathways. Similarly, Bonnano's (2004, 2006) work on resilience describes the concept in terms of people's ability to maintain a relatively stable trajectory of healthy functioning after they experience a traumatic event. Both bodies of work characterize hope and resilience as dynamic and suggest that they reside with, or are enacted by, individuals.

Another way to study hope and resilience is at the level of *dyads* or *relationships*. Partners in friendships, romantic associations, or work relationships can be hopeful or resilient together, as a unit. Acknowledging that relational partners are interdependent (see Kenny, Kashy, & Cook, 2006), this view conceptualizes each partner's hope or resilience as influencing that of the other partner. The effect of dyadic or relational hope or resilience, thus, can be assessed separate from, and might be greater or less than, the hope or resilience of the individuals who make up the dyad. Jordan (2006) offers a compelling rationale for looking at dyadic or relational resilience from the perspective of a therapist, arguing that relational resilience is essential to individuals' psychological, emotional, and physical well-being. If dyads can be hopeful or resilient, then so can *groups*. Families, groups of friends, and even societies can be seen as more or less hopeful or resilient. Like relational hope or resilience, the hope or resilience of a group or system involves the mutual influence of the individuals who are members of the group. It also involves the interplay of the group's subsystems. Because systemic hope or resilience is defined by numerous interdependent relationships, studying these two concepts at the group level is particularly complex. Indeed, nearly two decades ago, Walsh (1996) commented on this complexity and called for researchers and practitioners to confront the challenges involved in studying family resilience. She noted two reasons why researchers and practitioners need to take on these challenges: "(a) to identify potential relationship resources within and beyond the immediate household, throughout the kinship network and community; and (b) to attend to the temporal congruence of experiences over the life cycle and across generations" (p. 4). The reasons articulated by Walsh clearly apply to the study of resilience in a broad range of groups. Examining the resilience of group systems generates important information about relational resources within and outside the groups, how the groups go about attaining those resources, and how the experiences of group members change and are sustained over the life course.

Whether defined in terms of individuals, dyads, or groups, hope and resilience can be studied as antecedents, processes, or outcomes. Much of the literature examines hope and resilience as antecedents of—or precursors to—other variables. For instance, researchers might identify individuals, couples, or families who have been through a traumatic event and compare the ways those who are more and less resilient cope with the stress they have experienced. These studies position hope and resilience as characteristics or sets of skills that individuals, relationships, or groups possess prior to the onset of a stressor. The personality trait of hardiness (Kobasa, Maddi, & Kahn, 1982) is an example of such a characteristic. Individuals who are hardy tend to be more confident and better able to use social support to deal with stress than are those who are less hardy (Florian, Mikulincer, & Taubman, 1995).

Alternatively, hope and resilience can be conceived as processes. Scholars who conceptualize hope and resilience as processes define the concepts as qualities that are enacted by individuals, relational partners, or group members—often in the face of a traumatic event. The lead editor of this volume, Gary Beck, has described resilience in this way. Beck (2010) examined the resilience of romantic couples who experienced job loss. He developed a measure of interpersonal resilience that assesses the ways partners interact to generate resilience in their relationship and found that certain aspects of partners' communication mediated the association between job loss and relational qualities. Beck's participants, in short, jointly created resilience through their social interactions.

Yet another way to study hope and resilience is as outcomes. Because hope and resilience typically are seen as desirable, researchers and practitioners have set out to identify their predictors. What are the qualities, experiences, and processes that engender hope and resilience? Scholars have examined versions of this question using a variety of samples ranging from members of mental health agencies (Hodges, Hardiman, & Segal, 2003), to sexually abused adolescents (Williams & Nelson-Gardell, 2002) to disaster survivors (Bonanno, Galea, Bucciarelli, & Vlahov, 2007). Although communication processes are not included in these studies as often as demographic and social-structural variables, when they are included they are almost always key predictors of resilience. The social support people receive, the positive interactions they engage in, and the ability of individuals to express their thoughts and feelings about a traumatic event serve as resources or coping mechanisms that people employ to foster hope and resilience.

As suggested by the title of the current volume, the questions researchers ask about communicating hope and resilience and the findings generated by these questions are likely to be influenced by lifespan variables. Children certainly have different hopes than do adults and the processes that influence children's ability to hope may differ from those that influence the ability in adults. In a similar vein, the variables that encourage or discourage resilience in children and adolescents may differ from those that affect resilience in their adult parents. Furthermore, the ways relational partners and group members enact hope and resilience probably are affected by their age, the length of their relationship, and their stage in the life cycle. All of these variations, and others, are an indication of the complexity researchers must grapple with in studying hope and resilience. Decisions about whether to examine hope or resilience at the individual, dyadic, or group level—and whether to study hope and resilience as antecedents, processes, or outcomes—are likely to depend, in part, on the stage of the lifespan that researchers are investigating.

The Current Volume

The collection of chapters that Gary Beck and Thomas Socha have put together for the current volume reflect the complexity—and the promise—of scholarship on the communication of hope and resilience.

Beck and Socha open the volume with a chapter that frames research and theory on hope, resilience, and communication. In this first chapter, the volume editors use Murphy's Law ("Whatever can go wrong, will go wrong") as a springboard to explain their rationale for the book. They then carefully describe three assumptions that are foundational to theory on hope and resilience. Beck and Socha close their chapter by showing how existing theoretical work on hope and resilience can be used to highlight the role of communication in people's ability to function and manage stress.

Chapters Two through Five take many of the conceptual issues outlined by Beck and Socha and apply them to several different cognitive and affective processes related to hope and resilience. For instance, in Chapter Two, Manusov and Harvey-Knowles discuss how mindfulness promotes resilience. The authors begin by describing the ways mindfulness has been conceptualized by researchers and practitioners. They then examine research on mindfulness and show how the practice of mindfulness can positively influence health as well as relationship outcomes. Manusov and Harvey-Knowles round out their chapter with a description of various methods employed to assess mindfulness and then conclude with a discussion of some of the most well-known mindfulness training programs.

In Chapter Three, DiCioccio approaches hope and resilience through humorous communication. While the link between humor and both hope and resilience seems intuitive, DiCioccio acknowledges that humor can be used in positive and negative ways. She introduces several theories and models that are employed to explain how humor functions and shows how humor theory is associated with individuals' hope and resilience. DiCioccio also reviews research demonstrating that humor can function to create or encourage hope and resilience by promoting positive affect. This positive affect serves as a resource for individuals as well as a means for affiliating with others across the lifespan.

While Chapter Three emphasizes the association between positive affect and both hope and resilience, Chapter Four takes a very different approach. Specifically, the authors of Chapter Four, McLaren and Pederson, focus on hurt feelings. They review research on hurt and explore how hurt feelings can encourage hope, resilience, and personal growth. The authors discuss the challenges that people face in fostering hope and resilience after they have been hurt and after they have hurt others. They note the complexities associated with these challenges, discuss individual and relational variables that protect people from the impact of hurt, and describe strategies that individuals might use to repair their relationship following a hurtful episode.

The issues raised in Chapter Five follow nicely from those raised in Chapter Four. In Chapter Five, Metts and Ashbury discuss interpersonal transgressions. They provide a detailed description of transgressions and how transgressions are managed in close relationships through communication. The authors then turn to the literature on forgiveness. They define forgiveness and explain the ways forgiveness can function to modify the effects of transgressions. Metts and Ashbury tie their chapter together by showing how forgiveness, hope, and resilience can operate to help couples when they experience relationship transgressions.

Chapters Six through Eleven shift from concentrating on cognitive and affective processes associated with hope and resilience to focusing on different contexts in which hope and resilience may occur. Some of these settings are likely to be familiar to readers (e.g., the intersection of work and family life), whereas others are likely to be quite foreign (e.g., prison). What is common to these contexts is that all of them are influenced by, and constituted through, communication. As such, the authors argue that hope and resilience in each of these very different settings are accomplished through social interaction.

For instance, in Chapter Six, Peterson and McKenna describe hope and resilience in U.S. and Norwegian prisons. They introduce their chapter by providing background information on prisons and prisoners and by discussing how hope might be enacted in prison settings. The authors then juxtapose the ways hope and resilience manifest in U.S. and Norwegian prisons. The contrast they provide is striking. Peterson and McKenna use a very rich data set to show how the material and social aspects of prisons function to encourage (or discourage) hope and resilience in these two different social systems.

In Chapter Seven, Beck, Poole, and Ponche turn to a more familiar setting—the U.S. workforce—but deal with a situation that most people see as both unfamiliar and stressful. Specifically, the authors examine the employment transitions experienced by emerging adults and older adults in the aftermath of the 2008 economic collapse. They use theory on hope and resilience to explore the challenges faced by these two groups as well as the strategies they might employ to deal with those challenges. Beck and his coauthors also examine the unique qualities of each group that likely affect the way they navigate their employment transitions.

Buzzanell and Shenoy-Packer also look at individuals and work, but take a step back and more generally analyze work-family processes and resilience across the lifespan. They argue that work-family communication is a "key site" for the development and maintenance of resilience. These authors define resilience as a process that is constituted through communication and show how work-family processes demonstrate family members' resilience. Buzzanell and Shenoy-Packer outline five processes that can characterize resilience and offer a fascinating agenda for future research that includes examining power and authority in resilience processes as well as the co-production of resilience linked to work-family communication.

In Chapter Nine, Green examines power in a very different setting and with a very different group of people. He describes the stories of 22 individuals who were abducted as children from villages in Uganda by the Lord's Resistance Army. Green's goal in telling these stories is to illuminate the hope and resilience of those who were abducted both in terms of their experiences as abducted child soldiers and as free people who had returned to their villages. On his way to accomplishing this goal, the author provides a clear rationale for his method and carefully defines his role as a researcher and as a representative of—and for—his participants.

Merolla, like Green, analyzes hope and resilience associated with human trauma. The trauma described by Merolla, however, is caused by natural disasters. Merolla starts his chapter by examining research on the influence of natural disasters on individuals, families, and communities. He then shows how hope is created through communication and describes how it facilities coping and resilience. This author argues that individuals' hope—both before and after a natural disaster—buffers stressors, shapes goals, and promotes constructive recollections of traumatic events associated with the disaster.

In Chapter Eleven, Sparks, Hefner, and Rogeness turn readers' attention to healthcare settings as they analyze the role of hope and resilience in communication related to cancer. The authors review research on a broad range of variables that are likely to affect communication with cancer patients across the lifespan. They also examine how these variables may influence family members who are related to cancer patients. Sparks and her colleagues show how an understanding of the barriers to communication experienced by patients may enable researchers and practitioners to construct messages of hope and resilience that improve patients' well-being at every stage of life.

The "battles" engaged by people who have cancer are one of many types of war stories described by Socha and Torres in Chapter Twelve. These authors offer readers a characterization of war stories that addresses war in the traditional sense of the word (e.g., World War II, Vietnam), as well as the personal wars and battles that people wage in their everyday lives (e.g., with cancer, severe weather, or crime). Socha and Torres use Burke's (1969) dramatic pentad to analyze how accounts of resilience during war can serve as a means to promote hope. They argue that war stories are a form of communication that is employed across the lifespan to facilitate hope and resilience and, as such, that the stories represent an important area for future research.

The volume closes with a chapter by Palmer and Frey that focuses on the ways in which communication activism pedagogy can promote resilience and hope. The authors start by providing readers with a clear description of communication activism pedagogy, noting that its purpose is to draw students' attention to, educate them about, and encourage them to change social injustices such as poverty, racial discrimination, and gender violence. They then examine the connections between communication activism pedagogy and both hope and resilience, and explore the influences those connections can have on teachers, students, and community members. Palmer and Frey also note that communication activism pedagogy promotes civic hope and resilience and, as such, offers a means to challenge the conditions of unjust systems.

As evidenced by this brief review, each of the contributors to the present volume approaches the study of hope and resilience in a different way. They examine different individuals, relationships, and groups. Some treat hope and resilience as predictors, others treat them as processes, and yet others as outcomes. Some focus on a specific stage in the lifespan, others examine multiple stages. At the same time, the contributors share a common emphasis on communication. For these authors, social interaction is essential to hope and resilience. The agreement reflected in the current volume on the role of communication holds great promise for unravelling some of the complex challenges associated with studying hope and resilience.

References

Beck, G. A. (2010). *Interpersonal resilience in romantic relationships.* Unpublished doctoral dissertation. University of Texas at Austin, Austin, TX.

Bonanno, G. A. (2004). Loss, trauma, and human resilience: Have we underestimated the human capacity to thrive after extremely aversive events. *American Psychologist, 59,* 20–28.

Bonanno, G. A. (2005). Resilience in the face of potential trauma. *Current directions in psychological science, 14,* 135–138.

Bonanno, G. A., Galea, S., Bucciarelli, A., & Vlahov, D. (2007). What predicts psychological resilience after disaster? The role of demographics, resources, and life stress. *Journal of Consulting and Clinical Psychology, 75,* 671–682.

Florian, V., Mikulincer, M., & Taubman, G. (1995). Does hardiness contribute to mental health during a stressful real-life situation? The roles of appraisal and coping. *Journal of Personality and Social Psychology, 68,* 687–695.

Hodges, J. Q., Hardiman, E. R., & Segal, S. P. (2003). Predictors of hope among members of mental health self-help agencies. *Social Work in Mental Health, 2,* 1–16.

Jordan, J. V. (2006). Relational resilience in girls. In S. Goldstein & R. B. Brooks (Eds.), *Handbook of resilience in children* (pp. 79-90). New York, NY: Springer.

Kenny, D. A., Kashy, D. A., & Cook, W. (2006). *Dyadic data analysis*. New York: Guilford Press.

Kobasa, S. C., Maddi, S. R.., & Kahn, S. (1982). Hardiness and health: A prospective study. *Journal of Personality and Social Psychology, 42*, 168-177.

Patterson, J. M. (2002). Understanding family resilience. *Journal of Clinical Psychology, 58*, 233-246.

Snyder, C. R. (Ed.). (2000). *Handbook of hope: Theories, measures, applications*. San Diego, CA: Academic Press.

Walsh, F. (1996). The concept of family resilience: Crisis and challenge. *Family Process, 35*, 261-281.

Williams, J., & Nelson-Gardell, D. (2012). Predicting resilience in sexually abused adolescents. *Child Abuse & Neglect, 36*, 53-63.

• CHAPTER ONE •

Embracing the Insights of "Murphy": New Frontiers of Communication, Hope, and Resilience Across the Lifespan

Gary A. Beck
Thomas J. Socha
Old Dominion University

Murphy's law is a commonly expressed adage; "Whatever can go wrong, will go wrong." While most cannot help to say this phrase untainted by a dour tone, the story of its origin stands in stark positive contrast. Its namesake is World War II Air Force engineer, Captain Edward A. Murphy. The phrase is said to reflect one of the key principles that guides the careful process of fine-tuning the functioning of complex airplanes (Spark, 2006). The quality control that goes into aircraft design is a demanding and clearly essential process requiring high degrees of precision, regardless of outside pressures such as an ongoing war. Final responsibility for the optimal functioning of these modern miracles rests with teams of engineers, mechanics, and pilots who must tirelessly check and recheck their work with the understanding that even minor errors can lead to catastrophic losses of life and property. A pilot friend of the second author of this chapter summarized it this way, "There are no service stations in the sky." Although Murphy's mantra of imagining the worst and guarding against it is brought into particular relief in the production and maintenance of airplanes, it extends to all sorts of modern day vehicles from cars to elevators, as well as to medical procedures, the use of deadly force in war and law enforcement, human relationships, and much more. We contend that when seeking to bring about any significant outcome especially those dependent on a web of interconnected assumptions, procedures, and checks that it is wise for us to listen to Murphy.

Murphy's mantra invokes a special appreciation for the forces of chaos and change that are inherent in all of life's endeavors. Despite the best of intentions, honest motivations, and well-laid plans, flaws can emerge in design, function, and/or performance that require attention or "fixing." Embracing this way of thinking suggests an acceptance of imperfection as inescapable, where successful outcomes require active engagement in a process of revisions, and an open acceptance that despite our best efforts, we might have to return to the drawing table.

Consider the life and circumstances of Louis Zamperini: Olympian and World War II airman, subject of a popular book and movie. While even considering the significant challenges of Olympic competition, often most centered on are the 33 days he spent with fellow soldiers adrift at sea after a plane crash, only to be picked up by Japanese soldiers and taken to a prisoner-of-war camp. While he and his fellow soldiers developed strategies and camaraderie to manage the challenges they faced (the best they could), their ability to endure came from personal, social, and relational resources that undoubtedly existed prior to the circumstances. An attention to the spirit of Murphy's mantra informs not only the training of Louis and his fellow soldiers, but the shared values imparted by family and community growing up in small towns and inner cities. Despite geographic and economic differences, the common understanding is that we are better equipped for survival with each other, working for each other.

It is particularly fitting that we chose this common (albeit somewhat misunderstood) expression as a starting point for a volume where contributors gather to collectively begin to explore communication's role in resilience and hope across the lifespan. First, few would argue that throughout life there are unanticipated, unintended negative consequences; that is, "things go wrong": natural disasters, world-wide economic collapses, endless auto recalls, shaky confidence in relational institutions like marriage, expanding mobile media increasing isolation (Turkle, 2011), addictions, and much more. Such events can pose obstacles that range from minor disruptions in daily living to the loss of lives and property, to the destruction of entire communities as in post-Katrina New Orleans, to the untold loss of millions of lives as in WWII. While a fatalistic acceptance of Murphy's Law—an "Oh well, that's life" attitude—may seem expedient, on the positive side it is more prudent to heed Murphy's Law as a warning of the need to work toward minimizing pain and risk, while optimizing life's joys and rewards.

Second, the experience of when things "go wrong" is not exclusively negative. Unpredicted negative events, initially unwelcomed, have the potential to become learning experiences, resulting in a new lease on life, an appreciation of features initially outside of our perceptions, newfound connections in those who care to help, and perhaps even a new way of looking at things in general.

These watershed moments in life, these turning points, have the potential to be very important catalysts for personal growth and change. Importantly, an opportunity may present itself as a test, a test that a person may pass and feel more connected to some grander purpose for her or his life. As in the case of WWII veterans like Norwood Thomas of Virginia Beach, Virginia who was in the 501st Parachute Infantry Regiment, 101st Airborne that helped to liberate France on D-Day (Hixenbaugh, 2014). To the citizens of Normandy, France, especially those who were there for their arrival 70 years ago, Norwood and his fellow liberators are treated like aged, modern-day rock stars. And, the dwindling numbers of WWII vets like Thomas are grateful that someone still remembers and is appreciative for what they did for them on Omaha Beach in 1944—because as they continue to go about their daily lives they are unable to forget.

And third, this volume proposes a fresh, positive look at communication and its fundamental role in preventing and alleviating suffering in our world. Perhaps the purest biological need across all forms of life is the need to survive. However, we do not only seek to create future generations that just make it, rather we seek to strengthen ourselves and craft better lives for us and our offspring, that is, to thrive and flourish (Seligman, 2012). Cast this way, communication's role in societal development takes on a broader perspective: It goes beyond that of the outcomes of moments of interactions, examined as cross-sections, or "first order" reactions, toward communication's place in engineering better worlds that prompt "second order," anticipatory thinking. This approach is closely allied with the field of Applied Developmental Science (Lerner, Jacobs, & Wertlieb, 2005) where scholars from a growing number of fields accept that human development is life-long and use science as a means "to improve the life chances of the diverse infants, children, adolescents, families and communities of the world" (p. ix). Let's take a closer look at each of these foundational assumptions.

Foundational Assumptions

Murphy's perspective brings into focus at least three assumptions upon which future communication theorizing about resilience and hope can be built. First, when bad things happen communication can be a facilitating (or inhibiting) force in effectively managing bad things. Second, there is value in connection and communication when managing bad things. And, third, communicating resilience can be seen as "magic" and hope as "transformational."

Bad Things Happen

Experience teaches us that things do not always go as anticipated. Yet, by underemphasizing this fact, communication theorizing sometimes operates without a full sense of the ecological context of the worlds' in which we live. Or conversely, communication scholars zero in on moments of failure in isolation and how people react or respond to them. Relational development trajectories, for example, plot uniform incremental steps of increased interdependence, dialectics point to tensions in the dialogue we place within moments of exaggerated struggle. Specific communication behaviors are measured as *Band-Aids* to assess the impact of one versus another on some outcome variable. Survey cross-sections serve as indications of the importance of some phenomenon and corresponding communication behavior, while the ongoing flux of one's social life and personal needs are vastly more complicated. Socha (2009) argued that bad things happening is inevitable, but that taking a problems-approach is difficult and complex as numerous problems often occur at the same time. So instead of using communication to fix one problem at a time, or to plug leaks, it is better to use communication to build stronger structures that can stand the tests of time.

This volume touches on many bad things: war (Green, chapter 9; Socha & Torres, chapter 12), cancer (Sparks, chapter 11), relationship transgressions and hurt (McLaren & Pederson, chapter 4; Metts & Ashbury, chapter 5), involuntary unemployment (Beck, Poole, & Ponche, chapter 7), natural disasters (Merolla, chapter 10) and more. However, each seeks to begin to examine the role of communication and combinations of message strategies in building relationships and structures that have the potential to help us to bounce back from adversity.

Value of Connection and Communication

Access to resources, alternative perspectives, and a sense of personal and shared identity comes from our connection with others. The communication we use to reach out forges relationships and by extension communities. This interconnectedness is vital not only for day to day, routine functioning, but also corresponding changes with life circumstances as well. Relationships, fostered through communication, are composed of the utterances, dialogue, roles, and understandings reinforced through continued interaction. Therefore, the very building blocks of resilience-promoting responses end up constituting the relationships we develop by living our lives. And, on the front of hope, and following hope theory (Snyder, 2000), it is from others that we learn pathways thinking, that is, how to scale obstacles that impeded us, as well as realize that we are worthy of survival.

Those looking for concise-worded, specific messages of resilience or hope may be disappointed: The means by which communication contributes to either is more process-based and imbedded in context. Well-wishes, apologies, or even an uplifting speech gain meaning when considering the audience, the social, historical, and relational context, as well as the exigency for their creation. Additionally, utterances in isolation or retold devoid of the circumstance that prompted them (i.e., quoting out of context, or *contextomy*) may not retain the value they originally had to those who needed them. Instead, we posit that hope and resilience are fostered by the combination of positive, supportive, and meaningful interaction that is appropriate to the relationship and situation, as well as relevant to the stressor. Simply, there isn't likely a combination of magic words allow us to transcend, but a series of meanings created by features of our everyday discourse and the new paths we take as we navigate challenging circumstances.

While the value of communication and subsequent meaningful connection is imbedded in all the chapters, many call particular attention to the specific role that types of messages play in the process bolstering our responses to "bad things," as well as just making us happier. For example, humor can lift moods and relieve tension (DiCioccio, chapter 3), balance and boundaries can be effectively negotiated between work and family identities (Buzzanell & Shenoy-Packer, chapter 8), and our mindful presence throughout interaction with those closest can enrich those connections (more than we may realize) (Manusov & Harvey-Knowles, chapter 2). By emphasizing particular messages and uniquely communication phenomenon, we can gain a deeper appreciation regarding the centrality to communication in the resilience and hope processes. Overall, if demonstrating resilience or finding hope in the face of a challenging circumstance is most often a product of the meaningful connections we make with others, we see examples of how communication takes form toward this function in each of the chapters in this volume.

Resilience as "Magic," Hope as "Transformational"

The final foundational assumption ties directly into how phenomenal and at the same time taken for granted both resilience and hope can be. Ann Masten proposed the idea that resilience is in fact "ordinary magic" (2001), suggesting that our experience of resilience is hardwired into our experience of life. People display resilience on a daily basis, to the point that is more common than we think.

Consider how we only really notice resilience when it fails, either through the severity of the stressor (e.g., major illness diagnosis), the unexpectedness of the event (e.g., involuntary job loss), or both (e.g., severe car crash). Instead, as Masten and others would claim, people use their internal assets to accomplish challenging tasks, reach out to close others when necessary, and use additional external resources like loans, "expert" opinion on the Internet, or community or government agencies when the events exceed the threshold of what is "manageable."

While the instinct in this line of reasoning is to ponder about the conditions or circumstances that cause this "magic" to fail, there are more complete considerations: What does communication contribute to the process of resilience, or the ability of people to create these resilience patterns in their lives? And, if we can accept that bad (or at least unexpected) things are going to happen, how can we best prepare for them in positive ways?

This is where "hope" has potential to clarify ways forward. Rather than hope being situated in the land of dreams and wishful thinking, Hope theorists like Snyder suggest that hopeful thinking is emotionally and physically rewarding. Hopeful outcomes can be achieved by a clear sense of our goals, awareness of pathways or options toward achieving those goals, and agency or the belief and motivation that our efforts will push us toward those outcomes. Understanding where the process falters may create opportunities to revise the steps we take toward the lives we want.

Across the volume, the various chapters represent ways in which communication plays a vital role in enabling resilience and fostering hope. As the field digs deeper into a dialogue about these issues, we will also need to consider how we can educate future generations to create meaningful and lasting change in the worlds in which they live. Palmer and Frey (chapter 13) directly address this consideration, especially as educating future change leaders and inspiring others is truly a lifespan process.

To assist readers that are new to this line of thinking and introduce the chapters, the following sections will briefly clarify important details of resilience and hope theory, as well as how volume attempts to engage these ideas.

Foundational Theoretical Perspectives

It is our belief that the perspectives gained by resilience and hope theories provide additional insight into the role communication plays in human functioning and stressor management. While there are meaningful overlaps between hope and resilience, the following describes relevant background regarding each theoretical perspective.

Communication and Resilience Theory

Generally cast, resilience is the process of successful adaptation to adversity or stressors (Zautra, Hall, & Murray, 2008). Depending on the focus of study, researchers have investigated resilience as an individual trait (e.g., Block & Block, 1980), a dynamic process (Luthar et al., 2000; Buzzanell, 2010), or a desired outcome (Bonanno, 2004). Additional ecological conceptualizations cast an ecosystem's resilience as the capacity to absorb disturbances before meaningful changes occur in the system (Holling, Schilindler, Walker, & Roughgarden, 1995). Regardless of approach, we can consider resilience as evidenced by sustainability, recovery, or a combination of the two. If one thinks about the number of minute unanticipated changes that must occur in a given day as people interact and live their lives, daily functioning is some ways a micro-exercise of resilience: As mundane as it may feel at times, life isn't predictable in ways that don't require some degree of moment-by-moment improvisation. We strive to balance the system that comprises our life. Some of these experiential ripples are barely noticeable, while others threaten to capsize the boat.

And so our thoughts naturally move to these more significant events, and thus, the meaningful areas of inquiry as we consider resilience further: Effectively assessing risk or the stressor matters. Developmental scholars have examined risk factors to child development (e.g., abusive households, parenting, poverty), and despite initial emphasis on the demonstration of resilience as rare, people are more than capable of exceptional things, alternatively suggesting that resilience is common across the lifespan (Bonnano, 2004; Garmezy, 1991). Given the process of resilience is in fact common, what informs or contributes to this capacity to survive and (potentially) thrive?

If responding to adversity is universal, it must be acknowledged that the degree of response and the success of that response are not guaranteed. Thus, researchers have focused on different sources of protective (i.e., buffering) or promotive (i.e., compensatory or contributing) positive factors that help mitigate the experience of a stressor on relevant life outcomes. Cast across an ecological spectrum, factors include (but are not limited to): Trait *resiliency* (e.g., Block & Block, 1980), mental states like mindfulness (Manusov & Harvey-Knowles, chapter 2), emotional regulation, humor (DiCioccio, chapter 3), coping strategies (e.g., Bonnano & Mancini, 2008), social support, and community programs (Palmer & Frey, chapter 13). The literature associated with cataloging these positive factors further divides these into internally-based assets (e.g., intelligence, motivation), and externally-based resources (e.g., money, family, mentors, community). As anticipated, there are likely additive or synergistic effects of these assets and resources (e.g., Zimmerman, Rameriez,

Washienko, & Dyer, 1995), promoting wellbeing beyond what individual factors could do alone.

Thus clarifying the role positive resources play goes beyond just healthy or satisfying functioning. Indeed, many of the above listed assets and resources are surely beneficial to possess: However, what matters in regard to the presence of serious life stressors? If we accept that adversity is a part of everyday life, whether it is pleasant to acknowledge or not, shouldn't we have an interest in developing greater capacities for resilience? Developing the perspective of prevention (i.e., second order change) instead of merely intervention (i.e., first order change) (Watzlawcik, Weakland, & Fisch, 1974) opens up additional opportunities for communication scholars in their consideration of topics of study. Wilson & Gettings' (2012) excellent reframing of *stopping child abuse* to *nurturing children as assets* serves as a great example of shifting focus to programs that address problems before they manifest. In this regard, resilience isn't just *reactive*; it is inherently *proactive* in regards to understanding and managing stressors.

Communication and Hope Theory

In similar spirit, hope theory is derived from the search for the aspects of the individual and her/his behavior that contributes to overcoming obstacles and striving for goals. Snyder (1991) contributed the following definition: "Hope is a positive motivation state that is based on an interactively derived sense of successful a) agency (goal-directed energy), and b) pathways (planning to meet those goals)" (p. 287). If people are generally goal oriented, the capacity for them to realize those goals is derived from clarity about the goals themselves, the process associated with finding options for attaining that goal, and the requisite follow through. Evidence of hope cannot only be seen in daily talk and wishful thinking, but also in scholarship examining the role of hope in improved educational outcomes (Rand, Martin, & Shea, 2011; Snyder, 1999), as well as forms of relational functioning (Merolla, 2014).

Like resilience, the sources for our hopeful thinking come from a variety of places across our lifespan. As clarified in Snyder's (2002) *Elaborated Hope Model*, the origins of one's tendency to develop effective pathways ("waypower") and agency thinking ("willpower") starts in childhood and is reinforced through experiences later in life. Combined with one's trait-like emotional anchor point, this baseline approach helps inform a cost-benefit analysis of pursuing the goal in question. If worthwhile, the person pursues the goal by engaging in thoughts and actions toward achievement. Throughout this striving, iterative process, the person may experience a stressor, which may derail goal achievement. Eventual arrival at the goal, and thus successful management of the stressor, largely depends on competency at previous stages of the process.

Those that are deemed more competent at these various stages have been organized by an individual differences measurement of Trait Hope. "High hope" versus "low hope" individuals are able create goals that are extensions of previous experiences, approach goals with positive emotional mindsets, are attentive and mindful of the task at hand, and frame the experience of a stressor as a challenge (facilitating the development of alternate pathways and redirecting agency) (Snyder, Harris, et. al., 1991). A State Hope Scale was developed to account for variability in hopeful thinking given current experiences (Snyder et al., 1996). Similar to resilience thinking, hope proposes a process by which individuals approach goals, encounter stressors, and use resources or pathways to reach those goals.

Conclusion

While resilience and hope theory offer obvious potential for communication scholarship, there are still issues inherent to the concepts themselves that are "cause for pause." There is an established coping literature that looks at "stress management" as well as established coping processes. Our position is that investigation into living with life's stressors does not need to be directed down exclusively one path. The resilience and hope paradigms provide interesting alternative (and overlapping) vantage points, grounded in both ecological and practical phenomena.

The chapters in this volume highlight the variety of stressors that people may encounter in their lives. Some may seem more probable than others (e.g., health issues vs. particular kinds of natural disasters), where the need for resilience and hope is obvious for the people and communities most likely to be affected. What may be debatable is how if a stressor is required for resilience to be realized, or perceived obstacles to warrant a hope-fostering process, how serious do the consequences need to be? For instance is literal (or figurative) death required as a possible outcome to legitimize the experience of resilience? We can see this as true within those affected by natural disasters, war, poverty and crime, major health concerns, and domestic abuse, but what about those who overcome major transitions in their lives, such a temporary job loss, relational loss (i.e., divorce), or emotional trauma (e.g., social rejection, bullying). We can argue that those experiences too also feature "loss," especially as it relates to identity, and someone could very much mourn the "death" of a life they once knew, sense of identity, or innocence about the world. As Socha and Torres (this volume, chapter 12) highlight, we all have "war stories" to tell, of which some will involve war per se, but all of us have war stories broadly put where we have overcome significant obstacles and have lived to communicate about them.

The experience of resilience or hope that is required in war-torn Uganda, or the strength to rebuild a community decimated by a tsunami might be different than that required to get up after being bullied at school or the challenges of going through law school. In this way, the stressor informs not only the outcomes or goals worked toward (staying alive vs. feeling accepted), but also the type of resources that are appropriate to manage the stressor. In this way, communication research should then be as much an investigation of the stressor itself as it is about the overall process. We risk overlooking important lessons from the problem when we jump straight to how communication facilitates solutions.

In this spirit and across these circumstances, the chapters that follow present practical lessons for individuals, marriages, families, and relationship experts, as well as a variety of other practitioners. The trends we intended to trace across the chapters include seeing communication's role in challenging circumstances not in response, but also in the anticipation and in preparation. If we collectively value a better future for subsequent generations, many of the circumstances that lead to calamities in our personal health, relational lives, city infrastructure, and intercultural dialogue and community building are born from unaddressed and/or unanticipated issues. Unaddressed issues can come down to lack of resources, disregard for long-term consequences, or misaligned values. Unanticipated issues present an opportunity and a responsibility to learn form, adjust future planning, and educate our children to benefit from our trespasses. In this way, the practical import of hope and resilience communication research is one that informs improved and more effective ways of living happier and healthier lifespans *with each other*.

Regardless of the stressor, outcomes, or goals, no matter what the intensity or severity, the need and place for human connection knows no limits. Whether the connection comes from friends, family, community members, or strangers on the street, those relationships matter. Whether those messages come in the form of positivity, support, love, respect, appreciation, awareness, understanding, cooperativeness, or laughter, there is a place in the resilience process and hope for communication. The gray area that fills this place right now in our understanding of "what matters, when, where, and how" is not a sign of mystifying magic, but enormous potential for communication and allied discipline scholars.

References

Block, J. H., & Block, J. (1980). The role of ego-control and ego-resiliency in the organization of behavior. In W. A. Collins (Ed.), *Development of cognition, affect, and social relations: The Minnesota Symposia on Child Psychology* (Vol., 13, pp. 39-101). Hillsdale, NJ: Erlbaum.

Bonnano, G. A. (2004). Loss, trauma, and human resilience: Have we underestimated the human capacity to thrive after extremely aversive events? *American Psychologist, 59,* 20-28.

Bonnano, G. A., & Mancini, A. D., (2008). The human capacity to thrive in the face of potential trauma. *Pediatrics, 121,* 369-375.

Garmezy, N. (1991). Resilience and vulnerability to adverse developmental outcomes associated with poverty. *American Behavioral Scientist, 34,* 416-430.

Hixenbaugh, M. (2014, Fall). The heroes among us. *DistinctionHR, 23,* 123-131. Available at Virginia Pilot Media. www.distinctionhr.com

Holling, C. S., Schilindler, D. W., Walker, B. W., & Roughgarden, J. (1995). Biodiversity in the functioning of ecosystems: An ecological synthesis. In C. Perrings, K. G. Maler, C. Folke, C. S. Holling, & B. O. Jansson (Eds.), *Biodiversity and loss: Economic and ecological issues* (pp. 44-83). Cambridge, UK: Cambridge University Press.

Lerner, R. M., Jacobs, F., & Wertlieb, D. (Eds.). (2005). *Applied developmental science: An advanced textbook.* Thousand Oaks, CA: Sage.

Masten, A. (2001). Ordinary magic: Resilience processes in development. *American Psychologist, 56,* 227-238.

Merolla, A. J. (2014). The role of hope in conflict management and relational maintenance. *Personal Relationships, 21,* 365-386.

Rand, K. L, Martin, A. D., & Shea, A. M. (2011). Hope, not optimism, predicts academic performance of law students beyond previous academic achievement. *Journal of Research in Personality, 45,* 683-686.

Seligman, M. E. P. (2012). *Flourish: A visionary new understanding of happiness and well-being.* New York: Atria Books.

Snyder, C. R. (Ed.). (2000). *Handbook of hope: Theories, measures, applications.* San Diego, CA: Academic Press.

Snyder, C. R. (1999). Hope, Goal-Blocking Thoughts, & Test-Related Anxieties. *Pscychological Reports, 84,* 206-208.

Snyder, C. R. (2002). Hope Theory: Rainbows in the Mind. *Psychological Inquiry, 13,* 4, 249-275.

Snyder, C. R., Harris, C., Anderson, J. R., Holleran, S. A., Irving, L. M., Sigmon, S. T., et al. (1991). The will and the ways: Development and validation of an individual-differences measure of hope. *Journal of Personality and Social Psychology, 60,* 570-585.

Snyder, C. R., Sympson, S. C., Ybasco, F. C., & Borders, T. F., Babyak, M. A., & Higgins, R. L. (1996). Development and validation of the State Hope Scale. *Journal of Personality and Social Psychology, 70,* 321-335.

Socha, T. J. (2009). Family as agency of potential: Towards a positive model of applied family communication theory and research. In L. Frey & K. Cissna (Eds.), *Routledge Handbook of Applied Communication Research* (pp. 309–330). New York: Routledge.

Spark, N. T. (2006). A history of Murphy's Law. New York: Periscope Film.

Turkle, S. (2011). *Alone together: Why we expect more from technology and less from each other.* New York: Basic Books.

Watzlawick, P., Weakland, J., & Fisch, R. (1974). *Change: Principles of problem formation and problem resolution.* New York: W. W. Norton.

Wilson, S. R. & Gettings, P. E. (2012). Nurturing Children as Assets: A Positive Approach to Preventing Child Maltreatment and Promoting Healthy Youth Development. In T. J. Socha & M. J. Pitts (Eds.), *The Positive Side of Interpersonal Communication* (pp. 277–295). New York: Peter Lang.

Zautra, A. J., Hall, J. S., & Murray, K. E. (2008). Resilence: A new integrative approach to health and mental health research. *Health Psychology Review, 2,* 41–64.

Zimmerman, M. A., Ramirez, J., Washienko, K. M., Walter, B., & Dyer, S. (1995). Enculturation hypothesis: Exploring direct and protective effects among Native American youth. In H. I. McCubbin, E. A. Thompson, & A. I. Thompson (Eds.), *Resiliency in ethnic minority families: Vol. 1. Native and immigrant American families* (pp. 199–220). Madison: University of Wisconsin Press.

Section One
Contributing Processes

• CHAPTER TWO •

On Being (and Becoming) Mindful: One Pathway to Greater Resilience

Valerie Manusov
Jacquelyn A. Harvey-Knowles
University of Washington

In her book *The Gifts of Imperfection*, Brené Brown (2010) discusses people who she labels "wholehearted." Wholehearted people tend to be self-accepting and navigate well against some of the harder social patterns that we all face. Among the primary characteristics of the wholehearted are a resilient spirit, the capacity to let go of judgment, and the ability to cultivate some sense of internal peace and calm. These capacities show up in the ways that the wholehearted act across their lives. The ability to be wholehearted is not unlike the concept of hardiness, first developed by Salvatore Maddi (2004). Consistent with Brown's (2010) urging of us to dare greatly, Maddi (2004) writes that hardiness is an operationalization of existential courage: Those who are hardy are thought to have an air of resiliency and an ability to cope with, or even create opportunity from, stressful encounters. Such hardiness is apparent in certain children, often brought about in part because of what life has offered them, and it is seen in older adults who have developed the capacity to withstand hardship with open hearts over the course of their lives.

These characteristics—and their ability to show up early and affect us later in life—are also consistent with the concept of mindfulness, the focus of the present chapter. In one of his primary books on the subject, entitled *Full Catastrophe Living*, John Kabat-Zinn (1990) encouraged his readers to celebrate life in its "full catastrophe"; that is, to live fully with life's richness, including "the inevitability of all its dilemmas, sorrows, tragedies, and ironies" (p. 5). Being mindful is not about ignoring reality or life's hardships; rather, it is accepting their occurrence without fear. To do so, however, may be easier if we also are able "live intentionally and from moment to moment" (Kabat-Zinn,

1990, p. 19). Importantly, mindfulness can be increased through active engagement with mindfulness practices, making its tie to resilience closer to our reach. The act of being mindful, according to Kabat-Zinn, helps us to increase our capacity for resilience particularly in dealing with the stress that comes with living in the full catastrophe of our lives.

In addition to stress reduction, research suggests that living mindfully is beneficial in many ways across the areas and stages of our lives. In this chapter, we work to discuss mindfulness as a concept and as a practice from childhood to older ages, show some of the key variables that researchers have found to be linked with mindfulness, including positive health, relational, and communicative outcomes, and provide discussion of the ways in which mindfulness is measured—and how teaching mindfulness has been accomplished—to understand and encourage more mindfulness in our everyday lives and provide the grounds for additional research investigating mindfulness across the lifespan as an ongoing resilience practice.

Mindfulness as a Concept and a Practice

Gambrel and Keeling (2010) assert, accurately, that mindfulness "is hard to define and even harder to practice" (p. 413). Most people agree, however, that it includes at least two components: self-regulation of attention (i.e., noticing what one is noticing) and "an orientation that is characterized by curiosity, openness, and acceptance" (Bishop et al., 2004, p 232). These components stem primarily from Buddhist traditions, although most contemporary approaches to mindfulness are not tied necessarily to a larger theology (Gambrel & Keeling, 2010). Indeed, this separation is one area on which writings about mindfulness have been critiqued (see Stanley, 2012).

The most commonly used modern definition is by Kabat-Zinn (1994), who refers to mindfulness as "paying attention in a particular way: on purpose, in the present moment, and non-judgmentally" (p. 4). Rather than an automatic, or habitual, way of being in the world, mindfulness encourages us to observe actively but without judgment and to engage with rather than withdraw from life's vicissitudes. One result of this practice is an awareness that all thoughts are fleeting. Through our cultivation of mindfulness, thoughts become seen as distinct thoughts or stories and not as something real and immutable that must affect our behavior or views inherently. This is one way in which mindfulness may increase our overall ability to work throughout our lives with what comes into them.

We all have a degree of mindfulness, and as will be seen, our level of mindfulness can be measured, and also improved upon, should we wish to work on increasing its capacity. The degree to which people have what is called "dispositional mindfulness" varies, and this variation shows up early in life. Moreover, it starts to have positive effects early on: Greco, Baer, and Smith (2011) report on four studies with over 1400 children and found that young people with greater mindfulness had a higher quality of life, academic competence, and social skills and fewer physical complaints and behavior problems than did those with lower mindfulness scores. Likewise, Ciesla, Reilly, Dickson, Emanuel, and Updegraff (2012) found dispositional mindfulness in young adults was related to mood and susceptibility to stress.

Most of the correlational studies cited in this paper are based on assessments of our disposition to be more or less mindful. But Williams and Penman (2011) remind us that mindfulness is "not merely a good idea.... To be effective, mindfulness requires an embodied engagement on the part of anyone hoping to derive some benefit from it" (p. ix). Mindfulness practices vary, and in this chapter we will review some of the training techniques developed to teach mindfulness, including those for young people. Typically they include meditation practices, intentionally performed acts, such as eating and doing chores with awareness, and paying attention to and moving away from our habitual thoughts and evaluations of self and other.

Perhaps the most well-known method of mindfulness instruction is Kabat-Zinn's *Mindfulness Based Stress Reduction* (MBSR) training. MBSR courses typically consist of an 8-week program in which individuals learn various strategies designed to increase their capacity for being mindful. These include guided meditation, group discussions, mindful yoga, and daily take-home meditation assignments. People who have completed the program report increases in self-esteem, ability to cope with stressful life events, and overall energy levels as well as decreases in pain levels for a number of chronic conditions (Center for Mindfulness in Medicine, Healthcare, & Society, 2013). We will return later in this chapter to more discussion of mindfulness training; now, we discuss further some of the variables with which mindfulness is linked, highlighting those that reflect an increase in our resilience and well-being.

Mindfulness and Its Associations in Research

As just suggested, research with a variety of populations across the lifespan has shown that higher levels of mindfulness, in some cases brought about through mindfulness training, have positive outcomes, particularly in regards to health. When we are mindful, we are not ruminating over the past nor are we fearing what has yet to come. Rather, more mindful people attend to what needs attending to when it needs attending, and without the same degree of affect and reactivity that those less mindful bring to the events that challenge them.

Thus, being more mindful decreases the emotional and behavioral impact of difficult situations and is part of what may promote a more healthful way of being.

In this section, we provide some exemplars from this large body of health-oriented research, and we also summarize several studies that show how mindfulness is related to communication and relational outcomes. Importantly, however, positive outcomes are not always the first thing that occur as people engage in more mindfulness: As others have argued (e.g., Gambrel & Keeling, 2010; Huston, 2004), people engaging in mindfulness practices often feel overwhelmed at first, as the many thoughts and feelings they have are given more attention. But, over time, greater mindfulness decreases our reliance on these mental "stories," allowing us to become more resilient to what is difficult in our lives by giving the difficulty less emotional and cognitive "weight"; this is where positive outcomes are most likely to be seen.

Mindfulness and Health

Greeson's (2009) overview of the link between health and mindfulness reports research that connects mindfulness to better functioning immune systems, stress hormones, and overall health behaviors. A 2008 bibliography by Williams and Zylowska, with 94 pages of citations for mindfulness research, also lists work investigating the positive link between mindfulness and health issues such as HIV/AIDS coping, organ transplants, chronic fatigue, brain injury, and diabetes. For Kabat-Zinn (1990) the primary issue at stake is stress and the ways in which we handle it. Those who are more, using Maddi's (2004) word, hardy, have greater resources for coping with stress—are more resilient—and are therefore better able to fight disease and pain.

There are a number of possible explanations for why mindfulness works as it does. Some research suggests that increases in the brain's prefrontal cortex activity, and decreases in its amygdala activity, are associated with greater mindfulness, which provides evidence for why those who complete MBSR training report positive psychological benefits (Creswell, Way, Eisenberger, & Lieberman, 2007). Carlson, Speca, Patel, and Goodey (2003) found that the cultivation of mindfulness increases the emotional resiliency of those with debilitating illnesses. Brown and Ryan (2003) argue somewhat differently that one aspect of mindfulness—paying attention—may be particularly important for positive health outcomes. As they note, "[t]here are...many instances where attentional sensitivity to psychological, somatic, and environmental cues, a key component of mindfulness, is crucial to the operation of healthy regulatory processes" (p. 824). Among these, the authors list that lower levels of attention and the disregulation of behavior are linked with self-medicating and panic attacks.

Whatever the explanatory force, the results of studies on mindfulness suggest its physical and psychological benefits. In what is perhaps one of the most consistent health-related findings, Shapiro, Schwartz, and Bonner (1998) observed decreased anxiety and depression after mindfulness training in the medical students that they studied (see, also, Rosenzweig et al., 2003). Miller, Fletcher, and Kabat-Zinn (1995) saw the salutary effects on depression and anxiety in their sample of people with generalized anxiety and panic disorders. Brown and Ryan (2003) also reported correlations between self-reported mindfulness and lower neuroticism, self-consciousness, depression, negative affectivity, impulsivity, and angry hostility, and higher positive affectivity, life satisfaction, self-esteem, autonomy, and competence.

In general, it appears that people who have higher levels of mindfulness—whether brought about through training or inherent in the individual—are healthier psychologically. The consistency of these findings have led many to argue for the benefits of incorporating mindfulness training in therapy, particularly with people with certain psychological conditions such as borderline personality disorder (Linehan, 1993b) and eating disorders (Proulx, 2008). Gambrel and Keeling (2010), for instance, argue for the role of mindfulness in increasing the neurological capacity for bonding with and relating to others. This capacity for connection is another important aspect of people's resiliency and their hopefulness.

Other populations may likewise benefit from mindfulness training. Brotto and Heiman (2007), for instance, applied mindfulness to sexual arousal disorder in women. In their work, the authors incorporate mindfulness practices into a larger psychoeducational program (PED) that they designed for women with sexual dysfunction as a result of gynecologic cancer. The PED specifically asks the women to, at a particular point in the process, apply what they are learning about mindfulness to their sexuality. The authors' qualitative data suggested that the women in their study found engaging in mindfulness to be effective in the quality of their sexuality and their life generally. As well, Morone, Lynch, Greco, Tindle, and Weiner (2008) found mindfulness training helped older adults with lower back pain sleep better, improve attention, and report greater well-being, leading the authors to say that minfulness has "promising potential as a nonpharmacologic treatment of chronic pain for older adults" (p. 841).

Importantly, mindfulness training appears to also work well *early* in life. Ames, Richardson, Payne, and Leigh (2014) offered mindfulness training to adolescents who had moderate depression. After the 8-week course, the authors interviewed the young people in their study and found that the adolescents' depression and rumination were reduced, and their overall life quality increased. The authors also found that the adolescents thought that the training was something that was "acceptable" to them, that it was a set of practices people in their age group could undertake. Likewise, Sibinga et al. (2013) studied young urban men who were given mindfulness training in schools and found it lowered the young adults' stress and rumination. Moreover, Jennings and Jennings (2014) discerned that using a modified, shorter training could be taught effectively by peers and worked well for adolescents to increase their mindfulness and decrease problematic thoughts.

Mindfulness and Relationships

As can be seen from many of the studies mentioned already, mindfulness has its place in bettering ourselves (making us healthy and more able to cope, largely through stress reduction). Gambrel and Keeling (2010) argue specifically that "[t]he mindfulness process of awareness, acceptance and choice [also] has powerful implications for personal relationships" (p. 416). One of the most overarching claims is that mindfulness is likely to have positive effects on relationship satisfaction.

Wachs and Cordova (2007) are among those who tested this relationship between mindfulness and relational quality or satisfaction. In their correlational study of married pairs, the authors found that couple members higher in mindfulness were more satisfied in their relationships; they were also likely to have higher scores on perspective taking, empathic concern, and lack of distress. Barnes, Brown, Krusemark, Campbell, and Rogge (2007), using a longitudinal method, reported similarly that greater trait mindfulness correlates positively with relational satisfaction, along with an increased capacity to respond constructively to relational stress and less concern about an upcoming conflict discussion. In the observational component of their study, the authors also saw that those with higher state mindfulness predicted higher communication quality (i.e., lower verbal aggression and higher verbal support) during a conflict discussion. In our own correlational study (Harvey-Knowles, Manusov, & Crowley, 2013), we learned that certain components of mindfulness, most notably withholding of judgment and ability to describe (see descriptions of these variables below under the "Kentucky Inventory of Mindfulness Skills") positively predicted self-reports of more constructive, and negatively predicted less constructive, forms of conflict with their relational partners. Withholding of judgment also predicted increased satisfaction and commitment in both same- and opposite-sex couples.

The consistency of these findings has led some researchers to explain the connection between mindfulness and relational satisfaction. Jones, Welton, Oliver, and Thoburn (2011) found that *attachment* may work as an explanatory mediator for the relationship between mindfulness and satisfaction, such that higher degrees of dispositional mindfulness may be related to feelings of security and safety, also known to be important resilience factors. These feelings may, in turn, bring about greater satisfaction. Wachs and Cordova (2007) argue that *skillfulness of emotion* and *regulation of anger* mediate the mindfulness-satisfaction link, as did Pepping, Davis, and O'Donovan (2013), though they credit somewhat different ways in which this occurs. Goodall, Trejnowska, and Darling (2011) likewise reported a link among these variables.

There is also an important connection between mindfulness, compassion, and empathy (Wachs & Cordova, 2007). Shapiro et al. (1998) reported that mindfulness increased the degree of self- and other-compassion—and the degree of empathy—people felt. This finding was repeated by Dekeyser, Raes, Leijssen, Leysen, and Dewulf (2008), who studied a Dutch rather than a U.S. adult sample. Because of the link between empathy and whether or not couples can forgive one another for relational transgressions, we, along with our colleague, investigated whether mindfulness serves as a mediator between empathy and perspective-taking as a predictor for forgiveness in commited couples, and we found significant supporting results (Crowley, Manusov, & Harvey-Knowles, 2014); specifically, in our study, only those who were empathic *in a mindful way* were able to forgive their partners for a real or imagined transgression. Researchers have also looked for mediating effects in other arenas. In particular, Allen and Kiburz (2012) investigated a sample of working parents; they were interested in the relationship between trait mindfulness and the work-life balance. They found this link was mediated by sleep quality and vitality. It is not surprising that it is easier to engage in mindfulness when one has enough rest.

Overall, mindfulness as a trait and mindfulness training are both strong predictors of positive health and relational outcomes, although they may be mediated by other variables. Whether it is stress or anxiety reduction, or well-being in families, higher levels of mindfulness tend to make people better able to navigate what comes into their personal and relational lives across their lives. Indeed, Gehart and McCollum (2007) state that mindfulness works directly as a form of personal and social resilience by taking an "alternative stance" to the inherent suffering that life provides. That is, those with greater mindfulness think in ways that are less fearful and are more open to events as they unfold. It may have even more specific characteristics with some populations. For example, McHugh, Simpson, and Reed (2010) assert that aging can be tied to "over-selectivity" or the tendency to allow only a few environmental cues to control behavior. The authors found that mindfulness training increased the ability of the elderly group they studied to be more resilient to over-selectivity by retargeting attention.

To better understand how these findings were drawn, we offer an overview of many of the measures used to assess trait and/or state mindfulness and follow this with an overview of the primary ways in which mindfulness as a practice is taught. Our hope is that this review will encourage more research into mindfulness across the lifespan as well as more engagement with the acts of mindfulness in people's everyday lives.

Measuring Mindfulness

As mindfulness is a complex, multifaceted construct, so too are the ways it can be measured and used to enhance how we engage with life. The research just reviewed depends largely on one of two ways of considering mindfulness: as an existing state or trait or as something to be taught. This section presents some of the myriad measures that have been developed to tap into existing mindfulness in an array of ways. Whereas we do not take a stand on which of these is most effective, we do provide published critiques when they are available.

Mindful Attention Awareness Scale. The Mindful Attention Awareness Scale (MAAS; Brown & Ryan, 2003) is a 15-item measure that gauges individuals' tendency to be attentive to, and aware of, present-moment experiences in day-to-day life. The scale measures dispositional (i.e., trait) mindfulness and is meant to capture one's capacity for being mindful overall, rather than whether one has differential levels of various aspects of mindfulness (such as remaining nonjudgmental or nonreactive, etc.). The MAAS is intended for the general adult population rather than specific population subgroups. It uses a 6-point Likert-type scale (1-almost always to 6-almost never) to measure how often respondents report being preoccupied, acting on "auto-pilot," and/or lacking attention in the present moment. Responses closer to 6 are indicative of higher levels of mindfulness. As such, the actual items used in the MAAS are worded in a manner suggestive of mindlessness rather than mindfulness. Sample items include "I find it difficult to stay focused on what's happening in the present" and "It seems I am 'running on automatic' without much awareness of what I'm doing." An example study using the MAAS is Barnes et al.'s (2007) study of couples' mindfulness, satisfaction, adaptive responses, and self-control.

The MAAS is one of the more popular measures of mindfulness because it can be administered to a wide variety of populations. Those who take the measure can, but need not, be experienced in meditation. As Van Dam, Earlywine, and Borders (2010) assert, however, the negative wording of the MAAS items (e.g., "I do not pay attention") may be problematic given many individuals' limited ability to gauge when their own mindfulness is absent. These researchers also argue that the potential for response bias is strong. Grossman (2011) makes similar claims, while also arguing that there is a lack of evidence for construct and content validity of the scale and the samples used to validate the measure (primarily undergraduate students) were inadequate.

The Freiburg Mindfulness Inventory. The Freiburg Mindfulness Inventory (FMI; Buchheld, Grossman, & Walach, 2001) is a 30-item scale designed to gauge mindfulness levels in individuals who have experience with meditation and Buddhist psychology. Results found the FMI to be consistent and reliable. It uses four response options: rarely, occasionally, fairly often, and almost always. Examples of scale items include "I know that I am not identical to my thoughts" and "I am aware of how brief and fleeting my experience is." Walach, Buchheld, Buttonmuller, Kleinknecht, and Schmidt (2006) later developed a 14-item short form of the FMI. Although the FMI was found to have four distinct factors—mindful presence, non-judgmental acceptance, openness to experiences, and insight—the authors suggest that it be used to measure a unidimensional construct of mindfulness, as the four factors were found to be closely interrelated.

The Kentucky Inventory of Mindfulness Skills (KIMS; Baer, Smith, & Allen, 2004) is a 39-item self-report scale that assesses trait-mindfulness in individuals using a 5-point Likert-type scale (never or rarely true to always or almost always true). The scale examines four aspects of mindfulness: "observing, describing, acting with awareness, and accepting without judgment" (Baer, Smith, Hopkins, Krietmeyer, & Toney, 2006, p. 29). Observing consists of individuals' ability to recognize and focus on internal and external stimuli, such as taking note of sounds, smells, or sights. Describing is the ability to identify and express present-moment experience. Acting with awareness involves attending to only one aspect of the present-moment. Withholding of judgment includes refraining from evaluating, or negatively judging, present-moment occurrences.

Baum et al. (2010) state that the KIMS should be used only in looking at the four subscales independently, as the KIMS does not measure a hierarchical mindfulness construct. Sample items in the KIMS are "I notice changes in my body, such as whether my breathing slows down or speeds up" and "When I'm doing something, I'm only focused on what I'm doing, nothing else." The KIMS "measures a general tendency to be mindful in daily life and does not require experiences with meditation" (Baer et al., 2006, p. 29). Dekeyser et al. (2008) used this measure to find associations with empathy and self-expression in a variety of social situations.

Mindfulness Questionnaire. The mindfulness questionnaire (MQ; Chadwick, Hember, Mead, Lilley, & Dagnan, 2005), also known as the Southampton Mindfulness Questionnaire, is a 16-item instrument assessing how well individuals respond to distressing thoughts and images. All items begin with this stem: "Usually when I have distressing thoughts or images," after which each scale item is listed. Sample items include "I am able to accept the experience" and "I feel calm soon after." Items are measured on a 7-point scale (agree totally to disagree totally). Although the scale measures four aspects of mindfulness—letting go, mindful observation, nonjudgment, and nonaversion—the authors do not recommend using the scale as a uni- rather than a multi-faceted measure. Chadwick et al. report that the scale showed significant differences between meditators and non-meditators, with meditators reporting higher mindfulness levels. This scale can, however, be used for individuals regardless of their level of experience with mindfulness practices.

Five-Factor Mindfulness Questionnaire (FFMQ). The Five-Factor Mindfulness Questionnaire (Baer, Smith, Hopkins, Krietmeyer, & Toney, 2006) was developed from existing mindfulness scales. The authors used the MAAS, FMI, KIMS, and MQ, along with another less-used measure known as the Cognitive Affective Mindfulness Scale (CAMS; Feldman, Hayes, Kumar, & Greeson, 2004), to develop the FFMQ after having undergraduate students take all five measures. The FFMQ is able to measure changes in mindfulness after a treatment intervention, making it useful for examining both state and trait-mindfulness. Many of the individuals in their sample (approximately 70%) had no previous experience with meditation. As such, the FFMQ can be used with any population and/or lifespan cross-section regardless of whether people have been introduced to mindfulness concepts.

A factor analysis suggested a 5-factor structure to mindfulness: observing, acting with awareness, describing, nonjudgment, and nonreactivity. The first four components are the same components that the KIMS measures. Nonreactivity assesses individuals' ability to refrain from reacting negatively to undesired stimuli. Sample questions in the FFMQ include "In difficult situations, I can pause without immediately reacting." and "I notice visual elements in art or nature, such as colors, shapes, textures, or patterns of light and shadow." Successful uses of this measure include Shaver et al.'s (2007) study of the role of attachment style. In 2011, Bohlmeijer and colleagues developed a short form for the FFMQ.

Toronto Mindfulness Scale. The Toronto Mindfulness Scale (TMS; Lau et al., 2006) was not a part of the FFMQ but is a 13-item measure designed to estimate mindfulness levels in individuals who have experience with meditation. It is a two-factor scale that gauges awareness of thoughts and sensations in the present moment (decentering) as well as the degree to which one is open, curious, and accepting of such thoughts and sensations (curiosity). Because Kabat-Zinn (1994) argues that mindfulness is a variable state of mind and that meditation is a prime avenue through which individuals increase their capacity to be mindful, the TMS was designed to be completed after respondents are instructed to sit and meditate for a period of at least 15 minutes. Sample items of the TMS include the following: "I was aware of my thoughts and feelings without over-identifying them" and "I noticed subtle changes in my mood."

Later, a trait-version of the TMS was developed (Davis, Lau, & Cairns, 2009), giving researchers the ability to use both measures to better understand whether individuals are particularly mindful during or immediately following a meditation session and whether this mindfulness diminishes after time. In converting the state-TMS to a trait-measure, the wording of all 13 items was changed to reflect more enduring perceptions. For example, "I was curious to see what my mind was up to from moment to moment" for the original TMS, was altered to "I am curious to see what my mind is up to from moment to moment." The trait-TMS can be administered to individuals regardless of whether they have experience with meditation.

Child and Adolescent Mindfulness Measure (CAMM). Although most measures created to assess trait or state mindfulness are thought to be useful—or at least easily adaptable—to all populations, Greco et al. (2011) recently developed a measure specifically of child and adolescent mindfulness. Using four studies to develop and validate their measure, the authors produced a sound 10-item scale geared to assessing mindfulness skills in school age children and adolescents. As noted elsewhere in this chapter, the authors found correlations between CAMM scores and greater quality of life, academic performance, and social skills, among other things, suggesting greater hope for young people with higher levels of mindfulness.

The CAMM has received additional testing, and it revealed some differences in what mindfulness "looks like" in children as compared to their older peers. In their study of Dutch school children and adolescents, de Bruin, Zijlstra, and Bogels (2013), found that CAMM can be used as a single factor measure; but they also discovered a two-factor solution. The authors note that "for children as well as adolescents, a main component referring to 'present-moment non-judgmental awareness' arose, but for children a second component of 'supressing thoughts and feelings' arose whereas for adolescents 'distractability or difficulty paying attention' became apparent" (p. 1).

Mindfulness Interventions

The measures just reviewed conceptualize mindfulness as a state of mind or a general disposition to act with awareness, and this may change over the course of our lifetimes as we are transformed by our experiences. But we can also learn to become more mindful, and several organized practices have been developed that encourage increased mindfulness. To provide greater insight into mindfulness interventions, this section provides an overview of the most common programs used when mindfulness interventions are included in research endeavors, and it includes some more specialized trainings that speak to lifespan issues. They also offer ideas for places to go to learn more mindfulness in one's own life.

Mindfulness Based Cognitive Therapy

We discussed Kabat-Zinn's (1990) MBSR earlier in this chapter. Mindfulness Based Cognitive Therapy (MBCT; Segal, Williams, & Teasdale, 2002) is another type of mindfulness training that employs an 8-week course. In MBCT training, participants attend therapeutic sessions designed to increase their knowledge of mindfulness and relaxation techniques, while also completing at-home MBCT exercises (Galante, Iribarren, & Pearce, 2012). The creators of this approach developed specific week-by-week instructions for completing the program, as the initial purpose of MBCT was that of a preventive measure toward depressive-symptom relapse. Ma and Teasdale (2004) found that MBCT training has the capacity to reduce depressive relapse by up to half.

Similar to many MBSR implementation approaches, MBCT participants are typically either recruited from individuals already enrolling in a training course, or individuals are actively (sometimes randomly) recruited to participate (see Rimes & Wingrove, 2013). With this approach, individuals are generally evaluated on a number of dependent measures both before and after a training intervention to assess whether MBCT is associated with particular outcomes. With MBCT (and MBSR) trainings, results should be interpreted cautiously, as people who are willing to participate in such lengthy and in-depth interventions may be non-representative of the overall population. Importantly, MBCT can be adapted to and used successfully with adolescents (Ames et al., 2014).

Mindfulness-Based Relationship Enhancement

Another program, Mindfulness-Based Relationship Enhancement (MBRE), was developed by and used in Carson, Carson, Gil, and Baucom's (2004) experimental study of nondistressed couples but is similar in form to the two programs just reviewed. Carson et al. had their treatment group engage in eight weekly mindfulness sessions involving meditation and other couple-oriented practices such as dyadic eye-gazing, mindful touch, and various communication practices. The control group did not engage in such practices, but was offered the option to partake in MBRE training after study completion. The treatment group reported higher levels of relational satisfaction, closeness, relatedness with partner, and optimism, among other variables, than did the wait-list control group. This study was one of the few controlled interventions with the purpose of enhancing relationships for couples who are already well-functioning (most studies tend to focus on distressed couples). McBee (2003) outlines how to adapt the MBSR to nursing home populations.

Mindfulness-Based Childbirth and Parenting Program

The Mindfulness-based Childbirth and Parenting program (MBCP) was created in an effort to promote family well-being (Duncan & Bardacke, 2010) and, likewise, adapted from the Kabat-Zinn's (1990) MBSR training. The program is offered to pregnant women and/or their partners (or other sources of support). Those who enroll attend weekly three-hour sessions for a total of nine weeks. Sessions focus on coping skills, preparation for childbirth, and mindfulness in relation to various birthing and post-birth processes, as well as psychological adjustment after birth for the mother. Results from Duncan and Bardacke (2010) suggest that this type of training is associated with increased mindfulness, decreased pregnancy anxiety, and increased positive affect.

Dialectical Behavior Therapy

Dialectical Behavior Therapy (DBT; Linehan 1993a) is a type of behavioral intervention that consists of increasing skills such as emotion regulation, interpersonal effectiveness, and tolerance of distress (Lindenboim, Comtois, & Linehan, 2007). It was first developed in an effort to treat those diagnosed with borderline personality disorder (Neacsiu, Ward-Ciesielski, & Linehan, 2012). With DBT, individuals take part in both individual and group therapeutic sessions where they engage typically in "skills coaching" each week. Mindfulness is a core component of DBT training and is generally the first skill taught to participants (Linehan, 1993a). Unlike the previous interventions discussed in this chapter, DBT emphasizes informal mindfulness practices (e.g., mindful eating) over formal practices such as sitting meditation. Studies that have implemented DBT training typically use randomized controlled trials in which participants who meet the criteria for borderline personality disorder are recruited. The drawback of DBT is that it can range in length from a few months to a year; therefore involvement with and studies using DBT are quite complex and often require a significant financial investment.

Acceptance and Commitment Therapy

Acceptance and commitment therapy (ACT; Hayes, Strosahl, & Wilson, 1999) was designed to bring awareness to individuals' internal thoughts and sensations. As evidenced by its name, ACT promotes acceptance of positive and negative experiences rather than a focus on reducing negative psychological or physical issues that arise (Brady & Whitman, 2012), similar to the concept of hardiness (Maddi, 2004). So, for example, if an individual feels a negative emotion, that person is asked to reflect upon, and embrace, the emotion, rather than push it away (Brady & Whitman, 2012). Often, those who learn ACT do so in therapeutic or academic settings; nonetheless, there are self-help books available as well.

Correlational and experimental studies exist looking at the relationships between ACT and various health outcomes. In such studies, the Acceptance and Action Questionnaire (AAQ; Hayes et al., 2004) is the most commonly employed measurement. The AAQ "measures the degree to which an individual fuses with thoughts, avoids feelings, and is unable to act in the presence of difficult private events" (Hayes, Luoma, Bond, Masuda, & Lillis, 2006, p. 18). In training interventions, ACT is approached in a different manner than other mindfulness-based therapies. Hayes and colleagues (2006) assert that many ACT studies use an "inductive, technique-building, principles-focused treatment development approach: conduct micro-studies on each of the key ACT processes...to see if each is psychologically active and works in a fashion that accords with the theory" (p. 14).

Overall, there are myriad ways to teach people to be more mindful. Many of these were created with particular populations in mind, such as clinical patients or couples, but others are useful for, at least, most adults. As research continues to assess the people that mindfulness helps, the contexts in which it is most useful, and the stages in our lives where we can best learn it, more intervention modes will likely develop. As evidenced above, the benefits of mindfulness, particularly as tied to resilience over the lifespan, are many. One would be hard-pressed to find another construct that has been shown to increase individuals' well-being in so many different ways and with so much consistency (but see Stanley, 2012).

Conclusion

Research on mindfulness interventions suggests quite clearly a promising road to resilience in which most individuals—at all stages of the lifespan—experience increases in the quality of both their health and their life-satisfaction. For example, recent research on changing parents' mindfulness (including non-judgmental acceptance of the child and listening with full attention) shows that it affects parents' relationship with their adolescents (Coatsworth, Duncan, Greenberg, & Nix, 2010); moreover summer programs exist for adolescents themselves to learn mindfulness practices early in their lives, and reseach also shows mindfulness training can be done at school and with peers (e.g., Jennings & Jennings, 2013). Although work with younger children is still limited, some has focused on specific populations, finding, among other things, that caregivers of autistic children who learn to be more mindful report increased parenting satisfaction and decreased child aggression, suggesting how the change in one person's mindfulness may affect another's behavior (Singh et al., 2007).

In the 2008 bibliography mentioned previously, Williams and Zylowska provide a list of the populations studied already by mindfulness researchers. In addition to couples and families with children and adolescents, they list research on bilingual groups, people from inner cities, prisoners, teachers, and other workplaces. Shapiro, Brown, and Astin (2008) argue for the integration of meditation into higher education, and mindfulness used in college Communication classrooms has been found to enhance the student experience (Huston, Garland, & Farb, 2011).

Whereas many of the interventions discussed here involve a great deal of time and expense, this is changing. A number of mindfulness practices can now be learned on one's own for relatively little financial investment through the use of books written by authors of some of these therapies or those well trained in them (e.g., Williams & Penman, 2011). It is rare that such an opportunity arises, and it illustrates the importance of continued research on how and why mindfulness works and what other areas of our lives it may come to benefit.

References

Allen, T. D. & Kiburz, K. M. (2012). Trait mindfulness and work-family balance among working parents: The mediating effects of vitality and sleep quality. *Journal of Vocational Behavior, 80*, 372-379.

Ames, C. S., Richardson, J., Payne, S., & Leigh, E. (2014). Mindfulness-based cognitive therapy for depression in adolescents. *Child and Adolescent Mental Health, 19*, 74-78.

Baer, R. A., Smith, G. T., & Allen, K. B. (2004). Assessment of mindfulness by self-report: The Kentucky inventory of mindfulness skills. *Assessment, 11*, 191-206.

Baer, R. A., Smith, G. T., Hopkins, J., Krietemeyer, J., & Toney, L. (2006). Using self-report assessment methods to explore facets of mindfulness. *Assessment, 13*, 27-45.

Barnes, S., Brown, K. W., Krusemark, E., Campbell, W. K., & Rogge, R. D. (2007). The role of mindfulness in romantic relationship satisfaction and responses to relational stress. *Journal of Marital and Family Therapy, 33*, 482-500.

Baum, C., Kuyken, W., Bohus, M., Heidenreich, T., Michalak, J., & Steil, R. (2010). The psychometric properties of the Kentucky Inventory of Mindfulness Skills in clinical populations. *Assessment, 17*, 220-229.

Bishop, S. R., Lau, M., Shapiro, S., Carlson, L., Anderson, N. D., Carmody, J., et al. (2004). Mindfulness: A proposed operational definition. *Clinical Psychology: Science and Practice, 11*, 230-241.

Bohlmeijer, E., ten Klooster, P. M., Fledderus, M., Veehof, M., & Baer, R. (2011). Psychometric properties of the Five Facet Mindfulness Questionnaire in depressed adults and the development of a short form. *Assessment, 8*, 308-320.

Brady, V. P., & Whitman, S. M. (2012). An acceptance and mindfulness-based approach to social phobia: A case study. *College Counseling Case Studies, 15*, 81-96.

Brotto, L. A., & Heiman, J. R. (2007). Mindfulness in sex therapy: Applications for women with sexual difficulties following gynecologic cancer. *Sexual and Relationship Therapy, 22*, 3-11.

Brown, B. (2010). *The gifts of imperfection: Letting go of who we should be and embracing who we are.* Center City, MN: Hazelden.

Brown, B. (2012). *Daring greatly: How the courage to be vulnerable transforms the way we live, love, parent and lead.* New York: Gotham.

Brown, K. W., & Ryan, R. M. (2003). The benefits of being present: Mindfulness and its role in psychological well-being. *Journal of Personality and Social Psychology, 84*, 822-848.

Buccheld, N., Grossman, P., & Walach, H. (2001). Measuring mindfulness in insight meditation (Vipassana) and meditation-based psycho-therapy: The development of the Freiburg Mindfulnesss Inventory (FMI). *Journal for Meditation and Meditation Research, 1*, 11-34.

Carlson, L. E., Speca, M., Patel, K. D., & Goodey, E. (2003). Mindfulness-based stress reduction in relation to quality of life, mood, symptoms of stress, and immune parameters in breast and prostate cancer outpatients. *Psychosomatic Medicine, 65*, 571-581.

Carson, J. W., Carson, K. M., Gil, K. M., & Baucom, D. H. (2004). Mindfulness-based relationship enhancement. *Behavior Therapy, 35*, 471-494.

Center for mindfulness in medicine healthcare and society (2013). Stress reduction program. Retrieved from: http://www.umassmed.edu/content.aspx?id=41254.

Chadwick, P., Hember, M., Mead, S., Lilley, B., & Dagnan, D. (2005). *Responding mindfully to unpleasant thoughts and images: Reliability and validity of the Mindfulness Questionnaire.* Unpublished manuscript.

Ciesla, J. A., Reilly, L. C., Dickson, K. S. Emanuel, A. S., & Updegraff, J. A. (2012). Dispositional mindfulness moderates the effects of stress among adolescents: Rumination as a mediator. *Journal of Clinical Child and Adolescent Psychology, 41*, 760-770.

Coatsworth, J. D., Duncan, L. G., Greenberg, M. T., & Nix, R. L. (2010). Changing parents' mindfulness, child management skills and relationship quality with their youth: Results from a randomized pilot intervention trial. *Journal of Child and Family Studies, 19*, 203-217.

Creswell, J. D., Way, B. M., Eisenberger, N. I., & Lieberman, M. D. (2007). Neural correlates of dispositional mindfulness during affect labeling. *Psychosomatic Medicine, 69*, 560-565.

Crowley, J. P., Manusov, V., & Harvey-Knowles, J. A. (2014, May). *How we forgive: The mediating role of mindfulness in the forgiveness process*. Paper presented to the International Communication Association, Seattle.

Davis, K. M., Lau, M. A., & Cairns, D. R. (2009). Development and preliminary validation of a trait version of the Toronto Mindfulness Scale. *Journal of Cognitive Psychotherapy, 23*, 185-197.

de Bruin, E. I., Zijlstra, B. J. H., & Bogels, S. M. (2013). The meaning of mindfulness in children and adolescents: Further validation of the Child and Adolescent Mindfulness Measure (CAMM) in two independent samples from The Netherlands. *Mindfulness*. doi: 10.1007/s12671-013-0196-8

Dekeyser, M., Raes, F., Leijssen, M., Leysen, S., & Dewulf, D. (2008). Mindfulness skills and interpersonal behaviour. *Personality and Individual Differences, 44*, 1235-1245.

Duncan, L. G., & Bardacke, N. (2010). Mindfulness-based childbirth and parenting education: Promoting family mindfulness during the prenatal period. *Journal of Child and Family Studies, 19*, 190-202.

Feldman, G. C., Hayes, A. M., Kumar, S. M., & Greeson, J. M. (2004). *Development, factor structure, and initial validation of the Cognitive Affect Mindfulness Scale*. Unpublished manuscript.

Galante, J., Iribarren, S. J., & Pearce, P. F. (2012). Effects of mindfulness-based cognitive therapy on mental disorders: A systematic review and meta-analysis of randomised controlled trials. *Journal of Research in Nursing, 18*, 133-155.

Gambrel, L. E., & Keeling, M. L. (2010). Relational aspects of mindfulness: Implications for the practice of marriage and family therapy. *Contemporary Family Therapy, 32*, 412-426.

Gehart, D. R., & McCollum, E. E. (2007). Engaging suffering: Towards a mindful re-visioning of family therapy practice. *Journal of Marital & Family Therapy, 33*, 214-226.

Glomb, T. M., Duffy, M. K., Bono, J. E., & Yang, T. (2011). Mindfulness at work. *Research in Personnel and Human Resources Management, 30*, 115-157.

Goodall, K., Trejnowska, A., & Darling, S. (2012). The relationship between dispositional mindfulness, attachment security and emotion regulation. *Personality and Individual Differences, 52*, 622-626.

Greco, L. A., Baer, R. A., & Smith, G. T. (2011). Assessing mindfulness in children and adolescents: development and validation of the Child and Adolescent Mindfulness Measure (CAMM). *Psychological Assessment, 23*, 606-614.

Greeson, J. M. (2009). Mindfulness research update: 2008. *Complementary Health Practice Review, 14*, 10-18.

Grossman, P. (2011). Defining mindfulness by how poorly I think I pay attention during everyday awareness and other intractable problems for psychology's (re)invention of mindfulness: Comment on Brown et al. (2011). *Psychological Assessment, 23*, 1034-1040.

Harvey-Knowles, J. A, Manusov, V., & Crowley, J. P. (2013, November). *Minding your matters: Predicting relational satisfaction, commitment, and conflict styles from trait-mindfulness*. Paper presented to the National Communication Association Convention, Washington, DC.

Hayes, S. C., Luoma, J. B., Bond, F. W., Masuda, A., & Lillis, J. (2006). Acceptance and Commitment Therapy: Model, processes and outcomes. *Behavior Research and Therapy, 44*, 1-25.

Hayes, S. C., Strosahl, K., & Wilson, K. G. (1999). *Acceptance and commitment therapy: An experiential approach to behavior change*. New York: Guilford.

Hayes, S. C., Strosahl, K. D., Wilson, K. G., Bissett, R. T., Pistorello, J., Toarmino, D., Polusny, M. A., Dykstra, T. A., Batten, S. V., Bergan, J., Stewart, S. H., Zvolensky, M. J., Eifert, G. H., Bond, F. W., Forsyth J. P., Karekla, M., & McCurry, S. M. (2004). Measuring experiential avoidance: A preliminary test of a working model. *The Psychological Record, 54,* 553-578.

Huston, D. C., Garland, E. L., & Farb, N. A. S. (2010). Mechanisms of mindfulness in communication training. *Journal of Applied Communication Research, 39,* 406-421.

Jennings, S. J., & Jennings, J. L. (2014). Peer-directed, brief mindfulness training with adolescents: A pilot study. *International Journal of Behavioral Consultation and Therapy, 8,* 23-24.

Jones, K. C., Welton, S. R., Oliver, T. C., & Thoburn, J. W. (2011). Mindfulness, spousal attachment, and marital satisfaction: A mediated model. *The Family Journal, 19,* 357-361.

Kabat-Zinn, J. (1990). *Full catastrophe living: Using the wisdom of your body and mind to face stress, pain, and illness.* New York: Random House.

Kabat-Zinn, J. (1994). *Wherever you go there you are: Mindfulness meditation in everyday life.* New York: Hyperion.

Kabat-Zinn, J., & Chapman-Waldrop, A. (1988). Compliance with an outpatient stress reduction program: Rates and predictors of program completion. *Journal of Behavioral Medicine, 11,* 333-352.

Kobasa, S. C. (1979). Stressful life events and health: An inquiry into hardiness. *Journal of Personality and Social Psychology, 37,* 1-11.

Lau, M. A., Bishop, S. R., Segal, Z. V., Buis, T., Anderson, N. D., Carlson, L., Shapiro, S., Carmody, J., Abbey, S., & Devins, G. (2006). The Toronto Mindfulness Scale: Development and validation. *Journal of Clinical Psychology, 62,* 1445-1467.

Lindenboim, N., Comtois, K. A., & Linehan, M. M. (2007). Skills practice in dialectical behavior therapy for suicidal women meeting criteria for borderline personality disorder. *Cognitive and Behavioral Practice, 14,* 147-156.

Linehan, M. M. (1993a). *Cognitive-behavioral treatment of borderline personality disorder.* New York: Guilford.

Linehan, M. M. (1993b). *Skills training manual for treating borderline personality disorder.* New York: Guilford.

Ma, S. H., & Teasdale, J. D. (2004). Mindfulness-based cognitive therapy for depression: Replication and exploration of differential relapse prevention effects. *Journal of Consulting and Clinical Psychology, 72,* 31-40.

Maddi, S. R. (2004). Hardiness: An operationalization of existential courage. *Journal of Humanistic Psychology, 44,* 279-298.

McBee, L. (2003). Mindfulness practice with the frail elderly and their caregivers: Changing the practitioner-patient relationship. *Topics in Geriatric Rehabilitation, 19,* 257-264.

McHugh, L., Simpson, A., & Reed, P. (2010). Mindfulness as a potential intervention for stimulus over-selectivity in older adults. *Research in Developmental Disabilities, 31,* 178-184.

Miller, J. J., Fletcher, K., & Kabat-Zinn, J. (1995). Three-year follow-up and clinical implications of a mindfulness meditation-based stress reduction intervention in the treatment of anxiety disorders. *General Hospital Psychiatry, 17,* 192-200.

Morone, N. E., Lynch, C. S., Greco, C. M., Tindle, H. A., & Weiner, D. K. (2008). "I felt like a new person." The effects of mindfulness meditation on older adults with chronic pain: Qualitative narrative analysis of diary entries. *The Journal of Pain, 9,* 841-848.

Pepping, C. A., Davis, P. J., & O'Donovan, A. (2013). Individual differences in attachment and dispositional mindfulness: The mediating role of emotion regulation. *Personality and Individual Differences, 54*, 453-456.

Proulx, K. (2008). Experiences of women with bulimia nervosa in a mindfulness-based eating disorder treatment group. *Eating Disorders: The Journal of Treatment & Prevention, 16*, 52-72.

Rimes, K. A., & Wingrove, J. (2013). Mindfulness-Based Cognitive Therapy for people with Chronic Fatigue Syndrome still experiencing excessive fatigue after cognitive behavior therapy: A pilot randomized study. *Clinical Psychology and Psychotherapy, 20*, 107-117.

Rosenzweig, S., Reibel, D., Greeson, J., Edman, J., Jasser, S., McMearty, K., et al. (2007). Mindfulness-based stress reduction is associated with improved glycemic control in type 2 diabetes mellitus: A pilot study. *Alternative Therapies in Health and Medicine, 13*, 36-38.

Segal, Z., Williams, J. M. G., & Teasdale, J. D. (2002). *Mindfulness-Based Cognitive Therapy for depression: A new approach to preventing relapse.* London: Guilford.

Shapiro, S. L., Brown, K. W., & Astin, J. A. (2008). Toward the integration of meditation into higher education: A review of research. *Center for Contemplative Mind in Society*, 1-45.

Shapiro, S. L., Schwartz, G. E., & Bonner, G. (1998). Effects of mindfulness-based stress reduction on medical and premedical students. *Journal of Behavioral Medicine, 21*, 581-599.

Sibinga, E. M. S., Perry-Parrish, C., Chung, S., Johnson, S. B., Smith, M. Ellen, J. M. (2013). School-based mindfulness instruction for urban male youth: A small randomized controlled trial. *Preventative Medicine, 57*, 799-801.

Singh, N. N., Lancioni, G. E., Joy, S. D. S., Winton, A. S. W., Sabaawi, M., Wahler, R. G., et al. (2007). Adolescents with conduct disorder can be mindful of their aggressive behavior. *Journal of Emotional and Behavioral Disorders, 15*, 56-63.

Stanley, S. (2012). Mindfulness: Toward a critical relational perspective. *Social and Personality Psychology, 6*, 631-641.

Van Dam, N. T., Earlywine, M., & Borders, A. (2010). Measuring mindfulness?: An item response theory analysis of the Mindful Attention Awareness Scale. *Personality and Individual Differences, 49*, 805-810.

Wachs, K., & Cordova, J. V. (2007). Mindful relating: Exploring mindfulness and emotion repertoires in intimate relationships. *Journal of Marital & Family Therapy, 33*, 464-481.

Walach, H., Buchheld, N., Buttenmuller, V., Kleinknecht, N., & Schmidt, S. (2006). Measuring Mindfulness: The Freiburg Mindfulness Inventory (FMI). *Personality and Individual Differences, 40*, 1543-1555.

Williams, M., & Penman, D. (2011). *Mindfulness: An eight-week plan for finding peace in a frantic world.* New York: Rodale.

Williams, J. C., & Zylowska, L. (2008). *Mindfulness bibliography.* Los Angeles, CA: Mindful Awareness Research Center, UCLA Semel Institute.

• CHAPTER THREE •

"We Could Sure Use a Laugh": Building Hope and Resilience Through Humorous Communication

Rachel L. DiCioccio
University of Rhode Island

Humor is a ubiquitous experience that permeates all aspects of our lives. We communicate humor in our romantic, family, friendship, and work relationships through a variety of forms, for a multitude of relationship purposes. Often taken for granted, the complexity of humor communication is undeniable; it can simultaneously entertain, shock, encourage, and offend us. As an integral aspect of our relationships, the vast nuances of humor far exceed the mundane "knock-knock" joke and bring to light a potent communication tool. Humor, when used appropriately, can create or shift the emotional charge of an interaction. Whether through subtle means or overt contrast, humor has a direct impact on the emotional state of relational partners.

Our use and interpretation of humorous communication develops across our lifespan. From infancy to adulthood, we are exposed to and changed by the many forms and functions of humor. At an early age, we are taught the social value of having a "good" sense of humor and encouraged to and rewarded for successfully demonstrating humorous acts and messages. As we mature into adulthood, our ability to be funny and make others laugh is cast as a positive attribute, allowing us to engage others and making us more socially attractive. We are also acutely aware however, of the hurtful nature of humor, when it is intentionally employed to mock us. This type of humor can leave us embarrassed and bruised by someone's humorous remarks. During any period in our lives it is recognized that "humor serves as a social tool that fosters positive feelings and encourages a sense of kinship yet it can also act as a demonstration of aggression" (DiCioccio, 2012, p. 94). A significant corpus of research mirrors what we learn through our own life experiences, that humor can be employed for both "positive purposes (i.e., to reduce tension and provide support) and negative purposes (i.e., to create tension and attack and demean)" (Cann, Zapata, & Davis, 2009, p. 455). Research on positive humor recognizes numerous beneficial outcomes including "...bolstered psychological well-being (Martin, 2001); increased relationship satisfaction (Butzer & Kuiper, 2008; Ziv & Gadish, 1989); enhanced relational closeness (Alberts, Yoshimura, Rabby, & Loschiavo, 2005; Ziv, 1988); and reduced conflict in romantic relationships (Bippus, 2003; Campbell, Martin, & Ward, 2008)" (DiCioccio, 2012, p. 96). Attending to the negative outcomes of humor, researchers have examined "such consequences as marital dissatisfaction (DeKoning & Weiss, 2002); conflict escalation (Bippus, 2003); strengthened ethnocentrism (Miczo & Welter, 2006); and lower job satisfaction (Avtgis & Taber, 2006)" (DiCioccio, 2012, p. 96). The particular interest of this chapter centers on humor as a means of building hope and resilience, and therefore will focus on how the use of positive humor generates positive affect in others.

As the above summary suggests, there are many ways in which humor creates positive affect. It can be used to entertain and engage others, and often acts a social lubricant between interactants. The emotion that is produced through positive humor can have both short- and long-term benefits for the interaction, the individuals involved, and the relationship. To illustrate a short-term outcome, consider a situation in which a child comes home from school with a lesser grade on an art project than she desired. Her older brother teases saying, "C'mon, you knew old Mr. Cambridge never liked me or my art so he's still taking it out on me!" The younger sister giggles a bit, and her mood is lightened. Additionally, this exchange lightens the sibling relationship, and lifts the sister's self-esteem.

So how does humor serve to elevate and enhance the mood of an interaction? It is obvious that in order for a humorist to succeed at creating positive affect, they need to have a repertoire of humor competence. They must pay attention to delivery, timing, and the appropriateness of the message itself. In the preceding example, if the big brother had teased his sister not using self-deprecating but more a more attacking joke like "you know you could never draw anything recognizable anyhow—all your drawings look like a stick figure and a tree," the humor would be inappropriate and actually serve to hurt the sister's self-concept, and their relationship would suffer some injury. To convey humor successfully, the humorist must also be cognizant of the need to uplift others. How humor generates positive affect in others speaks to the intentionality behind its use. Although it is possible for positive affect to result from humor as a random product of circumstance, for the most part, it reflects the concerted efforts and goal directed intentions of the source. In other words, we purposefully consider both why we want to improve the mood of the receiver, as well as how and with what messages we will accomplish the task. In order to uplift the emotional state of an interaction, a humorist must take on a positive persona to evoke reciprocal positivity in the receiver as well as having some perceptiveness and empathy toward the receiver. A sweeping assertion supported by the literature on emotional contagion, is the notion that successful humor and the creation of positive affect is a product of mutual mood elevation—we build and feed on each other's use of humor and the corresponding emotion. An individual's intention to create a positive mood in a receiver depends on the demonstration of one's own positive affect, which in turn, is bolstered by the receiver's reciprocated emotional state. Here in the spiral of enhancing and reciprocity lies the connection between humor and resilience.

This chapter serves to recognize how humor communication functions as a cathartic act to promote positive emotion, and, in turn, fosters and bolsters hope and resilience. In order to link extant theory and research in humor with resilience, the following chapter will first introduce humor theory to lay the groundwork, identify the linkages between humor theory and hope and resilience theory, and, finally, discuss contextual research that illuminates humor as a mechanism to promote hopefulness and resilience across the lifespan.

Defining and Theorizing Humorous Communication

How do we define humor communication? Scholars have generated multiple conceptualizations of humor, all of which recognize humor "...as a communicative act that can serve single or multiple cognitive emotional, and relational functions" (DiCioccio, 2013, p. 53). As a communicative act, humor aids in accomplishing interpersonal goals that fulfills relationship needs and expectations. Rancer and Graham (2012) suggest that the value and power of humor resides in the negotiated meaning between relational partners. Martin (2007) conceptualizes humor as a "broad term that refers to anything people say or do that is perceived as funny and tends to make others laugh, as well as the mental processes that go into both creating and perceiving such an amusing stimulus and also the affective response involved in the enjoyment of it" (p. 5). Focusing on the prosocial aspect of humor, Booth-Butterfield and Booth-Butterfield (1991) suggest that humor includes "intentional verbal and nonverbal messages and other forms of spontaneous behavior that elicit laughter, chuckling and taken to mean pleasure, delight and/or surprise, in the targeted receiver" (p. 206). Together, these definitions underscore the activity of mutually engaging in humor communication; what is done by one person conjointly with another to influence, sustain, or change the emotional climate of an interaction.

As a starting point, the delineation of the central theoretical perspectives and models of humor will help to situate humor as an act of hope and resilience. Extant humor research has produced numerous theories and models to explain the production and interpretation of humor. However, for the purposes of this chapter, only a few prominent theories and models will be discussed. Three widely accepted types of theories of humor include arousal/relief/release, incongruity, and superior/disparagement.

The first set is arousal/relief/release theories, which focus on the physiological and psychological release created by humor (Graham, Papa, & Brooks, 1992; Martin, 2007). This perspective suggests that the emotional arousal and laughing created through humor, is a positive and enjoyable experience that results in the release of energy (Berlyne, 1969). The relief one experiences may be in the form of cognitive release, reducing anxiety, or a physical release that reduces tension.

Incongruity theory is the second type of theory and centers on the cognitive process we employ to interpret, understand, and appreciate a humorous message (Rancer & Graham, 2012). According to this theory, humor is the product of the juxtaposition of contrasting or dissimilar concepts. When confronted unexpectedly with a message that is incongruent with our expectations, the contradiction can be seen as humorous. In other words, we laugh at things that catch us off guard and surprise us.

Finally, the last theoretical set encompasses superiority-disparagement theories. This type of theory suggests that humor occurs when we are able to take pleasure in another's inadequacy or inferiority. From this perspective, humor is viewed as a type of aggressive communication. The butt of the joke or locus of aggression is "put down," which in turn " elevates a person above the target of humor" (Graham, Papa, & Brooks, 1992, p. 162). This theoretical perspective underscores the negative and damaging effect of humor on the individual and relationship.

Contemporary models of humor expand theoretical attempts to explain how and why humor works by highlighting the multiple functions accomplished by humor communication. Meyer's (2000) model of humor positions four functions of humor along a continuum ranging from the most unifying to the most divisive forms. This continuum reflects the varying degrees of positive and negative outcomes that result from humor. On the positive or unifying end of the continuum are two functions, identification and clarification. Identification is the most unifying function, reflecting humor used to strengthen relational bonds by emphasizing interconnectivity and underscoring the meaning held in common by relational partners. Clarification humor, also a positive function but slightly less unifying, reveals a speaker's perspective regarding a cultural belief or rule without specifically putting down or demeaning the violator of the social norm. These two forms of humor serve to foster positive interaction by encouraging an affiliative and cohesive relationship between communicators. At the divisive end of the humor functions continuum lie enforcement and differentiation humor. The enforcement function is characterized by teasing and put down humor used to highlight a receiver's violation of a social rule or norm. For example, imagine a large family gathering for a family dinner. As family line up to serve themselves from the buffet, an adult son cuts the line in front of his mother. The man's brother chides him, "Of course, Rick, you deserve to be in front of mom because you sat and watched TV while mom slaved to prepare this meal. You most definitely should go first!" In this example, the brother teases Rick for being rude and acting inappropriately. Finally, differentiation demonstrates the most divisive form of humor. Disparaging the receiver through the use of ridicule and mocking, the differentiation function aims to draw a distinct contrast between the speaker and the receiver. The conceptualization of this continuum "...sets humor functions on a single polarized array with prosocial humor positioned at one end and antisocial humor at the other" (DiCioccio, 2012, p. 95).

Another contemporary model addresses the styles of using humor. Developing and validating the Humor Styles Questionnaire, Martin, Puhlik-Doris, Larsen, Grey, and Weir (2003) delineated "four dimensions relating to different uses or functions of humor in everyday life" (p. 51). These four styles are subsumed under two overarching forms of humor: adaptive humor and maladaptive humor. Adaptive humor reflects the positive and social expression of humor used to foster well-being and fortify interpersonal relationships. The opposite dimension is maladaptive humor. This negative style employs the hostile expression of humor in order to at minimum undermine another individual and potentially inflict permanent damage on the relationship.

Martin et al.'s (2003) synthesizing psychological model posits that humor is the product of the integration of two central functions and two broad styles of humor. The main functions distinguish humor that "enhances the self" and humor that "enhances one's relationship with others" as an individual's intention to demonstrate humor. Serving as a defense strategy, self-enhancing humor is used to protect oneself against stress and adversity. Relationship-enhancing humor serves an interactive function that is meant to support relational partners by minimizing tension and conflict, and strengthening cohesion. Martin et al.'s model also introduces two styles of humor: benevolent and hostile. Humor can be benevolent or considerate to the self and to others, or it can be detrimental to the self or one's relationship. Martin et al.'s integration of these proposed functions and styles of humor results in four types of humor use: affiliative, self-enhancing, self-deprecating, and aggressive.

Affiliative humor is accomplished by "off-the-cuff" banter that affirms the self and the other, as well as their relationship. Self-enhancing humor focuses on one's own needs to be happy and healthy by helping to advance "a humorous outlook on life" (p. 71). Used to gain others' approval and inclusion, self-deprecating humor inflicts self-disparaging attacks. Last, aggressive humor utilizes ridicule and sarcasm to hurt and degrade others. As with the first model, Martin et al.'s psychological model underscores the duality of humor as both a positive and negative communication tool. The latter two models discussed provide useful insight into the functionality of humor and the role it plays in building resilience. Next, the relationship between positive emotion and resilience will be discussed through the lens of relevant humor theories and models.

Positive Emotion and Humor: Fostering Hope and Resilience

The constructs of resilience and hope represent two powerful mechanisms for achieving psychological health and well-being. Hope may be defined as a positive motivational state that is derived from a sense of accomplishment in recognizing one's desired goals and being able to successfully meet those goals (Snyder, 2002). The concept of resilience refers to a person's ability to manage and overcome stress and adversity (Rutter, 1999). Across one's lifespan, it is inevitable that we will be faced with trauma and hardship, including death, illness, loss of employment, and other unexpected stressors. The distress brought on by these negative experiences can significantly damage an individual's emotional health, psychological well-being, and relational stability. To avoid and diminish these consequences, one must positively adapt in the face of adversity—be resilient and hopeful. To bounce back from a low emotional state requires the levers of gaining hope.

Hope is a cognitive state that centers on a person's goal-directed thoughts. These goals can be short or long term, vary in importance, and can range from simple to impossible (Grewal & Porter, 2007). Snyder (1995, 2002) identifies two essential components of hope: agency (goal-directed energy) and pathways (planning to meet goals). In order for individuals to have high-hope cognitions, they must engage in both agency and pathways. They must recognize the necessary end goals but also actively pursue the means for accomplishing these goals. Agency defines one's motivation to "begin and continue using a pathway through all stages of the goal pursuit" (Snyder, 2002, p. 252). Pathways "entails the production of one's plausible route, with the concomitant sense of confidence in the route" (Snyder, 2002, p. 252). Although conceptualized as a thought process, engaging in high-hope cognition influences one's emotional state as well. "Higher-hope persons, with their elevated sense of agency and pathways for situations in general, approach a given goal with a positive emotional state, a sense of challenge, and a focus on success rather than failure" (Snyder, 1995, p. 355). A person's perceptions of his/her goal achievement influence his/her emotional response to the experience. The process of moving along one's path to goal attainment generates subsequent emotions that reflect the judgments and interpretation of the success or failure of the goal pursuit activities. "As such, positive emotion should flow from perceptions of successful goal pursuit" (Snyder, 2002, p. 252).

Resilience reflects the coping process people employ to bounce back from traumatic life events and successfully move forward with their lives. "Resilience evokes the promise of something good resulting from misfortune, hope embedded in adversity" (Dyer & McGuiness, 1996). Resilience has been conceptualized as a dynamic process that relies on the protective factors a person has at their disposal (Bonanno, 2004; Dyer & McGuiness, 1996; Luthar & Cicchetti, 2000). Protective factors include the healthy skills and competencies that serve as resources during times of stress. Collectively, protective factors "...are those that modify the effects of risk in a positive direction" (Luthar & Cicchetti, 2000, p. 585). The skills valuable in building resilience include individual, interpersonal, and familial competencies (Dyer & McGuiness, 2004). Individual skills that can protect against adversity include a positive and easygoing temperament and a high sense of self-worth. Interpersonal skill centers on the ability to build positive rapport with others and familial skill is derived from emotionally sound relationships with family members. Consistent across all three competency domains is the concept of positive emotion. Whether it is our own upbeat, positive outlook, or the emotion generated through our interaction with others, positive emotion serves as a central mechanism for fostering psychological resilience.

Positive emotion is an essential aspect of both hope and resilience as they fuel the process and embody the idea of psychological health and well-being. Positive emotions are multifaceted responses that "incorporate muscle tension, hormone release, cardiovascular changes, facial expression, attention, and cognition, among other changes–that unfold over a relatively short time span" (Fredrickson & Cohn, 2008, p.778). These physiological and cognitive tendencies center on an experience or circumstance specific to the person, and that is important and meaningful at the moment it is experienced. Positive emotions are associated with other beneficial cognitive functions such as flexibility, openness, and creativity. Fredrickson (1998, 2001) introduced the broaden-and-build theory of positive emotion as a way of conceptualizing how positive emotion benefits our psychological health. The broaden-and-build theory suggests that positive emotions are the key to establishing enduring personal resources.

Fredrickson's (1998, 2001) broaden-and-build theory posits that positive and negative emotions directly affect a person's adaptive skills, and, in turn, result in different cognitive and physiological outcomes. Specifically, "...negative emotions narrow one's momentary thought-action repertoire by preparing one to behave in a specific way (e.g., attack when angry, escape when afraid). In contrast, various discrete positive emotions (e.g., joy, contentment, interest) broaden one's thought-action repertoire, expanding the range of cognition and behaviors that come to mind" (Tugade & Fredrickson, 2004, p. 321). In other words, while negative emotions limit the options and skills available for reacting to a particular situation, positive emotions maximize the intellectual, emotional, and social resources a person has at his/her disposal. Take for example a father who returns home after just being laid off from his job. Only utilizing negative emotions, the father is angry and anxious, and when asked by his children why he is home so early, his response is short and hostile, upsetting his children and underscoring his negative emotional state. If in the same situation the father relies on positive emotions, he responds to the childrens' question with a joke or humours comment that makes everyone laugh– "I came home early so I could play video games but don't tell mom" – he stands a greater chance of alleviating stress in the moment, which in turn could allow him to step back from the situation and possibly see it from a different perspective. Fredrickson, Tugade, Waugh, and Larkin (2003) defined personal resources resulting from positive emotions to include "...physical resources (e.g., physical skills, health, longevity), social resources (e.g., friendship, social support networks), intellectual resources (e.g., expert knowledge, intellectual complexity), and psychological resources (e.g., trait resilience, optimism, creativity)" (p. 367). The relationship between positive emotions, personal resources, and coping is best explained by an upward spiral of mutual influence. According to McGhee (2010), "There is evidence that positive emotion initiates a reciprocal relationship with coping in which the experience of positive emotion enhances coping, which-in turn-leads to greater positive affect" (p. xxv). The positive emotions experienced in the moment broaden the options and resources we have for coping with stress. Successfully managing stress fosters positive emotions that increase the likelihood we will be emotionally sound in the future. Tugade and Fredrickson (2004) endorse the notion of successful stress management and suggest the broaden-and-build theory of positive emotion provides a useful framework for understanding resilience. One factor that hypothetically distinguishes high- from low-resilient individuals is the ability to experience and generate positive emotion during times of stress and trauma. Higher resilience is associated with greater generation and experiencing of positive emotion. Experiencing ongoing positive emotions can build an arsenal of personal resources that increases our flexibility and adaptability when managing adversity (McGhee, 2010).

Humor communication constitutes one such personal resource. In a chapter on the role of humor in stress reduction, Kuhn, Nichols, and Belew (2010) summarized the healing power of humor nicely: "Humor has now been shown to effectively reduce stress, boost immunity, relieve pain, decrease anxiety, stabilize mood, rest the brain, enhance communication, inspire creativity, maintain hope, bolster morale, sustain resilience, and provide a long-term perspective" (p. 655). The ability to see events around you as humorous and to evoke humor in others is integral to the creation of positive emotions. The health benefits introduced by humor are, in part, a product of the positive emotional states that accompany the experience of humor and laughter. "The essence of humor is its spontaneous expression of emotion and attitude. Whenever we smile or laugh we are expressing feelings for which we might not have the words" (Kuhn, Nichols, & Belew, 2010, p. 659). The notion of having a "healthy" sense of humor is accompanied by other positive temperament qualities such as joy, optimism, happiness, and love. So, humor is one of many strategies for generating positive emotions and the subsequent benefits.

According to Earvolino-Ramirez (2007), "The quality of having a sense of humor about life situations and about one's self is constant across all resilience studies of all ages" (p. 77). Humor is a vital strategy for encouraging hopeful thinking, reducing the intensity of stressful situations, and shifting the emotional charge of adversity (Richardson, 2002; Rutter, 1999). Although in this chapter, humor is primarily discussed as a mechanism to foster hope and resilience while leading people through times of challenge and crisis, it is important to recognize the broader benefit of humor—to proactively build a reserve or cushion of emotional strength and versatility. In this way, humor is a daily tool that constantly enhances one's psychological well-being and in challenging and stressful times it can be a vital skill and asset in helping people move forward.

Martin and Lefcourt (1983) conducted a series of studies examining the moderating effects of different measures of a subject's sense of humor. They found strong support for the hypothesis that humor reduces the impact of stress. Overall, subjects who scored high on different humor measures also reported lower mood disturbance when experiencing negative life events. Martin and Lefcourt (1983) also found that "for humor to moderate the effects of stress, the individual must also place a high value on humor and more importantly, produce humor particularly in the stressful situations that he or she encounters in daily life" (p.1322). Resilient individuals are able to employ humor and maximize positive emotion when working to manage traumatic experiences.

Engaging in humor during adverse situations benefits individuals in two ways. First, positive emotions generated through a humorous exchange work to minimize and counter the negative emotions brought on by stress. A second benefit of humor is the experience of engaging with another person. Humor is "a useful interpersonal skill that helps to establish and maintain social standing and friendship" (Kumpfer, 1999, p. 209). This social activity underscores one's supportive relationships and social network that can assist an individual in the process of bouncing back and being resilient (Bonanno & Keltner, 1997). In this way, humor fosters personal assests by bolstering an individual's emotional state, as well as interpersonal resources, by strengthening his/her relationships and support systems.

Humor serves to modify stress by not only generating positive emotion and mood elevation, but also helping to reorganize one's cognitive perspective regarding a negative experience. Engaging in humor helps us to reframe conditions that are unacceptable and undesirable, casting them in a more tolerable light. Kuhn et al. (2010) suggest that "humor can act as a shock absorber that lessens the jolt of absorbing new and unfamiliar things" (p. 660). In this way, humor serves to broaden one's outlook on and interpretation of the adverse event. Building an overall positive and humorous outlook on life supports more open-mindedness and creative attributions that cultivate more effective coping strategies. In this capacity, humor promotes an adaptive coping tactic "similar to positive reinterpretation and perspective taking" (Martin, 2001, p. 506). By introducing alternative perspectives and options for understanding and reacting to a situation, our flexibility and elasticity increase, and our hopefulness and resiliency are augmented.

Arousal/relief and incongruity theories provide a starting point to understand how the nature of humor is recuperative, promoting more resilient and hopeful thought processes. Arousal/relief theories center on the reduction of tension experienced because of humor. "The physiological benefits of laughter most closely align with this theoretical perspective as many negative health conditions are exacerbated by stress and laughter has been shown to reduce the symptoms of such conditions" (Wilkins & Eisenbraun, 2009, p. 351). Numerous studies recognize the stress reduction properties of laughter that enhance physical health. For example, laughter and humor improve pulmonary function (Kimata, 2004a), strengthen immunity (Berk, Felton, Tan, Bittman, & Westengard, 2001), and reduce blood glucose levels in patients with diabetes (Hayashi, Hayashi, Iwanaga, Kawai, Ishii, Shoji, & Murakami, 2003). Collectively, these studies support the notion that laughter has direct physical benefits. Relief can also be experienced through the release of cognitive tension and anxiety (Wilkins & Eisenbraun, 2009). The positive mental state of amusement and joyfulness can provide a release or break from anxiety and depressive mood states.

Incongruity theory suggests that humor resides in the violation of an accepted pattern or expected outcome. Being able to see humor in the absurd, the ironic, and that which is out of place, in part reflects a "good" sense of humor. Vilaythong, Arnau, Rosen, and Mascaro (2003) found that individuals exposed to comedic videos that depicted slapstick humor reported higher levels of hope on the Snyder State Hope Scale in contrast to those who watched neutral videos. Recognizing, understanding, and enjoying the oddities and quirks illuminated with humor contribute to an overall lightheartedness and hopeful perspective. Humor derived from incongruities, or experiences that seem out of place for their context, is conducive to aid in the reappraisal of a threatening event, broadening the lens of interpretation (Martin, 2001, 2007). The cognition necessary to recognize the incongruity of a humorous act is also essential to perspective-taking and open-mindedness. These skills are linked in numerous ways to communication competence.

The relationship between humor and coping can also be explained through the lens of functional humor models. Humor accomplishes multiple functions. What forms of humor are pivotal to generate positive emotion and promote hope and resilience? Martin (2001) posits that "certain forms or styles of humor may be more adaptive and health enhancing than others" (p. 506). It is logical to assume that the aggressive and maladaptive forms of humor, such as sarcasm and self-deprecating humor, would be counter-productive to encouraging a hopeful and resilient state of mind. Utilizing the model posited by Martin et al. (2003), we can identify the functions of humor that allow for the positive reframing of a negative event, and that support a more effective approach to coping.

Martin et al. (2001) conceptualizes self-enhancing humor as the humor employed to maintain an optimistic and upbeat demeanor. The very nature of this type of humor embodies the promotion of hope and resiliency. Self-enhancing humor functions to bolster and sustain a positive attitude towards one's day-to-day life. Being skilled at utilizing self-enhancing humor and appreciating the benefits it produces provides a preemptive tool for managing adverse events. As Cann and Etzel (2008) suggest, individuals "high on self-enhancing humor...would be best able to use their sense of humor to more positively construe stressors and therefore experience less stress" (p.159). Seeing the humor in one's everyday life is partly an act of hopefulness. Embracing a humorous way of thinking can color perceptions of the stressful nature of a life event—how intense, severe, and manageable it is.

In a study examining the relationship among humor, personality qualities, and stress, Cann and Etzel (2008) concluded that for study participants greater use of self-enhancing humor was associated with higher reported levels of hope, happiness, and optimism, and lower perceptions of stress. This type of humor arms a person with a sense of control and stability overall, especially during stressful situations. Nezu, Nezu, and Blissett (1988) state that "...it is possible that people who use humor to cope with stress do so as a function of their positive evaluations concerning self-efficacy and personal control" (p. 524). Self-efficacy and personal control reflect a person's sense of agency and his/her confidence in a chosen pathway. In this way, humor can buttress one's belief that goal attainment is possible, and motivate him/her to see the process to completion. Nezu et al. (1988) suggests that humor can be fundamental in shifting one's view of a stressful event—seeing it is as a challenge rather than as a threat. Having a humorous temperament can reinforce one's self-assurance and certainty in his/her ability to cope, by adopting a mindset that "I can survive and manage this."

Affiliative humor (Martin et al., 2001) focuses on humor used to establish and underscore liking, affinity, and interpersonal closeness. Employing humor to foster relational bonds can also have positive implications for a person's ability to manage stress. These close relationships provide a support network that can help carry a person through difficult periods and challenges. Unlike aggressive and negative humor, these two social forms of humor maximize relational resources that aid in the coping process. As Cann and Etzel (2008) posit, "Greater use of affiliative humor should increase the available social support networks, providing resources to facilitate dealing with potential stressors" (p. 160). Humor promotes emotional support and social intimacy that may inhibit, or at minimum, reduce the likelihood of crippling anxiety and depression when one must manage a traumatic situation. In this way, affiliative and positive humor mitigate feelings of isolation and detachment that undermine effective coping.

Contextualizing Research on Humor, Hope, and Resilience Across the Lifespan

A significant corpus of research explores the influence of humor on the management of stress and coping. Humor as a mechanism of hope and resilience has been examined in a variety of contexts and in conjunction with numerous personality and relational variables. The following discussion is by no means an exhaustive review of the research on humor and coping. Rather, the intention is to recognize and touch upon some of the prominent contexts in which the resilience-promoting properties of humor have been explored, and to present some significant research findings that inform our understanding of this powerful relationship. Extracting a selected few contexts from the broad sweep of lifespan, highlights the constancy of humor to effect hope and resilience.

One context that has received attention from communication, nursing, and psychology scholars is that of adolescences and the young adult life stage. Learning how to manage and adapt to adversity is a part of growing up. Unfortunately, adolescents and young adults are not sheltered from the stressors of life, and, therefore, must learn to cope with the anxiety and trauma that result from such life events as peer pressure and bullying, illness, and family struggles. Erickson and Feldstein (2007) utilized the Humor Styles Questionnaire to measure adolescent humor and assess the relationship between humor and coping, defense style, depression, and adjustment during adolescence. Applying an approach versus avoidance model of adolescent coping, Erickson and Feldstein explored if and how humor functions to manage stress. They found that positive, adaptive humor was associated with better coping. Affiliative and self-enhancing humor were positively associated with mature defense strategies (maintaining one's ego and sense of reality), and approach coping (the act of directly engaging to alter a stressor and to adjust positively). In a study of college students, Booth-Butterfield, Booth-Butterfield, and Wanzer (2007) determined that the adaptive quality and coping function of humor enactment held for less intense and nontraumatic day-to-day situations. In their study, high humor-oriented students who were also employed reported greater coping efficacy and job satisfaction.

Adolescence, coping, and humor use has also been examined with regard to cancer and pediatric illness. Dowling, Hockenberry, and Gregory (2003) conducted an exploratory investigation to observe the moderating effect of sense of humor on the relationship between childhood cancer stressors and one's psychological adjustment to having cancer, immunity, and infection. Guided by the framework of the transactional theory of stress, appraisal, and coping, 43 children undergoing outpatient chemotherapy completed self-reports of sense of humor, cancer stressors, and psychosocial adjustment, as well as physiological measures for immunity and infection. Results revealed "a direct relationship such that children with a high sense of humor had greater psychological adjustment, regardless of the amount of cancer stressors experienced" (p. 284).

Several studies argue the benefits of humor as a nursing intervention essential for helping children dealing with long-term illness. In a qualitative case study, Frankenfield (1996) identified a nurse's use of humor to reduce the anxiety and stress for a pediatric oncology patient. Dowling (2002), in her descriptive discussion of strategies of nurses to incorporate humor into their care plan for pediatric patients, also details numerous case examples of young patients benefitting from the humorous exchanges they experienced with medical professionals.

Humor has also been studied in adult interpersonal relationships navigating high-stress conditions. Horan, Bochantin, and Booth-Butterfield (2012) looked at the romantic relationships of police officers as one such type of relationship. They suggest that the high-stress work conditions of law enforcement officials can lead to greater stress in their romantic relationships and they hypothesized that humor is a useful coping strategy to manage this stress. Participants who were currently in a romantic relationship with a police officer reported their perceived stress, the frequency and nature of conflict with their partner, their self-report and other-report of humor orientation, and their use of humor to cope with stress. Findings revealed that self-reports of high humor orientation were associated negatively with reported levels of stress and conflict. Additionally, results "revealed that source's reported use of humor to cope mediated the relationships between self-reported HO levels and stress and conflict" (p. 566). In other words, the expression of humor during conflict and challenging times is particularly effective in minimizing stress.

In a study on effective coping with interpersonal transgressions, LaBelle, Booth-Butterfield, and Weber (2013) investigated the impact of humorous communication on relationship satisfaction following an interpersonal transgression. LaBelle et al. accepted a 2007 (McCollough et al., 2007, p.127) definition of interpersonal transgressions to include "nontraumatic social interactions that victims nonetheless perceive to be morally wrong and personally hurtful" (p. 222). They hypothesized that humor orientation would be related positively to coping with the stress brought on by interpersonal transgressions. Their findings underscore previous research, supporting their assertion "that higher HO is associated with greater perceived efficacy in coping with everyday stress, as well as the perception that humor can be effectively used to cope with interpersonal hurt" (p. 227).

Centering on the opposite end of the life continuum is the topic of humor and older adults and palliative care. During this life stage, elderly people are more likely to be confronted with issues related to terminal illness, financial crises, and serious decision-making. The later or end of life stage provides a unique set of conditions for examining the use of humor to foster hope and resilience. In a study examining the relationship between age, humor production, coping efficacy, and life satisfaction, Wanzer, Sparks, and Frymier (2009) found that "these variables function in complex ways for older adults" (p.133) Although overall, humor use declined for older adults in comparison to college-age students, for older adults, high humor orientation was positively associated with effective coping and greater sense of life satisfaction. Westburg (2003) investigated how humor benefits institutionalized elderly people and their professional caregivers in an assisted living facility. Utilizing the pathways and agency conceptualization of hope (Snyder, 2002), Westburg sought to examine the differences in humor use between more- and less-hopeful individuals. Analysis of participants' self-reports on the Hope Scale and the open-ended Funny Bone History Questionnaire revealed several differences between elderly residents and the staff. Most notably, residents reported higher levels of hope than the staff responsible for their care. One of the most significant findings distinguishing high from low hopeful individuals pertained to perceptions of sources of laughter. "The majority of the higher-hope residents and staff said 'most things' or 'real life' situations made them laugh, whereas none of the lower-hope residents responded this way" (p. 24). This suggests that for high-hope individuals, humor is mainly driven by an internal state of mind rather than an outside stimulus—they are able to see the humor in the day-to-day situations that arise. Westburg (2003) suggests that "The ability to find humor in everyday situations as a source of humor seems to be an inner strength that helps these people to feel positive when faced with the stressors of institutional living" (p. 24). In this way, humor sturdies one's confidence in and determination to move forward and successfully manage an adverse event.

Finally, Dean and Gregory (2004) conducted an ethnographic study in order to characterize the circumstances where humor and laughter occurred, the functions humor performed, and the instances when humor and laughter were inappropriate. Using extended observations and informal interviews with patients and their families, Dean and Gregory (2004) concluded that humor was ever present and that patients, families, and caregivers experienced a wide range of humor behaviors to manage the serious situations. Specifically, observations revealed that humor served three central functions: 1) building relationships, 2) contending with circumstances, and 3) expressing sensibility. These results support the argument that humor, especially during end-of-life transitions, is key in facilitating emotion and underscores the notion that "the predominant sense of good humor is related to palliative care philosophy, the significance of quality of life, and the importance of relationships" (p. 145).

Conclusion

The power of humorous communication as a mechanism for building hope and resilience is undeniable. Humor has a profound impact on our emotional state, our management of stress, and our ability to cope with the adversity inherent in daily life. Central to the hope and resiliency literature is the concept of positive emotion. Positive emotions fortify our psychological well-being and they are irrefutably a product of engaging in humor. This chapter delineates the connections between positive emotion, humor theories, and the functions of humor as they relate to coping. Specifically, the functions of self-enhancing and affiliative humor (Martin et al., 2001) provide a useful lens for interpreting the particular forms of humor that sustain and bolster a sense of hopefulness and resilience. The psychological benefits of coping and managing stress through humor are acknowledged in a variety of contexts throughout the communication, psychology, and nursing literature. In the final section of this chapter, the predominant bodies of research examined, adolescence, romantic relationship, work, and older adulthood, serve to contextualize the recuperative properties of humor across the lifespan. The theory and research discussed in this chapter draw upon a dispersed body of literature to recognize and endorse the critical role humor plays in buoying our hope and emboldening us to be resilient in times of adversity.

References

Berk, L. S., Felton, D. L., Tan, S. A., Bittman, B. B., & Westgard, J. (2001). Modulation of neuroimmune parameters during the eustress of humor-associated mirthful laughter. *Alternative Therapies, 7*, 62–76.

Berlyne, D. E. (1969). Laughter, humor, and play. In G. Lindzey & E. Aronson (Eds.), *Handbook of social psychology* (2nd ed., Vol. 3) Reading, MA: Addison-Wesley.

Bonanno, G. A. (2004). Loss, trauma, and human resilience: Have we underestimated the human capacity to thrive after extremely aversive events? *American Psychologist, 59*, 20–28.

Bonanno, G. A., & Keltner, D. (1997). Facial expressions of emotion and the course of conjugal bereavement. *Journal of Abnormal Psychology, 106*, 126–137.

Booth-Butterfield, S., & Booth-Butterfield, M. (1991). The communication of humor in everyday life. *Southern Communication Journal, 56*, 205-218.

Booth-Butterfield, S., Booth-Butterfield, M., & Wanzer, M. (2007). Funny students cope better: Patterns of humor enactment and coping effectiveness. *Communication Quarterly, 55*, 299-315.

Cann, A., & Etzel, K. C. (2008). Remembering and anticipating stressors: Positive personality mediates the relationship with sense of humor. *Humor, 21*, 157-178.

Cann, A., Zapata, C. L., & Davis, H. B. (2009). Humor style and relationship satisfaction in dating couples: Perceived versus self-reported humor styles as predictors of satisfaction. *Humor, 24*(1), 1-20.

Dean, R. K., & Gregory, D. M. (2004). Humor and laughter in palliative care: An ethnographic investigation. *Palliative and Supportive Care, 2*, 139-148.

DiCioccio, R. L. (2012). Humor as aggressive communication. In R. L. DiCioccio (Ed.). *Humor communication: Theory, impact, and outcomes.* (pp. 93-108). Dubuque, IA: Kendall Hunt.

DiCioccio, R. L. (2013). Make me laugh, make me listen: Using humor to accomplish interpersonal influence. In C. J. Liberman (Ed.). *Casing persuasive communication.* (pp. 51-65). Dubuque, IA: Kendall Hunt.

Dowling, J. S. (2002). Humor: A coping strategy for pediatric patients. *Pediatric Nursing, 28*, 123-131.

Dowling, J. S., Hockenberry, M., & Gregory, R. L. (2003). Sense of humor, childhood cancer stressors, and outcomes of psychosocial adjustment, immune function, and infection. *Journal of Pediatric Oncology Nursing, 20*, 271-292.

Dyer, J. G., & McGuiness, T. M. (1996). Resilience: Analysis of the concept. *Archives of Psychiatric Nursing, X* (5), 276-282.

Earvolino-Ramirez, M. (2007). Resilience: A concept analysis. *Nursing Forum, 42*, 73-82.

Erickson, S. J., & Feldstein, S. W. (2007). Adolescent humor and its relationship to coping, defense strategies, psychological distress, and well-being. *Child Psychiatry Human Development, 37*, 255-271.

Franenfield, P. K. (1996). The power of humor and play as nursing interventions for a child with cancer: A case report. *Journal of Pediatric Oncology Nursing, 13*, 15-20.

Fredrickson, B. L. (1998). What good are positive emotions? *Review of General Psychology, 2*, 300-319.

Fredrickson, B. L. (2001). The role of positive emotion in positive psychology: The broaden-and-build theory of positive emotion. *American Psychologist, 56*, 218-226.

Fredrickson, B. L., & Cohn, M. A. (2008). Positive emotions. In M. Lewis, J. M. Haviland-Jones, & L. F. Barrett (Eds.). *Handbook of emotions.* (p. 777-796). New York: The Guilford Press.

Fredrickson, B. L., Tugade, M. M., Waugh, C. E., & Larkin, G. R. (2003). What good are positive emotions in crisis? A prospective study of resilience and emotions following the terrorist attacks on the United States on September 11th, 2001. *Journal of Personality and Social Psychology, 84*, 365-376.

Graham, E. E., Papa, M. J., & Brooks, G. P. (1992). Functions of humor in conversations: Conceptualization and measurement. *Western Journal of Communication, 56*, 161-183.

Grewal, P. K., & Porter, J. E. (2007). Hope theory: A framework for understanding suicidal action. *Death Studies, 31,* 131-154.

Hayashi, K., Hayashi, T., Iwanaga, S., Kawai, K., Ishii, H., Shoji, S., & Murakami, K. (2003). Laughter lowered the increase in postprandial blood glucose. *Diabetes Care, 26,* 1651-1652.

Horan, S. M., Bochantin, J., & Booth-Butterfield, M. (2012). Humor in high-stress relationships: Understanding communication in police officers' romantic relationships. *Communication Studies, 63,* 554-573.

Kimata, H. (2004a). Effect of viewing a humorous vs. nonhumorous film on bronchial responsiveness in patients with bronchial asthma. *Physiology & Behavior, 81,* 681-684.

Kuhn, C. C., Nichols, M. R., & Belew, B. L. (2010). The role of humor in transforming stressful life events. In T. W. Miller (Ed.). *Handbook of stressful transitions across the lifespan.* (p. 653-662). New York: Springer.

Kumpfer, K. L. (1999). Factors and processes contributing to resilience: The resilience framework. In M. Glantz & J. Johnson (Eds.), *Resilience and development: Positive life adaptations.* New York: Plenum Press.

LaBelle, S., Booth-Butterfield, M., & Weber, K. (2013). Humorous communication and its effectiveness in coping with interpersonal transgressions. *Communication Research Reports, 30,* 221-229.

Luthar, S. S., & Cicchetti, D. (2000). The construct of resilience: Implications for interventions and social policies. *Development and Psychopathology, 12,* 857-885.

Martin, R. A. (2001). Humor, laughter, and physical health: Methodological issues and research findings. *Psychological Bulletin, 127,* 504-519.

Martin, R. A. (2007). *The psychology of humor: An integrative approach.* Burlington, MA: Elsevier Academic Press.

Martin, R. A., & Lefcourt, H. M. (1983). Sense of humor as a moderator of the relation between stressors and moods. *Journal of Personality and Social Psychology, 45,* 1313-1324.

Martin, R. A., Puhlik-Doris, P., Larsen, G., Gray, J., & Weir, K. (2003). Individual differences in the use of humor and their relation to psychological well being: Development of the Humor Styles Questionnaire. *Journal of Research in Personality, 37,* 48-75.

McGhee, P. (2010). *Humor: The lighter path to resilience and health.* Bloomington, IN: AuthorHouse.

Meyer, J. C. (2000). Humor as a double-edged sword: Four functions of humor communication. *Communication Theory, 10,* 310-331.

Nezu, A. M., Nezu, C. M., & Blissett, S. E. (1988). Sense of humor as a moderator of the relation between stressful events and psychological distress: A prospective analysis. *Journal of Personality and Social Psychology, 54,* 520-525.

Rancer, A. S., & Graham, E. E. (2012). Theories of humor. In R. L. DiCioccio (Ed.). *Humor communication: Theory, impact, and outcomes.* (pp. 3-10). Dubuque, IA: Kendall Hunt.

Richardson, G. E. (2002). The metatheory of resilience and resiliency. *Journal of Clinical Psychology, 58,* 307-321.

Rutter, M. (1999). Resilience concepts and findings: Implications for family therapy. *The Association of Family Therapy, 21,* 119-144.

Snyder, C. R. (1995). Conceptualizing, measuring, and nurturing hope. *Journal of Counseling & Development, 73,* 355-360.

Snyder, C. R. (2002). Hope Theory: Rainbows in the mind. *Psychological Inquiry, 13,* 249-275.

Tugade, M. M., & Fredrickson, B. L. (2004). Resilient individuals use positive emotions to bounce back from negative emotional experiences. *Journal of Personality and Social Psychology, 86,* 320-333.

Vilaythong, A. P., Arnau, R. C., Rosen, D. H., & Mascaro, N. (2003). Humor and hope: Can humor increase hope? *Humor, 16,* 79-89.

Wanzer, M., Sparks, L., & Frymier, A. B. (2009). Humorous communication within the lives of older adults: The relationships among humor, coping, efficacy, age, and life satisfaction. *Health Communication, 24,* 128-136.

Westburg, N. G. (2003). Hope, laughter, and humor in residents and staff at an assisted living facility. *Journal of Mental Health Counseling, 25,* 16-32.

Wilkins, J., & Eisenbraun, A. J. (2009). Humor theories and the physiological benefits of laughter. *Holistic Nursing Practice, 23,* 349-354.

• CHAPTER FOUR •

Fostering Hope in a Hurtful World: The Role of Communication in Promoting Hope and Resilience in the Face of Difficult Experiences

Rachel M. McLaren
The University of Iowa

Joshua R. Pederson
University of Alabama

People across their lifespan frequently experience acts that evoke the emotion of hurt, from elementary-aged children teasing each other in the schoolyard to romantic partners criticizing one another (Leary, Springer, Negel, Ansell, & Evans, 1998; Shapiro, Baumeister, & Kessler, 1991). The people most likely to hurt us, and the people we are most likely to hurt, are individuals with whom we have ongoing relationships (Miller, 1997). Not surprisingly, most of the research on hurt has focused on it as a negative relational experience, because feeling hurt can result in relational damage and a host of other negative outcomes, such as lowered self-esteem, lingering pain, and even relational termination (Mills, Nazar, & Farrell, 2002; Vangelisti & Young, 2000). Hurt feelings can leave emotional scars that last for years to come; in one study, about three quarters of a sample of older adults reported betrayals that occurred between 20 and 30 years ago (Jansson, Jones, & Fletcher, 1990). And yet, other research shows that some negative experiences only have short-term effects (e.g., Frederick & Loewenstein, 1999).

What factors affect people's ability to move beyond hurtful experiences? In this chapter, we explore the ways to promote positive outcomes in the midst of and in the aftermath of hurtful events. For example, hearing constructive critiques from close others could prompt people to reflect on the content of that feedback and possibly make changes in their lives. Even when hurtful messages are delivered with negative intentions, they still provide people with feedback about themselves, their relationships, and their interactions (Vangelisti & Hampel, 2012). Although it may not be possible or preferable to find the silver lining in all hurtful experiences, we consider the features of hurtful events that increase the likelihood of experiencing positive outcomes over the life course. In the following pages, we discuss the research on hurt and the factors that could protect against the negative impact of hurt. Then, we consider the challenges and possibilities people encounter when seeking to instill hope and resilience following a hurtful experience, from the perspectives of the deliverers of hurtful messages, the recipients, and the social network members.

Hurt: Definitions and Functions

Hurt is a distinct emotion that is evoked from social acts that convey relational devaluation. It is a social emotion, meaning that hurt occurs in the context of social encounters or relationships. Hurt feelings can range in intensity from a slight sting to a more intense feeling of emotional injury (Vangelisti, 1994), which can hurt in ways similar to physical pain (e.g., MacDonald & Leary, 2005). There are several types of messages and events that can elicit hurt, from jokes and questions to accusations, threats, and deception (Vangelisti, 1994). In addition to messages, scholars have identified actions that are hurtful, such as disassociation and betrayal (e.g., Leary et al., 1998). Vangelisti and colleagues (2005) found eight reasons that people feel hurt, with relational denigration and humiliation resulting in the most intense hurt feelings, among other causes, such as aggression, discouragement, or shock. The common thread within hurtful incidents is that they convey rejection or relational devaluation (e.g., Fitness, 2001; Leary & Leder, 2009).

In addition to the types of incidents that elicit hurt feelings, research has identified many predictors of the intensity of hurt feelings, such as the form of the message. For example, people report being less hurt by humorously phrased messages (Young & Bippus, 2001; see Beck & Socha, chapter 3) and have more negative appraisals of hurtful messages conveyed with greater intensity or force (Young, 2004). Sometimes it is the deliverer's negative vocal tone that elicits hurt feelings, not necessarily the content of the message. Relational context also matters, such that people are more intensely hurt by family members as compared to other relationship types (Vangelisti & Crumley, 1998). Relational characteristics can affect hurt as well; relational turbulence, or feeling like one's relationship is in turmoil, corresponds with more intense feelings of hurt, greater perceptions of intentionality, and more negative emotions in general (McLaren, Solomon, & Priem, 2011). On the other hand, when people are satisfied, hurtful messages tend to have less of an impact on the relationship (Vangelisti & Crumley, 1998). Finally, attributions also influence hurt; if the victim feels that the offender's behavior was purposefully hurtful, victims tend to feel stronger hurt feelings than if the message was judged as unintentional (Vangelisti & Young, 2000). When people feel more hurt, this can lead to a number of communicative responses, including both avoidance and direct communication (Feeney, 2005; Theiss, Knobloch, Checton, & Magsamen-Conrad, 2009). Thus, there are many factors that can influence the experience of hurt, including the features of the message, the relationship, and the situation.

Hurt feelings are frequent experiences in people's lives, but why do people convey hurtful messages? Vangelisti (2009) articulated three functions of hurtful messages: informative, supportive, and persuasive. Hurtful messages can be informative in that they convey feedback to the recipient. Informative statements are a type of hurtful message characterized by a disclosure of unwanted information ("I'm not ready to move forward in this relationship," Vangelisti, 1994). As Vangelisti and Hampel (2012) argue, hurtful messages give feedback or information to the recipient about themselves, the interaction, and their relationship. For example, accusations ("You're a cheater"), evaluations ("Your friends are much cuter than you"), and criticisms ("You have no style") are all types of hurtful messages that can provide feedback to individuals about their own personal qualities. Furthermore, people can gain feedback about their relationship with the deliverer of the hurtful message, such as how much that person values their relationship (Vangelisti & Hampel, 2012). Finally, hurtful experiences provide a person with information about the nature of their interaction. Often the nonverbal behaviors that accompany a hurtful message convey whether the overall context of the interaction is negative or positive (Vangelisti & Hampel, 2012).

In addition to being informative, hurtful messages can also function in supportive ways. First, people may inadvertently say something hurtful when they intend to be supportive. For example, in one study (McLaren, Priem, & Solomon, 2008), a participant wrote down that she was having a "low self-esteem day" and her boyfriend said, "I could date someone on this campus who is prettier than you, smarter, in better shape, and with a better personality, but I chose you." She recognized that he was trying to be supportive, but he ended up hurting her feelings by confirming her insecurities. Hurt might function in a more legitimately supportive way when people, such as coaches or parents, deliver feedback that is hurtful ("You're really slacking and need to pick up the pace"), but they do so because they have the recipient's best interest in mind (Vangelisti & Hampel, 2012). Even though the message is hurtful, when it occurs in the context of a supportive relationship, people can interpret it as an indication of how much that person cares (Vangelisti, 2009).

The third function of hurt is to be persuasive, either directly or indirectly (Vangelisti, 2009). Sometimes, people intentionally hurt others in order to gain compliance or to win a conflict. For example, tactics such as threats and accusations can be used to retaliate and purposefully cause emotional injury to others (Vangelisti, 1994). Furthermore, hurling criticisms are conflict strategies that can be used in an effort to equalize power. Using hurt as a persuasive tool can be effective, but is not likely to promote positive outcomes because it can lead to cycles of reciprocity of negative affect (e.g., Levenson, Carstensen, & Gottman, 1994). When people feel hurt, they might react by retaliating and trying to hurt the other person back (Vangelisti, 2007).

Although hurt is typically framed as negative, some interesting possibilities open up when we consider how hurt can promote hope, resilience, and growth across different stages in life. The lifespan perspective emphasizes developmental advances and increases throughout one's life (Pecchioni, Wright, & Nussbaum, 2005). Hurtful experiences can prompt personal growth as individuals develop adaptive ways of handling difficult situations. People's ability to effectively understand and control emotions increases with age (Lawton, Kleban, Rajagopal, & Dean, 1992; Labouvie-Vief & DeVoe, 1991). Furthermore, compared to middle-aged married couples, older married couples discuss conflicts with less negative emotion (i.e., anger, disgust, whining) and avoid escalation by remaining neutral instead of negative (Carstensen, Gottman, & Levenson, 1995). As people age and relationships grow, people seem to develop ways of effectively manage their own emotions as well as constructively respond to conflicts. Perhaps this is due to repeated exposure to hurtful conflicts, which gives people ample opportunity to hone their skills for managing negative emotions. Next, we review the literature on hurt for the individual and relational factors that can mitigate the intensity of hurt feelings and build resources to give individuals hope in the midst of hurtful experiences.

Individual and Relational Factors that Protect Against the Negative Impact of Hurt

There are several characteristics of recipients that could minimize the impact of hurt. First, people with secure attachments are often able to appraise hurtful events in constructive ways, allowing them to keep the hurtful experience in perspective, and engage in self-soothing with emotion-regulation techniques (e.g., Mikulincer & Shaver; 2004, 2007). This allows them to keep their "attention on constructive alternatives rather than becoming victims of rumination or catastrophizing" (Shaver, Mikulincer, Lavy, & Cassidy, 2009, pg. 109).

Furthermore, securely attached individuals should be able to constructively express hurt to the offender without being afraid that the person will leave them, allowing them to focus on effective relational repair (Shaver et al., 2009). On the other hand, anxiously attached individuals feel more intensely hurt, likely because of their fear of being abandoned and tendency to be hypersensitive to rejection (Feeney, 2005). Self-esteem is another personal characteristic that shapes the influence of hurt. For example, Vangelisti and colleagues (2005) found that self-esteem was negatively associated with the intensity of hurt reported by participants. Similarly, people who feel more secure in their self-identity are not as threatened by hurtful messages (e.g., Murray, Bellavia, Rose, & Griffin, 2003).

Another way to promote hope and positive outcomes is to invest in the relationship as a way to strengthen it against future harms. Research shows that relational quality affects how people interpret and respond to their partner's negative or dissatisfying behaviors (e.g., Fincham & O'Leary, 1983). Individuals in high-quality relationships tend to engage in less relational distancing (McLaren & Solomon, 2008) and report feeling less intensely hurt than people in dissatisfied relationships (Vangelisti & Crumley, 1998). Furthermore, individuals in satisfied relationships interpret honest but hurtful messages as less threatening (Zhang & Stafford, 2008) and tend to make more benign attributions for negative relationship events. People with high structural commitment to their relationship might be motivated to interpret hurtful events in a way that minimizes their negative impact, because they feel that they have to stay in the relationship (Vangelisti, 2007).

This research discussed above has implications for individual and relational qualities that make people better able to cope with hurt in productive ways. People can mitigate the negative impacts of hurt on themselves when they have secure relationship attachments and high self-esteem. Because hurtful messages are often ambiguous in their meaning, people have choices about how to interpret them. When people are confident about themselves and secure in their relationships, they tend to interpret potentially hurtful messages in ways that minimize the negative impact. In addition, by engaging in relationship maintenance behaviors and trying to keep one another satisfied, experiences of hurt should have less of a negative impact than if the relationship was in distress. Moreover, they may even be able to go a step beyond preventing harm and even promote relational improvement. In a study of hurt between romantic partners, relational quality was positively associated with relational improvement following a hurtful experience, even after controlling for the intensity of hurt experienced (unpublished data, McLaren & Solomon). Future research could continue to probe factors that could promote relational improvement following hurtful events. Now that we have examined the factors that can minimize hurt for receivers, next we draw on politeness theory to discuss ways that senders can minimize hurt feelings.

Minimizing Hurt: Applying Politeness Theory

If people are able to put forethought into their messages before saying them, they could choose to craft their message in a way to minimize hurt. This likely depends on the function of the message; if people want to be informative or supportive, but still need to convey a message that might be hurtful, they could use politeness strategies to deliver the message in a kinder manner. Hurtful messages are inherently face-threatening because they signal individual and relational devaluation as well as challenges to one's idea of self (Goldsmith & Donovan-Kicken, 2009). Face is the desired public image that people create through interactions with others (Goffman, 1967). Negative face is the desire for freedom of action and imposition. Positive face is a desire for approval or claims that are consistent with one's self-image or personality. Criticisms, disapproval, complaints, accusations, and insults can threaten both negative face and positive face because these types of messages are prone to questioning a person's sense of self (Brown & Levinson, 1987). During interactions people often practice what Goffman (1967) calls "facework," which is when people try to act in consistent ways with the public image they are trying to promote, while at the same time attending to the face needs of others. We apply research from face work (Goffman, 1967) and politeness theory (Brown & Levinson, 1987) to suggest ways to reduce the face threat of hurtful messages, which could increase the likelihood of also creating feelings of optimism and hope for moving forward (e.g., Young & Bippus, 2001; Young, 2004).

According to politeness theory (Brown & Levenson, 1987), there are five communicative strategies for minimizing face threats (arranged from most to least threatening). If a speaker goes on record he/she directly expresses the comment without adding anything to the message to address the conversational partner's face needs (e.g. "You really look like you've gained weight in the last year. You should go on a diet."). Instead, a deliverer of hurt could use positive politeness and redress the threat by providing positive face for the hearer. For example, the message should include the other and show commonality (e.g. "Sometimes during the holidays, I gain weight from overindulging. Any chance you feel the same and want to go on a diet with me?"). Another possibility is using a negative politeness strategy, by acknowledging the hearer's freedom of action and self-determination. Such strategies are "characterized by self-effacement, formality, and restraint" (Brown & Levinson, 1987, p. 70) (e.g. "I know you might not be interested, but I am so excited about this new diet and I'd love to tell you about it."). Finally, an off-record strategy tries to hint at the threatening message without actually having to say it. The off-record strategy is indirect and relies on subtle hints to get the message across (e.g. "Look at this photo of us from our wedding! We look so healthy!"). Although there are many factors that influence the effectiveness of politeness strategies, attending to face needs during difficult interactions can minimize negative consequences of potentially hurtful messages. Of course, the final option is not to convey the message at all, which would eliminate the chance of hurting either partner's face, but the downside is that the suggestion or criticism is not communicated (Brown & Levinson, 1987).

Along the same lines, deliverers should consider both their verbal and nonverbal communication when conveying hurtful messages. First, the message intensity or illocutionary force affects how the hurtful message is appraised (Young, 2004). Tracy, Van Dusen, and Robinson (1987) argue that the difference between "good" criticism and "bad" criticism rests on the perception of the harshness and negativity of the language. Individuals could refrain from using especially vivid language when conveying a potentially hurtful message and choose more moderate language with less nonverbal emphasis instead. Another option is to use humor, a type of "off the record" politeness strategy, to soften the threat to a recipient's face. Humorously phrased messages elicit less hurt (Young & Bippus, 2001). For example, a person could say, "All those fad diet plans scare me by saying you will lose 10 pounds in a week. It's not a race! I bet you and I could come up with a better diet plan." Finally, couching hurtful messages in an overarching attempt to show concern, provide comfort, or offer help could lead to more favorable appraisals of hurtful messages (Young, 2004).

It should be noted that the above suggestions operate in positive ways only if the deliverer is sufficiently motivated and skilled enough to try to minimize the recipient's level of hurt. Competent communicators who need to deliver critical messages, such as complaints, are able to do so without interfering with the goals of others (Cupach & Carson, 2012). Communicating with interpersonal competence requires the sender to craft a message that is effective in meeting one's goals and appropriate for the situation. There are many situations in which a deliverer wishes to evoke hurt, and sometimes, as much hurt as possible. The knowledge from politeness theory could be used to inflict extreme hurt, perhaps by using bald on-record strategies to deliver a hurtful message. Thus, the utility of politeness theory for minimizing hurt depends on people's level of motivation, skill, and desire to deliver hurtful messages in as kind a way as possible.

Feedback as a Site of Hurt Feelings

Sometimes people need to convey critiques or criticisms to another person to provide feedback about skills, behaviors, or performance. Feedback is important in many situations across the lifespan, such as in job performance reviews, in schools, and in parenting. If handled well, feedback has the ability to be extremely beneficial. People expect and need to receive feedback from others, because it can be difficult for people to see their own faults and limitations. An outsider's perspective is crucial for this reason; without it, many opportunities for growth and change would be missed. But, feedback is a "high-stakes game;" if it is handled poorly, it can wreak havoc on individual's self-image, egos, and relationships (Sutton, Hornsey, & Douglas, 2012, p. 1). Thus, figuring out how to craft feedback messages in such a way as to convey one's point without causing unnecessary harm is challenging. In this section, we examine why feedback can be hurtful and then we discuss ways to increase the likelihood that feedback will be received positively and result in growth.

For parents, feedback is an important part of socializing their children and helping them develop into adults (Grusec & Davidov, 2010). It can also be part of the discipline process, when parents explain to children why their behavior was not in line with expectations or rules. Unfortunately, giving feedback to children, especially adolescents, has a high likelihood of causing hurt feelings and conflict. Adolescents, as compared to parents, are especially hurt by events that convey criticism, perhaps because these messages imply incompetence when teens are in a period of trying to establish independence (McLaren & Sillars, 2014). Even if the feedback is an attempt to help adolescents improve their performance, such as their grades in school, it can cause hurt feelings for two reasons. First, hearing negative feedback can convey a sense of relational devaluation. Second, it points to a deficiency, at least from the parent's point of view, about the adolescent's skills, abilities, or efforts.

In a study of hurtful events in parent-adolescent relationships, discussing grades and homework in school was a hurtful topic (McLaren & Pederson, 2014; McLaren & Sillars, 2014). One parent said, "Do you need to go to Sylvan Learning Center or something? Because you're obviously not getting it." An adolescent said she was hurt when her mom proofread her paper and said she did a "really poor job on it" and it was "really crappy." When the mother provided her version of the story, she stated: "I told her I was disappointed in her and that it was unacceptable for her to let her homework go until the last minute. I wanted her…to learn to look at the big picture and manage her time well." Another parent also hurt her adolescent son's feelings when helping with homework: "I yelled at him that even a child in kindergarten could put sentences together better than him. I also said that even his two younger brothers can put sentences together better than him." Sometimes these incidents cause retaliation and mutual hurt. Another parent was giving her daughter feedback on her musical performance. The daughter said she was hurt because her mom was "just pointing out what I was doing wrong and nothing anything I was doing right." Then, the daughter retaliated by hurting her mother, saying "I hate you" and "I wish you would die."

In all three of the above examples, parents were providing their children with feedback, ostensibly with good intentions, but it still caused hurt feelings and sometimes prompted ongoing conflict. These scenarios are not limited to parent-child interactions. How can parents, or other people such as managers, administrators, teachers, supervisors, or coaches, provide feedback in ways that maximize the chances for growth without exacerbating the problem or harming the relationship? The influence of feedback depends both on the person's trust in the source of the feedback and the perceived importance of the feedback (Earley, 1986). Thus, trying to preserve the relationship is important for increasing the likelihood of the feedback having an effect on the recipient. If parents intentionally insult or criticize their children as part of their feedback, this can be counter-productive because it undermines the relationship between the parent and the child. More research from communication scholars is especially needed in this area, in an effort to develop effective strategies to teach parents how to give feedback to their children without causing serious damage and long-term hurt for the people involved. In the next section, we apply hope theory in an effort to generate strategies for giving feedback that will result in growth and improvement.

Promoting Feelings of Hope During Hurtful Feedback

Hope can be defined as a positive motivational state, where people confidently think about specific plans or pathways to reach a desired goal (Snyder, 2002). Pathways are considered the specific routes that people take to get to their goals and people have different levels of confidence in their ability and motivation to reach their goals. When people encounter obstacles, agency thinking is especially important because it can help people focus in on developing the best alternate pathways to their goals (Snyder, 1994). Research shows when people have low hope, they do not use the feedback from goal nonattainment to try to improve their future efforts; instead, they ruminate about not achieving the goal and doubt themselves (Michael, 2000; Snyder, 1999). Thus, one option for increasing the chances that feedback promotes growth is to increase people's hope, so that they are more likely to use the feedback to diagnostically develop alternative pathways to achieving goals.

In order to promote hope in giving feedback, there are some challenges that need to be addressed. First, the recipient has to be open to hearing the feedback. Specifically, they have to agree that the goal is unrealized, the current pathway is not working, or the current efforts are not sufficient. In some cases, the deliverer will also have to convince the receiver that the goal is important and worthy of pursuit (such as in the case of parents trying to convince their children to try harder in school because learning and getting good grades are important goals). Getting a person to hear and accept feedback can be especially challenging because people are more likely to reject negative feedback and attribute the cause to outside sources (Leary & Terry, 2012). In order to convince a person that the cause is an internal one, and something they can control, the deliverer of the feedback will likely elicit negative emotions and pushback from the recipient. Yet, doing so is also important so that the recipient will be prompted to take initiative in making changes.

Nonetheless, one way this might be done is by scheduling a predetermined time to give feedback, because people react more positively to expected feedback. When feedback is expected, people can psychologically prepare for it (Leary & Terry, 2012). For example, perhaps a soccer team agrees that on Fridays, the coach will meet individually with each member to provide comments about how the player is doing. In the case of supervisor-supervisee relationships, there are often formal reviews already in place in the organization, but they could also create more informal opportunities to discuss feedback. Of course, a major caveat here is that the feedback is delivered in a competent way.

The next step is convincing the target that he or she has the ability and the appropriate pathways to achieve the goal. For example, if a person receives criticism about his or her piano playing skills, the deliverer might be able to simultaneously convey the comment and promote hopeful feelings in the person by emphasizing the individual's abilities and pathways as a means to become a better player. For example, a music teacher might tell his student, "Your tempo is off and your timing is irregular. Have you been using your metronome when you practice? Let's come up with a plan so you can perfect this piece in time for the recital." Perhaps the student has been spending a lot of time practicing, but was rehearsing with the wrong tempo. The suggestion to use a metronome to help with tempo is a new pathway that can produce better results. By helping the student to map out a plan for improvement, the mentor could foster hope in the student, even though they are conveying hurtful feedback.

We'd like to point out two areas of caution regarding feedback. First, feedback does not always work. Despite people's best efforts, sometimes people choose not to listen to feedback and might have to learn lessons the hard way. Although parents, supervisors, coaches, and mentors would much prefer to protect others from harm, sometimes people might have to make mistakes (i.e., fail a class, make poor decisions) and experience tough consequences to prompt changes in their behavior. Doing so might help them to develop resilience, which can be defined as the ability to respond competently or gain positive outcomes, despite having experienced difficult situations or threats to one's adaptation or development (e.g., Brooks, 2006; Masten, 2001). Perhaps in learning lessons the hard way, people might develop resilience in the face of a stressor and take an active role in creating their own unique pathways to getting out of bad situations and back on track to achieving their goals.

Second, although extremely harsh feedback should be avoided, so should undeserved praise. Despite the popularly-held assumption that building and protecting high self-esteem is most beneficial for a range of outcomes (e.g., performance in school or work, increased happiness, etc.), people with inflated self-appraisals have a tendency to respond to critical feedback with aggression and violence (Baumeister, Smart, & Boden, 1996). In other words, "the higher (and especially the more inflated) the self-esteem, the greater the vulnerability to ego threats" (Baumeister et al., 1996, p. 29). Therefore, delivering hurtful messages, while attending to pathways for instilling hope, can work to mitigate the potential harms of inflated self-esteem by developing appropriate responses to critical feedback and assets for building resilience. Bolstering a person's self-esteem and giving undeserved praise is unlikely to promote desirable outcomes. Furthermore, by avoiding critical messages to protect the recipient's self-esteem, feedback givers could rob people of an opportunity to learn to deal with criticism and build resilience in times of struggle. Future research could address the implications and outcomes of instilling false hope when individuals withhold critical messages.

Relational Repair Following Hurtful Messages

The above sections all included factors that could minimize the impact of hurtful messages. After a person has already been hurt, what should people do to repair these relationships? In the following sections, we utilize research on apologies and forgiveness to discuss options for deliverers and recipients of hurtful messages, some of which could instill hope and resilience for both parties by promoting recovery and growth. We also consider communicative responses to hurt. Finally, we discuss the role that social network members play in helping people to recover from hurt.

Hurtful messages can be seen as a type of relational transgression, and there is large body of research that examines offenders' responses to transgressions (Beck & Socha, chapter 5; Metts & Cupach, 2007). When offenders realize they have hurt someone's feelings or when the victim confronts them, the offender might offer an account of what happened and/or they might apologize (Metts, 1994). Apologies are the most common response to committing a relational transgression and can be an effective way to repair a relationship (Metts, 1994). Apologies that are sincere and explicitly take responsibility for the negative behavior are the most likely to lead to positive outcomes (e.g., Bachman & Guerrero, 2006). Apologies can diminish hurt feelings, provide the victim with an assurance that the offender recognizes the negative behavior, and hope that the offender will not commit a similar act in the future. One caveat is that accounts and apologies should be honest reflections of what the offender thinks, not just strategic attempts to get off the hook.

A victim's reaction to hurt is likely to depend on the offender's account and/or apology following the hurt. If a victim decides to extend forgiveness to the offender, this can open up pathways toward resilience by bringing relief to negative emotions (McCullough, Worthington, Jr., & Rachal, 1997) and working to restore relationships (Waldron & Kelley, 2008). Forgiveness is a process involving a change from negative to pro-social cognitions, emotions, and motivations toward a transgressor (e.g., Enright, 1991; McCullough et al., 1997). Forgiveness provides a host of positive psychological and relational outcomes, including greater satisfaction with life, more positive mood (Bono, McCullough, & Root, 2008), increased trust in the partner, and greater relational satisfaction (Wieselquist, 2009). Forgiveness can also help foster reconciliation (Karremans & Van Lange, 2004) and discourage future transgressions against the forgiver (Wallace, Exline, & Baumiester, 2008). Thus, forgiveness can improve individual and relational outcomes following hurtful experiences.

Throughout the life course, forgiveness can operate as a mechanism for positive individual and relational change. The resentment, anger, avoidance, and revenge people feel after hurt can create roadblocks to relational repair, and possibly decrease hope. Forgiveness works against the negative effects of hurtful experiences, as people consider alternative pathways for moving forward, such as reconciliation, allowing them to shed their anger and resentment (Waldron & Kelley, 2008). For example, several scholars have suggested that forgiveness works as an effective coping strategy for children being bullied (e.g., Egan & Todorov, 2009; Flanagan, Vanden Hoek, Ranter, & Reich, 2012). If children can forgive their bully, which does not involve condoning the behavior, they might be able to regain hope, rather than becoming cynical and distrustful of people. For adults experiencing divorce, forgiving the ex-spouse can make space for new goals and pathways, such as believing that that new and healthy relationships are possible. Without forgiveness, ex-partners might get stuck in cycles of anger and bitterness, which could hinder their ability to pursue future romantic partners. In some cases, forgiveness allows for reconciliation of a damaged relationship.

Communicative Responses to Hurt

People who feel hurt might respond in a number of ways, which can be characterized by whether they approach or avoid the offender and whether the responses are constructive or destructive. Hurt is somewhat unique in that it produces motivations to both approach and avoid (McLaren & Steuber, 2013; Miller & Roloff, 2014). For example, people might want to approach the offender to try to understand what happened or they might want to avoid them in an effort to protect themselves from future harm (MacDonald, 2009). Another study characterized responses to hurt as being constructive, such as asking for an explanation, or destructive, such as expressing anger (Feeney, 2004). In this section, we discuss the research on communicative responses to hurt and the ways that these responses might promote resilience.

First, approach tactics can be either constructive or destructive, depending on how they are enacted. For example, calmly discussing the hurtful incident or disclosing one's hurt feelings (Feeney, 2004) could result in an open discussion about the hurt, where an offender might offer an apology or clarify his/her intentions. This could prompt the victim to re-appraise the event and perhaps reduce their hurt feelings or help them feel more positively about the offender going forward. Some research suggests that hurt feelings make people more likely to use direct communication (Theiss et al., 2009) and to use integrative responses to hurt (McLaren & Steuber, 2013). If people do talk openly and constructively about the hurtful event, their relationship could be enhanced (McLaren & Steuber, 2013).

Other scholars have emphasized that because hurt signals people's vulnerability, they might respond destructively, by attacking the offender, defending themselves, or expressing anger (Bachman & Guerrero, 2006; Leary et al., 1998). In fact, people who felt extremely hurt were more likely to use destructive communication compared to those who were less hurt (Bachman & Guerrero, 2006). These sorts of approach responses are likely to ignite a cycle of negative reciprocity and further escalate the conflict (e.g., Levenson, Carstensen, & Gottman, 1994).

Avoidance behaviors could also have positive or negative effects on the individual or relationship. Understanding the factors that differentiate the constructive avoidant responses from the destructive ones is complex, perhaps because the same behaviors can be enacted for very different reasons, such as being loyal or neglecting the relationship (Rusbult, 1987). Avoiding the offender could function constructively, because it prevents victims from using other destructive behaviors, which serves to reduce the overall negative effects of hurt on the relationship (Feeney, 2004). Other research shows the opposite: avoidant responses to being hurt generally seems to increase long-term relational harm (McLaren & Steuber, 2013). More specifically, when avoidance means that people are ruminating about the hurtful event, ongoing relational problems ensue (Feeney, 2004).

Avoidance and rumination are often mutually reinforcing, because when people ruminate, they perceive conflicts to be more severe, and severe conflicts are often avoided. People ruminate about hurtful events in an effort to understand and make sense of their experience, but doing so can prolong feelings of hurt (Miller & Roloff, 2014). That is, to the extent that ruminating means that people are re-living the incident, hurt feelings are unlikely to be resolved. Furthermore, rumination is often associated with biased ways of perceiving conflicts, but the anticipation of discussing a conflict reduces these biases (Cloven & Roloff, 1991; 1993). Thus, if people realize they are ruminating about a hurtful event, having a conversation about it is important step and could open up possibilities for mitigating biases and resolving hurtful conflicts. Future research could explore connections between ruminating, hope, and the ability to develop alternative pathways to meet goals.

Social Support Following Hurtful Messages

In addition to the interactions between the offender and the victim, people can become resilient after hurt by talking to close others about the experience. Because hurtful messages can cause psychological, physiological, and emotional distress (Vangelisti & Crumley, 1998; Priem, McLaren, & Solomon, 2010), people are in need of social support, which can buffer or reduce the amount of suffering individuals feel from life stressors (Cohen & Wills, 1985). Social support can be defined as information or messages that help make a person feel loved, cared for, and included. Individuals rely on social networks when problems occur in their relationships (e.g., Eaton & Sanders 2012; Klein & Milardo, 2000). The most frequent and valuable sources of support come from close relational partners (e.g., Cohen & Wills, 1985; Gottlieb, 1978), including family, friends, and romantic partners (Goldsmith & Parks, 1990; Felmlee, 2001). These network members can provide comfort and support for a person who has been hurt and ideally increase the chances that the victim will reap positive outcomes from the experience.

The perception that one has people that can provide advice, encouragement, and comfort in times of need goes a long way to building resilience even before an individual encounters a hurtful experience. For example, research shows a positive association between perceived approval and support from one's social network and romantic partners' love, satisfaction and commitment (Parks, Stan, & Eggert, 1983; Sprecher & Felmlee, 2000). Additionally, individuals who perceive they have more support for their marriage are less likely to report intentions to divorce or separate (Bryant & Conger, 1999). The perception of the quantity and quality of support should work to buffer against the negative effects of hurtful experiences because people feel confident that they will have support to overcome such negative experiences. Thus, people should invest time and energy into developing their support networks before they encounter stressors, so that they will have a rich system to rely on when needed.

Research also demonstrates the importance of enacted support, or the reception of certain types of supportive messages for a particular situation and context. Social network members can provide many types of support including emotional, esteem, informational, and tangible support (Burleson, 1994). Burleson (2009) argues that the positive influence of supportive communication depends on multiple features of the message. One such feature, high verbal person centeredness, is often considered the gold standard for emotional support. Messages high in person centeredness recognize and legitimize the distressed person's feelings as well as to help the person articulate and elaborate reasons for why the person might be feeling that way (Burleson, 1994). When people are hurt, hearing messages high in person-centeredness could make them feel understood and supported.

Another way supportive communication helps people to build resilience is through re-appraisal, which is a process where an individual re-assesses his or her original judgment about the meaning of a stressor or their options for coping with it (e.g., Lazarus, 1999). If people change their appraisals of the situation, their emotions should change as well (Burleson & Goldsmith, 1998). The comforting process should get the victim thinking about new ways to view the offender's behavior and the situation that might alter the person's initial appraisals (Burleson & Goldsmith, 1998). Jones and Wirtz (2006) found that when people received messages high in person-centeredness, they talked more about their thoughts and feelings using positive emotion words, which influenced reappraisal and ultimately resulted in an improved emotional outlook on the situation that was initially upsetting them.

For an example of reappraisal with regard to a hurtful incident, we turn to unpublished data from a study focused on social network members talking to one another about hurtful experiences. One participant discussed how a friend helped her process through her hurt feelings and reappraise them: "She listened and voiced her opinions on the situation as to why it might be the way it is and what I could try and do to make the situation better. She helped guide me from this abstract place of thought where I felt angry and frustrated to a more aware place where I was sad and then trying to bring to a place where I could take action with the situation and get what I want or at least figure out what I want" (Pederson & McLaren, 2012). As this quote demonstrates, social network members can help comfort the victim and prompt reappraisals that could minimize hurt feelings and help the victim recover from the experience.

Although social network members are the ones that most likely provide social support, a more challenging possibility is that the deliverer could attempt to comfort the person who is feeling hurt (Caughlin, Scott, & Miller, 2009). This is considerably more difficult to do, because the person who is attempting to provide comfort is also the one who evoked the emotional pain. Nonetheless, people could attempt to offer conciliatory remarks aimed at legitimizing the hurt person's feelings, such as "I can see why that would hurt your feelings." But, offenders should tread lightly when attempting to be supportive after hurting someone, because remarks could come across as insincere or mocking given the context and could further exacerbate the situation (Caughlin et al., 2009). Future research should continue to explore how social network members play a role in developing hope and resilience during the process of coping with hurtful experiences.

Final Thoughts

Much of the research on hurtful messages has focused on the resulting negative outcomes for individuals and relationships. And yet, experiences of hurt present opportunities to foster relational and personal growth. People can gain feedback about themselves and others and decide how to best move forward. Even in the midst of delivering hurtful messages, there are strategies people can use to mitigate the impact of the hurt feelings. Furthermore, research shows that there are a number of compensatory factors that can buffer against the negative outcomes of hurt. Communication scholars are in a prime position to explore how people can transition from patterns of destructive hurt to more growth-producing hurt in various contexts throughout the lifespan. Parents can learn to give their children resources for building resilience and pathways for hope when faced with hurtful messages. Coworkers can provide constructive criticism in ways that promote collective responsibility for encouraging harmony. Social network members can provide resources for promoting resilience and hope after hurt, through comforting and reappraisals processes. Research should continue to identify the tools people need to bolster resilience and hope-producing qualities in themselves and their relationships. Although hurt feelings cannot be prevented, they can be experiences that ultimately help people to grow and thrive across their lifespan.

References

Bachman, G. F., & Guerrero, L. K. (2006). Forgiveness, apology, and communicative responses to hurtful events. *Communication Reports, 19*(1), 45-56. doi:10.1080/08934210600586375

Baumeister, R. F., Smart, L., & Boden, J. M. (1996). Relation of threatened egotism to violence and aggression: The dark side of high self-esteem. *Psychological Review, 103*(1), 5-33. doi:10.1037/0033-295X.103.1.5

Bono, G., McCullough, M. E., & Root, L. M. (2008). Forgiveness, feeling connected to others, and well-being: Two longitudinal studies. *Personality and Social Psychology Bulletin, 34*(2), 182-195. doi:10.1177/0146167207310025

Brooks, J. E. (2006). Strengthening resilience in children and youths: Maximizing opportunities in the schools. *Children and Schools, 28*(2), 69-76. doi:10.1093/cs/28.2.69

Brown, P., & Levinson, S. C. (1987). *Politeness: Some universals in language usage.* New York: Cambridge University Press.

Bryant, C. M., & Conger, R. D. (1999). Marital success and domains of social support in long-term relationships: Does the influence of network members ever end? *Journal of Marriage and Family, 61*(2), 437-450. doi:10.2307/353760

Burleson, B. R. (1994). Comforting messages: Significance, approaches, and effects. In B. R. Burleson, T. L. Albrecht, & I. G. Sarason (Eds.), *Communication of social support: Messages, interactions, relationships, and community* (pp. 3-28). Thousand Oaks, CA: Sage.

Burleson, B. R. (2009). Understanding the outcomes of supportive communication: A dual-process approach. *Journal of Social and Personal Relationships, 26,* 21-38. doi:10.1177/0265407509105519

Burleson, B. R., & Goldsmith, D. J. (1998). How the comforting process works: Alleviating emotional distress through conversationally induced reappraisals. In P. A. Andersen & L. K. Guerrero (Eds.), *The handbook of communication and emotion* (pp. 245-280). Thousand Oaks, CA: Sage.

Carstensen, L. L., Gottman, J. M., & Levenson, R. W. (1995). Emotional behavior in long-term marriage. *Psychology and Aging, 10,* 140. doi:10.1037/0882-7974.10.1.140

Caughlin, J. P., Scott, A. L., & Miller, L. E. (2009). Conflict and hurt in close relationships. In A. L. Vangelisti's (Ed.), *Feeling hurt in close relationships* (pp. 143-166). New York: Cambridge University Press. doi:10.1017/CBO9780511770548.003

Cloven, D. H., & Roloff, M. E. (1991). Making sense of interpersonal conflict: Communicative cures for the mulling blues. *Western Journal of Speech Communication, 55,* 134-158. doi:10.1080/10570319109374376

Cloven, D. H., & Roloff, M. E. (1993). Sense-making activities and interpersonal conflict II: The effects of communicative intentions on internal dialogue. *Western Journal of Communication, 57,* 309-329. doi:10.1080/10570319309374456

Cohen, S., & Wills, T. A. (1985). Stress, social support, and the buffering hypothesis. *Psychological Bulletin, 98*(2), 310-357. doi:10.1037/0033-2909.98.2.310

Cupach, W. R. (2007). "You're bugging me!": Complaints and criticisms from a partner. In B. H. Spitzberg & W. R. Cupach (Eds.), *The dark side of interpersonal communication* (2nd Ed., pp 143-168). Mahwah, NJ: Lawrence Erlbaum.

Cupach, W. R., & Carson, C. L. (2012). Criticism through the lens of interpersonal competence. In R. M. Suton, M. J. Hornsey, & K. M. Douglas (Eds.), *Feedback: The communication of praise, criticism, and advice* (pp.139-152). New York: Peter Lang.

Earley, P. C. (1986). Trust, perceived importance of praise and criticism, and work performance: An examination of feedback in the United States and England. *Journal of Management, 12*(4), 457-473. doi:10.1177/014920638601200402

Eaton, J. & Sanders, C. B. (2012). A little help from our friends: Informal third parties and interpersonal conflict. *Personal Relationships, 19*(4), 623-643. doi:10.1111/j.1475-6811.2011.01381.x

Egan, L. A., & Todorov, N. (2009). Forgiveness as a coping strategy to allow school students to deal with the effects of being bullied: Theoretical and empirical discussion. *Journal of Social and Clinical Psychology, 28*(2), 198-222. doi:10.1521/jscp.2009.28.2.198

Enright, R. D., & The Human Development Study Group. (1991). The moral development of forgiveness. In W. Kurtines & J. Gewirtz (Eds.), *Handbook of moral behavior and development* (Vol. 1, pp. 123-152). Hillsdale, NJ: Lawrence Erlbaum Associates.

Feeney, J. A. (2004). Hurt feelings in couple relationships: Towards integrative models of the negative effects of hurtful events. *Journal of Social and Personal Relationships, 21*(4), 487-508. doi:10.1177/0265407504044844

Feeney, J. A. (2005). Hurt feelings in couple relationships: Exploring the role of attachment and perceptions of personal injury. *Personal Relationships, 12*, 253-271. doi:10.1111/j.1350-4126.2005.00114.x

Felmlee, D. H. (2001). No couple is an island: A social network perspective on dyadic stability. *Social Forces, 79*(4), 1259-1287. doi:10.1353/sof.2001.0039

Fincham, F. D., & O'Leary, K. D. (1983). Causal inferences for spouse behavior in maritally distressed and nondistressed couples. *Journal of Social and Clinical Psychology, 1*, 42-57. doi:10.1521/jscp.1983.1.1.42

Fitness, J. (2001). Betrayal, rejection, revenge, and forgiveness: An interpersonal script approach. In M. Leary (Ed.), *Interpersonal rejection* (pp. 73-103). New York: Oxford University Press.

Flanagan, K. S., Vanden Hoek, K. K., Ranter, J. M., & Reich, H. A. (2012). The potential of forgiveness as a response for coping with negative peer experiences. *Journal of Adolescence, 35*(5), 1215-1223. doi:10.1016/j.adolescence.2012.04.004

Frederick, S., & Loewenstein, G. (1999). Hedonic adaptation. In D. Kahneman, E. Diener, & N. Schwarz (Eds.), *Well-being: The foundations of hedonic psychology* (pp. 302-329). New York: Russell Sage Foundation.

Goffman, E. (1967). *Interaction ritual: Essays on face-to-face behavior.* Garden City, NY: Anchor Books.

Goldsmith, D. J., & Donovan-Kicken, E. (2009). Adding insult to injury: The contributions of politeness theory to understanding hurt feelings in close relationships. In A. L. Vangelisti's (Ed.), *Feeling hurt in close relationships* (pp. 50-72). New York: Cambridge University Press. doi:10.1017/CBO9780511770548.003

Goldsmith, D. J., & Parks, M. R. (1990). Communicative strategies for managing the risks of seeking social support. In S. W. Duck & R. C. Silver (Eds.), *Personal relationships and social support* (pp. 104-121). London: Sage.

Gottlieb, B. H. (1978). The development and application of a classification scheme of informal helping behaviors. *Canadian Journal of Behavioral Science, 10*, 105-115. doi: 10.1037/h0081539

Grusec, J. E., & Davidov, M. (2010). Integrating different perspectives on socialization theory and research: A domain-specific approach. *Child Development, 81*, 687-709. doi: 10.1111/j.1467-8624.2010.01426.x

Hansson, R., Jones, W., & Fletcher, W. (1990). Troubled relationships in later life: Implications for support. *Journal of Personality and Social Psychology, 7*, 451-463. doi: 10.1177/0265407590074003

Jones, S. M., & Wirtz, J. G. (2006). How does the comforting process work? An empirical test of an appraisal-based model of comforting. *Human Communication Research, 32*, 217-243.

Karremans, J., & Van Lange, P. A. M. (2004). Back to caring after being hurt: The role of forgiveness. *European Journal of Social Psychology, 34*, 207-227. doi:10.1002/ejsp.192

Klein, R. C. A., & Milardo, R. M. (2000). The social context of couple conflict: Support and criticism from informal third parties. *Journal of Social and Personal Relationships, 17*(4-5), 618-637. doi:10.1177/0265407500174008

Kowalski (1996). Complaints and complaining: Functions, antecedents, and consequences. *Psychological Bulletin, 119*, 179-196. doi:10.1037/0033-2909.119.2.179

Labouvie-Vief, G., & DeVoe, M. (1991). Emotional regulation in adulthood and later life: A developmental view. In K. W. Schaie, & M. P. Lawton (Eds.), *Annual review of gerontology and geriatrics* (Vol. 11, pp. 172-194). New York: Springer.

Lawton, M. P., Kleban, M. H., Rajagopal, D., & Dean, J. (1992). Dimensions of affective experience in three age groups. *Psychology and Aging, 7*, 171-184. doi:10.1037/0882-7974.7.2.171

Lazarus, R. S. (1999). *Stress and emotion: A new synthesis.* New York: Springer.

Leary, M. R., & Leder, S. (2009). The nature of hurt feelings: Emotional experience and cognitive appraisals. In A. L. Vangelisti's (Ed.), *Feeling hurt in close relationships* (pp. 15-33). New York: Cambridge University Press. doi:10.1017/CBO9780511770548.003

Leary, M. R., Springer, C., Negel, L., Ansell, E., & Evans, K. (1998). The causes, phenomenology, and consequences of hurt feelings. *Journal of Personality and Social Psychology, 74*, 1225-1237. doi:10.1037/0022-3514.74.5.1225

Leary, M. R., & Terry, M. L. (2012). Interpersonal aspects of evaluative feedback. In R. M. Sutton, M. J. Hornsey, & K. M. Douglas (Eds.), *Feedback: The communication of praise, criticism, and advice* (pp.15-28). New York: Peter Lang.

Levenson, R. W., Carstensen, L. L., & Gottman, J. M. (1994). Influence of age and gender on affect, physiology, and their interrelations: A study of long-term marriages. *Journal of personality and social psychology, 67*, 56-68. doi:10.1037/0022-3514.67.1.56

MacDonald, G., & Leary, M. R. (2005). Why does social exclusion hurt? The relationship between social and physical pain. *Psychological Bulletin, 131*, 202-223. doi:10.1037/0033-2909.131.2.202

Masten, A. S. (2001). Ordinary magic: Resilience processes in development. *American Psychologist, 56*(3), 227-238. doi:10.1037//0003-066X.56.3.227

McCullough, M. E., Worthington, E. L., Jr., & Rachal, K. C. (1997). Interpersonal forgiving in close relationships. *Journal of Personality and Social Psychology, 75*, 1586-1603. doi:10.1037/0022-3514.75.6.1586

McLaren, R. M., & Pederson, J. R. (2014). Relational Communication and Understanding in Conversations About Hurtful Events Between Parents and Adolescents. *Journal of Communication, 64*, 145-166. doi: 10.1111/jcom.12072

McLaren, R. M., Priem, J. S., & Solomon, D. H. (2008, July). *Layers of Identity and Experiences of Hurt: A Theme Analysis.* Paper presented at the meeting of the International Association for Relationship Research, Providence, RI.

McLaren, R. M., & Sillars, A. (2014). Hurtful episodes in parent-adolescent relationships: How accounts and attributions contribute to the difficulty of talking about hurt. *Communciation Monographs.*

McLaren, R. M., & Solomon, D. H. (2008). Appraisals and distancing responses to hurtful messages. *Communication Research, 35*, 339-357. doi:10.1177/0093650208315961

McLaren, R. M., Solomon, D. H., & Priem, J. S. (2011). Explaining variation in contemporaneous responses to hurt in premarital romantic relationships: A relational turbulence model perspective. *Communication Research, 38*, 543-564. doi: 10.1177/0093650210377896

McLaren, R. M. & Steuber, K. R. (2013). Emotions, communicative responses, and relational consequences of boundary turbulence. *Journal of Social and Personal Relationships, 30*, 606-626. doi:10.1177/0265407512463997.

Metts, S. (1994). Relational transgressions. In W. R. Cupach & B. Spitzberg (Eds.), *The dark side of interpersonal communication* (pp. 217-240). Hillsdale, NJ: Erlbaum.

Metts, S., & Cupach, W. R. (2007). Responses to relational transgressions: Hurt, anger, and sometimes forgiveness. In B. H. Spitzberg & W. R. Cupach (Eds.), *The dark side of interpersonal communication* (2nd ed., pp. 243-273). Mahwah, NJ: Erlbaum.

Michael, S. T. (2000). Hope conquers fear: Overcoming anxiety and panic attacks. In C. R. Snyder (Ed.), *Handbook of hope: Theory, measures, and applications* (pp. 355-378). San Diego, CA: Academic.

Mikulincer, M., & Shaver, P. R. (2004). Security-based self-representations in adulthood: Contents and processes. In W. S. Rholes & J. A. Simpson (Eds.), *Adult attachment: Theory, research, and clinical implications* (pp. 159-195). New York: Guilford.

Mikulincer, M., & Shaver, P. R. (2007). *Attachment in adulthood: Structure, dynamics, and change.* New York: Guilford.

Miller, C. W., & Roloff, M. E. (2014) When hurt continues: Taking conflict personally leads to rumination, residual hurt and negative motivations toward someone who hurt us. *Communication Quarterly, 62*(2), 193-213. doi:10.1080/01463373.2014.890118

Miller, R. S. (1997). We always hurt the ones we love: Aversive interactions in close relationships. In R. M. Kowalski (Ed.), *Aversive behaviors in interpersonal relationships* (pp. 11-29). New York: Plenum Press.

Mills, R. S. L., Nazar, J., & Farrell H. M. (2002). Child and parent perceptions of hurtful messages. *Journal of Social and Personal Relationships, 19*, 731-754. doi:10.1177/0265407502196001

Murray, S. L., Bellavia, G. M., Rose, P., & Griffin, D. W. (2003). Once hurt, twice hurtful: How perceived regard regulates daily marital interactions. *Journal of Personality and Social Psychology, 84*, 126-147. doi:10.1037/0022-3514.84.1.126

Parks, M. R., Stan, C. M., & Eggert, L. L. (1983). Romantic involvement and social network involvement. *Social Psychology Quarterly, 83*, 116-131. doi:10.2307/3033848

Pecchioni, L. L., Wright, K. B., & Nussbaum, J. F. (2005). *Life-span communication*. Mahwah, NJ: Lawrence Erlbaum.

Pederson, J., & McLaren, R. M. (2012, July). *Sharing forgiveness: Exploring how social network members process hurtful experiences*. Paper presented at the meeting of the International Association for Relationship Researchers, Chicago, IL.

Priem, J. S., McLaren, R. M., & Solomon, D. H. (2010). Relational messages, perceptions of hurt, and biological stress reactions to a disconfirming interaction. *Communication Research, 37*, 48-72. doi:10.1177/0093650209351470

Shapiro, J. P., Baumeister, R. F., & Kessler, J. W. (1991). A three-component model of children's teasing: aggression, humor, and ambiguity. *Journal of Social and Clinical Psychology, 10*, 459-472. doi:10.1521/jscp.1991.10.4.459

Shaver, P. R., Mikulincer, M., Lavy, S. & Cassidy, J. (2009). Understanding and altering hurt feelings: an attachment-theoretical perspective on the generation and regulation of emotions. In A. L. Vangelisti (Ed.), *Feeling hurt in close relationships* (pp. 92-119). New York: Cambridge University Press. doi:10.1017/CBO9780511770548.003

Snyder, C. R. (1994). *The psychology of hope: You can get there from here*. New York: Free Press.

Snyder, C. R. (1999). Hope, goal blocking thoughts, and test-related anxieties. *Psychological Reports, 84*, 206-208. doi:10.2466/pr0.1999.84.1.206

Snyder, C. R. (2002). Hope theory: Rainbows in the mind. *Psychological Inquiry, 13*, 249-275.

Sprecher, S., & Felmlee, D. H. (2000). Romantic partners' perceptions of social network attributes with the passage of time and relationship transitions. *Personal Relationships, 7*, 325-340. doi:10.1111/j.1475-6811.2000.tb00020.x

Sutton, R. M., Hornsey, M. J., & Douglas, K. M. (2012). Introduction. In R. M. Sutton, M. J. Hornsey, & K. M. Douglas (Eds.), *Feedback: The communication of praise, criticism, and advice* (pp.1-5). New York: Peter Lang.

Theiss, J. A., Knobloch, L. K., Checton, M. G., Magsamen-Conrad, K. (2009). Relationship characteristics associated with the experience of hurt in romantic relationships: A test of RTM. *Human Communication Research, 35*, 588-615. doi:10.1111/j.1468-2958.2009.01364.x

Tracy, K., Van Dusen, D., & Robinson, S. (1987). "Good" and "bad" criticism: A descriptive analysis. *Journal of Communication, 37*, 46-59. doi:10.1111/j.1460-2466.1987.tb00982.x

Vangelisti, A. L. (1994). Messages that hurt. In W. R. Cupach & B. H. Spitzberg (Eds.), *The dark side of interpersonal communication* (pp. 53-82). Hillsdale, NJ: Erlbaum.

Vangelisti, A. L. (2007). Communicating hurt. In B. H. Spitzberg & W. R. Cupach (Eds.), *The dark side of interpersonal communication* (2nd Ed., pp 121-142). Mahwah, NJ: Lawrence Erlbaum.

Vangelisti, A. L. (2009). Hurt feelings: Distinguishing features, function, and overview. In A. L. Vangelisti (Ed.), *Feeling hurt in close relationships* (pp. 3-11). New York: Cambridge University Press. doi:10.1017/CBO9780511770548.003

Vangelisti, A. L., & Crumley, L. P. (1998). Reactions to messages that hurt: The influence of relational contexts. *Communication Monographs, 65,* 173–196. doi: 10.1080/03637759809376447

Vangelisti, A. L. & Hampel, A. D. (2012). Hurtful interactions as feedback. In R. M. Sutton, M. M. Hornsey, & K. M. Douglas (Eds.), *Feedback: The handbook of praise, criticism, and advice* (pp. 153–167). New York: Peter Lang.

Vangelisti, A. L., Maguire, K. C., Alexander, A. L., & Clark, G. (2007). Hurtful family environments: Links with individual, relationship, and perceptual variables. *Communication Monographs, 74,* 357–385. doi: 10.1080/03637750701543477

Vangelisti, A. L., & Young, S. L. (2000). When words hurt: The effect of perceived intentionality on interpersonal relationships. *Journal of Social and Personal Relationships, 17,* 393–424. doi: 10.1177/0265407500173005

Vangelisti, A. L., Young, S. L., Carpenter-Theune, K. E., & Alexander, A. L. (2005). Why does it hurt? The perceived causes of hurt feelings. *Communication Research, 32,* 443–477. doi: 10.1177/0093650205277319

Waldron, V. R., & Kelley, D. L. (2008). *Communicating forgiveness.* Thousand Oaks, CA: Sage.

Wallace, H. M., Exline, J. J., & Baumeister, R. F. (2008). Interpersonal consequences of forgiveness: Does forgiveness deter or encourage repeat offenses? *Journal of Experimental Social Psychology, 44,* 453–460. doi:10.1016/j.jesp.2007.02.012

Wieselquist, J. (2009). Interpersonal forgiveness, trust, and the investment model of commitment. *Journal of Social and Personal Relationships, 26,* 531–548. doi: 10.1177/0265407509347931

Young, S. L. (2004). Factors that influence recipients' appraisals of hurtful communication. *Journal of Social and Personal Relationships, 21,* 291–305. doi: 10.1177/0265407504042833

Young, S. L., & Bippus, A. M. (2001). Does it make a difference if they hurt you in a funny way?: Humorously and non-humorously phrased hurtful messages in personal relationships. *Communication Quarterly, 49,* 35–52. doi: 10.1080/01463370109385613

Zhang, S., & Stafford, L. (2008). Perceived face threat of honest but hurtful messages in romantic relationships. *Western Journal of Communication, 72,* 19–39. doi: 10.1080/10570310701828628

• CHAPTER FIVE •

Unfolding the Transgression Scene: From Distress to Hope and Resilience

Sandra Metts
Illinois State University

Bryan Asbury
University of Iowa

The transgression scene is one episode within the ongoing narrative of relationship partners and the the larger family system within which they are embedded. Family relationships, perhaps more than any other, are predicated on the fundamental assumption of trust and when a transgression calls this trust into question, members must work through the issues to reach insight and understanding to restore this trust (Hargrave, 1994). The process can be complicated and depends on the nature of the transgression, the family role of the transgressor, his or her reconciliation attempts, and the ability of other family members to respond with empathy and constructive communication. As challenging and multilayered as the process may be, its restorative consequences depend ultimately on the forgiveness experienced and sincerely expressed by those who were hurt or angered by the transgression. When the pain and resentment are gone and trust in the offender is restored, the family can work together to move forward with hope and resilience.

Hope and resilience are culturally imbedded within relational transgression scenes, particularly through anticipatory scripts. While relational transgressions are inevitable, the cultural belief (or hope) is that strong relationships will survive. Wedding vows include a commitment to the future, "for better or for worse," in which the hope of that relationship exists in the belief that it will survive, or remain resilient, through times plagued with inevitable challenges, including transgressions. For familial relationships, hope and resilience are the backdrop that animates transgressions as serving pro-social functions such as teaching the children life lessons. The discipline of "tough love," for example, moves beyond the realm of the transgression to a broader framing of these otherwise anti-social behaviors to find the pro-social functions they can serve (Lasch, 1977). The love in "tough love" is entrenched with hope and resilience (and more specifically hope for resilience)—the children will not only endure the transgressive interaction but will thrive because of it. The children will undergo the tough to receive the love and the hope is that these transgressions are for this greater good. In both wedding vows and tough love, the connection between transgressions, hope, and resilience is apparent in these anticipatory messages. Hope and resilience are anticipated before a transgression occurs and reappear under the regenerative conditions of forgiveness following a transgression.

The goals of this chapter are threefold: (1) to characterize the transgression scene by clarifying the transgression construct and the role of communication in managing transgressions, (2) to define forgiveness and the transformative functions it serves, and (3) to integrate the roles of forgiveness, resilience, and hope in reconciling and restoring troubled family relationships or, when restoration is not possible as in the case of divorce, moving forward to new experiences with confidence and positive attitude.

Transgressions: Let the Scene Begin

Transgressions can occur in virtually every aspect of our daily life. Co-workers may exhibit rude or disrespectful behavior or a neighbor may discipline another family's child in an inappropriate way. Even a babysitter may learn private information about a family and share that information with others. However, the arena in which transgressions are least expected, but are most likely to elicit strong emotional responses, are close relationships. The interdependence that characterizes close relationships such as romantic relationships, families, and friendships necessarily links the behaviors of those involved. We can fire a wayward babysitter, but coping with the untoward acts of a close other requires competent communication from both parties. This communication is effective to the extent that it clarifies what the transgression is, negotiates its meaning for the relationship and the persons involved, and constructs a path toward reconciliation if possible and desirable. When the transgression scene involves multiple actors, for example, members of the immediate and even extended family, the scene is further complicated. Age and emotional maturity of the actors, the role played in the scene as transgressor or victim, as well as the types of relationships between and across family members (e.g., biological versus stepparent) create a particularly challenging communication context.

In order to examine more fully these complicated issues in couples and families, we begin this section with a summary of the types of actions and behavior that researchers have identified as types of transgressions in dyadic close relationships before moving to the nature of transgressions within families. We then turn to a more focused discussion of communicative responses to transgressions.

Transgressions in Close Relationships: Romantic Partners and Friends

An integration of the research on close relationships suggests three general approaches to offensive actions or untoward behaviors (Metts & Cupach, 2007). The broadest and most inclusive approach uses the term *transgressions*, defined as messages, actions, events, or behaviors that violate an implicit or explicit relationship norm or rule that presumably determines appropriate behavior within a particular relationship (Boon & Sulsky, 1997; Metts, 1994; Roloff, Soule, & Carey, 2001). Explicit rules are those that have been established as a result of behaviors or events that have emerged within the relationship or are established to avoid such behaviors or events. For example, if a friend or partner brings up an issue in public that is embarrassing or painful, the pair will establish a rule that the issue should be avoided. To bring it up again violates that rule and is considered a transgression. Other explicit rules are established prior to any event or action. As a couple moves from casual dating to a serious relationship, rules concerning emotional and sexual exclusivity are typically established. Although the phrase, "going steady" is no longer widely used, similar statements about the nature of the relationship make the boundaries clear, even on social media. Implicit norms and rules tend to be those that are accepted as cultural mandates for the proper conduct in relationships (e.g., honesty is the best policy). Of course, a couple might make adjustments to these more generic rules and decide, for example, that they will not be sexually exclusive, but that they will be emotionally exclusive (Metts, 1994).

Perhaps the prototypical example of a rule violation in close relationhips is deception. It is a particularly complicated transgression. Not only is it, by definition, the intentional violation of the rule of truthfulness and openness, but it is also enacted in different types of messages and is motivated by different, but often overlapping goals (Metts, 1989; Metts & Cupach, 2007). More specifically, deception can be enacted as a falsification or lie that fully distorts the truth. It can also be enacted as omission or concealment that fully hides the truth, or as equivocations, exaggerations, or understatements that manipulate the degree of full honesty about an issue. Moreover, deception is motivated by three, often overlapping, goals: protect self, protect partner, and protect the relationship. Needless to say, when the discovery of deception is the event that initiates the transgression scene, participants are faced with the challenges of determining what the truth actually is, why it was falsified or concealed, and how to restore trust in the integrity of the deceiver before reconciliation can even be addressed.

A second approach to transgressions is more narrowly focused on actions, behaviors, or messages that are perceived by a close other to be hurtful. These *hurtful messages* devalue the importance, specialness, or integrity of the relationship or the partner/friend (Beck & Socha, chapter 4; Vangelisti & Young, 2000). These messages are still rule violations, but are associated with a particular category of implicit rules that mandate the demonstration of regard, respect, caring, and concern for a relationship or partner. Nonverbal actions such as a broken promise or forgetting an important obligation can be hurtful, but verbal messages are particularly hurtful when the language used has high intensity, for example, harsh or abrasive language used in a criticism or complaint (Young, 2004). Acts of disregard are also more hurtful when perceived to be intentionally performed (Vangelisti & Young, 2000).

A third approach to transgressions is also more narrowly focused on a particular type of action that not only violates a rule and induces hurt or anger in the victim, but also has ethical or moral implications. This category of transgressions is termed *infidelity* and/or *betrayal*. In romantic relationships, infidelity may be sexual involvement with someone other than the partner, emotional involvement with another person, or both. Infidelity is a particularly challenging transgression for couples to resolve because it not only arouses strong negative emotions in the offended partner (e.g., hurt, anger, repulsion, fear; Hall &Fincham, 2006), but also introduces a third party who threatens the very stability of the relationship.

In addition, some scholars believe that infidelity exhibits unique gendered profiles in terms of responses such as distress, jealousy, and relational termination. Although the debate among scholars continues, and the specifics of the research are beyond the scope of this chapter, a brief summary offers two competing lines of argument based on the method of analysis. First, when respondents are asked to choose between sexual and emotional infidelity as the most distressing or most likely to evoke jealousy, men tend to select sexual infidelity and women to select emotional infidelity. From an evolutionary perspective, researchers argue that men experience more jealousy over sexual infidelity because of concerns for paternity and women experience more jealousy over emotional infidelity because of concerns for loss of resources (Shackelford, Buss, & Bennett, 2002). From a sociological perspective, scholars argue that sex-role scripts allow, and even encourage, men to demonstrate their sexual expertise without the need to frame sexual involvement within an emotional context. By contrast, sex role scripts mandate that women should be sexually conservative unless motivated by the desire to demonstrate emotional affection. Thus, a man who learns that his partner has been sexually unfaithful may assume that she is also emotionally involved, but a woman who learns that her patner has been sexually unfaithful may assume that he is still emotionally committed to her (Hendrick & Hendrick, 1995).

However, when alternative measures are used, for example, Likert scales that assess degree of distress or jealousy associated with both types of transgressions and recalled responses to actual infidelity experiences (rather than hypothetical scenarios), the findings do not support sex differences. Both men and women report sexual and emotional infidelity as equally distressing (Carpenter, 2012). Moreover, when a partner's sexual and emotional infidelity involves a former dating partner, both men and women report more difficulty in achieving forgiveness than when the rival is a stranger (Cann & Baucom, 2004).

In sum, it is likely that both men and women do reflect cultural norms regarding gender role expectations in response to infidelity when considering hypothetical scenarios and predicting possible jealous feelings. However, when experiencing the actual occurrence of infidelity committed by a partner who was valued, trusted, and presumably committed to the relationship, the flood of simultaneous and oscillating emotions that occur during the transgression scene and beyond, including anger, hurt, resentment, and fear, are not easily categorized within gender role scripts. The conclusion that is consistent across studies is that infidelity is one of most challenging and difficult transgressions to forgive and move beyond.

As indicated in Table 1, the research on transgressions broadly construed, and on hurtful messages and infidelity more specifically, has identified a substantial list of actions and behaviors that are commonly reported by respondents across relationship types and ages. Although the list moves from what are typically considered less severe transgressions to more severe, it is important to note that the severity of any transgression is determined by the parties involved and influenced by the particular features of that event within the relational context. In addition, an event may include a primary transgression as well as other offensive actions associated with that transgression. For example, both emotional and sexual infidelity may include deception as well as a lack of sensitivity and disregard for the relationship.

Table 5.1. Summary of Transgression Categories

Transgression Categories	Description
Inappropriate interaction	Rude or inappropriate comments, often during conflict; ill-conceived humor
Lack of sensitivity	Thoughtless, disrespectful, inconsiderate behavior
Lack of support	Failure to offer assistance, demonstrate concern, or be emotionally responsive when expected and appropriate
Disregard and neglect	Not privileging the primary relationship; choosing other people or activities over partner or changing plans
Broken promises and rule violations	Failure to keep a promise, changing plans with no explanation, or violating a specific established rule within the relationship
Privacy violations	Not keeping sensitive information private, or violating privacy boundaries
Deception	Intentionally leading a partner to believe something that is not true, typically for self-protection or personal gain
Hurtful messages	Intentional or unintentional actions or statements that communicate a devaluation of partner (sense of rejection) or devaluation of the relationship
Relational depreciation	Reducing commitment implicitly or explicitly; indifference toward or personal attacks directed to partner
Abuse/Aggression	Verbal or physical threats; verbal or physical aggression or violent acts
Abrupt termination	Terminating a relationship with no warning and no explanation; no discussion of relational issues precedes the unilateral decision to terminate
Extrarelational involvement	Sexual or emotional involvement with persons other than one's partner
Relational threat confounded by deception	Sexual or emotional involvement with persons other than one's partner, which is further intensified by the use of deception to conceal the involvement

Transgressions in the Family

Although less scholarly attention has been directed specifically to types of transgressions within family units and across generations, an integration of the empirical research with intervention training programs tested by clinical psychologists and therapists yields an informative profile. For example, several scholars have noted the concern of parents to assure that their children do not violate social and moral norms that are reflective of the rule violations for adults listed in Table 1 such as not telling lies, not making rude comments, and not saying things that hurt other people's feelings (Holden, Coleman, & Schmidt, 1995). In addition, however, parents also recognize that more severe transgressions committed by their children require strong disciplinary responses, particularly when a serious transgression involves aggression. In a study designed to validate the Parent Discipline Scale, Lopez, Schneier, and Dula (2002) identified four categories of children's behaviors that parents believed warranted discipline: (1) Safety non-aggressive transgressions (e.g., crossing the road without looking), (2) safety aggressive transgressions (e.g., beating up a younger child), (3) social non-aggressive transgressions (e.g., watching television instead of doing homework), and (4) social aggressive transgressions (e.g., vandalizing school property with peers). Among the findings were the greater endorsement of power assertive and induction discipline techniques in the case of aggressive and safety violations as well as greater use of power assertive and induction discipline for the violations that involved aggressive social violations compared to non-aggressive social violations.

In families, the transgression scene is further complicated by the fact that parents interact with each other as well as with their children and rules can be violated at multiple levels. For example, an implicit or explict rule may exist within a family that both parents will agree on a disciplinary response before administering discipline to a child for his or her misconduct. If a parent moves forward with unilateral discipline, a rule has been violated. Moreover, if the discipline is considered inappropriate by the uninformed parent, he or she may criticize the other parent in front of the child (violating a rule of appropriate interaction) and the child gets caught in the middle of a parental dispute, violating another rule of proper parenting (Kiefer, Worthington, Myers, Kliewer, Berry et al., 2010). In addition, family well-being is negatively affected by parental conflicts that do not involve the children but rise to the level of interpersonal transgressions when they "entail feelings of injury and resentment, and attributions of blame, on the part of one or both parties" (Hoyt, McCullough, Fincham, Maio, & Davila, 2005, p. 376). These types of conflict can reduce family cohesion by dividing family members' loyalty in much the same way that persistent alcohol misuse by a family member can reduce family cohesion by reducing trust for the offending parent or sibling (Scherer, Worthington, Hook, Campana, West, & Gartner, 2012).

Although most attention given to family transgressions is focused on parents and children, grandparents and older adult siblings also experience transgressions. In general, these offenses are consistent with those experienced by other adults. For example, when a sample of older adults (mean age = 70.1 years) were asked to recount a serious and unresolved interpersonal transgression in preparation for a forgiveness intervention trial, they described instances of emotional and/or verbal abuse, being emotionally neglected by a partner, broken commitments, and infidelity (Allemand, Steiner, & Hill, 2013).

The Role of Communication in Managing Transgressions

Once a transgression is committed, revealed, or discovered, the stage is set for the scene to unfold. As a metaphorical backdrop, several aspects of the transgression and the transgressor determine the direction of the enactment. More specifically, the severity of the offense and the perceived blameworthiness (i.e., degree of intentionality) of the transgressor are two important influences on the offended person's response (Merolla & Zhang, 2010). In addition, when the transgression is committed outside of the offended person's awareness, as is the case for instances of infidelity, the method of discovery is also important. For example, if the transgressor reveals the infidelity to his or her partner, anger, hurt, and resentment are somewhat less intense than when the infidelity is revealed by a third party or discovered by the victim (Metts & Cupach, 2007) and the likelihood of forgiveness is greater (Afifi, Falato, & Weiner, 2001).

Given these variations in the backdrop of the transgression scene, variations in specific messages are inevitable. However, at the broadest level, these episodes are characterized by three phases: the reproach, the account, and the evaluation (Miller, Worthington, Hook, Davis, Gartner, & Frohne, 2013). During the *reproach* phase, the victim seeks an explanation for the offense using aggravating or mitigating strategies. Aggravating strategies imply that a justification for or denial of the offense is expected. The emotional tone tends to be accusatory and angry with no indication of empathy for the offender. Mitigating strategies imply that an excuse, explanation, or apology is expected. The emotional tone tends to be calm, possibly sad, and reflects empathy for the offender. During the *account* phase the offender offers an excuse, justification, a denial, or an apology. An excuse minimizes one's control over the situation; a justification minimizes the importance of the offense. A fully developed apology expresses remorse, accepts responsibility, offers restitution if necessary, and promises better behavior in the future. During the *evaluation* phase, the offended person considers the appropriateness and sincerity of the transgressor's account, accepting or rejecting it.

As might be expected, communicative choices in each phase influence a subsequent phase. For example, mitigating reproaches that are gentle in tone followed by sincere apologies expressing remorse are the sequence most likely to lead to relationship reconciliation and forgiveness in romantic relationships (Miller et al., 2013) and marriage (Fincham, Hall, & Beach, 2006). Likewise, when the account phase includes an explanation and apology that evokes empathy from the offended person during the evaluation phase, family members are more likely to reconcile, retain family cohesion, and experience forgiveness (Keifer et al., 2010). Finally, when a friend's account for his or her hurtful behavior includes not only an apology, but also conciliatory efforts to compensate the offended friend (e.g., do a favor, give a gift), the trangressor is perceived as fair, just, and sympathetic (i.e., agreeable); the friendship feelings are strengthened and forgiveness is experienced (Tabak, McCullough, Luna, Bono, & Berry, 2012).

Taken together, research on the role of communication during the transgression scene underscores the nature of messages sent by both transgressor and victim, as well as the cumulative nature of these interactions in the ongoing drama of the family. That is, an aggressive and hostile reproach is likely to elicit an aggressive response or withdrawal from the transgressor that intensifies the hostility and tension within the family. Drawing on Gottman's cascade model of marital conflict to characterize unsuccessful forgiveness episodes, Worthington (1998) argues that in families where the normal principle of forbearance is violated by extreme or repeated offenses, and communication is marked by accusation, defensiveness, and stonewalling, unforgiveness is more likely than forgiveness. By contrast, a mitigating reproach is more likely to lead to "sincere acknowledgement" including a sincere apology, acknowledgement of responsibility, and expressions of remorse that facilitate empathy and the process of forgiveness (Merolla & Zhang, 2010; Miller et al., 2013).

Given the interdependent nature of family relationships, it is not surprising that the cumulative effects of transgressor and victim interaction episodes leave their mark. Over time, a global quality of affection or disaffection permeates the relationship and "sentiment override" shapes the interpretation of messages more strongly than objective assessments (Weiss, 1980). This is not to say that trust cannot be restored and forgiveness granted, but it does suggest that hope and resilience are critical elements in both the enactment of the transgression scene and its ultimate consequences.

Fortunately, whatever the circumstances of the transgression and the qualities of the scenes through which it is managed, once the victim has experienced sincere forgiveness, he or she can exit the emotional constraints of the transgression scene. Indeed, the experience of forgiveness facilitates related positive emotions such as happiness and contentment, which allow the victim to more forward with strength, optimism, and insightful sense-making strategies (Kelley, 2012). Without forgiveness, lingering resentment and vengeful rumination continue to impact both the victim's metal health and his or her communication. We turn now to a more detailed discussion of forgiveness.

Forgiveness: Exit Scene, Stage Left

In much the same way that the concept of transgression is multifaceted, the concept of forgiveness has been conceptualized in multiple ways. McCullough (2000) defines forgiveness as a motivational/decisional model in which an individual becomes less motivated to avoid a relational offender or seek retribution for a transgression and increasingly more motivated toward benevolence. Forgiveness has also been conceptualized as a process. Holter, Magnuson, and Enright (2010) define forgiveness as a transformation of negative emotions such as anger, resentment, and hurt to positive regard for the transgressor (although not necessarily the act). This conceptualization of forgiveness requires an individual to re-orient himself or herself to the transgressor so that negative emotions are replaced with positive emotions and empathy (Fincham, Paleari, & Regalia, 2002).

Implied in these conceptualizations of forgiveness is the key to its positive consequences as well as its complexity. First, the positive consequences of experiencing forgiveness entail a regeneration of hope, or the belief that impediments can be overcome. It restores the optimism that one has agency in reaching goals and the ability find the pathways that will facilitate the process (Snyder, 2000). When goals are achieved, positive emotions are experienced and, reciprocally, positive emotions open a person to finding resources that facilitate goal achievement. Thus, using the transgression as a motivation to better understand, evaluate, correct, and appreciate the marriage, the parent-child or sibling relationship may be inspired by the hope that arises after forgiveness.

Second, forgiveness is a particularly complex type of emotion. Not only is it a secondary or blended emotion, but also a transformative emotion (Knobloch & Metts, 2013). Like other blended emotions, forgiveness has no culturally recognized facial or physiological display pattern. When expressed nonverbally, forgiveness is displayed in component units, such as a smile of relief that attends the letting go of anger and/or hugs as a sign of affection that replaces the avoiding postures associated with disgust, resentment, or repulsion. Also, unlike the basic emotions of anger, sadness, fear, and happiness, forgiveness requires sophisticated cognitive appraisal to process and label the arousal that moments, days, or years before was negatively valenced but has transformed into arousal that is positively valenced. As a result, the commuication of forgiveness reflects the nuances of this cognitive reappraisal process.

As Kelly (1998) noted, the communication of forgiveness can be direct, indirect, and conditional. Direct forgiveness is explicitly communicated to the forgiveness-seeking transgressor (e.g., having a long talk about the transgression, saying "I forgive you," or using a third party to say all is forgiven). Indirect forgiveness is communicated indirectly through words (e.g., diminishing the severity by saying "it's actually not that big of a deal" or using humor) or through nonverbal gestures (e.g., hugging, showing new and positive emotion, or behaving "normally" again). Conditional forgiveness is communicated to the transgressor but is accompanied with conditions (e.g., saying "I forgive you as long as you never let it happen again"). Although negative emotions are transformed into positive and the transgressor is forgiven, the desire to avoid future hurt and distress motivates the warning comment. In a sense, the forgiving person foregrounds his or her resilience and belief that the impediments to the relationship have been overcome, but acknowledges that these qualities, like forgiveness, are only conditional.

In contrast to sincerely felt forgiveness, two less forgiving responses to a transgression can occur: pseudo-forgiveness and unforgiveness. Pseudo-forgiveness involves an individual communicating forgiveness while maintaining the negative emotions and anti-social motivations toward the transgressor (Al-Mabuk & Downs, 1996). An individual may tell a friend that the transgression is forgiven while that individual harbors anger, hurt, and resentment or avoids that friend. Unforgiveness is the perpetuation of negative emotions (e.g., anger, resentment, or hatred) and anti-social motivations (e.g., avoidance or retaliation) (Worthington & Wade, 1999). The key distinction between pseudo-forgiveness and unforgiveness is the perception of forgiveness. In pseudo-forgiveness, the transgressor, and possibly the victim, believe that forgiveness has occurred. Both pseudo-forgiveness and unforgiveness maintain the negative emotional and motivational relational states that lead to negative consequences. Without true forgiveness, vengeful rumination controls the victim and prevents psychological healing while motivating the conflictual communication that characterizes relational interactions (McCullough, Bellah, Kilpatrick, & Johnson, 2001). These negative conditions are framed by Grudge Theory (Baumeister, Exline, & Sommer, 1998). The only escape from a grudge is true forgiveness.

Forgiveness has also been approached as an interactive process in which both the victim and the transgressor play pivotal roles in the process by which forgiveness is negotiated. Rusbult, Hannon, Stocker, and Finkel (2005) argue for a model of interdependence-based forgiveness in which both the the victim and the transgressor play active and important roles in determining forgiveness. A closer look at the factors that predict forgiveness in close relationships supports a conceptualization of forgiveness as an interactive process.

The first factor that predicts forgiveness are qualities of the individual who has been offended. Two characteristics associated with the forgiver are personality and gender. For example, the Big Five model of personality has been linked to forgiveness dispositions such that neuroticism negatively correlates and agreeableness positively correlates with forgiveness (Mullet, Neto, & Riviere, 2005). In addition to personality, forgiveness scholars have explored gender with mixed results. Women are found to be more likely to be forgiving than men across the lifespan (Miller, Worthington, & McDaniel, 2008). In contrast, male newlyweds are found to be more forgiving than their wives (Miller & Worthington, 2010). The existence of sex or gender differences in disposition toward forgiveness has been questioned by recent research that finds no significant differences between men and woman across the lifespan (Fehr, Gelfand, & Nag, 2010), although the general tendency to forgive does increase across the lifespan for both sexes (Allemand, 2008). As Allemand explains, the enhanced emotion regulation skills that develop over the lifespan and a limited time perspective that places one's focus on elements of the "now" in terms of maintaining important relationships may facilitate forgiveness among older adults compared to younger adults. The second factor that predicts forgiveness is relational equity. If a victim of transgression has previously been a transgressor in that relationship and been forgiven, that person is more likely to be forgiving of his or her partner (Morse & Metts, 2011). Relational justice can explain this predictive factor of forgiveness (Exline, Worthington, Hill, & McCullough, 2003). An individual who has been forgiven for a previous transgression is likely to experience an indebtedness to the person who has forgiven him or her. An apology does not always fully compensate for the cost (e.g., stress, hurt, or damage) of a transgression that results in an "injustice gap." Reciprocating forgiveness for a current transgression can be the only way to narrow this injustice gap. Simply put, a victim may feel obliged to forgive if he or she has previously been forgiven.

The third factor is the most consistent predictor of forgiveness and entails the actions of the transgressor. As noted above, the communication of a sincere apology (Bachman & Guerrero, 2006) and repentence expressed as a promise to do better in the future (Exline & Baumeister, 2000) predict greater forgiveness among adults. Interestingly, the positive consequences of an apology are also evident in children. Smith and Harris (2011) conducted a lab experiment in which a child (the confederate) kept stickers for him or herself or shared them with the subject (a child aged 4-7 years old). The children who had been told they would be given the stickers were disappointed when they did not receive them. However, those children who received an apology from the confederate child reported feeling better, rated the offending child as more remorseful and nicer compared to those children who did not receive an apology.

Although the interactive profiles that characterize the experience and expression of forgiveness continue to emerge and will no doubt begin to incorporate social networking venues as interactive locations, the consequences of forgiveness are well established. Forgiveness has important and lasting impact on both the transgressor and the offended person(s) as well as the relationship.

For the transgressor, self-forgiveness is achieved when he or she acknowledges the wrongdoing, accepts responsibility, and ultimately is able to replace negative self-criticism with acceptance of his or her self-worth in spite of, or separate from, the transgression (Hall & Fincham, 2005). Self-forgiveness is a motivational response to the socially adaptive, emotional response of shame that is experienced following a transgression (Woodyatt & Wenzel, 2013a). Shame motivates the transgressor to increase pro-social behaviors that can restore social belonging and acceptability. The emotional response of shame is intended to be temporary and self-forgiveness is the means through which an individual can resolve the feelings of shame that motivated that transgressor to sincerely apologize. Self-forgiveness is important because long-term shame can be damaging for the individual and the relationship. Woodyatt and Wenzel (2013c) argue that the resolution of shame is linked to self-trust. Additionally, self-forgiveness is a necessary condition for interpersonal restoration; both parties, offender and offended, must forgive the transgressor in order for the relationship to move beyond the transgression (Woodyatt & Wenzel, 2013b).

For the offended person and the relationship, forgiveness is associated with psychological well-being (e.g., Bono, McCullough, & Root, 2008), physical health (e.g., Friedberg, Suchday, & Srinivas, 2009), and enhanced relational quality and satisfaction (e.g., Kachadourian, Fincham, & Davila, 2004). Indeed, although a severe transgression can diminish commitment in a romantic relationship, longitudinal research indicates that over time, the experience of forgiveness mediates this effect (Ysseldyk & Wohl, 2012). Moreover, the assumption that an individual who forgives is subject to future victimization (e.g., forgiveness of abuse promotes more abuse) has not been supported by the research. Research indicates that not only is the forgiveness of a transgression not linked to an increased likelihood of future transgressions (Wallace, Exline, & Baumeister, 2008), but, in fact, that true forgiveness in the face of a sincere apology deters future transgressions (Murphy & Helmer, 2013). Cobb and colleagues (2013) argue that the hope a relationship will grow and improve in quality, as a product of the forgiveness process, actually does improve the relationship and decreases the likelihood of future transgressions. True forgiveness has many benefits for the victims of relational transgressions and provides the bridge to hope and resilience. We turn now to a description of that process.

And the Play Moves On: Transforming the Transgression Scene to One of Hope and Resilience

An integration of the research summarized to this point yields a clear pattern of sequential effects: revelation of the transgression evokes negative emotions for the transgressor and the victim(s) as well as threatening the stability of the relationship or cohesion of the family. Communicative negotiation of the meaning of the transgression and the transgressor's expressions of remorse and promise of better behavior in the future facilitates forgiveness. Forgiveness for self and others then mediates the negative consequences of the transgression. Of course the severity of the offense increases the salience of each phase in this process toward achieving forgiveness.

Perhaps more important for the enduring consequence of a transgression is the link between forgiveness and the two positive directions for the post-transgression future: hope and resilience. That link is provided by the functional interdependence among forgiveness, the positive emotions it elicits, hope, and resilience. To clarify the nature of this functional interdependence we begin with the Broaden and Build theory of positive emotion.

The fundamental premise of the Broaden and Build theory of positive emotions (Fredrickson & Branigan, 2005) is that action tendencies accompany the cognitive and physiological experience of emotion. For example, physiological tension and increased flow of blood to large muscles accompany the action tendency to attack when angry or flee when afraid. The action tendency associated with happiness and related positive emotions is to approach and engage with the environment. The scope of attention is broadened and solutions to problems are more readily available from the thought-action repertoires. This highly functional asset in the wake of a transgression is only possible when forgiveness has transformed the restrictive and inhibiting action tendencies of the negative emotions initially experienced. Once the positive emotions arising from forgiveness are experienced, for both the transgressor and the victim(s), the possibility of hope and resilience is increased. "To the extent that positive emotions broaden people's momentary thought-action repertoires, they promote the discovery and development of people's strengths and resources, which serve as enduring reserves that can be accessed in times of need" (Fredrickson & Branigan, 2005, p. 329). The discovery of one's strengths and resources are, in fact, the very core of hope.

Hope is a positively valenced affective state or psychological orientation that entails the expectation that a desired goal is available and obtainable (Lazarus, 1999). The belief that a successful path to accomplish the desired goal is available is referred to as the "way" and the belief that one has the agency or ability to find and implement that path is referred to as "will" (Magaetta & Oliver, 1999). Both elements facilitate the difficult challenge of moving forward constructively after a transgression. In much the same way that positive emotions facilitate the process of understanding the transgression and coping with its implications at the time, hope provides a constructive long-term coping strategy in its focus on future goals and their achievement. Of course in the case of a transgressions, the belief that the rule violation, hurtful message, or infidelity will not occur again is sometimes proven wrong. Fortunately, to the extent that the initial and subsequent events are managed constructively, good will and relational satisfaction can be maintained. This is the critical function served by resilience.

Resilience is the ability to cope with adversity and move forward in life by reevaluating the negative consequences of an event or by moving past it. Resilience is, to some degree, a relatively stable aspect of an individual's social orientation or personality, instilled in part from parental influences during early childhood experiences with stress and disappointment (Luthar, Cicchetti, & Becker, 2000). Even into the later years of adulthood, people who are able and willing to use available resources and to view social situations beyond their own concerns are more resilient (van Kessel, 2013). In addition, however, resilience is also a situated response to a particular adverse event that necessitates concerted effort to rebound and move forward (Dyer &

McGuinness, 1996). The availability of social or emotional support, practical resources, and social networks facilitate this type of resilience. Whether a personality trait or a situational accomplishment, in the wake of a transgression resilience functions to enhance the experience of hope for a better future and to allow all parties to move forward. Even if the transgression occurs again, resilience facilitates constructive coping and the reinvigoration of hope. In short, hope and resilience are interdependent and reciprocal tools in the reconstruction of relationships and families or, alternatively, in the reconstruction of separate lives that are open to new experiences rather than stalled in the erosion of rumination and regret.

Conclusion

Transgressions in close relationships are inevitable because people are flawed; they speak before thinking, act impulsively, and seek gratification inappropriately. Yet, they are also understanding and empathetic. Friends forgive, romantic partners forgive, parents forgive, and children forgive. The hope and resilience that follow in the wake of a forgiven transgression can facilitate relational improvement from its state prior to the experience or discovery of the transgression. Relational partners and family members can become more attentive to each other, clarify and negotiate relational rules, and envision a more positive and hopeful future. Future research could explore the ways in which hope and resilience are maintained in relationships plagued with cycles of transgressions and forgiveness to explore whether hope and resilience diminish or develop over time. Hope and resilience are important individual and relational features that guide enactment of the transgression scene, facilitate productive coping, and generate the new relationship scripts that promote growth and enrichment across the lifespan.

References

Afifi, W. A., Falato, W. L., & Weiner, J. L. (2001). Identity concerns following a severe relational transgression: The role of discovery method for the relational outcomes of infidelity. *Journal of Social and Personal Relationships, 18,* 291–308.

Al-Mabuk, R. H., & Downs, W. R. (1996). Forgiveness therapy with parents of adolescent suicide victims. *Journal of Family Psychotherapy, 7,* 21–39.

Allemand, M. (2008). Age differences in forgiveness: The role of future time perspective. *Journal of Research in Personality, 42,* 1137–1147.

Allemand, M., Steiner, M., & Hill, P. L. (2013). Effects of a forgiveness intervention for older adults. *Journal of Counseling Psychology, 60,* 279–286.

Aune, R. K., Metts, S., & Hubbard, A. S. E. (1998). Managing the outcomes of discovered deception. *Journal of Social Psychology, 138,* 677–689.

Bachman, G. F., & Guerrero, L. K. (2006). Forgiveness, apology, and communicative responses to hurtful events. *Communication Reports, 19*, 45-56.

Baumeister, R. F., Exline, J. J., & Sommer, K. L. (1998). The victim role, grudge theory, and two dimensions of forgiveness. In E. L. Worthington (Ed.), *Dimensions of forgiveness: Psychological research and theological perspectives* (pp. 79-104). Philadelphia, PA: Templeton Foundation Press.

Boon, S. D., & Sulsky, L. M. (1997). Attributions of blame and forgiveness in romantic relationships: A policy capturing study. *Journal of Social Behavior and Personality, 12*, 19-44.

Cann, A., & Baucom, T. R. (2004). Former partners and new rivals as threats to a relationship: Infidelity type, gender, and commitment as factors related to distress and forgiveness. *Personal Relationships, 11*, 305-318.

Carpenter, C. J. (2012). Meta-analysis of sex differences in responses to sexual versus emotional infidelity: Men and women are more similar than different. *Psychology of Women Quarterly, 36*, 25-37.

Cobb, R. A., DeWall, C. N., Lambert, N. M., & Fincham, F. D. (2013). Implicit theories of relationships and close relationship violence: Does believing your relationship can grow relate to lower perpetration of violence? *Personal Social Pscyhology Bulletin, 39*, 279-290.

Dyer, J. G., & McGuinness, T. M. (1996). Resilience: Analysis of the concept. *Archives of Psychiatric Nursing, 10*, 276-282.

Exline, J. J., & Baumeister, R. F. (2000). Expressing forgiveness and repentance. In M. E. McCullough, K. I. Pargament, & C. E. Thoresen (Eds.), *Forgiveness: Theory, research, and practice* (pp. 133-155). New York: Guilford Press.

Exline, J. J., Worthington, E. L., Hill, P., & McCullough, M. E. (2003). Forgiveness and justice: A research agenda for social and personality psychology. *Personality and Social Psychology Review, 7*, 337-348.

Fehr, R., Gelfand, M. J., & Nag, M. (2010). The road to forgiveness: A meta-analytic synthesis of its situational and dispositional correlates. *Psychological Bulletin, 136*, 894-914.

Fincham, F. D., Hall, J., & Beach, S. H. (2006). Forgiveness in marriage: Current status and future directions. *Family Relations, 55*, 415-427.

Fincham, F. D., Paleari, F. G., & Regalia, C. (2002). Forgiveness in marriage: The role of relationship quality, attributions, and empathy. *Personal Relationships, 9*, 27-37.

Fredrickson, B. L. & Branigan, C. (2005). Positive emotions broaden the scope of attention and thought-action repertoires. *Cognition and Emotion, 19*, 313-332.

Friedberg, J. P., Suchday, S., & Srinivas, V. S. (2009). Relationship between forgiveness and psychological and physiological indices in cardiac patients. *International Journal of Behavioral Medicine, 16*, 205-211.

Hall, J. H., & Fincham, F. D. (2005). Self-forgiveness: The stepchild of forgiveness research. *Journal of Social and Clinical Psychology, 24*, 621-637.

Hargrave, T. D. (1994). *Families and forgiveness: Healing wounds in the intergenerational family*. New York: Routledge.

Hendrick, S. S., & Hendrick, C. (1995). Gender differences and similarities in sex and love. *Personal Relationships, 2*, 55-65.

Holden, G. W., Coleman, S. M., & Schmidt, K. L. (1995). Why 3-year-old children get spanked: Parent and child determinants as reported by college-educated mothers. *Merill-Palmer Quarterly, 41*, 431-452.

Holter, A. C., Magnuson, C. M., & Enright, R. D. (2010). Application and assessment of interpersonal forgiveness. In E. Mpofu & T. Oakland (Eds.), *Rehabilitation and health assessment: Applying ICF guidelines* (pp. 453-472). New York: Springer.

Hoyt, W. T., McCullough, M. E., Fincham, F. D., Maio, G., & Davila, J. (2005). Responses to interpersonal transgressions in families: Forgivingness, forgivability, and relationship-specific events. *Journal of Personality and Social Psychology, 89*, 375-394.

Kachadourian, L. K., Fincham, F., & Davila, J. (2004). The tendency to forgive in dating and married couples: The role of attachment and relationship satisfaction. *Personal Relationships, 11*, 373-393.

Kelley, D. L. (1998). The communication of forgiveness. *Communication Studies, 49*, 1-17.

Kelley, D. L. (2012). Forgiveness as restoration: The search for well-being, reconciliation, and relational justice. In T. J. Socha & M. J. Pitts (Eds.), *The positive side of interpersonal communication* (pp. 193-209). New York: Peter Lang.

Kiefer, R. P., Worthington, E. L., Myers, B. J., Kliewer, W. L., Berry, J. W., et al. (2010). Training parents in forgiving and reconciling. *The American Journal of Family Therapy, 38*, 32-49.

Knobloch, L. K., & Metts, S. (2013). Emotions in relationships. In L. Campbell & J. Simpson (Eds.), *Oxford Handbook of Close Relationships*. Oxford, UK: Oxford University Press.

Lasch, C. (1977). *Haven in a heartless world: The family besieged*. New York: Basic Books.

Lazarus, R. S. (1999). Hope: An emotion and a vital coping resource against despair. *Social Research, 66*, 653-678.

Leary, M. R., Springer, C., Negel, L., Ansell, E., & Evans, K. (1998). The causes, phenomenology, and consequences of hurt feelings. *Journal of Personality and Social Psychology, 74*, 1225-1237.

Lopez, N. L., Schneider, H. G., & Dula, C. S. (2002). Parent Discipline Scale: Discipline choice as a function of transgression type. *North American Journal of Psychology, 4*, 381-394.

Luthar, S., Cicchetti, D., & Becker, B. (2000). The construct of resilience: A crucial evaluation and guidelines for future work. *Child Development, 71*, 543-562.

Magaletta, P. R., & Oliver, J. M. (1999). The hope construct: Will, and Ways: Their relations with self-efficacy, optimism, and general well-being. *Journal of Clinical Psychology, 55*, 539-551.

McCullough, M. E. (2000). Forgiveness as human strength: Theory, measurement, and links to well-being. *Journal of Social and Clinical Psychology, 19*, 43-55.

McCullough, M. E., Bellah, C. G., Kilpatrick, S. D., & Johnson, J. L. (2001). Vengefulness: Relationships with forgiveness, rumination, well-being, and the Big Five. *Personality and Social Psychology Bulletin, 27*, 601-610.

Merolla, A. J., & Zhang, S. (2010). In the wake of transgressions: Examining forgiveness communication in personal relationships. *Personal Relationships, 18*, 79-95.

Metts, S. (1989). An exploratory investigation of deception in close relationships. *Journal of Social and Personal Relationships, 6*, 159-179.

Metts, S. (1994). Relational transgressions. In W. Cupach & B. Spitzberg (Eds.), *The dark side of interpersonal communication* (pp. 217-239). Mawah, NJ: Erlbaum.

Metts, S., & Asbury, B. E. (2009). Transgressions. In H. Reis & S. Sprecher (Eds.), *The SAGE encyclopedia of human relationships* (1644-1647). Thousand Oaks, CA: Sage.

Metts, S., & Cupach, W. (2007). Responses to relational transgressions: Hurt, anger, and sometimes forgiveness. In B. Spitzberg & W. R. Cupach (Eds.), *The darkside of interpersonal communication* (pp. 243-274). New York: Routledge.

Miller, A. J., & Worthington, E. L. (2010). Sex differences in forgiveness and mental health in recently married couples. *Journal of Positive Psychology, 5*, 12-23.

Miller, A. J., Worthington, E. L., & McDaniel, M. A. (2008). Gender and forgiveness: A meta-analytic review and research agenda. *Journal of Social and Clinical Psychology, 27*, 843-876.

Miller, L. M., Worthington, E. L., Hook, J. N., Davis, D. E., Gartner, A. L., & Frohne, N. A. (2013). Managing hurt and disappointment: Improving communication of reproach and apology. *Journal of Mental Health Counseling, 35*, 108-123.

Morse, C., & Metts, S. (2011). Situational and communicative predictors of forgiveness following a relational transgression. *Western Journal of Communication, 75*, 239-258.

Mullet, E., Neto, F., & Riviere, S. (2005). Personality and its effects on resentment, revenge, forgiveness, and self-forgiveness. In E. L. Worthington (Ed.), *Handbook of forgiveness* (pp. 159-181). New York: Routledge.

Murphy, K., & Helmer, I. (2013). Testing the importance of forgiveness for reducing repeat offending. *Australian & New Zealand Journal of Criminology, 46*, 138-156.

Roloff, M. E., Soule, K. P., & Carey, C. M. (2001). Reasons for remaining in a relationship and responses to relational transgressions. *Journal of Social and Personal Relationships, 18*, 362-385.

Rusbult, C., Hannon, P. A., Stocker, S. L., & Finkel, E. J. (2005). Forgiveness and relational repair. In E. L. Worthington (Ed.), *Handbook of forgiveness* (pp. 185-202). New York: Routledge.

Scherer, M., Worthington, E. L., Hook, J. N., Campana, K. L., West, S. L., & Gartner, A. L. (2012). Forgiveness and cohesion in familial perceptions of alcohol misuse. *Journal of Counseling and Development, 90*, 160-168.

Shackelford, T. K., Buss, D. M., & Bennett, K. (2002). Forgiveness or breakup: Sex differences in responses to a partner's infidelity. *Cognition and Emotion, 16*, 299-307.

Smith, C. E., & Harris, P. L. (2011). He didn't want me to feel sad: Children's reactions to disappointment and apology, *Social Development, 20*, 1-14.

Snyder, C. R. (2000). *Handbook of hope: Theory, measures, and applications.* San Diego, CA: Academic.

Tabak, B. A., McCullough, M. E., Luna, L. R., Bono, G., & Berry, J. W. (2012). Conciliatory gestures facilitate forgiveness and feelings of friendship by making transgressors appear more agreeable. *Journal of Personality, 80*, 503-536.

Van Kessel, G. (2013). The ability of older people to overcome adversity: A review of the resilience concept. *Geriatric Nursing, 34*, 122-127.

Vangelisti, A. L., & Young, S. L. (2000). When words hurt: The effects of perceived intentionality on interpersonal relationships. *Journal of Social and Personal Relationships, 17*, 393-424.

Wallace, H. M., Exline, J. J., & Baumeister, R. F. (2008). Interpersonal consequences of forgiveness: Does forgiveness deter or encourage repeat offenses? *Journal of Experimental Social Psychology, 44,* 453–460.

Weiss, R. L. (1980). Strategic behavioral marital therapy: Toward a model for assessment and intervention. In J. P. Vincent (Ed.), *Advances in family intervention, assessment and theory* (Vol. 1, pp. 229–271). Greenwich, CT: JAI Press.

Woodyatt, L., & Wenzel, M. (2013a). A needs-based perspective on self-forgiveness: Addressing threat to moral identity as a means of encouraging interpersonal and intrapersonal restoration. *Journal of Experimental Social Psychology, 50,* 125–135.

Woodyatt, L., & Wenzel, M. (2013b). Self-forgiveness and restoration of an offender following an interpersonal transgression. *Journal of Social and Clinical Psychology, 32,* 225–259.

Woodyatt, L., & Wenzel, M. (2013c). The psychological immune response in the face of transgressions: Pseudo self-forgiveness and threat to belonging. *Journal of Experimental Social Psychology, 89,* 951–958.

Worthington, E. L. (1998). An empathy-humility-commitment model of forgiveness applied within family dyads. *Journal of Family Therapy, 20,* 59–76.

Worthington, E. L., & Wade, N. G. (1999). The psychology of unforgiveness and forgiveness and implications for clinical practice. *Journal of Social and Clinical Psychology, 18,* 385–418.

Young, S. L. (2004). Factors that influence recipients' appraisals of hurtful communication. *Journal of Social and Personal Relationships, 21,* 291–303.

Ysseldyk, R., & Wohl, M. J. A. (2012). I forgive therefore I'm committed: A longitudinal examination of commitment after a romantic relationship transgression. *Canadian Journal of Behavioural Science, 44,* 257–263.

Section Two
Contexts

• CHAPTER SIX •

(Re)Envisioning Hope & Resilience in U.S. and Norwegian Prisons

Brittany L. Peterson
Ohio University

Timothy P. McKenna-Buchanan
Manchester University

> [Do] you know [what] the big difference between Norway and America is?...in America you have lots of people never coming out of prison; in Norway everybody has a date we go out. So then you have to be careful because if you make too much fuss they move that date. In America you get [a] life time [sentence], and then you don't really give a shit. So you do what you want.
> —Mark, Inmate in the Norwegian Prison System

On July 22, 2011, Anders Behring Breivik went on a rampage, detonating bombs in Oslo and opening fire on labor-party youth on the island of Utoya. At the end of the day, 77 people lay slain (Lewis & Lyall, 2012, August 24). Breivik claimed that he was protecting Norway from its growing affinity toward multiculturalism, Islam in particular. He was sentenced to 21 years in prison, Norway's maximum sentence (Kriminalomsorgen, 2013), and has since been serving time in what is known to be one of the most humane prison systems in the world (Christie, 2000, 2004; Pratt, 2008). Perhaps ironically, Breivik publically penned his criticisms of these facilities complaining to the media about the conditions in the prison. The New York Times reported that Breivik was displeased with "his three-cell suite with a television and exercise equipment" and "would like butter, a new pen, more comfortable handcuffs and a view" (Sayare, November 9, 2012). The sarcasm in the above quote is palpable, in part because the intentions and implementation of prison sentences in the U.S. and Norway vary dramatically. The United States is infamous for its high incarceration rates, and the "enormous prison population is *not* a source of shame. It is seen as a sort of inevitable answer to crime, if anything, a sign of strength and efficiency" (Christie, 2004, p. 114 emphasis in original). Conversely, Norway is known for its "exceptionalism in an era of penal excess" (Pratt, 2008, p. 119). Norwegians pride themselves on their humane approach to incarceration. These starkly different environments, or *scenes* (Burke, 1945), likely lend themselves to varied communicative organizational practices.

Burke (1945) explains that "a thing is determined insofar as it is limited by the boundaries of other things, determined by whatever outside itself marks its terminations" (p. 143). In essence, the "scene" is determined by the here and now of everyday life. It is "the background of the act, the situation in which it occurred" (Burke, 1945, p. xv). The scene is flexible and can change when new agents enter or exit and with the passage of time. In this chapter, we "begin afresh" by drawing on qualitative interviews conducted with U.S. and Norwegian incarcerated individuals, correctional staff, and prison teachers to explore *hope* and *resilience* in two different scenes: U.S. and Norwegian prisons (Burke, 1945, p. xvi). We concur with Hylland and Eriksen (2001), who explain that "culture is the patterns of thinking, habits, and experiences that human beings share and that make it possible to understand each other" (p. 60). As such, we argue that the cultural elements of these scenes are resources that inform our understanding, hope, and resilience among involuntary members in prison and across individuals attached to these scences (e.g., correctional officers, family, and society at large). Most fundamentally, we posit that the way hope and resilience are created, expressed, and experienced throughout an incarcerated individual's life may have nuanced levels of complexity based on the cultural scene (see Gunnestad, 2006). In line with this thinking, we take a moment to set the scene by outlining the stark contrasts between the U.S. and Norwegian prison systems.

Setting the Scene

According to the U.S. Bureau of Justice Statistics (BJS) in 2012, 6.9 million people (2.9% of the U.S. adult population) were under some type of correctional supervision (e.g., probation, jail, prison, or parole; Glaze & Herberman, December 2013). That is, 1 out of every 35 adults was in some way directly tied to the correctional system in the United States with 1 in every 50 adults being under parole/probation and 1 in every 108 adults being housed in a prison or jail correctional facility (Glaze & Herberman, December 2013). Of those, approximately 1.57 million were incarcerated in state or federal prisons, 83,603 in local jails, and 137,220 in private prisons (Carson & Golinelli, December 2013). In 2011, there were 716 inmates incarcerated in the state or federal system for every 100,000 in the population (ICPS World

Prison Brief, 2013). These high incarceration levels come at a cost, on average $25,000 to incarcerate an individual for one year (Schmitt, Warner, & Gupta, 2010). In all, the U.S. spent $75 *billion* on federal, state, and local corrections in 2008 (Schmitt, Warner, & Gupta, 2010).

Conversely, Norway's prison population as of January 2013 was a measly 3,649 people (ICPS World Prison Brief, 2013) with nearly 1/3 of those individuals serving time for narcotics or drug related charges (Statistics Norway, Imprisonment, 2009). Admittedly, Norway's total population of 4.7 million is markedly smaller than the U.S. population, estimated 316 million as of July 2013 (The World Fact Book, U.S., 2013; The World Fact Book, Norway, 2013). Still, when the numbers are distilled, the differences between the two countries are startling. In Norway, 72 *out of every* 100,000 people in the population are incarcerated (ICPS World Prison Brief, 2013), whereas in the U.S. 716 *out of every* 100,000 individuals are incarcerated (ICPS World Prison Brief, 2013). Moreover, Norway, unlike the United States, does not have the death penalty (Christie, 2004). Under normal conditions, the longest sentence that Norwegians can serve is 21 years, and the average time served is only 5.5 months (Kristoffersen, 2007). Finally, the recidivism rates in Norway are strikingly lower: 20% of individuals reoffended after two years (report generated in 2010) (Kriminalomsorgen, 2013), when compared to those in the United States, where 43% reoffended within a three-year period between 2004–2007 (The PEW Center on the States, 2011, April). Simply put, the U.S. incarcerates a higher percentage of its population and has a higher rate of recidivism than Norway.

Presumably, the numerical differences outlined above have meaningful implications for the construction of hope and resilience in these two different scenes. In order to highlight the intricacies of the scene in these two cultures we will first provide an overview of hope and resilience.

Hope and Resilience in Prison

Hope can be understood as a positive motivational state that is the result of goal-directed energy and the plans to meet those goals (Snyder, Irving, & Anderson, 1991). Lazarus (1999) explains, "A fundamental condition of hope is that our current life circumstance is unsatisfactory—that is, it involves deprivation or is damaging or threatening" (p. 664). Hope, then, enables us to shift our focus away from the current negative events and circumstances toward the potential positive outcomes that can arise in the midst of an unsatisfactory situation. For most individuals, incarceration provides one such example of an undesirable life circumstance. When incarcerated individuals cling to hope, they increase their "perceived capacity to derive pathways to desired goals, and motivate...[themselves] via agency thinking to use those pathways" (Snyder, 2002, p. 249).

Etymologically, resilience is the ability to regain *original* shape after being bent, compressed, or stretched. In prisons, though, it is far more likely that resilience manifests as a competent response to the pervasive stressors of prison life. This view of resilience resonates with Masten (2001) who refers to resilience as "a class of phenomena characterized by good outcomes in spite of serious threats to adaptation or development" (p. 228). Richardson (2002) adds that resilience is "the process of reintegrating from disruptions in life" (p. 39). Thus, for incarcerated individuals, resilience likely involves accepting current circumstance and subsequently figuring out a path for restoration and literal reintegration back into society. These individuals need to figure out how to pick up the pieces of their broken lives, mend their communication networks (Koschmann & Peterson, 2013), and survive on the outside.

Although past research has taken a more quantitative and individualistic approach to hope (see Snyder, 2002) and resilience (see critique Buzzanell, 2010), Buzzanell (2010) suggests that as communication scholars we incorporate an additional angle to our analyses that is "fundamentally grounded in messages, d/Discourse, and narrative" (Buzzanell, 2010, p. 2). Individual experiences and expressions of hope and resilience are inextricably tied to the larger Discourse of the culture and the individual narratives lived. Moreover, hope and resilience are often experienced across the lifespan in concert with other people. In correctional institutions, inmates' experiences of hope and resilience are indelibly bound to their families (e.g., children, siblings, parents) and those incarcerated around them. Ultimately, we want to envision how the composition of different scenes shape incarcerated individuals' understanding of hope and resilience in prison and re-envision more hopeful and resilient ways of living in light of this.

Accordingly, our central guiding research question is: *In what ways do incarcerated individuals speak about hope and resilience in prison in the U.S. and Norway?*

The data in this chapter were drawn from aproject on involuntary membership in prison organizations.[1] The first author spent approximately 5 months acquiring approvals to conduct research with this protected population. She worked with the Institutional Review Board (IRB)[2] at her current institution to determine the best course of action for crafting the full-board IRB submission. One of the initial complicating factors was that the IRB required site approval prior to submission of the proposal and both of the research sites required the IRB approval prior to approving access. Ultimately, the first author was able to aquire a conditional approval document from both the Texas Department of Criminal Justice (TDCJ)[3] and the Norwegian Correctional Services Office (Kriminalomsorgen) that satisfied the IRB's requirements. Notably, the first author's study was approved in four separate phases: 1). Norwegian employees, 2). Norwegian inmates, 3). U.S. employees, 4). U.S. inmates. These phases arose based on ease of approval (i.e., employees are not a protected population and did not require full IRB board approval) and logistical timing (i.e., the Norway data collection was slotted to occur first). As such, the first author initially submitted her proposal for Norwegian employees with the understanding that she would ultimately submit ammendments for Norwegian inmates and the U.S. participants in the study. As the approvals were granted, the first author worked with a colleague in Norway to facilitate the access to a local prison. In the U.S., however, she began making cold-calls to the various prison facilities in Texas. The wardens at each facility had the power to determine whether or not they would grant her access and facilitate her data collection in the U.S.

Ultimately, the first author conducted a total of 62 interviews ($N = 62$) with incarcerated individuals ($n = 41$), correctional officers ($n = 10$), prison teachers ($n = 8$), and prison wardens ($n = 3$) in both the U.S. ($n = 48$) and Norway ($n = 14$) across 4 separate prison organizations. The interviews totaled 70 hours and 21 minutes and resulted in 1,367 single-spaced pages of transcribed text. In addition, the first author recorded 58 pages of field notes during her time in the prisons, which were used to inform this analysis. We have edited some of the Norwegian narratives (e.g., minor tense and grammatical changes) to improve readability. The first author worked from an etic coding scheme, seeking out illustrations of hope and resilience in the stories shared (Lindlof & Taylor, 2011)[4]. Unless otherwise noted, the narratives below are drawn from inmates; discourse and data drawn from field notes, wardens, correctional officers, or prison teachers are identified in kind.

(Re)Envisioning Hope and Resilience

The participants in our study painted a complicated picture of the experience of hope(lessness) as well as resilience and/or the lack there of. Throughout the narratives, the participants talked directly and indirectly about the ways in which these constructs are intertwined. At times the discussion of hope preceded resilience; other times the opposite was true. Often, the interviewees shared their stories in such a way that made it impossible to detangle the constructs. Below we share the lived experiences of our participants.

U. S. Prisons' Hope and Resilience

Incarcerated individuals in the U.S. shared stories with varying degrees of hopefulness and hopelessness. To begin, glimmers of hope shone through in the conversations with the inmates. They hoped for parole or early release. They hoped to get their lives straightened out, to get off the streets, out of their gangs, off of the drugs. They hoped to break the cycle of incarceration and the bad behavior they had embraced in the past. They hoped, prayed, and yearned for a second chance. At least some of them did.

David was one of those people. His hope resided in his vision to start a bar grill business upon release:

> My main thing is, I wanna do something. And to anybody when I say this, it might sound crazy, you know, like it's impossible. But nothing, that's another things I've learned, nothing's impossible. So I wanna do something that's gonna pay back. You know, and not just anything, because I hope to make it huge, as much as I can.

Other inmates dreamed, but on a smaller level. Reggie and Frankie talked about the hope they had to be paroled one day and Terrell hoped this was his last stop. The word "hope" was prevalent in the U.S. inmate interviews. Many incarcerated individuals were hoping for something, to be somewhere, to get something, or to be someone else.

At times, hope seemed to be born out of fear. Jimmy explained, "I seen old people in here walking around with a cane, I just be like, man, I hope that's not me one day man." The examples of hope are best distilled in Cuba's poignant words as he pondered the question, "what gets you through the day?" "Hope, you gotta have hope."

Conversely, some of the inmates were suspicious of hope. They believed hope to be a false emotion that would never truly be realized. Terrell explained that,

> Some people pretty much fantasize on how they are going to be when they get out and I am not that type of person to live in a fantasy world. I know [when] I get out, it [is] not going to [be] no walk in the park. So I am not even looking for a walk in a park when I get out. I know that really it is better for me to invest in myself because you can get high hopes…and move too fast. And they realize that nothing going their way. They can't think properly so they go to anything…and they fall back.

Hope, in absence of a realistic lens, can be almost dangerous. Norbert, a prison teacher, explained this sentiment best when he said "hope in prison is deadly because you can really get wrapped up in it, and you're just setting yourself up to get crushed." Terrell and Norbert seemed to suggest that too much hope can lead inmates down an undesirable pathway, one where they believe they are invincible and unrealistically imagine that everything will go exactly they way they plan. And although hope can be dangerous, hopelessness can be far worse.

Amid the hopefulness that permeated some of the interviews, undertones of hopelessness simmered. Some inmates acted on their hopelessness in an effort to end it all. Phil said that he witnessed nearly 50 suicide attempts during his time behind bars. In one particularly disturbing story, he explained how a mentally ill inmate responded to his hopeless situation:

> There's a backlog for the mentally ill offenders. They don't have anywhere to put em...The officers aren't trained to deal with them...So I saw a mentally ill offender cut his eyeball out with a razor blade. And the officer was just egging him on, you know, tormenting him, kicking on his door. And the inmate, he had a razor blade...finally he just pulled his eye lid out like that and sliced the eyelid off and stuck it on the glass on the window like that...More officers came in kept egging him on and finally he just reached and stuck his finger into his eye and pull it out and cut it off.

And although this particular inmate was unsuccessful in his suicide attempt, many others succeeded. Correctional Officer Wanda explained that some inmates try to starve themselves to death. Warden Tex concurred and said that he has seen people hang themselves with twisted toilet paper and jump off roofs. In his interview, Warden Tex related one particularly graphic story:

> He had taken that little bitty razor blade and cut a square out of his neck because it was so small that he couldn't reach in there... took his finger and pulled that artery out and then just cut it...He fell face down in the cell. "Bam" [Warden Tex smacked his hands together]. This was at nighttime. Well, the officer working the wing ... was underneath the stairways filling out some reports, and the way he know it, something was starting falling on the paper he was writing. And it was blood...So he went up there, and of course, he was dead...bled out.

Through these stories you can almost envision the tension between hopefulness and hopelessness. It is a tension that extends far beyond what many of us could ever understand. The lived emotions are palpable especially in the case of Duncan who accidently killed his newborn son in a shaking incident. Duncan's story emanated with both hopefulness *and* hopelessness as he shared, "everybody has been supportive, and my wife, she [has] still been by my side through all of this. So I thank God for that." Still, a few moments later he continued:

"but I got some family that don't [support me] ...I can't say how they think about this situation or what they may think but like my brothers... (they been locked up before so I am the last out of the 3 to come down to the penitentiary), and at first they weren't even writing me. So I was like "ok you all must be holding grudges or something about my situation."
...I can't see my niece when I get out because [my sister-in-law] feels that I am a threat to the kids or whatever but that's not the case...Still, my mother, my father, my step dad, [and] my wife, they all been supportive so them really the only ones that I really worry about.

Plainly, three generations of Duncan's family were affected by his actions, and Duncan explained that his choices would continue to affect his family relationships long after his release. In the excerpt above, Duncan seemed to almost reframe his view of hope in order to embrace a resilience-promoting mindset by shifting his focus away from his unsupportive siblings toward his supportive parents and wife. As is evident in the excerpt above there is space for resilient moments surronding hope.

Where hope emerged as more of an emotional tension, resilience manifested in an embodied response. In the context of prison, resilience is often affiliated with an inmate's post-release life in terms of his or her successful reintegration to society. The epitome of resilience would occur when an inmate does *not* recidivate but instead reacclimates to his or her life on the outside. Within the confines of the prison walls, resilience looks slightly different. Most often, it surfaced in discussions of surviving prison by escaping the hold of gangs, participating in mentorship programs, finding God, or simply, discovering a new reason to keep moving forward.

One particular program that several of the inmates spoke about that helped shape their resiliency was called the "GRAD" program, Gang Renouncement and Disassociation. Jacob explained that when he made up his mind to leave his gang, he signed up for and successfully completed the nine-month program. Phil also went through the GRAD program after eleven and a half years in ad seg (administrative segregation), otherwise known as the hole. Phil's story is an ultimate one of resilience. For eleven years he lived in a cinderblock cell, with steel doors and no windows only allowed to leave for 1 hour of solo recreation time per day. But he demonstrated resilience. Phil maintained his sanity by studying criminal law and helping other inmates (via mail) with post conviction habeas corpus.

Other inmates participated in peer eduction programs where older, more seasoned veterans of the prison system mentored younger, more naïve inmates. These partnerships helped to foster reslient attitudes and behaviors. Clarence explained how he came to be a peer educator and how it helped him to give back to his community:

They just don't let anyone be a peer educator. You got to be somebody that have certain type of standing on your unit. Officers pretty much respect you, your not a trouble maker, and so they call you [and ask], "ok, you want to be a peer educator?" You can say yes or no. If you tell them yes they going to put you through a seven-day course. Somebody from the free world come in teach you. You get certified you get a certificate, and it's a good thing. I love doing it...I felt like, "man I took so much away from my community. I took so much from when I got first got locked up. I was in so much drama and so much stuff that I feel like I owe, I owe a lot. I am in debt to society, and this is one of the ways I can pay my debt. So I love doing it."

In addition to escaping gangs and and paying back a debt to society as a form of resilience, several inmates cited God as the source or reason for their resilience. They talked about how God enabled them to turn from their former ways toward a new beginning. Alex explained that:

[Faith] is priority with me because I believe my peace and joy don't have to come from my surrounding circumstances. Even in spite of the midst of a bad circumstantial situation I still have peace and joy...Me re-establishing my relationship with God and prioritizing my life had been the best thing that I could have done. I don't look at this so much as being me arrested, I think I was rescued and given the opportunity to get it right.

Still other inmates credited their resilience to memorable moments that propelled them forward. Alan, a college-aged former student, killed two girls in a drunk driving accident. After his conviction, Alan worked with the district attorney to create a public service announcement that aired in the state of Texas. Shackled, he also spoke at his former high school about the dangers of drinking and driving in an effort to stop future generations of students from following his path. Alan's participation in the video, part of the Shattered Dreams series, led to renewed resilience and a refreshed vision for his future. Likewise, Vince shared a touching narrative about how the birth of his son was a memorable moment that shook him to the core and ultimately encouraged him to move toward real change in his life:

Eight days after he was born I got arrested...him being brought in the world changed my whole outlook on my criminal behavior attitude. Cause I said now that I done created life, I no longer live for me, I live for him too. So now my decision-making is based on him...When I would normally get attitude and be wantin' [to] fight in those [cell] blocks...I leave it alone cause now I'm trying to get outta here for him.

The embodied experience of resilience was typically born out of a memorable moment, a striking change, or an impactful person. Inmates talked about these life-changing experiences as being the pre-cursors to true resilience, that is resilience that endures, that is lasting, and that helps individuals successfully navigate the transition back to society. Notably, this type of resilience is born on the inside. True resilience, then, is not reactionary. Instead, inmates start preemptively working toward meaningful resilience while incarcearted to better prepare them for the challenges they might encouter upon release.

In the above stories, we have attempted to tease out specific examples of hope and unique instances of resilience. Yet, in the actual interviews, these two constructs were indivisible. Many inmates, like Benji, intermixed their feelings of hope with the desire to be resilient upon release.

> When I get out... I just want to make a difference. Like I said, I want to do something I am proud of and make my family proud. I don't want to come back. I don't want to do this the rest of my life. [The] recidivism rate in at a penitentiary is horrible. Guys come back. My dad, I think it was his fifth time coming back, something like that...I don't want to do that...There is opportunities and classes there, but you have to seek them out and take advantage of them. That's why I am [in] college. That's why I took "overcomes." I go to AA programs. They have a program called changes, different parenting classes, and things like that. You just want to take them, and he never took advantage of any of that. And I think that has pushed me to get off my butt and not just sit in my cell all day and watch TV.

A handful of the inmates dreamed, some even dreamed big. Unfortunately, the stories often sounded like pipe dreams that these individuals were telling themselves in order to survive. Rarely were they well thought out, tangible plans that could be put into practice upon release. We suspected, sadly, that many of these hope and dreams would indefinitely remain abstract. Layering on the lens of hope theory (Snyder, 2002), the inmates spoke about hope in terms of their goals and dreams that were support by agency thinking. The missing link, however, was often the articulation of clear pathways to reach those goals. Perhaps then, the prescence or absence of viable pathways or their specificity might be related to inmate success upon release (i.e., successful reintegration, continued hope, and enduring resilience).

In sum, feelings of hope and stories of resilience albeit present, were not the norm in U.S. prisons. More often than not, jaded, frustrated inmates shared their stories about the broken system and its oppressive nature. Many rants were shared during the hours spent in the three American facilities. There was a lot of anger, pain, and brokenness. Such was not the case in the Norwegian prison.

Norwegian Prisons' Hope and Resilience

Although, the *word* "hope" was much less pervasive in the interviews with Norwegian inmates and staff, the *sentiment* of hope permeated our conversations. It was almost as if discussing hope was a non-issue; it was the status quo. Hope was much more simple, pure, and present. In Norway, hope was engendered through the enactment of normalcy. Hope, then, was pervasive in the inmates' ability "to maintain the mundane, the regularities in life" that were not always present in the U.S. inmates' narratives (Buzzanell, 2010, p. 3). For instance, inmates were allowed to take leave (aka vacations from prison or furloughs). The duration of leave was determined by inmate behavior as well as time accrued. Matt, an inmate, explained that he had 18 days of leave during a year period (and that inmates can apply for up to 50 days of leave each year). Typically, individuals take leave for two to three days at a time, visiting their family in other parts of the country. They sign themselves out of the prison, arrange transportation—typically via train—spend time doing "normal" activities, and return to the confines of the prison when their "vacation" is up. When Matt's house burned down, Warden Grant allowed him to take leave to get his affairs in order. Matt explained that he appreciated his leave time because it enabled him to remain in touch with the outside world, and ulimately, better prepare him for life post-release.

Small degrees of normalcy were also afforded to the families of the inmates. Families were allowed to visit for entire days (as opposed to the closely measured moments prescribed in U.S. facilities). In addition, Eric said that his children could play in the prison gym. He, and others, were allowed to have conjugal visits with their significant others. In fact, one of the more prominent topics of discussion with Warden Grant was the importance of conjugal visits in prison. He spent a good amount of time talking about the renovations of the prison visiting rooms so that the inmates and their loved ones will have a more comfortable space to have sex:

> We are making [a room] with a bed. It is possible to make a bed that they can get clean sheets and they can get condoms. So we are saying to the inmates if you have that kind of visit with your wife, it's ok, we should do the best we can to get to make this a good time for you.

The warden's desire to go above and beyond to improve the inmates' intimacy in the prison speaks to the hospitable incarceration practices that foster hopeful realities.

In addition, inmates created hopeful situations by comparing their circumstances to other incarcerated individuals. Perhaps unsurprisingly, the

Norwegian inmates focused almost exclusively on comparing their experiences to those of U.S. inmates. They drew their knowledge, in large part, from the extensive media and entertainment industry coverage of U.S. prison facilities and conditions. As such, individuals incarcerated in Norway were well aware of the negative stigma imbued on U.S. prisons and the desirablilty of their own arrangements, under the circumstances. They talked about their paths with more hopeful undertones than their American counterparts. For instance, incarcerated individual Mark said somewhat apathetically: It's not dangerous to be in prison. It's just terribly boring. Nothing happens. It's like watching paint dry. If you don't behave like a complete idiot, you won't ever be in any physical danger. Norway is not like America (laughter)."

Matt, also an inmate, concurred that "prison is not a terrible place to be." He went on to say that he heard the bad stories, the horror stories, about it. And most of those stories had originated with American television shows portraying the experience. Matt believed that ultimately attitude was the determining factor in the prison experience and that prison, by and large, was a "good place."

Correctional officer Adam agreed with the inmates. He explained that before working in prison, he thought he would be breaking up non-stop fights like in American movies and news stories. When he arrived, he learned that most inmates kept to themselves and followed the rules. Adam explained "inmates have a carrot in front of them. They know that if they behave nicely for this sentence, they can go outside and can maybe meet their wives and children... so maybe that motivates them." Adam's words are quite representative of the attitude of most incarcerated individuals in Norway. The system is set up in such a way to encourage hope. They are able to taste freedom during their prison leave time. And as Mark so poignantly points out:

> "in America you have lots of people never coming out of prison; in Norway everybody has a date we go out. So then you have to be careful because if you make too much fuss they move that date. In America you get [a] life time [sentence], and then you don't really give a shit. So you do what you want."

The maximum sentence of 21 years in Norway when compared to the life sentences doled out in the U.S., have significant psychological, emotional, and practical implications. As Mark suggests, it motivates Norwegian inmates to keep it together so they can start to live the freedom they have glimpsed from the few precious days of leave they spend outside the barbed wire fences.

Although the word hope was rarely spoken during the interviews with Norwegian inmates and staff, those same individuals were never without a story of resilience. While serving time, inmates were expected to get their situations in order so that they could demonstrate resilience upon release.

Adam, a correctional officer, and Warden Grant both explained that the Norwegian prison system believes it is important for inmates to "go out to the society again" (Adam) and practice being a good citizens while incarcerated. The rationale? Inmates who spend time outside of the prison walls during their incarceration are far more likely to be well adapted and resilient than those who remain locked up for the duration of their sentence. In addition to developing resilience through release, Norwegian prisons foster resilience through formal and informal counseling.

Correctional officers Chris and Adam both affirm the importance of these activities. Chris talked about informal mentoring through small talk centered on sports. Adam, on the other hand, discussed more formal mentoring and its positive outcomes: "We encourage them to talk about it to do something with their lives because we want of course that every inmate here will have a good life outside that they are not addicted to drugs or have to do crime to to live outside." Chris, an inmate, talked about the importance of these counseling sessions in the recovery process. He explained that the first time he went through the official drug mentoring program that he was not ready to change. And change is an essential precursor to being resilient outside the confines of the prison walls. However, during his next stint in prison, he appreciated the program. He said it was good because you were able to work on yourself and that if you went in with an open mind, change was possible. In fact, Chris told the story of one of his friends who initially enrolled in the drug counseling program to earn what Americans understand as "good time" (i.e., completing a program or class in exchange for early release from prison). At the culmination of the program, Chris's friend was a believer. He had started the program with ulterior motives but it ended up engendering real change in him that will hopefully lead to the demonstration of resilience post-release.

Finally, Bjorn's narrative was the ultimate story of resilience. Bjorn was a prison teacher who strove to motivate and encourage his students to have "faith in themselves as a person without doing criminal activities." During his time as a prison teacher, Bjorn held one moment particularly close to his heart. Here's his story:

> For me it's quite clear because I had two pupils…[who] were in prison for the first time. They had about a year and a half sentence which was nearly finished when they took part in that group…We had many good discusions…They were bright. They were good young men with opportunities…I used all my force to tell them don't waste young lives on criminal activities. Once again, don't do the same mistakes when you get out. Get some education. Get a real life…[Two years later] I saw those two guys.

> They were students at the university. One of them was studying to be a nurse. The other one was taking the same education that I have myself.

How rewarding it was to have two of his former incarcerated pupils really turn their lives around by working toward college degrees. While remembering this success story, Bjorn, got a bit emotional. He believed in his students and daily saw them embody resilience in his classroom and beyond.

In sum, the underlying cultural expectation in Norway is that people can reform. The inmates are given hope through the system. They taste freedom and can recognize an end in sight. As such, they can demonstrate resilience and experience restoration "from [the] disruptions in life" (Richardson, 2002, p. 39). Thus far, we have taken a cursory look at the stories of hope(lessness) and resilience shared by incarcerated individuals. But we have yet to investigate the ways in which these experiences are shaped, in large part, by the cultural scenes that envelop them. Following, we turn our attention to the importance of the scene to explain some of the intricacies present in our data. We re-envision the cultural scene as having both material and social substance.

Sensemaking the Scene

Norwegian and American inmates' feelings of hope and resilient triumphs are fundamentally shaped by the material and social substance of their respective scenes. The materiality and social fiber of the scenes offer a level of explanation for aforementioned differences between U.S. and Norwegian prison organizations.

Material

Norway differed from the U.S. in terms of the material substance of the scene. In other words, the physical structures of prison were unique to each country. Norway's physical structure was different from that of the U.S. on many levels. To begin, the prison was located in a neighborhood surrounded by houses just a few blocks from a school. If it weren't for the tall chain link fences and the secured entryway, the prison could have been passed for any other public service building. In addition, the interior structure of the prison housed some significant amenities as an excerpt from the first author's field notes suggests:

> We were able to get a view of the C block. It was impressive. I felt more like I was in a college dorm than a prison cell. Chris's room was pretty decent sized. He had pictures (and calendars with semi nude women) on the walls, schoolbooks, a nice flat screen TV and DVD player, and a computer. He also had his own shower and toilet.

Honestly, I could probably live in that space. That was my first thought. It was a lot nicer than I expected.

The U.S. cells on the other hand were a bit different. They exuded punishment. The cells were designed in such a way to promote discomfort, and of course, denial of the niceties of life. In the United States there were two types of living spaces in the prison: one was a large barracks-style room that boasted approximately 150 beds partitioned off in smaller groups (e.g., 4 beds) by cement half walls. The other style was traditional cell style. An excerpt from the first author's field notes paints a picture of cell space in the United States:

> The cell was incredibly small, no bigger than the inside of a large SUV... On the right there were two bunk beds. Steel, bolted to the wall. Then right at the very back wall on the left, was the toilet. What surprised me about this toilet was that it wasn't like the ones I'd seen in other facilities (steel, no parts) but rather, it was a "normal" looking toilet with a seat and all... looked like it could be broken off and used as a weapon. There were drawers, two of them, underneath the lower bunk. It's all they get to store their personal belongings in. Notably, there was NOT a ladder to get up to the top bunk. I'm not sure how they go about hoisting themselves up there.

Through these descriptions, we have painted two drastically different scenes. In Norway, resilience still shines through the C block window. The personalized artifacts and nonverbal expressions in the prison cells give the impression of a hopeful future. The scene has been structured to foster the importance of reintegration back into society and a desire to bounce back in spite of the difficulties. However, the hope in the U.S. cells is dusted in discomfort and denial. The standard, replicable beds rob inmates of their individuality in lieu of order and structure. The industrial bars that lock up each prisoner do not allow much hope for reintegration. It is evident that the stories of hope(lessness) and resilience are inextricably bound to the materiality of the scene. We will now explore the social substance of the scene as that provides us additional clues that add to our cultural understanding.

Social

In addition to material differences in scene, there are also social substance differences. Norwegians and Americans largely have different views on the position of inmates within the society. Norwegians embrace incarcerated individuals as human beings first and foremost. In fact, Norwegian prison teachers like Linda seemed flabbergasted when I asked what they "called" the inmates. I was fully expecting to get answers similar to the U.S. (e.g., offender, inmate, prisoner); instead, Linda and others simply said, "they are my students." In the U.S., on the other hand, inmates are saddled with a distasteful stigmatized identity. These social differences first became apparent in the conversations shared with the Norwegian correctional officers. In general, their families were not worried about them working in prison (unlike those of their American counterparts). The job of a correctional officer was highly regarded, esteemed even, equated to the level of a police officer or firefighter. They were envisioned as caregivers, counselors, and protectors of those within and outside the prison walls. According to correctional officers Adam and Cory, it came with significant training (3 years in the academy) and prestige. The job of a correctional officer, unlike in the U.S., was not a "dirty job" (see Tracy & Scott, 2006).

Perhaps one reason for the stark difference between the esteem of a correctional officer in the U.S. and one in Norway is the degree of taint or stigma associated with their respective roles. Goffman (1963) explains that individuals like correctional officers who are close to stigmatized others experience a degree of "courtesy stigma" through their association with inmates (p. 30-31). In Norway, that taint is not as great as it is in the U.S. Moreover, there are varied degrees of social distance, or the amount of stratification or "space" that divides different groups or classifications of individuals, across the two scenes. Pratt (2008a) explains that social distance in Scandinavian prisons is extremely low. Officers and inmates often share meals at the same table. Similarly, the social distance between inmates and individuals in the "free world" is also noticeably smaller in Norway than in western countries (Christie, 2004; Pratt, 2008). Cory, a Norwegian correctional officer, illustrated this point beautifully:

> I can meet the people (inmates) and find out that he is a real nice guy, and we work together good. And I can go back later and find out that he has been a murder--one or two persons... I think it's quite hard to actually put a word on it because it's a real thing. Because when we are sitting in the outside world, if me and my friends are together, I can hear my friends saying that he shouldn't be alive or he's a bastard. And it's awful that he had murdered two people and everything, and I can sit beside them I can actually agree with them no problem...But when I come in here, I am at work, and this is my job, and I have to be professional. I am not entitled to judge them because they have already been judged by the sentence. They are already put in here, so it's not mine to like go in and punish them further because that's already been done. But I can maybe prevent I say maybe this from happening again or maybe I can just give him a little bit sense to prevent him from doing it again.

When juxtaposing this quote with one from a U.S. correctional officer, the perceptions of social distance differences are quite clear. Nilsa explained the differences between the correctional officers and the inmates:

> It's like, you're in gray and we're in white, and that's how they're gonna put it. You're in gray and we're in white...Like say there was a policy change, you as an officer can't possibly see the effects on them because you don't live as an offender. And they tell you that, "Well at least you get to go home...Well you forfeited that right." You don't sit there and argue with them, but they forfeited that right when they did what they did.

In sum, the social distance between correctional officers and incarcerated individuals in U.S. and Norwegian prisons is strikingly different. In Norway there is room for hope because inmates are not labeled in patently different ways than they were on the "outside." Indeed, the scene in Norway is not littered with as much social stratification or social distance than is present in the U.S. Moreover, in Norway, inmates experience a sense of resilience as societal, familial, and often personal judgments are kept in the past and not carried over into the present. Conversely, in the U.S. hope is not seen between the gray and white uniforms that create social distance. And narratives of resilience in the prison system are few. The stigma has far reaching effects that extend beyond the prison walls and into the post-release lives of the formerly incarcerated. These individuals are seemingly (re)incarcerated every time they fill out a job application that asks whether or not they have felony convictions in their past (Khimm, 2013, July 21) and every time an election passes and they are unable to vote (Lee, 2012; ProCon.org, 2013). Thus, the social substance of the scene further showcases the intricacies of hope(lessness) and resilience in the U.S. and Norway.

On the whole, the material and social substance of the scene complicate our understanding of hope and resilience in these cultures. However, in taking this scenic approach, we have perhaps unintentionally omitted the agency of those whose stories we share. As such, we have left room for future dramaturgical exploration, which we address below.

Future Research: From Dramatism to Dramaturgy

In this chapter we focused on the pentadic view from the perspective of scene. Yet, by examining the narratives of hope and resilience with a scenic lens, we arguably have neglected actor agency and the role of the audience. Goffman (1959) envisions people as actors who, "have to conduct themselves in ways that met the requirements of real situations, which are theatrical in construction" (p. 255). In the U.S., there still seems to be a very sharp division between the front stage where inmates actively perform and back stage where they are able to step out of character. There are explicitly appropriate ways of acting and being when in front of varied audiences such as family, correctional officers, or even other inmates, however fewer descriptions of what happens in the back stage when the lock clicks. Norwegian prisons, on the other hand, do not seem to have the same stark division between the stages. In fact, they more accurately reflect the way in which Goffman talks about the fluid nature of these stages. He explains that while there is a tendency for a region to become identified as the front stage or back stage of a performance, there are many regions that function at one time and in one sense as a front stage and at another time and in another sense as a back stage (Goffman, 1959). This fluidity while apparent is interesting to explore as it can pose interesting challenges of constant negotiation for individuals in prison settings.

Whereas dramatism's strength is in its exploration of motives from varied angles to "begin afresh" (Burke, 1945, p. xvi), dramaturgy's strength is grounded in its attention of the agentic nature of the performance of "everyday life" (Goffman, 1959). As such, future research should take up Goffman's (1959) dramaturgical perspective as a new perspective on the experience of hope and resilience in prisons.

Hope for a Resilient Future

This research has highlighted the varied experiences and expressions of hope and resilience in U.S. and Norwegian prisons. The meaningful material and social elements of the cultural scenes suggest that Norway is doing something right. Where the Norwegian inmate narratives reverberated with swells of hope and resilience, the U.S. narratives merely whispered them. These findings may be due, in large part, to the fact that in Norway the material and social scenes *in prison* closely mirrored those *outside of prison*. In other words, incarcerated individuals were not materially nor socially divided from the rest of society in that way that U.S. inmates were (and are) throughout their lifespan.

It is possible that some of these divisions might be diminished if we adopt systematic changes, hence, Koschmann and Peterson's (2013) recommendations to re-envision the incarceration problem as fundamentally a communication problem. That is, we need to recognize that incarcerated individuals are cut off from their social networks and need help to successfully navigate the reentry process into society and experience the possibility of resilience. This help needs to come throughout the lifespan. Clearly, support during incarceration is important; however, equally as important is the continued aid through the reintegration process. Thus, practically we argue that incarcerated individuals in the U.S. prison system need supportive partners, mentors, prison teachers, and the like to help them move toward a more hopeful future outside the prison walls.

In addition, we want to encourage scholars to consider how the clarity (or lack thereof) in incarcerated individuals' goals, pathways, and agency thinking might have tangible consequences for reintegration and recidivism. Conceivably, the high recidivism rate in the U.S. could be related to inmates' ill-articulated plans that are not constructed in meaningful, hope-promoting ways. Thus, future scholarship should seek to augment the high-low hope dichotomy by considering the role of clarity in the construction of hope.

Finally, more hopeful futures might be envisioned through wide-spread implementation (and study) of alternative programs that encourage inmate success (e.g., restorative justice, family support programs, reentry partnerships, etc.). For instance, the Girl Scouts Beyond Bars program is designed to serve girls with incarcerated mothers. These young girls (ages 5-17) are able to connect with their moms and receive counseling services and social support during their time in the program, all in an effort to break the cycle of incarceration that is often deeply engrained in family units (Grant, 2006, see also Girl Scouts, 2014).

Perhaps most importantly, we need to envision ways in which hope and resilience can open up space for enriching the lives of incarcerated individuals within and beyond the confines of prison. Or in the words of Liz, a prison teacher in the U.S. system, we need to let inmates know why we are really there: "You know why we're really there? We're really there to show them that they're loved...They're not forgotten about. They're not shut away forever. That somebody on the outside hopes for a better life for them." In short, it is up to us to help encourage hopefulness and foster resilience. We need to be part of the solution.

Notes

1 These data were part of the first author's dissertation conducted under the direction of Larry Browning at the University of Texas at Austin. It was funded in part by the Jesse H. Jones Endowed Centennial Fellowship from the University of Texas at Austin and the High North Fellowship awarded by the Bodø Graduate School of Business at Bodø University.

2 Before beginning this study, the first author worked with the Institutional Review Board (IRB) at her home institution, the Texas Department of Criminal Justice, and Kriminalomsorgen, which is the national correctional services office in Norway, to ensure that all of the proper documents were in place to conduct research using this protected population. The informed consent document was written in grade school level English. In

addition, the informed consent document was translated into Norwegian for the inmates incarcerated in Norway. The first author was accompanied by a colleague fluent in Norwegian for all of the interviews in Norway, and while the interviews primarily took place in English, some translation did occur.

3   The research contained in this document was coordinated in part by the Texas Department of Criminal Justice (Research Agreement #586-AR09). The contents of this report reflect the views of the author and do not necessarily reflect the views or policies of the Texas Department of Criminal Justice.

4   The data in this study were analyzed with the help of the software NVivo. The first author used the software to search key words in the transcripts including but not limited to: hope, hopeless, hopefulness, resilience, future, plan(s), goal(s), etc. From these queries, examples of hope and resilience emerged. In addition, the first author read through the transcripts looking for poignant stories of hope and resilience shared by the participants. The analytic approach resonates with what Lindlof and Taylor (2011) call etic coding, whereby the researcher evaluates the scene "through the conceptual categories provided by our disciplinary knowledge and theory" (p. 95).

References

Beck, G. A. (2013). Buffering the impact of involuntary job loss: The role of interpersonal resilience in romantic relationships. Manuscript submitted for publication.

Burke, K. (1945). *Grammar of motives.* New York: Prentice Hall.

Buzzanell, P. (2010). Presidential address—Resilience: Talking, resisting, and imagining, new normalcies into being. *Journal of Communication, 60,* 1-14. doi:10.1111/j.1460-2466.2010.01469.x

Carson, E. A., & Golinelli, D. (2013, December). *Prisoners in 2012: Trends in admissions and releases, 1991-2012* (U.S. Department of Justice. Office of Justice Programs. Bureau of Justice Statistics Publication No. NCJ 243920). Washington, DC: U.S. Government Printing Office. Retrieved from: http://www.bjs.gov/index.cfm?ty=pbdetail&iid=4842

Christie, N. (2000). *Crime control as industry* (3rd ed.). New York: Routledge.

Christie, N. (2004). *A suitable amount of crime.* New York: Routledge.

Girl Scouts. (2014). *Girl Scouts Beyond Bars.* Retrieved June 15, 2014, from: http://www.girlscouts.org/beyondbars

Glaze, L. E., & Herberman, E. J. (2013, December). *Correctional populations in the United States, 2012* (U.S. Department of Justice. Office of Justice Programs. Bureau of Justice Statistics Publication No. NCJ 243920). Washington, DC: U.S. Government Printing Office. Retrieved from: http://www.bjs.gov/index.cfm?ty=pbdetail&iid=4843

Goffman, E. (1959). *The presentation of self in everyday life.* New York: Doubleday Anchor.

Goffman, E. (1963). *Stigma: Notes on the management of spoiled identity.* New York: Simon & Schuster.

Grant, D. (2006). Resilience of girls with incarcerated mothers: The impact of Girl Scouts. *The Prevention Researcher, 13* (2), 11-14.

Gunnestad, A. (2006). Resilience in a cross-cultural perspective: How resilience is generated in different cultures. *Journal of Intercultural Communication, 11,* 1.

Hylland Eriksen, T. (2001). *Small places, large issues. An introduction to social and cultural anthropology* (2nd ed.). London: Pluto Press.

International Centre for Prison Studies (ICPS). (2013). World prison brief: Norway. Retrieved October 8, 2013, from: http://www.prisonstudies.org/info/worldbrief/wpb_country.php?country=158

International Centre for Prison Studies (ICPS). (2013). World prison brief: U.S. Retrieved October 8, 2013, from: http://www.prisonstudies.org/info/worldbrief/wpb_country.php?country=190

Kim, S. (2013, July 21). States push to provide some ex-felons a second chance. *MSNBC.* Retrieved from: http://www.msnbc.com/all-in/states-push-provide-some-ex-felons-secon

Koschmann, M., & Peterson, B. L. (2013). Rethinking recidivism: A communication approach to prisoner reentry. *Journal of Applied Social Science, 7,* 188-207. doi:10.1177/1936724412467021

Kriminalomsorgen. (2013). Norwegian directorate for correctional service. Retrieved October 8, 2013, from: http://www.kriminalomsorgen.no/english.293899.no.html

Lazarus, R. S. (1999). Hope: An emotion and a vital coping resource against despair. *Social Research, 66,* 665-669.

Lee, T. (2012, October 8). States deny millions of ex-felons voting rights. *Huffington Post.* Retrieved from: http://www.huffingtonpost.com/2012/10/08/felon-voting-rights_n_1924535.html

Lewis, M., & Lyall, S. (2012, August 24). Norway mass killer gets the maximum: 21 years. *The New York Times.* Retrieved from: http://www.nytimes.com/2012/08/25/world/europe/anders-behring-breivik-murder-trial.html

Lindlof, T. R., & Taylor, B. C. (2011). *Qualitative communication research methods* (3rd ed.). Thousand Oaks, CA: Sage.

Masten, A. S. (2001). Ordinary magic: Resilience processes in development. *American Psychologist, 56,* 227-238. doi:10.1037//0003-066X.56.3.227

The PEW Center on the States. (2011, April). *State of recidivism: The revolving door of America's prisons.* Public safety performance project. Retrieved October 8, 2013, from: http://www.pewtrusts.org/uploadedFiles/wwwpewtrustsorg/Reports/sentencing_and_corrections/State_Recidivism_Revolving_Door_America_Prisons%20.pdf

Pratt, J. (2008). Scandinavian exceptionalism in an era of penal excess. Part I: The nature and roots of Scandinavian exceptionalism. *British Journal of Criminology, 48,* 119-137. doi:10.1093/bjc/azm072

ProCon.org (2013). Felon Voting. Retrieved October 30, 2013, from: http://felonvoting.procon.org/viewresource.php?resourceID=286

Richardson, G. E. (2002). The metatheory of resilience and resiliency. *Journal of Clinical Psychology, 58,* 307-321. doi:10.1002/jclp.10020

Sayare, S. (2012, November 9). Life in a prison suite doesn't agree with a mass killer. *The New York Times.* Retrieved from: http://www.nytimes.com/2012/11/10/world/europe/norway-killer-breivik-complains-about-prison.html?_r=0

Schmitt, J., Warner, K., & Gupta, S. (2010, June). *The high budgetary cost of incarceration*. Center for Economic and Policy Research. Washington, DC: U.S. Government Printing Office.

Snyder, C. R. (2002). Hope theory: Rainbows in the mind. *Psychological Inquiry, 13*, 249-275. doi:10.1207/S15327965PLI1304_01

Snyder, C. R., Irving L., & Anderson, J. R. (1991). Hope and health: Measuring the will and the ways. In C. R. Snyder & D. R. Forsyth (Eds.), *Handbook of social and clinical psychology: The health perspective* (pp. 285-305). Elmsford, NY: Pergamon.

Tracy, S. J., & Scott, C. (2006). Sexuality, masculinity, and taint management among firefighters and correctional officers. *Management Communication Quarterly, 20*, 6-38. doi:10.1177/0893318906287898

The World Fact Book. (2013). Norway. CIA. Retrieved October 1, 2013, from: https://www.cia.gov/library/publications/the-world-factbook/geos/no.html

The World Fact Book. (2013). United States. CIA. Retrieved October 1, 2013, from: https://www.cia.gov/library/publications/the-world-factbook/geos/us.html

• CHAPTER SEVEN •

Employment Transitions in the Aftermath of Economic Collapse: Emerging and Older Adults

Gary A. Beck
Ashley M. Poole
Lisa M. Ponche
Old Dominion University

An especially relevant problem for working-age populations around the globe is the turbulent nature of worldwide economic markets and the related lack of employment opportunities. In a recent case of art imitating life, *The Internship* (2013) is on the surface a dubious big-screen example of these larger economic issues affecting two unique subgroups across the lifespan. After all, the movie stars comedic actors Owen Wilson and Vince Vaughn as ever-goofy, crude, but also lovable salespeople scrambling for a new break after their sales careers become obsolete. Presented limited and undesirable opportunities on the job market, the two take a chance at a competitive internship at Google, the preeminent technology company of the early 2010s.

The plot thrusts these two comparatively older salesmen in direct competition with millennials, armed with vastly superior familiarity with technology and digital ingenuity. Eventually placed in a team with several millennial outcasts, Wilson and Vaughn's characters develop an awkward but necessary alliance to vie for the coveted jobs at Google. In the end (saving the reader from any major spoilers) these characters combine the strengths of the younger team members (e.g., technological savvy, coding ability) with that of the older characters (e.g., street smarts, likeability, and persuasion) in an attempt to respond to the movie's central question: What does it take to survive in our modern era's professional world?

In the aftermath of the 2008 worldwide economic collapse, there weren't many satisfying answers to that question. It seemed that only those with enough training to be relevant and enough experience to make them invaluable were enjoying continued employment. And even those qualifications didn't guarantee safety, as innovation makes some occupations unnecessary (as *The Internship's* protagonists experienced, as apparently endangered "wristwatch salesmen"). High school, college graduates, and the recently unemployed were met with the discouraging ratio of way too little jobs to way too many applicants. Not helping that ratio was the lack of natural job turnover: When the economy collapsed it took investments and retirement saving accounts down with it, sinking the dream of an early retirement at a particular level of comfort. Older adult workers either needed to retire anyway and settle with a lesser vision of their "golden years," or continue to work until things rebounded. With many choosing the latter, those higher paying positions in the company remained occupied. And those unfortunate to retire before the collapse either needed to downsize their lifestyles and future plans or dust off the resume and return to the workforce.

Recent signs, as of 2014, have indicated improved economic stability and consumer confidence. As of July 2014, the U.S. unemployment rate fell to 6.1%; the lowest since September 2008. Moreover, an unprecedented 200,000 positions were added in June, marking the fifth straight month of both broad and accelerating job creation—the best the U.S. economic market has witnessed since the 1990's tech boom (Bureau of Labor Statistics, 2014). This change in economic fortunes has gradually resulted in more disposable income for purchases and with it the associated higher demand for product. This increase in demand *usually* leads to hiring more employees to help manage the swell in business. Such news is, at the very least, most welcome. Yet cynicism lingers, especially when some recent global estimates still suggest that 202 million people remain unemployed (40%, 75 million, are youth ages 16-24) (WEF, 2013). Any further job market recovery is likely predicated upon increased familiarity with post-recession policies, risks, and opportunities.

Despite reasons to be skeptical, hope grows for those with motivation and a willingness to adapt. Young people, disillusioned by the job market have taken to service, such as *Teach for America* or *AmeriCorps*, working part time or freelance, or enlisting in the military. Others have documented their resultant experience of personal and professional rediscovery, as is the case with those behind the lemonademovie.com, or the motivating college campus speaking series and documentary "Build Your Dreams" (Irvin & Hiden, 2013). These efforts highlight a clarification of professional motivations and emphasis on exercises of self-reflection, notions echoed in both the post-recession discourse and re-employment strategies of both emerging and older adults.

Utilizing a Resilience and Hope Framework

It may appear that our salvation, or the answers for best managing the challenges of unemployment, come first from a necessary re-calibration of our expectations and pathways forward in this new era: An era that is focused around a technologically enhanced, knowledge-based, social media infused, and health-minded professional world. Still, unique contextual features for those situated in different spots along the lifespan face specific challenges.

The theoretical frameworks of resilience and hope theory may provide insight into these challenges and potential solutions. Both theories involve encountering challenges and harnessing resources to best manage life stressors. Resilience theory, cast within ecological, psychological, and developmental traditions (see Reich, Zautra, & Hall, 2012) generally suggests that promotive or protective factors (i.e., internal assets or external resources) help mitigate the effect of a stressor on particular life outcomes (e.g., happiness, employment status). While different disciplines emphasize alternative conceptualization and measurement strategies, most theoretical models identify resilience in relation to some serious life stressor, with emphasis on what helps mitigate or compensate for challenges to effective or competent functioning. For those going through employment troubles, helpful promotive or protective factors could be internal assets like optimism and drive, or external resources like social support from loved ones or colleagues, professional mentorships, or even a financial assistance.

Alternatively, hope theory (Snyder, 2002) suggests that hope is enacted when people establish clear goals, identify reasonable options or pathways for achieving those goals, and then sustain the necessary follow-through to make it happen (i.e., agency). Research clarifying hope's role in pursuing and achieving educational goals (Rand, Martin, & Shea, 2011; Snyder, 1999) holds promise for additional implications as students prepare for life after college. Together, resilience and hope theory generally suggest the proactive assessment of not only the challenging circumstance, but also the means by which solutions can be realized from variety of sources.

Additionally, if we utilize these theoretical perspectives to examine the context of employment challenges and transitions, we can make distinctions between seeking first and second order change (Watzlawick, Weakland, & Fisch, 1974). *First order change* involves intervening with challenges when they become obvious, with what we have at our disposal. Alternatively, *second order change* instead asks us to consider the source of the problem, and what may be used to prevent the problem from ever happening in the first place. Therefore instead of waiting for unemployment to start worrying about establishing and maintaining a professional identity, second order thinking would suggest actively cultivating it along with maintaining important professional ties, seeking career related training, and demonstrating professional competence (all while employed or still at school). While first order approaches are obviously necessary, second order change thinking opens up multitudes of preemptive options for addressing employment issues and the associated transitions. Worldwide economic circumstances are cyclical, and future generations would likely benefit from the lessons and preparations derived from second order thinking.

Mid-career adults, compared to other lifespan cross-sections, generally seem to be the most insulated from involuntary unemployment, clearly one of the worst effects of depreciated economic conditions. As a group, they possess the largest array of social capital: Years of experience, on the job specialized training, better overall financial conditions, and a cultivated network of interdependent industry colleagues (WEF, 2013). Therefore the following chapter will be focused on the bookends of the unemployment experience: Emerging Adults (18-29 year olds) and Older Adults (it varies, but usually 65 and older). Each of the following sections will aim to clarify the unique features of each lifespan cross-section as it relates to employment challenges, as well as sources of hope and resilience. Finally, implications for each will be summarized.

Emerging Adults Transition to Uncertain Employment

Despite the recent promising rise in job opportunities, a few lifespan cross-sections continue to fare unfavorably. Emerging adults, those between the ages of 18 and 29, represent one of the highest percentages of Americans unemployed, especially among young college graduates. Unemployment for this demographic as a whole is 8.8%, worse than the national average of 7.5% (Bureau of Labor Statistics, 2014). On average in 2013, only 17% of college graduates had a job waiting for them after college, down from 20% the year prior (Sum, et al. 2014). Furthermore, recent studies have suggested that fewer than half of U.S. college graduates between 2009 and 2011 found a job within 12 months of graduation (Stone, Van Horn, & Zukin, 2012), and because of this underemployment is on the rise.

The average number of college graduates reported to be underemployed jumped from 27% in 2007 to 37% percent in 2013, a seemingly poor return of investment on emerging adults' college tuition and time (Sum, et al., 2013). An estimated 37% of bachelor degree-holding emerging adults are in positions that require no more than a high school diploma (Vedder, Denhart, & Robe, 2013). With already bleak employment statistics in a rapidly changing job market, it is important to understand the unique features and challenges of emerging adulthood as it relates to employment transitions. Only then can researchers attempt to identify pathways for promoting resilience during what is perceived by many as a turbulent time of transitional uncertainty.

The last decade has seen a shift in terminology describing individuals between the ages of 18 and 29, specifically in postindustrial western societies. "Emerging adult" has been coined to describe the first wave of millennials to graduate high school and enter the work force, higher education, or some combination of both (Arnett, 2000). Salient to the conceptualization of emerging adulthood is the recent economic and cultural transformations in postindustrial societies. Additionally relevant to this definition is the cultivation and construction of social roles and personal traits that have been identified to occur more often among this age cohort than any other period of the life course.

As will be discussed below, the unique challenges facing this demographic necessitate emerging adults to reevaluate college to career pathways: Such introspection is crucial to successfully navigate employment transitions as well respond with resilience to the volatility of the modern job market. The uncertain context surrounding entry into adulthood makes long-term planning difficult. However the benefit of learning to successfully overcome the context of uncertainty can provide emerging adults the requisite skill sets to construct and manage their lifelong career path, which has been identified as an imperative skill amid the shift toward technologically-driven career markets.

College-to-career transitions have changed drastically over the last twenty years in the United States. The decision-making process relating to life choices among young adults has experienced a cultural shift. Emerging adulthood marks a time of uncertainty and imbalance. It is during this time that adult roles are postponed and emerging adults explore various paths in order to find meaningful and enduring life work. Between poor economic markets, an increase in higher education opportunities, and a decrease in immediate adult responsibilities, emerging adults have been provided with unprecedented opportunities for identity exploration. In prior generations, identity exploration was a pivotal characteristic typically (and solely) associated with adolescence.

Given these various contextual features, this period marks an important period for promoting resilience and fostering hope in emerging adulthood. Many emerging adults embrace the indeterminate nature of these years, yet others seemingly become stagnant in the face of uncertainty (Tanner, 2006; Murphy, Blustein, Bohlig, & Platt, 2010). For many, newfound identity is manifested through the exploration of a chosen career (Mortimer, Zimmer-Gembeck, Holmes, & Shanahan, 2002) suggesting that emerging adults may begin to feel a lack of esteem, self-worth, or loss of identity while sorting through career options during this transitional time period. Indeed, employment statistics provide not only a picture of career uncertainty, but also the potential for multiple career transitions in just the first decade of ones' career. Thus, college to career transition obstacles experienced by emerging adults likely constitutes a risky environment, promoting both adaptive and maladaptive outcomes (Arnett, 2000; Masten, 2001).

From this arises the need to understand the varying degrees of how emerging adults adapt and cope in the face of adversity in order to successfully transition from college to meaningful employment. While normative experiences during transitional life stages do not generally qualify as resilience (Masten, Obradovic, & Burt, 2006), today's route through higher education and beyond features many concurrent challenges. Additional stressors such as increasingly competitive college admissions, soaring tuition debt (and inadequate training about responsibly taking on debt), unequal access to the Internet and social networking, balancing interpersonal and work relationships, and biological vulnerabilities in the latter half of emerging adulthood provide additional parameters for researchers to consider as they investigate resilience during emerging adult transitions.

Further, extant research elucidates how challenging this period can be for emerging adults, especially considering their different paths (Osgood et al., 2005). Schulenberg, Bryant, and O'Malley (2004) suggested during college to career transitions emerging adults need varying levels of support from multiple network sources in order to successful transverse into adult roles, both personally and professionally. They state: "It can be a turning point: some young people who falter and flounder during the transition come from the ranks of well-functioning adolescents; likewise, some troubled adolescents demonstrate a turnabout through successful experiences with the new opportunities and tasks of this transition" (p.1120). The differences between these two and other emerging adult groups need to be further clarified within resilience theory, but the importance of social support (Wright et al., 2013), supportive learning environments (Kerssen-Griep, Trees, & Hess, 2008), and the role of hope has been well documented in educational settings (Rand, Martin, & Shea, 2011; Snyder, 1999).

Career pathways are no longer clearly linear, as once was the case in many job fields. Instead, modern innovative marketplaces are fast paced, diverse, and less predictable, warranting the need for awareness and adaptability among emerging adult job seekers. Employers expect potential employees to be well educated, experienced laborers who possess niche skill sets often learned from prior work experience. Moreover, employees that are rendered most valuable possess high levels of emotional intelligence deeming them as socially and cognitively flexible, agile as well as easily able to adapt to new and ever changing job roles. In spite of low employment opportunities among this age demographic currently, companies are actively looking for new, experienced young employees especially as the economy moves, albeit sluggishly, out of recession. Current trends show that experimental learning programs (e.g., internships, cooperative education, service learning, externships, job shadow programs) are the most sought-after experiences that recruiters look for in new graduate hires (McAtee, 2010). In 2005, the conversation rate of interns hovered around 35%, however the 2014 conversation rate rose to 51.2%, where employers made full-time offers to 64.8% of interns (NACE, 2014). Clearly, today's internships are tomorrow's jobs in our modern economy.

In the fast-paced, evolving digital workforce it is imperative to understand how to build and brand one's professional identity, starting at the beginning of emerging adulthood. All too often, college students assume their degree will be the winning ticket to a successful, self-satisfying career right out of college...and that professional identity development will take place upon employment. Being proactive and being flexible regarding opportunities during the beginning of emerging adulthood supports a hope theory framework for managing this important employment transition.

The idea of developing career flexibility (Ebberwein, 2008) suggests that emerging adults acknowledge the hallmark of today's workforce—change and choice—that promotes anticipation and preparation in spite of uncertain trajectories. It is a promising pathway for emerging adults to choose a potential career field, acknowledge limitations, define particular skill sets, and frame their career pathway as a life-long process versus a finalized destination. Often, emerging adults set limits too high, and when certain goals go unaccomplished a sense of defeat evokes feelings of failure. A commitment to some kind of work is a societal norm, but career flexibility acknowledges that multiple pathways are possible in spite of having to "choose" a career path (and stick to it). In doing so, emerging adults are encouraged to view their college-to-career transition as merely an initial data point. Several options and opportunities can be derived from career flexibility to support a more successful transition.

A recent study found that "realistic and well-informed expectations may play a central role in emerging adults' perceptions of both their current life satisfaction and experience of their transitions to the working world" (Murphy, Blustein, Bohlig, & Platt, 2010, p. 174). Career flexibility and adaptability allow emerging adults to identify a particular career pathway while simultaneously acknowledging the potential limitations and obstacles. Social support has been found to be one of the most consistent assets to current life satisfaction and successful transitions. However, this support should not be limited to family and friends. Implementing support from additional social network sources gained through one's academic career can also help support a successful transition. Several universities have begun implementing career transition programs that not only acknowledge the bumpy transition but also highlight key attributes emerging adults need in order to flourish after graduation (McAtee, 2010).

A recurring complaint from employers is that emerging adults are unable to translate learned abilities into the necessary skills needed in the workforce. The National Association of Colleges and Employers (2010) reported that competent communication, editing, and writing are three high-ranking skills needed by all employers regardless of career field. However, writing was found to be the second largest gap between what employers need and what new graduates actually deliver. In an attempt to fill this gap, Emory University found that using e-Portfolios across a student's college career helped strengthen not only writing skills, but fostered students' ability to translate meaning from what they were learning, develop the skills sets needed to identify their personal strengths and weaknesses, develop career pathways by writing professional development plans, research potential threats in their industry of interest, and conclude their development plans with goal-oriented tasks necessary to obtain their career goals. In doing so, students gained invaluable self-awareness through tangible experiences by setting and achieving desired goals, creating a track for themselves to transverse throughout their college careers (Borgen, Amundson, & Reuter, 2004). Graves and Epstein (2011) stated, "As a collecting place for the communication artifacts that students develop throughout the course, the e-portfolio allows students to construct professional identities and to display narratives significant to potential employers" (p. 346). Indeed, active curation of an online repository of one's student work appears to establish and reinforce an emerging professional identity.

Higher education programs that seek to reinforce emerging adults' resilience to the challenges of transitioning to the workforce should seek to develop the necessary student attitudes, skills, and strategies to successfully face unexpected disappointment, transition, and adversity in the workplace. A key attribute of resilience-promoting cognition is the ability to reframe a negative experience into a positive one, to re-cast, at face value. Change and transition in the 21st-century work force is inevitable and it will happen. Employers provide their employees with employment, without guarantees of stability. "Employers provide the opportunities, tools, and support to help employees develop their skills and main their employability; the employees have the responsibility of managing their careers, taking advantage of the opportunities they are given...the employees must be self-reliant" (Brown, p. 2, 1996). Thus, the onus of a career and long-term professional development is shifted to the employees, a process that must start much earlier in the career trajectory.

While college internships have been a time-tested attribute to gain workforce literacy, they are often overlooked and not mandated by all colleges and universities. Internships have been found to be not only a rewarding experience, but also a developmental tool for students to gain realistic expectations of work and ease the expectation-reality gap. Research suggests that while case studies and projects in the classroom help prepare students to gain awareness of typical workplace scenarios and challenges, the complexities of work life only become apparent through actual experience garnered through opportunities such as internships (D'Abate, Youndt, & Wenzel, 2009). Another alternative to internship opportunities could be "shadowing" employees, usually for shorter periods of time. Advanced soft skills, as previously noted, are in high demand among employers looking for new hires. Many college students, surprisingly, are unaware of the importance of this experience and their development during internship opportunities, compromising their transition efforts.

Lastly, modern estimates suggest that less than 20% of college graduates have a full-time job waiting for them after college. The role of career management centers in student career development after graduation is just as important as supporting current students to find work. Several research studies have implicated the importance of social support during college to career transitions, suggesting the potential need for added and extended support from college career centers. However, support from career centers would likely be most effective if initiated well before a college student's senior year or graduation. "Social support is the foundation for a satisfying transition, instilling a sense of empowerment and resilience to help dispel the mental roadblocks of shame, frustration, and procrastination that often accompany young alumni in their pursuit of employment" (Maietta, p. 31, 2012). Career services faculty may be most effective as a steady presence throughout the college experience, through the transition, and afterward.

One case study that provides ample evidence of how resilience can be promoted from college career centers is the Virtual Job Club implemented through career services at Nichols College (Dudley, MA). As a web-based job-search support program, the Virtual Job Club provides current seniors and recent college graduates a millennial-friendly online platform for discussion, career advice, workshops, and job listings. Students and alums using the Virtual Job Club are able to forge new relationships or rekindle old connections with fellow alumni, local businesses, professors, and college staff. Among participants, involvement was found to be a source of hope and optimism for unemployed recent graduates. No longer are job search frustrations isolated incidents: Having this large network support enables students to remain realistic and optimistic while benefiting from guidance and intergenerational advice from alumni and staff who have "been there." Bolles (2009) found that such networking has a 33% higher success rate than scanning Internet job boards and then flooding a specific career field with resumes. In addition, joining established networks reinforces a sense of community and accountability among the users. Such users develop additional motivation to follow through on community advice or leads, thus applying more time and effort to the job-hunt process.

While the above program provides an exemplar of social support for college students professionally, it is important for emerging adults to also focus on developing and maintaining their personal support network. Finding a balance between work and personal relationships is imperative for the healthy social development. The key for work-life balance is to develop an autonomous and competent professional identity outside of one's primary interpersonal relationships. Prior longitudinal studies provide evidence suggesting adaption and adjustment during transitional stages is greatly facilitated through social support, improving one's well-being and self-esteem (Galambos, Barker, & Krahn, 2006; Schulenberg, Bryant, & O'Malley, 2004). Additionally, the role of family, friendships, and romantic partners is crucial to helping emerging adults form realistic expectations of school to work transitions, helping to mediate outside stressors that in return increase current life satisfaction (Murphy, Blustein, Bohlig, & Platt, 2010).

In today's labor market, emerging adults must grasp the understanding that today's job market is centered on the idea of a "self-managed" career. The need to stay employable by possessing core qualities learned within a working environment versus solely obtaining specific educational knowledge is a difficult concept for many college students to grapple. A college degree is simply not enough to position emerging adults onto successful career paths. While this expectation was the norm for prior generations, recent experiences reflect a gap in today's college-to-career transition that must be addressed well before students reach graduation. While the argument can be made that the need for more well-rounded programs in college is necessary, it should be noted that emerging adults should be well informed at the beginning of their educational careers that changing job markets require a sense of identity, adaptability, and self-discipline. The implementation of both new and old methods of preparation is needed to inform emerging adults of the necessary skill sets they must decidedly adapt in order to transition successfully from college into the job force.

Older Adults' Later Career Transitions

Given our modern economic circumstances, older adults are finding the dream of a leisurely and comfortable retirement is in fact a "dream deferred." Despite their best efforts many will have serious challenges reaching a sunset lifestyle once considered a guarantee. Due to advancements in health technology and education older people are living longer, more active lives. People can now expect to potentially spend around a third of their life in retirement after leaving their main jobs (Owen & Flynn, 2004). The American Social Security program is fast headed for insolvency as baby boomers enter retirement (Gokhale, 2013). As a result, individuals have to rely on their own savings or family financial planning that many are simply not prepared for.

Therefore many older adults are discovering that as they reach retirement age they may not have planned properly for the financial strains they may be faced with in retirement. Gone are the days in which people remained loyal to one company throughout their lifetime and retired with a nice pension. Additionally, it is increasingly more common for older workers to be forced out of their jobs into taking an early retirement (Bender, 2011; Hyatt, 2006; Noone, O'Loughlin, & Kendig, 2013; Wang & Shi, 2014). Older adults may unfortunately find themselves woefully financially unprepared to retire. When such realities are aggravated by economic instability, older adults are increasingly finding that they must start anew: reentering the job market by finding a new job or career, or even going back to school to update outdated job skills.

The New Face of Retirees

By 2014, according to the system's own trustees, Social Security will be taking in less money from FICA taxes than it is obliged to pay out—a shortfall of $21 billion a year by 2015, rising to $252 billion by 2030, in inflation-adjusted dollars (Scientific American, 2000). A significant factor that will shape the future demographics of the U.S. population is the increase in older workers (Toosi, 2012). The baby boomer generation will be between the ages of 56 and 74 in the year 2020, and will represent a total of more than 97.8 million people over the age of 55 in the workforce. This is the largest ever group of older adults still in the labor market and the U.S. Census Bureau reports that this is primarily due to falling mortality rates and increasing life expectancies for the U.S. population, primarily due to a significant reduction in deaths from infectious diseases, heart conditions, strokes, and cancer (Toosi, 2012). Because we are living longer, we will need significantly more income than what was once needed when looking to retire.

Alternatively, if someone is living modestly within their means, they are more likely to be better prepared for retirement. Financial planning can be the key to ensuring a more comfortable, stress-free retirement. As the number of Americans over age 65 climbs from 37 million in 1998 to 64 million by 2025, the nation will have to grapple with the imbalanced Social Security system, rising medical costs, health care rationing, and age discrimination. The very nature of retirement will change (Scientific American, 2000). Many Americans may find themselves believing in an outdated notion about what it means to work hard their entire life and then retire.

In an analysis of well-being in retirement, one researcher found that one of the biggest determinants to retirees' well-being was the reason for retirement. If individuals voluntarily retired, they expressed much higher levels of well-being compared to those who retired involuntarily (Bender, 2011). Bender's study also found that retirees seem to value having income above what financial planners recommended, and that when they don't it has a direct effect on their well-being. Thus a sudden loss of earning potential pre-retirement will have far-reaching ramifications. Research has increasingly focused on what Bender (2011) terms *retirement income adequacy*, or the financial resources that retirees need to be above in order to feel safe and not have it affect their well-being. Naturally, retires preferred pension-based income over that earned by reentering the workforce (often underemployment). Either way, it was important for these individuals to feel some sense of financial control as they enter retirement (Bender, 2011).

Offering long-time employees an early retirement package has traditionally been a popular way for companies to effectively reduce the number of employees and overall costs associated with those employees. In a survey conducted of 4,000 individuals at a large Swedish insurance agency in which workers age 55 and over were offered early retirement packages, researchers discovered that retirees reported a more positive attitude and fewer symptoms of distress than those who remained at work (Isaksson & Johansson, 2000). In this particular situation, workers who had reached the age of 55 or over were offered a choice on whether or not to accept an early retirement. Researchers concluded that being able to personally influence the outcome of the downsizing process was critical to subsequent adaptation. That said, those who did make the decision to stay in their job ended up being less satisfied over time and felt more uncertainty for their future (Isaksson & Johansson, 2000). Therefore, accepting an early-retirement package may be financially and personally beneficial for many and certainly should be viewed as a viable option when planning for retirement.

In a recent survey of baby boomers' retirement intentions, researchers identified health, social, and economic determinants for those who intended to retire completely, compared to those who are considering continuation of work either in a full-time or part-time capacity. Analysis of survey data concluded that feelings about part-time work, retirement transitions, and retirement are changing from the traditional views of retirement, or the retirement myth (Taylor, Pilkington, Feist, Dal Grande, & Hugo, 2014). Surprisingly, a large number of baby boomers suggested that they would be happy to work part time or never retire. Given worldwide economic issues, a reluctance to withdraw from the workforce may be driven by practical financial concerns; however, other quality of life factors may play a role in these decisions.

People close to traditional retirement age also may simply decide to change careers or lifestyles. There may not be many suitable examples for older adults making this type of transition. Researchers conducted a survey of 5,200 people in which they were asked about their job transition in mid-to-late working life and results indicated that little is being done to encourage more diverse forms of employment opportunities for those in later life (Owen & Flynn, 2004). In 2003, in a study sponsored by the Centre for Research into the Older Workforce, conducted through the University of Surrey in the United Kingdom, investigators developed a picture of how people experience job change (Owen & Flynn, 2004: Men tended to change jobs for financial reasons or simply for career reasons, while women were more likely to change in order to gain better work-life flexibility (see also Buzzanell & Shenoy-Packer, chapter 8). This research also indicated that retirement age continues to be seen as a time in which economic activity dramatically ends rather than a period in which leisure activities can be combined with a lighter workload (Owen & Flynn, 2004). These attitudes reflect lingering doubts about the variability of older adult career choices.

While emerging adult millennials may lament that they need to compete for jobs with more experienced veterans, older adult workers suffer from associations with outdated ideas and irrelevant skill sets. Upstart companies often value fresh perspectives and prioritize younger workers' low wage demands and their ability to relocate for work. That said, challenges for older workers reentering the workforce often manifest in three forms: age discrimination, technology and educational training, and social isolation.

Age Discrimination

Older workers are often faced with having to deal with preconceived notions and blatant stereotypes of what it means to be an "older worker." Such stereotypes project generalized cognitive, motivational, and physical age-related changes onto older workers unnecessarily. Indeed, research suggests that if an older worker perceives a climate of age discrimination in the workplace, there is a direct link to lowered performance levels (Kunze, Boehm, & Bruch, 2011). This represents a major challenge to older workers who are faced with either voluntarily having to change career paths or those who are forced to look for work in their later years.

There is an abundance of research pointing to the fact that age discrimination in older adult workers is indeed prevalent (Avolio & Barrett, 1987;

Haefner, 1977; Perry & Bourhis, 1998). In a review of existing research on age discrimination in the employment interview, investigators found that over the last 30 years there has been ample evidence that age discrimination takes place often during the job interview selection process (Morgeson, Campion, Reider, & Bull, 2008). Younger applicants were often viewed to have "future potential" and they were given higher overall evaluation ratings than those given to older applicants, even when their qualifications were the same (Avolio & Barrett, 1987). Workplaces with limited openings may be unwilling to invest training and time in older adult workers that may view employment as temporary or "stopgap." This can present enduring challenges to older adult workers seeking to transition between jobs or reenter the job market.

Technology and Educational Training

In addition to the challenges of age discrimination during interviews, many older adults may face barriers related to requisite technological skills as well as familiarity with modern job search methods. The job search process has shifted drastically given the rise of Internet job search websites and social media. Websites like Careerbuilder.com, Monster.com, Indeed.com, and LinkedIn are popular ways to search for available jobs and become aware of the subtleties surrounding openings within particular career fields. Applicants can then use such websites to contact potential employers for interviews, completing the process by uploading their cover letter, resume, and other required materials. Additionally, social networking and professional reputation is important to many employers when evaluating candidates. While some older adults are migrating to social media platforms, not all older adults may compare favorably with the familiarity and proficiency of younger applicants.

Given the rate of technological innovations to most industries, older workers potentially face challenges with insufficient skills. While continuing education is a possibility for some, the costs of enrollment are high. The reality is that going back to school can be a scary process that can become a job in itself, and one that demands money rather than pays it. Such barriers can serve as sufficient challenges for older adults' career or re-employment goals.

Social Isolation

While workplace stigma and outdated skill sets present serious challenges to one's professional identity, social isolation has the potential for additional personal consequences. One unique risk factor that that relates to older adults' well-being during this period is loneliness (Chen & Feeley, 2014). When older adults find that they are able to retire from working, they may be faced with relatively limited options in regard to maintaining social ties. As a result of leaving the workforce, older adults may experience a lost sense of self that they had while in the midst of their career. During this period following retirement from the workforce, individuals may struggle to establish a "new normal" around their changed sense of self (Conroy & O'Leary-Kelly, 2014). In this regard, maintaining patterns of interaction and daily rituals within the family may serve to help the older adult maintain "normalcy" and familiarity in a larger context of change (see Buzzanell & Turner, 2003, 2013).

Loneliness, combined with the loss of important work-related social ties can add to the struggles retirees face. In a study examining the effects of various sources of social support and social strain on loneliness and well-being in older adults, results indicated that social support from one's partner as well as friends alleviated loneliness. In this study, spousal support demonstrated a much stronger effect than friend support (Chen & Feeley, 2014). Thus, it can be critical that couples work together to communicate through their new lifestyle change to help lessen the impact of these factors.

Practical Recommendations

Understanding the unique challenges of both emerging and older adults further clarifies a surprisingly similar experience. Both age cohorts are seen in the marketplace as lacking something important, yet bring unique benefits to positions as well. In stressed economic markets, these outliers find themselves competing with the in between middle adults, who are by comparison often "just right." There is hope for the future however; not just in a burgeoning economic recovery, but in pursuing goal-oriented and mindful processes to prepare for the prospect of employment and professional development at any age. Insight into personal skills, character strengths, and professional competencies can help identify corresponding employment options. Dedicating oneself to the life-long development and enrichment of new skills, especially with emerging and evolving technologies, is a positive professional habit that someone of any age could benefit from.

Still, specific strategies given each cohort remain. Emerging adulthood is a unique generational cohort: It features an extended period of identity exploration, extended connection and reliance on parents, and delayed relational commitment. While this wandering can seem to outsiders as "self-absorbed," those years, if directed into a metaphorical journey, should guide the emerging adult through challenges that will test their internal assets and call for the identification of new external resources (as they wean themselves off of parents). This period, without the pressures of starting a family and supporting them, should allow for maximum opportunity to develop strengths and translate those into marketable skill sets. For some this could mean going to college or trade school, for others an apprenticeship, or perhaps another direction entirely. Depending on one's goals, the process for achieving these dreams can be considered pathways in hope theory (Snyder, 2002). If encouraged and provided with sufficient models and encouragement, all that would be missing is the motivation to follow through (and perhaps a little bravery).

The theme across the older adult unemployment experience is the potential for an unfortunate lack of preparation and unrealistic expectations. These, sometimes in combination, set up older adults for an uncertain and challenging future. Resilient aging (Hicks & Conner, 2013) suggests that instead of simply reaching retirement age and asking "what's next?," individuals plan for retirement throughout their adult life and live a smarter life pre-retirement. Resilience thinking would suggest that one nurture valued relationships, seek advice from financial and health professionals, and develop a plan to anticipate the changes and transitions that will need to be made both personally and professionally.

References

Arnett, J. J. (2000). Emerging adulthood: A theory of development from the late teens through the twenties. *American Psychologist, (55)*5, 469–480.

Atchley, R. C. (1999). Continuity theory, self, and social structure. In C. D. Ryff & V. W. Marshall, *Families and Retirement* (pp. 145–158). Newbury Park, CA: Sage.

Avolio, B. J., & Barrett, G. V. (1987). Effects of age stereotyping in a simulated interview. *Psychology & Aging,* 56–63.

Barnes-Ferrell, J. L. (2003). Beyond health and wealth: attitudinal and other influences on retirement decision-making. In G. A. Adams, & T. A. Beehr, *Retirement: Reasons, Processes, and Results* (pp. 159–187). New York: Springer.

Bender, K. (2011). An analysis of well-being in retirement: The role of pensions, health, and "voluntariness" of retirement. *The Journal of Socio-Economics, 41,* 424–433.

Bolles, R. N. (2009). *The job-hunter's survival guide: How to find hope and rewarding work even when "there are no jobs."* New York: Ten Speed Press.

Bonnal, M., Lira, C., & Addy, S. (2009). Underemployment and local employment dynamics: New evidence. *The Review of Regional Studies,* 317–335.

Borgen, W. A., Amundson, N. E., Reuter, J. (2004). Using portfolios to enhance career resilience. *Journal of Employment Counseling, 41,* 50–59.

Bureau of Labor Statistics (2014). The employment situation-September 2014 [News Release]. Retrieved from: http://www.bls.gov/news.release/empsit.toc.htm

Buzzanell, P. M., & Turner, L. H. (2003). Emotion work revealed by job loss discourse: Backgrounding-foregrounding of feelings, construction of normalcy, and (re)instituting of traditional masculinities. *Journal of Applied Communication Research, 31,* 27–57.

Buzzanell, P. M., & Turner, L. H. (2012). Crafting narratives for family crises: Communicative behaviors associated with effectively managing job loss. In L. Webb & F. Dickson (Eds.),

Communication for families in crisis: Theories, methods, strategies (pp. 281-306). Cresskill, NJ: Hampton Press.

Chen, Yixin, & Feeley, T. H. (2014). Social support, social strain, loneliness, and well-being among older adults: An analysis of the Health and Retirement Study. *Journal of Social and Personal Relationship, 31*, 2, 141-161.

Clarkberg, M., & Moen, P. (2001). Understanding the Time-Squeeze: Married Coupled Preferred and Actual Work Hour Strategies. *American Behavioral Scientist, 44*, 1115-1136.

Conroy, S. & O'Leary-Kelly, A. (2014). Letting go and moving on: Work related identity loss and recovery. *Academy of Management Review, 39*, 1, 67-87.

D'Abate, C. P., Youndt, M., & Wenzel, K. E. (2009). Making the most of an internship: An empirical study of internship satisfaction. *Academy of Management Learning & Education, 8*(4), 527-539.

Dawson, D., Winocur, G., & Moscovitch, M. (1999). The psychosocial environment and cognitive rehabilitation in the elderly. In D. T. Stuss, G. Winocur, & I. H. Robertson, (Eds.), *Cognitive Neurorehabilitation* (pp. 94-108). Cambridge, UK: Cambridge University Press.

Ebberwein, C. A. (2008). Career flexibility for a lifetime of work. In S. J. Lopez (Ed.), *Positive psychology: Exploring the best in people* (Vol.3) (pp.123-144). Wesport, CT: Praeger.

Erikson, E. H. (1963). *Childhood and society*. New York: Norton.

Galambos, N. L., Barker, E. T., & Krahn, H. J. (2006). Depression, self-esteem, and anger in emerging adulthood: Seven year trajectories. *Developmental Psychology, 42*:2, 350-365.

Gokhale, J. (2013). Social Security reform: Does privatization still make sense? *Harvard Journal on Legislation, 50*, 169-207.

Gonzalez Herero, V., & Extremera, N. (2010). Daily life activities as mediators of the relationship between personality variables and subjective well-being among older adults. *Personality and Individual Differences, 49*, 124-129.

Graves, N., & Epstein, M. (2011). Eportfolio: A tool for constructing a narrative professional identity. *Business Communication Quarterly, 74*: 3, 342-346.

Haefner, J. R. (1977). Race, age, sex, and competence as factors in employer selection of the disadvantaged. *Journal of Applied Psychology*, 199-202.

Havighurst, R. (1972). *Developmental tasks and education*. New York: Longman.

Hicks, M., & Conner, N. (2013). Resilient ageing: A concept analysis. *Journal of Advanced Nursing, 70*, 744-755.

Hyatt, J. (2006, April). The Art of the Second Act. *Money*, pp. 27-32.

Irvin, A., & Hiden, C. (2013). *Build your dreams: How to make a living doing what you love*. Philadephia, PA: Running Press.

Isaksson, K., & Johansson, G. (2000). Adaptation to continued work and early retirement following downsizing: Long-term effects and gender differences. *Journal of Occupational & Organizational Psychology, 73*, 241-256.

Kerssen-Griep, J., Trees, A. R., & Hess, J. A. (2008). Attentive facework during instructional feedback: Key to perceiving mentorship and an optimal learning environment. *Communication Education, 57*, 3, 312-332.

Kunze, F., Boehm, S., & Bruch, H. (2011). Age diversity, age discrimination climate and performance consequences—a cross organizational study. *Journal of Organizational Behavior, 32*, 264-290.

Maietta, H. N. (2012). Virtual job club: A social support network for recent graduates. *About Campus, 17*(3), 28-32.

Masten, A. S. (2001). Ordinary magic: Resilience processes in development. *American Psychologist, 56*:3, 227-238.

Masten, A. S., Obradovic, J., & Burt, K. B. (2006). Resilience in emerging adulthood: Developmental perspectives on continuity and transformation. In J. J. Arnett & J. L. Tanner (Eds.), *Emerging adults in America: Coming of age in the 21st century* (pp. 173-190). Washington, DC: American Psychological Association.

McAtee, J. F. (2012). Pathway programs to life after college. In G. S. McClellan & J. Parker (Eds.) *Stepping up to stepping out: Helping students prepare for life after college* (pp. 29-41). Hoboken, NJ: Wiley Periodicals, Inc.

Moen, P. (2007). Not so big jobs and retirements: What workers and retirees really want. *American Society on Aging, 31*, 31-36.

Morgeson, F. P., Campion, M., Reider, M., & Bull, R. (2008). Review of research on age discrimination in the employment interview. *Journal of Business Psychology, 22*, 223-232.

Mortimer, J. T., Zimmer-Gembeck, M. J., Holmes, M., & Shanahan, M. J. (2002). The process of occupational decision-making: Patterns during the transition to adulthood. *Journal of Vocational Behavior, 61*, 439-465.

Murphy, K. A., Blustein, D. L., Bohlig, A. J., & Platt, M. G. (2010). The college-to-career transition: An exploration of emerging adulthood. *Journal of Counseling and Development, 88*(2), 174-183.

National Association of Colleges and Employers (2014). Executive summary: 2014 Internship & co-op summary. Retrieved from: https://www.naceweb.org/intern-co-op-survey/

Newman, B. K. (1995). Career change for those over 40: Critical issues and insights. *The Career Development Quarterly, 44*, 64-67.

Noone, J., O'Loughlin, K., & Kendig, H. (2013). Australian baby boomers retiring 'early': Understanding the benefits of retirement preparation for involuntary and voluntary retirees. *Journal of Aging Studies, 27*, 207-217.

Osgood, D. W., Ruth, G. W., Eccles, J. E., Jacobs, J. E., & Barber, B. L. (2005). Six paths through the transition to adulthood: Fast starters, parents without careers, educated partners, educated singles, working singles, and slow starters. In R. A. Setterson, F. F. Furstenburg Jr., & R. G. Rumbaut (Eds.), *On the frontier of adulthood: Theory, research and public policy* (pp. 320-355) Chicago: University of Chicago Press.

Owen, L., & Flynn, M. (2004). Changing work: Mid-to-late life transitions. *Aging International, 29*, 333-350.

Perry, E. L., & Bourhis, A. C. (1998). A closer look at the role of applicant age in selection decisions. *Journal of Applied Social Psychology, 28*, 1670-1697.

Rand, K. L, Martin, A. D., & Shea, A. M. (2011). Hope, not optimism, predicts academic performance of law students beyond previous academic achievement. *Journal of Research in Personality, 45*, 683-686.

Reich, W., Zautra, A. J., & Hall, J. S. (Eds.). (2010). *Handbook of adult resilience.* New York: Guilford.

Schulenberg, J. E., Bryant, A. L., & O'Malley, P. M. (2004). Taking hold of some kind of life: How developmental tasks relate to trajectories of well-being during the transition to adulthood. *Development and Psychopathology, 16*, 1119-1140.

Scientific American. (2000, July). Social Insecurity. *Scientific American,* pp. 26-29.

Segrist, K. A., Tell, B., Byrd, V., & Perkins, S. (2007). Addressing needs of employers, older workers, and retirees: An educational approach. *Educational Gerontology, 33,* 451–462.

Snyder, C. R. (1999). Hope, Goal-Blocking Thoughts, & Test-Related Anxieties. *Psychological Reports, 84,* 206–208.

Snyder, C. R (2002). Hope theory: Rainbows in the mind. *Psychological Inquiry, 13:*4, 249–275.

Stone, C., Van Horn, C., & Zukin, C. (2012). Chasing the American dream: Recent college graduates and the great recession. John J. Heldrich Center for Workforce Development, Rutgers University.

Sum, A., Khatiwada, I., Trubskyy, M., Ross, M., McHugh, W., & Palma, S. (2014). The plummeting labor market of teens and young adults. Washington, DC: Brookings Institution.

Tajfel, H., & Turner, J. C. (1986). The social identity theory of intergroup behavior. In S. Worchel & W. G. Austin, *Psychology of Intergroup Behavior* (pp. 7–24). Chicago: Nelson-Hall.

Tanner, J. L. (2006). Recentering during emerging adulthood: A critical turning point in life span human development. In J. J. Arnett & J. L. Tanner (Eds.), *Emerging adults in America: Coming of age in the 21st century* (pp. 21–56). Washington, DC: American Psychological Association.

Taylor, A., Pilkington, R., Feist, H., Dal Grande, E., & Hugo, G. (2014). A survey of retirement intentions of baby boomers: an overview of health, social and economic determinants. *BMC Public Health, 14,* 314–355.

Teuscher, U. (2010). Change and persistence of personal identities after the transition to retirement. *International Journal of Aging and Human Development, 70,* 89–106.

Toosi, M. (2012). *Employment Outlook 2010–2020: Labor force projections to 2020. A more slowly growing workforce.* Washington, DC: U.S. Department of Labor.

Van Solinge, H. (2008). Adjustment to and satisfaction with retirement: Two of a kind? *Psychology and Aging, 23,* 422–434.

Vedder, R., Denhart, C., & Robe, J. (2013). Why are recent college graduates underemployed? University enrollments and labor-market realities. Center for College Affordability and Productivity. Retrieved from http://centerforcollegeaffordability.org/uploads/Underemployed%20Report%202.pdf

Wang, M., Henkens, K., & Van Solinge, H. (2011). Retirement adjustment: a review of theoretical and empirical advancements. *American Psychologist,* 204–213.

Wang, M., & Shi, J. (2014). Psychological Research on Retirement. *Annual Review of Psychology, 65,* 209–233.

Watzlawick, P., Weakland, J. H., & Fisch, R. (1974). *Change: Principles of problem formation and problem resolution.* New York: W. W. Norton and Co.

World Economic Forum. (2013). *Global agenda councils: Youth unemployment visualization 2013.* Retrieved from: http://www.weforum.org/community/global-agenda-councils/youth-unemployment-visualization-2013

Wright, K. B. Rosenberg, J., Egbert, N., Ploeger, Bernard, D., & King, S. (2013). Communication competence, social support, and depression among college students: A model of Facebook and face-to-face support network influence. *Journal of Health Communication, 18,* 1, 41–57.

• CHAPTER EIGHT •

Resilience, Work, and Family Communication Across the Lifespan

Patrice M. Buzzanell
Purdue University

Suchitra Shenoy-Packer
DePaul University

Resilience is a process that has gained attention in the last several years as natural disasters and other events have prompted scholars and practitioners to question how and why individuals, communities, and the global citizenry reconstitute their lives. In much literature, resilience is considered to be an individual or community capacity to adapt to changed situations (see Buzzanell, Shenoy, Remke, & Lucas, 2009). Yet, scholars have begun to realize that human resilience is processual, embedded in relationships, and developed not simply for present circumstances but also for the future (Black & Lobo, 2008; Buzzanell, 2010; Buzzanell et al., 2009; Lucas & Buzzanell, 2011, 2012). They have begun to see that resilience is neither an atypical life patterning nor simply overcoming adversity. Rather, resilience is a regular feature of life that is essential for well-being and sustainability in work and personal life areas (Buzzanell, 2010a, 2010b; Segrin, 2006).

In this chapter, we first discuss the intersections of human resilience and work and family communication across the lifespan. We maintain that work-family communication is a key site for the development and sustainability of resilience. We position resilience as a process that is constituted communicatively through the interrelationships of everyday talk in interaction and associated cultural formations or discourses, as well as through the material conditions with which people create, contest, and disrupt their realities (Alvesson & Kärreman, 2011; Ashcraft, Kuhn, & Cooren, 2009). By taking a constitutive approach, we emphasize the politicized and ongoing meaning making of realities (Brummans, Cooren, Robichaud, & Taylor, 2014;

Putnam & Nicotera, 2009). Furthermore, we acknowledge that resilience and work-family dynamics themselves are created in and through communication with all the linguistic choices, identity negotiations, and interactions that take place online and offline. This sensemaking and construction of realities occurs in particular moments across the lifespan and different contexts.

In the second half of our chapter, we present an agenda for scholarship and practice in resilience and work-family communication across the lifespan. Because resilience is an ongoing struggle and process that is (re)constituted communicatively in particular contexts, it offers means for hope and deep-seated change in work and family dilemmas that touch everyone's lives in some way.

Intersections of Resilience and Work-Family Communication

Only within the last decade have work-family issues become an important area of study within communication, bringing together organizational, interpersonal, family, feminist, conflict, and other communication contexts (e.g., Buzzanell, 2014; Golden, Kirby, & Jorgenson, 2006; Kirby & Buzzanell, 2014; Kirby, Golden, Medved, Jorgenson, & Buzzanell, 2003; Kirby, Wieland, & McBride, 2013; Medved, 2010). Communicative lenses offer different vantage points on work-family issues because scholars examine work-family intersections less for outcomes that could be achieved (e.g., work-family "balance" or lower work-to-family conflict and family-to-work conflict, see Kirby et al., 2003, 2013), and more as processes embedded within multi-level interaction. To describe how and when work-family scholarship, practices, and policies benefit from communication, we describe: (a) how work-family and resilience are constituted communicatively, then (b) how work-family scholarship has portrayed resilience across the lifespan.

How Work-Family and Resilience Are Constituted Communicatively

In this section, we provide a brief overview of communication research in work-life and work-family processes that highlight particular times when such issues are most salient as well as what these processes look like across the lifespan. In distinguishing a communicatively constituted approach to work and family issues, Kirby and Buzzanell (2014) summarized and reframed the ever-expanding current work and personal life theory and research being done by communication researchers to distinguish core themes. Their communication themes or processes focused on the organizing, career, and work aspects more so than personal life and family considerations in their five work-life processes or themes. First, in their "policy-ing" work-life in organizations process, they examined differences in national and organizational support for work-life challenges, including the Family and Medical Leave Act (FMLA) of 1993 and telework, as well as the underlying assumptions guiding policy generation, use, and revision. Second, in their "norm-ing" (or not) issues of work-life in organizations theme, they delved into the cultural expectations about appropriate behaviors for work-life management, specifically those embedded in workplace relationships and organizational culture. Third, in their discussion about (re)producing "ideal" workers and the primacy of work, they examined "how ideologies of success and ideal workers are (re)produced in organizations and the broader culture," considering how workers are socialized by various agents (e.g., family, organization members, media, and popular cultural discourses) to elevate work over other concerns in life. Fourth, in their constructing (gendered) (working) identities section, they depict the reasoning behind and strategies that women and men use to negotiate their roles as workers and caregivers. Fifth and finally, in their work-life process of acting practically and routinizing work and (personal) life, Kirby and Buzzanell discuss the everyday routines and technologies put to use in managing work-life issues. These themes act as a framework in which a communication approach to resilience is embedded. This five-theme structure can inform how resilience is cast in a more ecological way, bringing forth both the theoretical and pragmatic advantages of a resilience-centered approach to work and family scholarship.

How Work-Family Scholarship Portrays Resilience Across the Lifespan

In this section, we explore how resilience is depicted in work-family studies as well as how resilience is communicatively constituted in the work-family communication. Like the Kirby and Buzzanell overview for the *Handbook of Organizational Communication* (Putnam & Mumby, 2014), Buzzanell (2014) argues that communication scholars' ability to problematize the politicized and taken-for-granted nature of work-family communication along the lines of the five processes could transform organizational and family communication scholarship and everyday life. In rethinking these processes for the *Handbook of Family Communication* edited by Turner and West (2014), Buzzanell maintained Kirby and Buzzanell's original meta-theoretical overview of processes constituted communicatively, but reframed their work-life dynamics to focus more on family and to destabilize the primacy of work. For each, resilience processes and findings for work-family communication are applicable and are presented here.

First, for "policing family and work," scholars would emphasize family rather than organizational members' discourse and work-family practices associated with family leaves, alternative work arrangements, and policy implications in areas such as immigration, reproductive rights and health policies, food insecurity, and rural poverty. For our purposes, families' perceived or actual (in)abilities to form, enact, codify, and revise (or not) policy can be critical to the resources they have for their construction of family well-being and resilience (see Canary, 2008a; Canary, 2012; Canary & Cantú, 2012). Moreover, the overarching positive connotations attached to "resilience" belie the complexity of the process and the fact that some families have greater tangible and immaterial resources on which they can rely to construct a new normalcy in their lives (Green, 2013; Harrison, 2012). For instance, families exposed to chronic stressors and without sufficient support suffer long-term negative consequences for well-being although the bases, mitigating factors, and intervention results are not well understood (Bowes & Jaffee, 2013). However, other families might have assets internal to members or the group as a whole, such as memories of hard times that enable them to situate current circumstances within individual, family, and community lifespan perspectives.

Second, in norming (or not) family issues, Buzzanell focuses on family rituals, norms, spatio-temporal arrangements, and technology use that enable families to construct work-family communication. Resilience researchers strongly emphasize the roles of family rituals, stories, and traditions in positive adaptation after adversity (e.g., Black & Lobo, 2008; Burton, 2007; Marin, Bohanek, & Fivush, 2008; McCubbin & McCubbin, 1988; Notter, MacTavish, & Shamah, 2008). Maintaining daily and seasonal routines such as having an evening meal together or going on summer holiday after job loss sustains feelings and patterns of normalcy although the details of the events, such as members, sites, and artifacts, and the communication surrounding such events changes across lifespans and generations (Buzzanell & Turner, 2003). Even so, there are different types of losses and trauma with which families contend that affect how and why they might engage in (re)producing or changing (family) normative communication. When family demands exceed members' capabilities to handle work-family struggles, the imbalance may lead to crises that necessitate overhauls of existent practices. Although they would not wish for such struggles, these overhauls might coincide with improvements in family members' lives, such as when families come together upon terminal or life-threatening conditions, and the communication in their own lives and that of subsequent generations and others affected by such crises shifts (Buzzanell, 2004). Families who utilize themes of resilience develop a homeostatic balance or normalcy by "reducing demands, increasing capabilities, and/or changing meanings" (Patterson, 2002, p. 251; see also Buzzanell & Turner, 2003, 2013). Being able to negotiate these shifts and the various aspects of life is what sets families apart in their abilities to rebound from life's disruptive situations and to constitute resilience daily.

Third, in (re)producing ideal family members and work, Buzzanell focused on family and others' socialization messages about family in work-family interactions as well as hegemonic, embodied, and disruptive discourses constituting family in work-family contexts. Whereas Kirby and Buzzanell talked about ideal workers, in work-family communication the ideal family members in work-family and resilience situations may be those who recognize the difficulties in constructing good family relationships that can withstand and even thrive in difficult times. They may be those who socialize other family members into what it means, and the accompanying struggles, to be a good working mother and breadwinner, as well as good father who sees his (or her) role and choices as caregiving within webs of responsibilities (see Buzzanell, Meisenbach, Remke, Bowers, Liu, & Conn, 2005; Buzzanell, D'Enbeau, & Duckworth, 2010; Duckworth & Buzzanell, 2009; Medved, 2009; Medved & Rawlins, 2011; Meisenbach, 2010; Turner & Norwood, 2013). But they also may be family members who have withstood difficult times, built new lives, and sought to convey how to do so to others who face or likely may face similar circumstances over the course of their lifespans (e.g., constraints caused by finances, illness, intrafamily dynamics, work-life balancing issues, life transitions and movement, as well as relationship strains; McCubbin & McCubbin, 1988). For instance, using a life history approach, Bell and Nkomo (2001) describe how many African American women had family members and others—people from their community, church, or school system—who took an active interest in them and helped them cope with the harsh realities of everyday life. Through stories and advice, these people socialized these individual and their families into strategies and roles, such as work, family, and community roles, that differ from mainstream portrayals and promote resilience. When families weather difficult situations, including those about work-family challenges, research indicates that they can grow stronger and more resourceful as family units and as individual family members (Black & Lobo, 2008).

Fourth, in constructing (gendered) family identities, Buzzanell (2014; see also Kirby & Buzzanell, 2014) emphasized the gender work and gendered work (see Rakow, 1992), as well as intersectionalities of difference that pervade construction of family membership and identity in the broader community. For instance, in times of economic hardship, Buzzanell and Turner (2003) found that family members helped identify and support the individual who suffered job loss by affirming his or her gendered societal role even to the point that they would downplay their own contributions to family sustainability. For instance, the partners of men who lost their jobs often contributed substantially to family income yet referred to their own income, as did their children, by phrases like "pin money." Similarly, families and extended relationship networks are needed to offer support for individuals coming out in sexual-social orientations valued by others as non-normative (Kwon, 2013) or to develop "armor" against racial prejudice (Bell & Nkomo, 2001; Theron, 2013). Bell and Nkomo recount stories of Black women's upbringing in which caregivers invest considerable effort into cultivating resilience:

> Julia's and Patricia's parents had financial resources and personal connections at the time overt segregation was being dismantled. Consequently, they could expose their daughters to the arts, to historical monuments, and to finer restaurants within white America. However, they were highly selective of the place and events they chose. We call this selective exposure. These parents intentionally chose only those activities that would reinforce their daughter's positive self-images. At a time when black girls were growing up in segregated communities or were among a tiny handful of blacks living in otherwise exclusively white suburbs, selective exposure enabled them to gain deep insight into the social norms, behaviors, and attitudes of the white world. This element of their armor increased their self-confidence, enhanced their social skills and grace, and gave them the courage to comfortably move back and forth between the two cultural contexts. That is, they learned early in their lives how to be bicultural, interacting and engaging in both the white dominant culture and their own culture. (p. 96)

Resilience work similar to that depicted by Bell and Nkomo occurs in work and family contexts as family members and others create direct and indirect messages as well as contextual (ambient) cues to indicate that sustainable work-family interactions across the lifespan are ongoing negotiations that call upon different resources and networks over diverse online and offline spatio-temporal contexts (e.g., Gabor, 2011; Lim, 2013; Medved, 2004; Medved, Brogan, McClanahan, Morris, & Shepherd, 2006). For instance, U.S. college-aged children often text parents to keep in touch through concise wording that might hint at desires to visit home, to discuss problematic roommate and romantic relationships, or to request financial support without losing face that perhaps they were not as independent as they would like to admit. Likewise, family members may Facetime, use Google hangout, or Skype for easy access to family and friends, finding such information-rich contexts helpful when the message exchanges involve information seeking and giving about sensitive issues. Often family members need to see and hear others to ascertain exactly how people are and what they are doing, as opposed to hearing only what individuals say. In this regard, resilience is co-constructed through extended personal (and work) networks that function as resources in times of need and uncertainty (Buzzanell, 2010a).

Fifth and finally, acting practically and routinizing family and work life offered a means of replicating and disrupting the status quo within and for families. Through analyses of interview data asking employed women about their typical days, Medved (2004) found three practical action clusters— routinizing, improvising, and restructuring—through which "doing work and family ...[was about] doing relationships, not just taken for granted as a function of time management or organizational policies" (p. 140). These work-family processes are filled with contradictions, tensions, dilemmas, and opportunities. Women's (and their partners') strategies involved face-to-face work-family negotiations at regular intervals and on a daily basis (Medved, 2004), as well as use of technologies to routinize, improvise, restructure, and disrupt (Golden, 2009a, 2009b; Golden & Geisler, 2007; Lim, 2013). These ongoing conversations for meaning making and actionable tactics build resilience within interdependencies by providing tangible assistance within secure base relationships where people feel comfortable asking for assistance. As these and other studies show, the successful navigation of challenging and adverse situations requires more than simply managing that situation. Acting practically and routinizing work-family interactions for resilience involve changing positions and perspectives such that family members can learn to view them as opportunities for relational growth, learning, and family strengthening, as well as for development of network structures to nurture and reinforce resilience (e.g., use of peer groups, community, and school or work settings, see Walsh, 2003, 2007).

Besides elevating the primacy of family and personal life through the aforementioned themes, Buzzanell (2014) argues that work-family areas should be fused innovatively. These reframed processes depict how family and family communication are simultaneously privileged and marginalized, and with what consequences for the communicative constitution of resilience in work-family contexts. Within these work and family communication processes are questions about how resilience is constituted and how resilience may operate as a meta-process that integrates and transcends work-family orientations.

Agenda for Resilience and Work-Family Communication Across the Lifespan

Although resilience was mentioned in each of the work-family processes in the last section, there has not been focused attention on resilience per se in work-family communication studies. Buzzanell (2010) theorized that resilience can be examined in and of itself as a necessary process for everyday life and for pivotal periods of discontinuity, stress, and change in life, including work-family communication. In this section, we first lay out several resilience processes and their applicability to work-family contexts, then explicate an agenda for communication research on work-family resilience across the lifespan.

Human Resilience Processes in Work-Family Contexts

Resilience can be captured through five processes that would be appropriate for many contexts and that were alluded to in the research overview on work-family communication. Through these five processes, people engaged in: (a) crafting a new normalcy, (b) affirming or anchoring their most important identities during difficult times, (c) using and/or developing salient communication networks, (d) looking beyond conventional ways of thinking about and doing life by putting alternative logics to work, and (e) foregrounding productive action while backgrounding unproductive or negative feelings (Buzzanell, 2010). Thus resilience work is the effort put into these communicative processes such that people not only can adapt to their changed circumstances but also can (potentially) thrive and transform lived conditions through a new normal (see also Bonnano, 2004). Although a constitutive lens highlights the communicative processes involved in resilience work, this approach never neglects the real material conditions and human capacity resources (e.g., see Bowes & Jaffee, 2013; Green, 2013; for overview, see Buzzanell et al., 2009) that can enable and inhibit people's abilities to do resilience work and have productive outcomes.

A key aspect of Buzzanell's (2010) theory is that resilience processes are intertwined in various ways based on the context and on individuals' or collectivities' growth in this process. There may be different, layered, sequential, and merged processes over individual and family lifespans (e.g., Hammoud & Buzzanell, 2012; Lucas & Buzzanell, 2012; Villagran, Cazona, & Ledford, 2013). Moreover, resilience is never complete. Rather, resilience is an ongoing struggle and accomplishment. In some cases the loss that triggers resilience processes is irreversible, such as death. In other cases the loss might be characterized as more of a liminal state, caught between framings of temporariness but bordering on the permanent, such as families caught within prolonged refugee conflicts and living in refugee camps for decades (Hammoud & Buzzanell, 2012, 2013). In still other cases, the loss is ambiguous such as when family members, particularly children, find it difficult to make sense of people who are missing from their lives, that is, people who are no longer supposed to be part of their everyday family experiences (Afifi & Keith, 2004).

In other words, resilience develops and shifts over time much as work-family concerns and communication also change. Thus, multimethodological approaches that capture the complexities of resilience work over time (e.g., longitudinal, narrative, and ethnographic methods) combined with survey data (e.g., background, health, finances, education, and other key resources) would provide insight into the contexts in which resilience processes are learned and put into motion, including work and family communication across the lifespan.

Communication Research Agenda for Work-Family Resilience

Building upon the review of research linking work-family communication and resilience, we propose that future scholarship should delve more fully into (a) how power and authority are implicated, contested, and affirmed in resilience processes associated with work-family communication contexts; and (b) how people engage in the often ambiguous and contradictory ways in which resilience is coproduced.

How Power and Authority are Implicated, Contested, and Affirmed in Resilience Associated With Work-Family Communication Contexts. As with other human communication processes, power, resistance, authority, complicity, and contestation emerge as dialectic tensions that affect the ways in which resilience is constructed and the forms in which resilience is manifest in work-family contexts and communication. Many scholars have noted that processes related to power are messy, contradictory, embodied, and embedded in everyday actions and work-family organizing structures. Power is associated with: control of family and work storytelling, cultures, resources and rules, structures, everyday behaviors, legitimate arguments for policy use, ideologies, and preferred identity construction in resilience processes (e.g., Kärreman & Alvesson, 2009; Kirby & Krone, 2002; Liu & Buzzanell, 2005, 2007; Turner & West, 2014). Likewise, resilience processes affect how individual members and families perceive and implement power in tangible and intangible ways (e.g., control of material and symbolic resources), thus offering new directions for research in work and family communication across the lifespan.

In work-family communication and resilience, power and authority emerge in the ways in which family members express their identities and their use of particular resilience processes. For instance, Villagran et al. (2013) describe resilience as "an ongoing milspouse [military spouse] narrative of successful adaptation" in which adversity was reframed as "part of the job." They found that milspouse resilience was a constructed "set of processes involving new routines, alternative logics, social support, and interaction to intersubjectively negotiate a proactive state," replicating some of Buzzanell's (2010) key communication processes of resilience. However, milspouses seemed to reject "their legitimate right to experience or act on negative emotions" because of personal and others' concerted efforts to enforce positive talk and supportive spousal identities. They also found that resilience involved a "mindfulness about the relational context and circumstances that existed before their partner left, and a desire to share stories and enact processes to maintain their relationship despite separation," meaning that the physically absent partner and their relationship exerted influence on how and why they conducted themselves and their family life as they did during military deployments (see also Wilson, Wilkum, Chernichky, MacDermid Wadsworth, & Broniarczyk, 2011). These processes might be inherent in military culture and, by extension, to the family and cross-unit networks that form through relocations and deployments. Similarly, they may also be part of expatriate and diplomatic family situations and families whose members are mindful of an individual's work that requires high security clearances and sometimes unexpected separations, among other contexts. How such processes affect and are affected by different family members and family configurations, such as children's communication and the reported experiences of older family members who may have previously lived through wars and other challenging experiences, deserves greater attention. In particular, those with past lived experience similar to current trauma and/or in physical or online sites may re-live, re-collect memory fragments, and re-integrate past and current experience in complex resilience constructions (e.g., see Aden, Han, Norander, Pfahl, Pollock, & Young, 2009; Lucas & Buzzanell, 2011, 2012). Constitutive processes of resilience across the lifespan and for particular familial members and groups and under certain conditions (e.g., stroke), deserve greater attention.

Similarly, in certain kinds of loss, such as involuntary job termination and unemployment, the foregrounding of productive action, such as the need to apply for jobs and perform appropriate behaviors, and the maintenance of normalcy such as a "regular" work day and "normal" family routines, may be processes that occur before or simultaneously with family members' "requirements" to uphold the face and family status, such as head of household and breadwinner, for individuals who had suffered job loss (Buzzanell & Turner, 2003, 2013). Although there were no reported overt power displays in Buzzanell and Turner's (2003, 2013) interviews with family members, the adults and their children revealed the discursive framing and linguistic choices that they used to uphold the status of the individual who incurred job loss even when, as mentioned earlier in this chapter, their strategies subverted their own contributions to their families.

As a final example of how power and authority are implicated, contested, and affirmed in resilience associated with work-family communication contexts, Faris (2013) noted that former prisoners released to problem-solving reentry courts were able to create a new (more productive) normal through the support of reentry teams that included case workers, legal and social services experts, community members, and others. These team members encouraged prisoners to develop and maintain communication networks that could help them withstand difficulties and the stigma of prison. Through logics that the ex-prisoners would consider to be alternative or different from their habitual ways of processing and responding to information, these former prisoners were "learning to live again" by "rebuilding" their family relationships as well as other aspects of their lives (Faris, 2013). On their path toward resilience, they admitted their vulnerabilities and fears, and participated in the subtle and complex interplay of coercion and self-agency, required by the reentry court systems (Faris, 2013). In short, studying power processes in work-family communication and resilience could offer nuance to an area typically understood as overcoming obstacles and dealing with adversity by adapting to change in life domains, including work and family.

How People Engage in Ambiguous and Contradictory Resilience Coproduction

In this section, we explore and advocate for further research in how people engage in the often ambiguous and contradictory ways in which resilience is coproduced. As noted earlier, there are many types of loss, hardship, and obstacles that can prompt different forms and emphases in resilience processes. For instance, children who have lived through divorce suffer ambiguous loss, "unique kind of loss in that a loved one is technically present but functionally absent, creating a lack of closure and clarity" (Afifi & Keith, 2004, p. 67). Moreover, they may want their parents to be happy but experience dismay at the rapidity of courtship and remarriage, fostering a new normal that children are not yet prepared to accept or co-construct. Remarriage might consist of "the point of no return," meaning that birth parents probably would never reunite (p. 77). Outwardly they might be adapting but inwardly they may not be engaging in the processes that enable them to foster resilience. Children can overcome the hardships and uncertainties of post-divorce relationships more readily under certain communicative conditions. They can invest themselves in a positive new normal if their parents are able to communicate in ways that children perceived as competent, as not putting them in the middle of conflict, and as giving them time to heal wounds (Afifi & Schrodt, 2003; Schrodt & Afifi, 2007).

In a type of loss and hardship that is ongoing, Canary (2008b) and Buzzanell (2008) portray the lived experiences of families that include children who have disabilities. Their examination of these families' everyday experiences highlight the many contradictions, identity negotiations, and tensions that often center on ambiguous feelings of loss. Besides identity constructions, they both portray sensemaking, ironies in policy use, and co-creation of normal through storytelling that is so vital to resilience in families. Against a birthday party backdrop for a child (who had severe disabilities), Buzzanell's family was caught up in "necessary fictions" that both affirmed and disconfirmed a mother's need to view and treat her child as aware of and as an active participant in her surroundings. If the mother did not envision her child in this way (as aware and capable of enjoyment), then her efforts to provide a nurturing and stimulating (intellectually, physically, emotionally, and materially) environment might seem foolish to herself and to others. Likewise if she did not engage in these caregiving efforts then she and others could not consider her to be a good mother or have purpose in her life. The dilemma for others was struggling with ways to support the mother and child despite profound uncertainties and feelings of loss for the child that could have been. Caught between knowing and not knowing, caring deeply and pulling back, fear that something might happen to the child who was living on borrowed time and (sometimes) unspoken hope that the child would die peacefully, and much more, Buzzanell's story unfolds. In the end, it is love that enables these tensions to be sustained. It is the struggling with life's mysteries and traumas that brings family members' compassion, love, and appreciation for the life to the foreground. It is through this struggle that family members constitute and perform resilience, in as-yet underresearched ways.

Performing resilience also engenders a certain positivity or hope toward future outcomes. In this regard, hope, "defined as the percieved capability to derive pathways to desired goals, and motivate oneself via agency thinking to use those pathways" (Snyder, 2002, p. 249) can be a contributing factor in developing alternative goals and envisioning positive future outcomes. Snyder (see also Shorey, Snyder, Hockemeyer, & Feldman, 2002) explains that high-hope individuals (or individuals/families characterized by productive resilience processes in our case) thrive not only because they draw their capacities from proactive agentic thinking but also because of their consistent beliefs in plans of action or specific pathways toward reconstituting a new normal.

Although not analyzed as such in the published story, Buzzanell's (2008) "necessary fictions" speak to processes of crafting a new normal, relying on communication networks, usurping "normal" caregiving models and identity constructions, and anchoring identity constructions in familial love and hope. As such, Buzzanell's and Canary's (2008b) findings are consistent with communication research on resilience in families sharing information about chronic and debilitating health conditions (Stone, 2013), post-divorce stepfamilies (Afifi & Keith, 2004), people suffering addictions (Shenoy-Packer, 2013), and families undergoing periods of unemployment (Buzzanell & Turner, 2003, 2012; Lucas & Buzzanell, 2011, 2012). In these studies resilience consists of ongoing and multiple processes to handle major obstacles and challenges in family members' lives at present and for their futures.

Conclusion

In taking a communicatively constitutive approach to organizing and relationships, communication is situated as central to meaning production on individual, family, organizational, and broader levels. In taking the constitutive approach, researchers sort through ways in which power and authority are contested and how people in work-family situations where disappointments, obstacles, and trauma have occurred make sense of these happenings and the often ambiguous and contradictory ways in which resilience is coproduced.

Resilience is an ongoing struggle to create and sustain the new normal that comes from recognition that life cannot be the same as it was before the onset of a particular trauma or before recognition of ongoing hardship. Resilience also occurs when, despite the odds, there are flickers of possibilities for transformation and for the choice and agency that lends dignity to self and others (see Buzzanell & Lucas, 2013; Tracy & Rivera, 2010). To be viable, this new normal must incorporate that which family members value and that which offers security. For families, resilience might take the form of stories and rituals that are modified for members of every age and over the course of members' lifespans to sustain families through disappointment, major illness, death, destruction of home and/or neighborhood, job loss, and financial hardship (Buzzanell, 2010; Buzzanell & Turner, 2003, 2012; Marin, Bohanek,

& Fivush, 2008). It is the human capacity to communicatively constitute resilience that is fundamental to humanity and hope.

References

Aden, R., Han, M., Norander, S., Pfahl, M., Pollock, T., & Young, S. (2009). Re-collection: A proposal for refining the study of collective memory and its places. *Communication Theory, 19*, 311-336.

Afifi, T., & Keith, S. (2004). A risk and resiliency model of ambiguous loss in postdivorce stepfamilies. *The Journal of Family Communication, 4*, 65-98.

Afifi, T., & Schrodt, P. (2003a). "Feeling caught" as a mediator of adolescents' and young adults' avoidance and satisfaction with their parents in divorced and non-divorced households. *Communication Monographs, 70*, 142-173.

Alvesson, M., & Kärreman, D. (2011). Decolonializing discourse: Critical reflections on organizational discourse analysis. *Human Relations, 64*, 1121-1146.

Ashcraft, K. L., Kuhn, T. R., & Cooren, F. (2009). Constitutional amendments: "Materializing" organizational communication. In J. P. Walsh & A. P. Brief (Eds.), *The academy of management annals* (vol. 3, pp. 1-64). London: Routledge.

Bell, E. L. J. E., & Nkomo, S. M. (2001). *Our separate ways: Black and white women and the struggle for professional identity*. Boston: Harvard Business School Press.

Black, K., & Lobo, M. (2008). A conceptual review of family resilience factors. *Journal of Family Nursing, 14*, 33-55.

Bonanno, G. A. (2004). Loss, trauma, and human resilience: Have we underestimated the human capacity to thrive after extremely aversive events? *American Psychologist, 59*, 20-28.

Bowes, L., & Jaffee, S. R. (2013). Biology, genes, and resilience: Toward a multidisciplinary approach. *Trauma Violence Abuse, 14*, 195-208.

Brummans, B., Cooren, F., Robichaud, D., & Taylor, J. (2014). Approaches to the communicative constitution of organizations. In L. L. Putnam & D. K. Mumby (Eds.), *Handbook of organizational communication* (3rd ed., pp. 173-194). Thousand Oaks, CA: Sage.

Burton, L. (2007). Childhood adultification in economically disadvantaged families: A conceptual model. *Family Relations, 56*, 329-345.

Buzzanell, P. M. (2004). Metaphor in the classroom: Reframing traditional and alternative uses of language for feminist transformation. In P. M. Buzzanell, H. Sterk, & L. H. Turner (Eds.), *Gender in applied communication contexts* (pp. 179-193). Thousand Oaks, CA: Sage.

Buzzanell, P. M. (2008). Necessary fictions: Stories of identity, hope, and love. *Communication, Culture, & Critique, 1*, 31-39.

Buzzanell, P. M. (2010a). Resilience: Talking, resisting, and imagining new normalcies into being. *Journal of Communication, 60*, 1-14.

Buzzanell, P. M. (2010b). *Seduction and sustainability: The politics of feminist communication and career scholarship*. Washington, DC: Carrol C. Arnold Distinguished Lecture Series, National Communication Association. Available: http://www.natcom.org/uploadedFiles/Convention_and_Events/Annual_Convention/PDF-Convention-Carroll_C_Arnold_Lecture_2010.pdf

Buzzanell, P. M. (2014). Work and family communication. In L. H. Turner & R. West (Eds.), *The SAGE handbook of family communication* (pp. 320-336). Thousand Oaks, CA: Sage.

Buzzanell, P. M., D'Enbeau, S., & Duckworth, J. (2010). What men say about women: Fathers contemplate work-family choices and motherhood. In S. Hayden & L. O'Brien Hallstein (Eds.), *Contemplating maternity in the era of choice: Explorations into discourses of reproduction* (pp. 291-311). Lanham, MD: Lexington Press.

Buzzanell, P. M., & Liu, M. (2005). Struggling with maternity leave policies and practices: A poststructuralist feminist analysis of gendered organizing. *Journal of Applied Communication Research, 33,* 1-25.

Buzzanell, P. M., & Liu, M. (2007). It's "give and take": Maternity leave as a conflict management process. *Human Relations, 60,* 463-495.

Buzzanell, P. M., & Lucas, K. (2013). Constrained and constructed choice in career: An examination of communication pathways to dignity. In E. L. Cohen (Ed.), *Communication yearbook* (vol. 37, pp. 3-31). New York: Routledge.

Buzzanell, P. M., Meisenbach, R., Remke, R., Bowers, V., Liu, M., & Conn, C. (2005). The good working mother: Managerial women's sensemaking and feelings about work-family issues. *Communication Studies, 56,* 261-285.

Buzzanell, P. M., Shenoy, S., Remke, R. V., & Lucas, K. (2009). Intersubjectively creating resilience: Responding to and rebounding from potentially destructive organizational experiences. In P. Lutgen-Sandvik & B. Davenport Sypher (Eds.), *The destructive side of organizational communication* (pp. 530-576). New York: Routledge.

Buzzanell, P. M., & Turner, L. H. (2003). Emotion work revealed by job loss discourse: Backgrounding-foregrounding of feelings, construction of normalcy, and (re)instituting of traditional masculinities. *Journal of Applied Communication Research, 31,* 27-57.

Buzzanell, P. M., & Turner, L. H. (2012). Crafting narratives for family crises: Communicative behaviors associated with effectively managing job loss. In L. Webb & F. Dickson (Eds.), *Communication for families in crisis: Theories, methods, strategies* (pp. 281-306). Cresskill, NJ: Hampton Press.

Canary, H. (2008a). Creating supportive connections: A decade of research on support for families of children with disabilities. *Health Communication, 23,* 413-426.

Canary, H. (2008b). Negotiating dis/ability in families: Constructions and contradictions. *Journal of Applied Communication Research, 36,* 437-458.

Canary, H. (2012). Children with invisible disabilities: Communicating to manage family contradictions. In F. Dickson & L. Webb (Eds.), *Communication for families in crisis: Theories, methods, strategies* (pp. 155-178). New York: Peter Lang.

Canary, H., & Cantú, E. (2012). Making decisions about children's disabilities: Mediation and structuration in cross-system meetings. *Western Journal of Communication, 76,* 270-297.

Duckworth, J., & Buzzanell, P. M. (2009). Constructing work-life balance and fatherhood: Men's framing of the meanings of both work and family. *Communication Studies, 60,* 558-573.

Faris, J. (2013). Serving time by coming home: Communicating hope through a reentry court. In S. Hartnett, J. Wood, E. Novek (Eds.), *Working for justice: A handbook of prison activism and education.* Urbana, IL: University of Illinois Press.

Gabor, E. (2011). Turning points in the development of classical musicians. *Journal of Ethnographic & Qualitative Research, 5,* 138-156.

Golden, A. G. (2009a). Employee families and organizations as mutually enacted environments: A sensemaking approach to work-life interrelationships. *Management Communication Quarterly, 22*, 385-415.

Golden, A. G. (2009b). The gendered paradox of efficiency in ICT mediated work-life interrelationships: Caring more about work while working in more care. In S. Kleinman (Ed.), *The culture of efficiency* (pp. 339-354). New York: Peter Lang.

Golden, A. G., & Geisler, C. (2007). Work-life boundary management and the personal digital assistant. *Human Relations, 60*, 519-551.

Golden, A. G., Kirby, E. L., & Jorgenson, J. (2006). Work-life research from both sides now: An integrative perspective for organizational and family communication. In C. S. Beck (Ed.), *Communication yearbook* (vol. 30, pp. 143-195). New York: Routledge.

Green, A. (2013). Patchwork: Poor women's stories of resewing the shredded safety net. *Affilia: Journal of Women and Social Work, 28*, 51-54.

Hammoud, A., & Buzzanell, P. M. (2012). "The most vulnerable...[and] most resilient people": Communicatively constituting Palestinian refugees' resilience. In B. Omdahl & J. Harden Fritz (Eds.), *Problematic relationships at work* (pp. 215-234). New York: Peter Lang.

Hammoud, A., & Buzzanell, P. M. (2013, April). *Leading others toward imagining the possible: A Palestinian woman's story of resilience in a Jordanian refugee camp*. Paper presented to the Central States Communication Association, conference held in Kansas City, MO.

Harrison, E. (2012). Bouncing back? Recession, resilience and everyday lives. *Critical Social Policy, 33*, 97-113.

Kärreman, D., & Alvesson, M. (2009). Resisting resistance: Counter-resistance, consent and compliance in a consultancy firm. *Human Relations, 62*, 1115-1144.

Kirby, E. L. (2000). Should I do as you say, or do as you do?: Mixed messages about work and family. *The Electronic Journal of Communication, 10*(3-4). Retrieved from http://www.cios.org/EJCPUBLIC/010/3/010313.html

Kirby, E. L., & Buzzanell, P. M. (2014). Communicating work-life. In L. L. Putnam & D. K. Mumby (Eds.), *Handbook of organizational communication* (3rd ed., pp. 351-373). Thousand Oaks, CA: Sage.

Kirby, E. L., Golden, A. G., Medved, C. E., Jorgenson, J., & Buzzanell, P. M. (2003). An organizational communication challenge to the discourse of work and family research: From problematic to empowerment. In P. J. Kalbfleisch (Ed.), *Communication yearbook* (vol. 27, pp. 1-43). New York: Routledge.

Kirby, E. L., & Krone, K. J. (2002). "The policy exists but you can't really use it": Communication and the structuration of work-family policies. *Journal of Applied Communication Research, 30*, 50-77.

Kirby, E. L., Wieland, S. M. B., & McBride, M. C. (2013). Work-life conflict. In J. G. Oetzel & S. Ting-Toomey (Eds.), *The SAGE handbook of conflict communication: Integrating theory, research, and practice* (2nd ed., pp. 377-402). Thousand Oaks, CA: Sage.

Kwon, P. (2013). Resilience in lesbian, gay, and bisexual individuals. *Personality and Social Psychology Review, 17*, 371-383.

Lim, S. (2013, November). *Women, mobile media and "double work": When social transformation lags behind technological change*. Paper presented at the ICA Regional Conference in China, Shanghai, PRC.

Lucas, K., & Buzzanell, P. M. (2011). It's the cheese: Collective memory of hard times during deindustrialization. In J. M. Cramer, C. P. Greene, & L. M. Walters (Eds.), *Food as communication: Communication as food* (pp. 95-113). New York: Peter Lang.

Lucas, K., & Buzzanell, P. M. (2012). Memorable messages of hard times: Constructing short- and long-term resiliencies through family communication. *Journal of Family Communication, 12*, 189-208.

Marin, K., Bohanek, J., & Fivush, R. (2008). Positive effects of talking about the negative: Family narratives of negative experiences and preadolescents' perceived competence. *Journal of Research on Adolescence, 18*, 573-593.

McCubbin, H. I., & McCubbin, M. A. (1988). Typologies of resilience families: Emerging roles of social class and ethnicity. *Family Relations, 37*, 247-254.

Medved, C. E. (2004). The everyday accomplishment of work and family: Exploring practical actions in daily routines. *Communication Studies, 55*, 128-145.

Medved, C. E. (2009). Constructing breadwinning mother identities: Moral, personal, and political positioning. *Women's Studies Quarterly, 37*, 140-156.

Medved, C. E. (2010). Communication work-life research. In S. Sweet & J. Casey (Eds.), *Work and family encyclopedia*. Chestnut Hill, MA: Sloan Work and Family Research Network. Retrieved from http://repo.library.upenn.edu/storage/content/2/3kb6k5cb4ft7918c/1/Communication_Work-Life_Research.pdf

Medved, C. E., Brogan, S. M., McClanahan, A. M., Morris, J. F., & Shepherd, G. J. (2006). Family and work socializing communication: Messages, gender, and ideological implications. *Journal of Family Communication, 6*, 161-180.

Medved, C. E., & Rawlins, W. K. (2011). At-home fathers and breadwinning mothers: Variations in constructing work and family lives. *Women & Language, 34*(2), 9-39.

Meisenbach, R. J. (2010). The female breadwinner: Phenomenological experience and gendered identity in work/family spaces. *Sex Roles, 62*, 2-19.

Notter, M., MacTavish, K., & Shamah, D. (2008). Pathways toward resilience among women in rural trailer parks. *Family Relations, 57*, 613-624.

Putnam, L. L., & Mumby, D. K. (Eds.). (2014). *Handbook of organizational communication* (3rd ed.). Thousand Oaks, CA: Sage.

Putnam, L. L., & Nicotera, A. M. (Eds.). (2009). *Building theories of organization: The constitutive role of communication*. New York: Routledge.

Schrodt, P., & Afifi, T. (2007). Communication processes that predict young adults' feelings of being caught and their associations with mental health and family satisfaction. *Communication Monographs, 74*, 200-228.

Segrin, C. (2006). Family interactions and well-being: Integrative perspectives. *Journal of Family Communication, 6*, 3-21.

Shenoy-Packer, S. (2013, November). *Former substance abusers and the communicative construction of resilience in recovery*. Paper presented to the National Communication Association conference, Washington, DC.

Shorey, H. S., Snyder, C. R., Rand, K. L., Hockemeyer, J. R., & Feldman, D. B. (2002). Somewhere over the rainbow: Hope theory weathers its first decade. *Psychological Inquiry, 13*, 322-331.

Snyder, C. R. (2002). Hope theory: Rainbows in the mind. *Psychological Inquiry, 13*, 249-275.

Stone, A. (2013). Dilemmas of communicating about Alzheimer's disease: Professional caregivers, social support, and illness uncertainty. *Journal of Applied Communication Research, 41*, 1-17.

Theron, L. (2013). Black students' recollections of pathways to resilience: Lessons for school psychologists. *School Psychology International*, pp. 1-13.

Tracy, S., & Rivera, K. (2010). Endorsing equity and applauding stay-at-home moms: How male voices on work-life reveal aversive sexism and flickers of transformation. *Management Communication Quarterly, 24*, 3-43.

Turner, P., & Norwood, K. (2013). Unbounded motherhood: Embodying a good working mother identity. *Management Communication Quarterly, 27*, 396-424.

Turner, L. H., & West, R. (Eds.). (2014). *The SAGE handbook of family communication*. Thousand Oaks, CA: Sage.

Villagran, M., Cazona, M., & Ledford, C. (2013). The milspouse battle rhythm: Communicating resilience throughout the deployment cycle. *Health Communication, 28*, 778-788.

Wilson, S. R., Wilkum, K., Chernichky, S. M., MacDermid Wadsworth, S. M., & Broniarczyk, K. M. (2011). Passport toward success: Description and evaluation of a program designed to help children and families reconnect after a military deployment. *Journal of Applied Communication Research, 39*, 223-249.

• CHAPTER NINE •

Fear of the Unknown, Hope for the Unseen: Resilience of Child Soldiers in Uganda, East Africa

Erik W. Green
Concordia University Texas

On July 4, 2007 I conducted an online interview with Fr. Simon Wamelile—a Catholic priest in Tororo, Uganda—about the Lord's Resistance Army and potential steps toward conflict resolution. With urgency, he expressed, "Lord's Resistance Army are real and is a movement of monsters stationed in the northern Uganda and partly Eastern where I come from. Sometime back they came to Moroto and Soroti which are not very far from Mbale. They abduct children, women, young men and property. In 1999, they even abducted some fifty minor seminarians who up to date, some are not known whether alive or dead. A few managed to escape and others who were caught were killed. The children abducted are Ugandans mainly." Stories of the Lord's Resistance Army (LRA) are still told widely across majority of regions of Uganda, and the effect of this rebel group's violence is far reaching. In our interview, Fr. Wamelile argued that "[t]he worst form of conflict as experienced in part of Uganda is a result of lack of maturity, democracy, and dialogue which breaks down due to mistrust." While the issues of the conflict were cast as national and human rights problems, potential for overcoming barriers—a move toward *positive social change* (Cheney, 2005)—appeared to lie in addressing interpersonal communication dynamics. As a conflict and communication scholar, I had an opportunity to seek understanding of this conflict involving the Government of Uganda and the Lord's Resistance Army and what characterizes an avenue toward the maturity, democracy, and dialogue needed to foster trust—a call that my friend Fr. Wamelile pleaded for. Three years later I was standing on Ugandan soil.

Around the time I was reading the aforementioned interview responses on my computer screen in the comfort of my home in the United States, a woman in Gulu Uganda was rebuilding her life after escaping from the rebel LRA forces that held her captive for over 5 years. Josephine was only 15 years old when the rebels ambushed her village, gathered up the children, and held them captive. Josephine was taken away from her family. Rebel soldiers stole all food, cooking utensils, and clothing and set the huts of the village on fire. Josephine was forced—tied together with other abducted children—to walk an exhausting distance without food or rest through the the jungle—the bush—to reach a rebel army camp. She was surrounded by LRA members of varying age including 8- and 9-year-old girls that served as porters, adolescent boys with logs and machetes that served as soldiers-in-training, middle-aged men with assault guns that served as commanders, and women of all ages that served as the commanders' wives. This would be her new "family" for the next 5 years. Little did she know that she would eventually share her story of escape with an interpersonal communication researcher who lived 8,400 miles away.

Overview

This chapter focuses on the experience of children abducted by the Lord's Resistance Army (LRA) from villages in Uganda, East Africa who were able to escape and return to village life. Their stories highlight the richness of the concepts of hope and resilience. Their fear of the unknown gave way to the hope that arose out of this terrible situation. Even though the reality of a different life was initially unseen (i.e., they couldn't conceive of a better alternative), those who escaped the LRA at some point confronted a hope for a "new normal." My hope is to honor the 22 participants interviewed by accurately portraying the spirit of the stories of hope and resilience they shared with me.

I approach the concept of hope in line with Snyder's development of hope theory. As such, hope is defined as "a positive motivational state that is based on an interactively derived sense of successful (a) agency (goal-directed energy) and (b) pathways (planning to meet goals)" (Snyder, Irving, & Anderson, 1991, p. 287). Snyder (2000) suggests we have anchors that provide direction for hopeful thinking, cognitive routes we take to reach desired endpoints, motivation to take those routes, and barriers that can get in the way of achieving our goals. The concept of resilience is a bit more elusive. Hardy, Concato, and Gill (2004) defined resilience as "the capacity to remain well, recover, or even thrive in face of adversity" (p. 257). Masten and Coatsworth (1998) defined resilience as "manifested competence in the context of significant challenges to adaptation or development" (p. 206). Harvey and Delfabbro (2004) critiqued the latter definition as being too focused on competence, particularly in light of varying culturally-derived meanings of success in terms of competently dealing with adversity. Most recently, Buzzanell (2010) emphasized the communicative processes that characterize resillience. Building upon Richardson's (2002) conceptualization of resilience as "the process of reintegrating from disruptions in life" (p. 309), she suggested five communicative processes that function as the basis of resilience: (a) crafting normalcy, (b) affirming identity anchors, (c) maintaining and using communication networks, (d) putting alternative logics to work, and (e) legitimizing negative feelings while foregrounding productive action. I approach resilience in line with Buzzanell's communicative lens for this project.

This project sheds some light on what communication processes are involved with that difficult transition back to village life. In this chapter, I will provide a brief summary of the setting for readers not as familiar with the Northern Uganda conflict. Then I will address the theoretical lenses I looked at the participants' stories through to contribute to our understanding of agents and agency of hope and resilience. Finally, I will mention the unanticipated outcome from this project. To understand the richness of the participants' stories, we have to first look at the larger context in which they were created.

The Setting

The conflict between the Government of Uganda (GoU) and the Lord's Resistance Army (LRA) has perpetuated for over 25 years. The LRA has been charged with involvement in violations of human rights for over two decades, including killings, rape, and beatings of civilians. This conflict has led to more than 1.8 million people being moved into internally displaced persons' (IDPs) camps by the GoU in an effort to protect citizens and rout the rebel group (Amnesty International, 2008). In effect, Ugandan people have been forced off their own land and face the challenge now—after living for numerous years in the densely populated IDPs resulting in the loss of livestock—of reclaiming their original land and initiating a new livelihood. Children are particularly sought out by rebels due to their vulnerability to control and indoctrination. Somewhere between 25,000 (CSUCS, 2008) and 60,000 (Annan, Brier, & Aryemo, 2009) children have been forced into involvement with the LRA. There are a number of ways child soldiers are manipulated to serve the needs of the LRA. The UNICEF (2007) definition for what constitutes a child soldier includes any person below 18 years of age associated with an armed force or armed group that is used in any capacity—fighters, cooks, porters, messengers, spies, or for sexual purposes. In other words, as argued by

Betancourt and colleagues (2008) we have to move beyond sole images of boys with guns when talking about child soldiers.

Community/Cultural View of Justice

To understand the participants' stories it is important to know how the Acholi people view LRA crimes and the identity of children that are able to escape and return. Of particular interest are the findings of an attitude study on peace and justice conducted by Vinck and collegaues (2007). The researchers collected data through survey questionnaires between April to June 2007 in camps, new settlement sites, and villages in three sub-regions of northern Uganda (i.e., Acholi, Lango, & Teso). The respondents were in favor of a combination of restorative and distributive justice. Vinck and colleagues (2007) reported that "more than two-thirds of respondents said those responsible for committing violations of human rights and international humanitarian law in northern Uganda should be held accountable" (p. 4). Respondents' opinions differed regarding *how* violators should be held accountable. When asked what should happen to the LRA leaders who committed human rights abuses, overall, "52% of respondents preferred options such as forgiveness, reconciliation or reintegration for LRA leaders, while 40.9% of the respondents mentioned options including trials and/or punishment including imprisonment or death" (Vinck et al., 2007, p. 4).

Worden (2008) concluded that there was a dilemma with how to communicate justice in Uganda. When it comes to the top LRA leaders, follow-through on indictments becomes increasingly under the purview of the International Criminal Court (ICC). A more distributive (or punitive) system of justice is preferred for these top-level perpetrators. The warrants that were issued for Joseph Kony and his associates are in fact functioning as restraints toward further peace pact talks (Ojambo, 2008) as ICC threats drive these individuals deeper into the bush. Still, a large portion of LRA perpetrators can also be classified as victims. Since the conflict has been ongoing for over 25 years, many current LRA fighters are former children that were kidnapped and trained by Kony. The Acholi people are challenged with discerning whether or not to accept these individuals back into their community.

A restorative justice system through traditional, community-based justice mechanisms is preferred for lower-level perpetrators and those who have received amnesty. Those receiving amnesty would need to: a) confess their wrongdoing; b) apologize; and c) undergo traditional ceremonies to be reintegrated into the community (Vinck et al., 2007). The traditional ceremonies have particular significance—they often constitute the forgiveness and reintegration process.

Ceremonies and rituals, such as *mato oput* and *stepping on the egg* have historically sustained harmony among the Acholi people. Mato oput (drinking of the "bitter root") occurs within or between clans when wrongdoing (even murder) has been committed and the two parties have subsequently agreed to compensation and payment. Stepping on the egg is an act that symbolically breaks open a new life for wrongdoers and returns them back to innocence. According to Vinck and colleagues (2007) the people of Northern Uganda believe these rituals are effective if the root cause of the conflict is determined (99% said this was important), and truth is established (84% said this was important). In other words, *how* messages about the abduction, experience within the LRA, and request for forgiveness after escape are communicated within the community is critical. These rituals are communicative events that are immeasurably deep with meanings (Baxter, 2004). The *shared systems of meaning* around these rituals allow for paradoxical ideas (e.g., accountability and forgiveness) to both be conciliated paving the way for reintegration into community.

Community/Cultural View of Restoration

The presence of non-governmental organizations (NGOs) that work to rehabilitate former child soldiers provides unexpected hope to the returned children. Gulu Support the Children Organisation (GUSCO), World Vision–Uganda, Kitgum Concerned Women's Association (KICWA), and Concerned Parents Association have all focused on providing psychological and social support and capacity-building of communities.

The category of "child" became a critical force within the rhetoric of the NGO community in their restoration efforts. The children work through post-traumatic stress disorder (PTSD), psychological harm, nightmares, guilt, and confusion of identity upon their return (Jordans, Tol, Komproe, & de Jong, 2009). Cheney (2005) reminds us that these returned LRA members used "childhood" as a means for help from the NGOs. She relayed the story of Geoffrey, who "expressed his wish 'to be a child again, to go back to school' to recover the childhood stolen from him. This narrative helped engender pity and forgiveness from his community" (p. 37). Perhaps appealing to "childhood" offered a face-saving approach when coming back to village life (Goffman, 1959). Parallel with UNICEF's (2007) 18-year mark to define a child soldier, those that are able to escape the LRA have the label of "child" if under 18. In all, the NGOs bolster a community-wide legitimacy to the experience of abducted children and have become a part of the cultural narrative that allow for a claim of innocence as the children are seen as victims of the war rather than as culpable rebels.

Theoretical Lens
Lifespan Development

Clear-cut life stage categories are hard to come by in Acholi culture. The cultural roots of the community suggest a vague delineation of lifespan development. This ambiguity creates difficulty for how to view each child—as innocent victim of war or as culpable offender of violence.

In traditional Acholi culture, elders told stories around campfires (referred to as *fire circles*) that nurtured the moral code of the community. Family interactions around the *fire circle* in the evenings allowed opportunities for children to entertain elders and elders to tell stories to shape the moral frame of the children. Generational hierarchies in the Acholi culture historically gave decision-making authority to clan elders regarding when to wage war and who would be involved. Rituals were in place to cleanse warriors who killed their enemies (Finnstrom, 2001).

Kony's actions are breaking down Acholi culture by disrupting their intergenerational structure (Cheney 2005). Parents are unable to care for, raise, and discipline their children because of war (Rubin, 1998; Oloya, 2002). Connections to ancestral roots are lost as men, women, and children are pushed to internally displaced persons (IDP) camps (Amnesty International, 2008). As Angucia and colleagues (2010) put it, "The underlying concerns in this social problem include loss of relationships, trust, dignity and confidence, a legacy of individual and collective guilt, trauma and painful memories both among the children and in the community" (p. 220). O'Callaghan and colleagues (2012) put it this way:

> Time and again in the children's narratives they give examples of common conventions being inverted, social norms being perverted and the abnormal existing side-by-side with the normal. This juxtaposition has the effect of normalizing gratuitous violence and offering a rationale for inexplicable acts of cruelty. In Acholi culture the elderly are the custodians of knowledge and experience and afforded great respect. Yet, for the rebels, the elderly are an inconvenience, slowing their progress through the bush. (p. 92)

For many Northern Ugandans, the experience of being abducted in many ways grew them up. At the same time, they missed out on the opportunities to just be a kid. They struggle with the uncertainty of being viewed as children of lost innocence or culpable adults in the eyes of their village community. Even the Uganda People's Defense Force (UPDF)—the armed forces of Uganda—has been criticized for strategically choosing to use the "child" label when they rescue someone, but the "rebel" label when they kill someone (Cheney, 2005).

Interpretive Social Science

Interpretive social scientific approaches dig into the variability of communication phenomena to offer deep insights into unique aspects of communication as experienced by unique people (Rabinow & Sullivan, 1979). I was drawn to an interpretive approach as it brings participants' socially constructed worlds to light. Gergen (2001) stated that talk involves "the opening of new visions and alternative futures" (p. 63). In other words, participants were constructing the meaning of their experiences as they shared their story with the interpreters and me (Goffman, 1959). Through an interpretive lens, relational meanings were continually feeding back into stories as participants and I interacted—including me becoming a new part of their ongoing story of hope and resilience (Watzlawick, Beavin, & Jackson, 1967).

Telling Stories

Discovering or narrating a story often constitutes the *work* of interpretive communication research. Storytelling is complex. Goffman's (1959) dramaturgical perspective (i.e., life as a theater) suggests that these former child soldiers present various *faces* to their audience (e.g., researcher, village members, NGO workers) while telling their story. Rather than an analysis of the psychology of returned child soldiers these in-depth interviews were "face engagements" since the participants, interpreters, and I all focused our attention on the interaction at hand (Goffman, 1967, 1959). The focused gathering put primacy on the participants' stories. While telling stories these participants were making sense of their experiences nested within an overarching communal narrative about the LRA, ongoing violence, sporadic abductions, and returned escapees. My challenge was to maintain the *spirit* of participants' meanings of their lived experiences of hope and resilience while also putting those experiences into perspective with my understanding of the larger communal narrative of the Acholi culture (Goffman, 1981). Overall, I sought to shield my personal biases by having an air of curiosity about the participants' stories as they emerged (Putnam, 2005).

I conducted the interviews in Gulu, Northern Uganda in June and July of 2010. Personal friends—members of the Catholic Archdiocese of Tororo, Uganda—helped coordinate transportation to Gulu, translators to assist with the interviews, and accommodations for my stay. My snowball sampling procedure culminated in 22 completed in-depth interviews. These participants were screened by local school or church administrators and the interpreters to ensure they had a substantial story of abduction by the LRA, time in the rebel camp, and subsequent escape. While all participants spoke some English, their primary language was Luo. Some chose to conduct the interview in English, because of their wish to talk directly with me rather than through an interpreter. For those interviews conducted in Luo the goal of the translators was to express the spirit of the details of the participants' stories more so than providing a direct word-for-word exchange. The interviews ranged from 21 to 50 minutes.

I phrased interview questions to be objective and avoid implying anything negative about the participants' experiences. Furthermore, the interpreters and I were particularly attentive to ask questions in a way sensitive to participants' mood or emotions. As stated by de Kadt (1995), "the need to interpret 'linguistic' in a broad sense [is] to include *both* verbal and nonverbal channels" (p. 2). Due to the nature of the concepts studied the nonverbal channel was crucial for a better understanding of the messages conveyed by participants. We often reminded participants that they did not have to answer any question they were uncomfortable with and were allowed to stop participating at any time. All participants chose to continue. The names used in this chapter are pseudonyms. The next section unpacks the ideas of hope and resilience through their specific stories.

The primary aim was to explore ideas of hope and resilience of the escaped child soldiers of Northern Uganda. What communicative ways is hope nurtured? How is resilience fostered relationally as well as communally through various forms of communication?

Agents and Agency of Hope and Resilience

Hope was not a one-time event for these participants. It had to be nurtured. Resilience was not a trait that was either present or not. It was a process that emerged in interaction with others. To be clear, we cannot assume that simply escaping from the LRA provided hope for a better life. As Cheney (2005) suggested the rhetoric of "redemption" that is used by some of the NGOs working with these children sets up false ideals since many of these children are not necessarily going back to "better conditions." As other researchers found, some former child soldiers faced ambivalence upon return to village life and reported having difficulties with their communities (Annan, Brier, & Aryemo, 2009; Veale & Stavrou, 2007). Therefore, I discuss the participants' hope and resilience both with the LRA and upon return to village life [see Table 9.1].

My discussion builds upon the framework of communicating new normalcies into being (Buzzanell, 2010). Overall, potential for hope to be replaced by moments of despair was ever-present. Resilience emerged as these participants pushed past potential despair while with the LRA and chose productive action upon return to life in the village. Participants struggled with uncertainty about their identity and what it meant to be part of a "family." They wrestled with new definitions of "normal." They made sense of uncertainty through alternative logics. Finally, participants looked to transformative communicative rituals of both the rebel army and their village communities to move forward.

Table 9.1. Hope and Resilience of Child Soldiers

	With LRA	Upon Return to the Village
Resilience	Fear of the unknown	Fear of the unknown
	Resilience by being part of a "family"	Resilience by being part of a "family"
	Resilience in new rebel role	Resilience in "new normal"
	Resilience for physical survival (staying alive)	Resilience for emotional survival (rising above rejection & isolation)
Hope	Hope for the Unseen	Hope for the Unseen
	Hope that rebel rituals work	Hope that Acholi rituals work
	Hope for advancement in rank	Hope that "new normal" is real
	Hope for temporary acceptance	Hope for permanent acceptance
	Hope for escape	Hope to remain

Hope and Resilience While With the LRA

While with the LRA, new moral frameworks shaped what participants hoped for. The LRA communicates morality through discipline and violence. As Rubin (1998) wrote, "The moment they were snatched by the LRA, they entered a moral universe where everything they had been taught was flipped on its head. Killing was good. Kindness was bad" (p. 63). Ever-present in the participants' stories were examples of the use of family metaphors where LRA leaders are the head of families, abducted females are taken as wives and all other abductees are siblings that can be instructed, punished, or killed by commanders. LRA leaders maintain control by referring to themselves as teacher to foster respect from the children (Cheney, 2005). So, participants found hope in a better life within the LRA by way of compliance. When children obey orders and excel within this environment they are rewarded with advancement in rank.

Teddy's story highlights how her moral universe was flipped on its head when she was abducted at 8 years old.

> My dad was a soldier. When these people came they killed him. They gathered me and my sisters up and said they were taking us. They asked my mother if she wanted to go with us or be killed. She said she would go with them, but then they made her lay down and they shot her. I was so young I didn't know what was going on. At first I was laughing... I did not know what was going on. Then I saw my other sisters crying. The rebels said if you are crying you will also follow your mother. If you want to be alive you eat this mother of yours. I was scared. They gave us luggage to carry. Then these people took us with them in the bush.

The normative dynamic of instruction and compliance served as a basis for resilience in participants as they came to depend on their captors in the absence of any other parental relationship (Buzzanell, 2010; Dodge & Raundalen, 1991). They put alternative logics to work as another display of resilience to maintain the LRA lifestyle. Steal when you need to. Beat anyone that defies orders and puts the family at risk. Kill those that are holding you back or making you vulnerable to attack from the UPDF. Survival. Another participant, Thomas, shared one LRA ritual where rebel leaders put oil on his head, which would ensure his safety in the LRA. He experienced the protection of the leaders, which gave him strength. This was his family.

LRA leaders imposed affiliation with the family as an alternative anchor for hope by communicating that there was no other hope outside the rebel camp. Majority of participants shared that LRA leaders often said "no one wants you" and "you have nowhere else to go." Abducted children who were forced to watch their parents get shot or burned in their hut, in particular found validity in those "truths." This was their new reality—to survive and to advance. Kony's efforts to change the child soldiers' anchor for hopeful thinking is particularly salient in Rosemary's story of his response to a radio campaign that parents put together letting the abducted children know that the villages will take them back—that they are welcome home. Hearing these aired on the radio planted a seed of hope for the children. Rosemary said that in response, Kony had all the radios that were with the rebels gathered up and set on fire. He destroyed the medium through which hope was reaching the children. Yet, the message had already been planted in Rosemary's mind. A pathway was birthed for escape. The radio campain encouraged the children's agency to find a way home (Snyder, 2000).

Hope and Resilience Upon Return to Village

Upon return to village life, Acholi moral frameworks shaped what the participants hoped for. Ultimately the Acholi cultural moral frame helped these children see that the destructiveness of brutality that came with the hope for advancement and temporary acceptance in the LRA was far outweighed by the constructiveness of purpose and sense of community that came with the hope for escape and the possibility of permanent acceptance. Josephine's story highlights this constrast.

> While we were traveling through the bush we came upon someone that was a witch doctor. I was given a gun to kill this person. I said I did not know how to use a gun. They beat me and said, "you need to be trained to kill." So, when they are moving there are three groups. The first are those amateurs who do not know...who won't kill. Then there is the second group that was a bit...they were learning. Then the third group was a terrible group. They will move behind so in case you fall or if you do not do what they tell you they will just kill you or run you over...in the camp, some girls were given luggage to carry. Older girls were told to go over there and Kony's men would come by to choose a wife. So this man took me as a wife. I had two children of this man in the bush.

After many years within the rebel group, Josephine was able to escape when the rebels were attacked by UPDF.

> The first time when I got back from the bush, whenever I would go to sit, these people would get up and go away. They would say "you smell like Kony" [crying]. When I came to the village I was told to step on an egg, because they thought I was dead. Then they asked if I killed someone. If I had they would do something to send away the spirits and I would be cleansed. But I said I didn't kill and so was asked to just do stepping on the egg. But if I had killed then there would have been more things involved such as Mato oput.

Josephine was able to escape with her two children. Although her tears revealed the hurt that she still carries with her, upon return to the village she felt that she had a new start as an adult.

The hope for escape led participants to somewhat of a second-order hope that it *is* possible to have a change of heart, that the community rituals do work to release the evil spirits from their heart and that stepping on the egg could crack open a new life. It took ongoing motivation for participants to foreground productive action, thus nurturing resilience to live in this "new normal" that they had hoped for. Geofrey's story highlights how crafting normalcy and affirming identity anchors served as the basis of resilience in this second-order hope for a better future in the village community.

> As a child I lived with my uncle who drank too much alcohol. One day, I went to the well for water and there was one of those rebel soldiers there. I knew him because we used to play football (soccer) together although I did not recognize him as much from when he was younger. That boy called Kony's men to capture me...after many years,

there were these government soldiers nearby. One of the soldiers was drunk singing and shouting. One of the rebels got scared and started shooting. People scattered. Then, I hid under a bush.... some space where an animal had probably slept. I hid there. I was told by rebels, "If you ever run and we find you, we will kill you immediately. If you run we will shoot you." So I stayed hidden, even hid from government soldiers for a full day, until I heard there was no more noise. There were potatoes in my pocket and I collected rain water in a plant leaf. When I first came across people I would sit and wait so as to not be found. Finally I crossed a river and knew I was close to a village. I thought if I went to local authorities I would get arrested. So, I finally snuck back to this village I knew. When people recognized me I couldn't say I was with the rebels because the people would kill me. I came back to my uncle... the drunkard. When this uncle asked me where I was I told him the truth— "when we came back from church when I went to get water, at the well, rebels found me." This uncle said, "Do not tell anyone about this because people will arrest or kill you." So, I was sent to my Auntie, that I called my grandma. I didn't tell her I had been abducted, but instead helped her around her hut in the village with planting cassava. My mother had married another man that was a government soldier so I couldn't tell her about being abducted. My father was not around—he left when I was very young. Auntie said I should go start to study—go to school. This uncle criticized me for disappearing and then coming back to go study at a different school. Auntie was harsh to me too. She would talk about other rebel kids—saying "this son of Kony here and this son of Kony there"—so I would not tell her that I was with the rebels. I would just keep quiet. Then there was a man though that stayed by the hospital. This man saved me by making me see something better. He prayed for me and I told him all the things that had happened. This man said I should forget about them, and that God would give me a new life one day.

Helping his Auntie around her hut, planting cassava, and talking about school established a *normal* routine for Geofrey. Identity work also anchored Geofrey in contrast to the "son of Kony" label. His uncle helped protect his identity through silence. The man that prayed for Geofrey affirmed his identity as the recipient of a new life from God. What especially caught my attention during his interview was when Geofrey said, "you have to find one or two people who really understand the situation with the LRA—otherwise keep quiet." His statement brings to light the need for community-wide affirmation of a returned child soldier's new identity. Nearly all participants portrayed the significant role of traditional Acholi rituals in moving forward in village life. To live back in community, it was important for others in the village to affirm that the participant's identity was no longer attached to Kony or the rebel army. These rituals served as unifying community-wide events—a community level resource—for fostering resilience.

Rituals

In Acholi culture, rituals cleanse the children of evil spirits. Stepping on the egg is the most common. Sacrificing chickens or goats is also practiced. Rituals offer a pathway to release escaped children from being stuck in past experience. These rituals represent a fresh start—a new beginning. For example, Thomas shared that he no longer has bad dreams because of the ritual that cleansed him of evil spirits. A majority of participants shared that stepping on the egg represented a cracking open of new life. A couple of participants shared experiences of having a chicken killed and its blood sprinkled upon them. One participant shared a ritualistic killing of a goat, with its stomach cut, and the insides of the goat's intestines being smeared on him.

There are deep meanings in the lived experiences of hope and resilience inherent in these rituals. Baxter (2004) articulated the communicative significance of ritual. Based on Bakhtin's (1990) work on the dialogic self, she argued that "rituals, when powerfully enacted, are likely candidates as aesthetic moments" (Baxter, 2004, p. 13)—these fleeting moments when parties through dialogue can create wholeness amid fragmentation and disorder. Rituals gave some teeth to the process of death of past actions and the resurrection to a "new normal" at a community level. In these moments participants could finally be released of the bad spirits that "sit on their head." As Josephine demonstrated, she can focus on her "new husband" now and care for her children. She can nurture in them the freedom to choose an anchor for their own hopeful thinking that does not involve the LRA.

Rituals alone are not a magic pill completely wiping away all memories of the past. Participants expressed the essential role of agency toward productive action to rebuild Uganda. Even in the face of messages from naysayers that reminded them of their past involvement with the LRA—participants clung to their "new normal." These participants faced moments to truthfully embrace what the past was—not rationalizing it away or downplaying it—and celebrating a "new life." Hope emerged as the returnee knew that the resilience to make it through such terrible circumstances was available to others too. Overall, rituals were the community level starting point for participants to anchor their hope in a yet-to-be-seen better future (Snyder, 2000).

Hope for the Unseen

The participants communicated hope for a new and better unseen future in varying ways. For example, Thomas had an uncle that told him he could have a new heart. The Acholi rituals alone did not have a strong impact on

Thomas, but the message from his uncle was transformational and the primary source for his agency toward living a better life. Geofrey told the story of a man that came and "prayed for him" and told him he could have a new life. Betty spoke of her efforts learning to be a hairdresser to get past the negative feelings from watching her parents get killed, surviving with the LRA for years, escaping, and now working to be a good mother to her own children.

These returnees now are embodying the definition of hope as "a positive motivational state that is based on an interactively derived sense of successful (a) agency (goal-directed energy) and (b) pathways (planning to meet goals)" (Snyder, Irving, & Anderson, 1991, p. 287). They are making constructive contributions to the community now through education, skilled trade, and caring for living family members.

Josephine is an exemplary case. Through GUSCO she received four months of rehabilitative support. Then she came back to village life for two weeks of hairdressing training. She has a husband now and two children by him. Her husband will not have anything to do with her two children born of the rebel leader—and makes some reference to them being "devil babies"—yet this serves as a backdrop for highlighting the strength of resilience that emerged as she directed her energy toward her new anchor of hopeful thinking.

Cooperation of the entire community is needed to craft the new normal as a basis for resilience. In the best case, all members of the village encourage those affected by the LRA to share their experiences and then are trustworthy shareholders of the details of the stories shared. There are barriers to reaching this end. A common experience among all participants was being taunted by kids at school and in the village. Kids would say that participants "smelled like Kony" or "like the bush." These participants faced barriers to reaching their new normal. Often participants were *not* happy after their escape. Yes, the Acholi rituals presented a new beginning for them. Yet, the entire community plays a role in anchoring hope in a better unseen future even after traditional rituals have been performed. I want to be careful not to downplay circumstances that led to grief of these participants (e.g., as child soldiers some beat other adults and children to death). It is taking time for these participants to go through the process of silence, wrestling, death of the past, and into a new life.

Resilience continually emerges as the participants grieve, face shame, and ultimately break through to share their story of village life now. As Cheney (2005) found, "[l]ocal people actually want children to be culpable in some ways, if only to break the cycle of violence. Attention to children's agency may thus also contribute to the amelioration of war's circumstances, for children and the community at large." (p. 42). So, for the Acholi community there is a reverence that comes with truthfully acknowledging experiences, sincerely asking forgiveness, and then collectively setting aside aggressive and hostile tendencies that have perpetuated the violence in Northern Uganda. The Acholi people are crafting a "new normal." The well-being of their community now is dependent on relational and communicative efforts to continually nurture resilience. When the opportunity comes to scapegoat one member, the community has to resist. When the opportunity to blame arises, the community has to resist. Instead, they must hold to their cultural traditions of campfire dialogue—their fire circles that constitute formative interpersonal communication. It is the communal hope for a better future that holds the promise for not just changed lives, but a changed Acholi community.

I/Thou Perspective

According to Buber (1958) there are two ways we may address existence: (a) the "I" towards an "It" or object that is separate; or (b) "I" toward "Thou" where existence is in relationships without bounds. All of the participants mentioned the ability for Kony to change—reinforcing the view that *any* human can change. In other words, each participant could claim that their change was credible and true with the consistent belief that Kony too could change. Kony is not an "It" nor are they. The Acholi rituals hold the mysterious transcendence of paradoxical views of innocence and culpability occurring at a spiritual level. The stepping on the egg, the sacrifice of an animal, and the sprinkling of blood capture the "Thou" who has given release from the prison of past self. Now each participant can perform their self with dignity (Goffman, 1981, 1959). Their face has been restored. They can speak of their life past and celebrate their life now and the hope for a dignified contribution to their community.

When I asked Josephine what could bring about positive social change in Northern Uganda, she said:

> There will be no single act that can bring peace based on how I saw Kony act. Maybe only when he is dead. He can change, but these people should not try to go to him. It is best to just leave Kony alone. He is very sly and hard to understand. Instead the people of Northern Uganda should just continue to work and live life here.

> If someone comes back from either of the 3 groups, let them come back. It is okay. Just cleanse them because he has killed. After cleansing, if he has asked for forgiveness you should be ready to forgive because that is the only way to peace. That person should ask for forgiveness. If it is sincere, the community accepts them and that is the

way to peace. We should forgive those that come back so that the country can grow. Even Kony.

Cheney (2005) discovered similar perspectives from her research with returnees. When she asked how they would like their communities to view them, they said, "the community should look at us as something which is very important and receive us in a very normal way because we have been suffering in the bush. Some of us died in the bush...and God allowed us to return" (p. 38). As Cheney (2005) puts it, "[r]eturned LRA child soldiers thus embrace a potentially stigmatizing label in order to wear their survival as a badge of honor that makes them the same and yet sets them apart from other children in ways that facilitate forgiveness and even warrant special attention" (p. 38). These children are not just objects of war, but instead real people who should be understoodnd through a relational perspective.

An I/Thou perspective provides a communication lens to view relational resilience for these participants. I/It would direct attention toward a general and fixed resilience where actions are directed toward an object that can withstand so much (i.e., stay resilient) up to a point of fracture. For example, a window can get tapped only so many times by only so much increasing force until it shatters. A door latch can be opened and closed only so many times up to a point of functional failure. Or perhaps, Kony, his rebel leaders, or naysaying village members could attack an abducted/returned child soldier so many times until his or her spirit is broken. However, the participants did not necessarily have a fixed point for breaking. It is not as if they were born for a particular capacity for difficult life events. It is not as if life could only tap at them so many times with increasing force until they shatter. Instead, as others relate to them as a respected being with dignity, their resilience was birthed, nurtured, and maintained in increasing and unexpected ways. For example, a child soldier could hear a message on the radio that they are welcome home; have family members experience stepping on the egg with them to bring new life; hear village members grant them forgiveness; or experience a researcher giving them full attention while they tell their stories. Hope for the unseen is nurtured when participants are reminded of their dignity and worth despite past actions. These messages propel them toward the future and remind them of the reality of that new story they have yet to tell (i.e., a new anchor).

To promote the face—dignity and worth—of the participants, agents in their drama (Goffman, 1959) were able to respect silence, come alongside for the internal wrestling of innocence or culpability, celebrate (through ritual) the death of the old life, and communicate messages of hope and resilience for life within a "new normal." They were not constrained within a deterministic social label of "child soldier" any more. As Cheney (2005) suggested, we should actually use the label "war-affected children" rather than "returned child soldiers" to further bolster the reality by which these children view themselves. Through collective understanding by the Acholi people the integrity and dignity of these village members affected by the war can be maintained through the language used to tell their story (i.e., affirming identity anchors, Buzzanell, 2010).

Communication Scholars as Agents of Hope

There is one final unexpected insight from this research project. I approached each interview with gratitude that participants would agree to participate in my research, tell their stories to an outsider like me, and patiently work through language barriers. Unexpectedly, each participant expressed gratitude to me for coming from the United States to listen to their story. They found hope in the thought of more people beyond the borders of Uganda understanding their struggles. They expressed a positive effect from telling their stories about their difficult experiences (cf. Pennebaker, 1995). During interviews I often had a deep sense that participants, while they were telling their stories, recognized the power and potential of resilience in their lives. My interest in them nurtured hope that their suffering was not in vain and that they are worthwhile individuals. Life could begin to make sense again and be worthwhile. As scholars and practitioners, let us not underestimate our potential roles as instruments of hope and resilience in the storyline of those we work with. As O'Callaghan and colleagues (2012) urged, narratives present an opportunity for child soldiers to recast traumatic events in more constructive ways to gain purpose and meaning in life. Furthermore, the participants' experiences can live on through stories told around Acholi fire circles to serve as cultural lessons for future generations. The ontological security (Giddens, 1991) of participants seemed to be in need of attention so that their story told and story lived align. Renarrating their story offered an avenue for them to move toward that end.

I cannot study, talk about, or observe communication without engaging in communication. Similarly, participants cannot share stories with me without, in the process, also engaging in the actual communication that constitutes their developing stories. This reflexivity means that, in essence, the in-depth interview has the potential for shaping a new story lived. Aesthetic moments (Bakhtin, 1981) emerged during interviews that gave dialogic selves a new glimpse for understanding who they and the other(s) are in the situation. Bakhtin's concept of heteroglossia, or diversity of language within a culture, is relevant here, as language is never a product of a single unified tradition. The language of a culture is in continuous motion, so that the meaning of words subtly changes within each new context (Gergen, 2001). This project created a new context that allowed participants' meanings within their story to subtly change. As Pearce (1989) iterates, humans are both physical beings and on another level moral beings that live in a world of honor, integrity, dignity, and value. These interviews allowed participants to feel approached with honor, integrity, dignity, and value. In turn, their hope was nurtured.

I too am changed in the process of identifying the hope and resilience that emerged in the participants' stories. My approach to, and understanding of, life with its challenges and frustrations has been positively shaped by these war-affected children. They have given me new language for referring to them—the language that has allowed them to have a new anchor for hopeful thinking. I would be remiss to not mention the tremendous impact my visit to Uganda had on me. I feel some sorrow that I may never be able to let these participants know how much they have nurtured my own hope and resilience. My gratitude runs deep. As just one small token of thanks to them, I hope that my writing here has done an adequate job of honoring their life stories.

References

Amnesty International (2008). *Left to their own devices: The continued suffering of victims of the conflict in northern Uganda and the need for reparations.* London: Amnesty International.

Angucia, M., Zeelen, J., & de Jong, G. (2010). Researching the reintegration of formerly abducted children in Northern Uganda through action research: Experiences and reflections. *Journal of Community & Applied Social Psychology, 20*, 217-231.

Annan, J., Brier, M., & Aryemo, F. (2009). From 'rebel' to 'returnee': Daily life and reintegration for young soldiers in northern Uganda. *Journal of Adolescent Research, 24*(6), 639-667.

Bakhtin, M. M. (1981). *The dialogic imagination: Four essays by M. M. Bakhtin* (M. Holquist, Ed.; C. Emerson, & M. Holquist, Trans.). Austin: University of Texas Press.

Bakhtin, M. M. (1990). *Art and answerability: Early philosophical essays by M. M. Bakhtin.* (M. Holquist & V. Liapunov, Eds.; V. Liapunov & K. Brostrom, Trans.). Austin: University of Texas Press.

Baxter, L. A. (2004). Relationships as dialogues. *Personal Relationships, 11*, 1-22.

Betancourt, T., Borisova, I., Rubin-Smith, J., Gingerich, T., Williams, T. & Agnew-Blais, J. (2008). *Psychosocial adjustment and social integration of children associated with armed forces and armed groups: The state of the field and future directions.* Cambridge, MA: Psychology Beyond Borders and the Francois-Xavier Bagnoud Center for Health and Human Rights/Harvard School of Public Health.

Buber, M. (1958). *I and Thou.* New York: Scribner.

Buzzanell, P. M. (2010). Resilience: Talking, resisting, and imagining new normalcies into being. *Journal of Communication, 60*, 1-14.

Cheney, K. E. (2005). 'Our children have only known war': Children's experiences and the uses of childhood in Northern Uganda. *Children's Geographies, 3*(1), 23-45.

CSUCS (2008). *Child soldiers global report*. London: Coalition to Stop the Use of Child Soldiers.
de Kadt, E. (1995). "I must be seated to talk to you": Taking nonverbal politeness strategies into account. *Pragmatics and Language Learning, 6,* 2-12.
Dodge, C., & Raundalen, M. (1991). *Reaching Children in War: Sudan, Uganda, and Mozambique.* Bergen, Norway: Sigma Forlag.
Finnstrom, S. (2001). In and out of culture: fieldwork in war-torn Uganda. *Critique of Anthropology, 21*(3), 247-258.
Gergen, K. J. (2001). *An invitation to social construction.* Thousand Oaks, CA: Sage.
Giddens, A. (1991). *Modernity and self-identity: Self and society in the late modern age.* Cambridge, UK: Polity Press.
Goffman, E. (1959). *The presentation of self in everyday life.* Garden City, NY: Doubleday.
Goffman, E. (1967). *Interaction ritual.* Garden City, NY: Anchor.
Goffman, E. (1981). *Forms of Talk.* Oxford, UK: Basil Blackwell.
Hardy, S. E., Concato, J., & Gill, T. M., (2004). Resilience of Community-Dwelling Older Persons. *Journal of the American Geriatrics Society, 52*(2), 257-262.
Harvey, J., & Delfabbro, P. H., (2004). Psychological resilience in disadvantaged youth: A critical overview. *Australian Psychologist, 39*(1), 3-13.
Jordans, M., Tol, W., Komproe, I., & de Jong, J. (2009). Systematic review of evidence and treatment approaches: Psychosocial and mental health care for children in war. *Child and Adolescent Mental Health, 14*(1), 2-14.
Masten, A. S., & Coatsworth, J. D. (1998). The development of competence in favourable and unfavourable environments: Lessons from research on successful children. *American Psychologist, 53,* 205-220.
O'Callaghan, P., Storey, L., & Rafferty, H. (2012). Narrative analysis of former child soldiers' traumatic experiences. *Educational & Child Psychology, 29*(2), 87-97.
Ojambo, F. (2008, December 9). Uganda's Museveni Willing to Hold Talks With Kony, Vision Says. *New Vision.*
Oloya, O. (2002, February 19). Are the Acholi mum for fear of rocking the boat? *New Vision.*
Pearce, W. B. (1989). *Communication and the human condition.* Carbondale: University of Southern Illinois Press.
Pennebaker, J. W. (1995). *Emotion, disclosure, and health.* Washington, DC: American Psychological Association.
Rabinow, P. & Sullivan, W. M. (1979). *Interpretive Social Science: A Reader.* Berkeley: University of California Press.
Richardson, G. E. (2002). The metatheory of resilience and resiliency. *Journal of Clinical Psychology, 58,* 307-321.
Rubin, E. (1998, March 23). Our children are killing us. *New Yorker,* 56-64.
Simon Wamelile, interview, July 4th, 2007. Priest at Kamuge-Olinga Parish in Archdiocese of Tororo, Uganda.
Snyder, C. R. (2000). Hypothesis: There is hope. In C. R. Snyder (Eds.), *Handbook of Hope: Theory, Measures and Applications* (pp. 3-21). San Diego, CA: Academic Press.
Snyder, C. R., Irving, L., & Anderson, J. R. (1991). Hope and health: Measuring the will and the ways. In C. R. Snyder & D. R. Forsyth (Eds.) *Handbook of social and clinical psychology: The health perspective* (pp. 285-305). Elmsford, NY: Pergamon Press.

Veale, A., & Stavrou, A. (2007). Former Lord's Resistance Army child soldier abductees: Explorations of identity in reintegration and reconciliation. *Peace and Conflict: Journal of Peace Psychology, 13*(3), 273-292.

Vinck, P., Pham, P., Stover, E., Moss, A., & Wierda, M. (2007). *Research note on attitudes about peace and justice in northern Uganda.* Human Rights Center, University of California-Berkley, Payson Center for International Development, Tulane University, and International Center for Transitional Justice.

Watzlawick, P., Beavin, J. H., & Jackson, D. D. (1967). Some tentative axioms of communication. In *Pragmatics of human communication: A study of interactional patterns, pathologies, and paradoxes* (pp. 48-71). New York: W. W. Norton & Company.

Worden, S. (2008). The Justice Dilemma in Uganda. *USI Peace Briefing.* Washington, DC: United States Institute of Peace.

• CHAPTER TEN •

When All Seems Lost: Building Hope Through Communication After Natural Disasters

Andy J. Merolla
Baldwin Wallace University

Natural disasters greatly affect people's lives. They demolish people's sense of normalcy, interfere with their long-term goals, and, at their worst, take lives and destroy communities. The effects of disasters, moreover, can be felt across generations and take many years to recover from. Yet, even when all seems lost, humans appear to have a remarkable capacity for recovery and renewal (Joseph, 2011; Shalev & Errera, 2008). This chapter explores the complex ways that disasters affect people and the ways people respond to disaster-related trauma. Special focus is placed on the concept of hope and its role in disaster readiness and recovery. In particular, the chapter aims to show how hope is created through communication and contributes to coping and resilience. It is argued that hope mitigates the initial onslaught of stressors, shapes immediate and post-disaster goal pursuits, and promotes adaptive recollections of events in ways that support personal growth and strong communities. The chapter begins by reviewing existing literature on the commonness of disasters, as well as the effects of disasters on individuals, families, and communities.

Natural Disasters and Contemporary Life

As evidenced by the news reports we watch on TV or read about online, natural disasters are quite common. From "superstorms" and tsunamis to tornadoes and wildfires, disasters occur daily. According to the Centre for Research on Epidemiology of Disasters (CRED), between 2001 and 2011 there was an average of 384 disasters per year across the globe (Guha-Sapir, Vos, Below, & Ponserre, 2012). Millions of people are affected by these events. In 2011, for instance, over 200 million people, in 101 nations, were directly affected by disasters, with losses estimated to be over $300 billion (Guha-Sapir et al., 2012). In 2012, in the United States alone, there were 11 severe weather and climate events that resulted in losses of at least $1 billion (National Oceanic and Atmospheric Association, 2012).

Due to population increase, migration patterns, and climate change (among many other factors) disaster frequency and magnitude will likely increase over time. Understanding, let alone predicting, the effects of disasters, however, is complicated by many issues. Consider, for instance, the importance of geographic location. Whereas a May 2008 earthquake in China's Sichuan province, with a magnitude of 7.9, killed approximately 70,000 people and caused losses for millions more (New York Times, 2009), a May 2013 earthquake off Russia's eastern coastline, with an even larger magnitude of 8.2, took no lives and did little damage (Gutterman, 2013). In the United States, Alaska has the highest number of earthquakes each year, yet those earthquakes typically (though not always) affect relatively few people because they occur in unpopulated areas (U.S. Geological Survey, 2013). In California, however, the second highest earthquake-affected state, earthquake damage is much higher due to the denser population. Clearly, where people live matters (Bonanno, Brewin, Kaniasty, & La Greca, 2010), and when people migrate to areas, such as coastlines, fault lines, river banks, and mountainsides, their susceptibility to the effects of natural disasters rises (Berger, Kousky, & Zeckhauser, 2008). The consequences of geography are also intertwined with many other factors, especially economic ones. As Cavallo and Noy (2010) reported, the effects of disasters tend to be greater in poorer nations than in richer ones.

Before moving on, it is important to briefly define disasters and consider their different forms. The aforementioned CRED defines a disaster as any event that "overwhelms local capacity, necessitating a request to a national or international level for external assistance" (Guha-Sapir et al., 2012, p. 7). Natural disasters often have identifiable meteorological, hydrological, or geophysical causes. Technological disasters, in contrast, are considered human-generated, and include events such as industrial accidents, war, and terrorism (Shaw, Espinel, & Shultz, 2012). Despite the utility of categorizing disasters in this manner, many disaster events cannot be viewed as strictly natural or technological. The 2011 Tohoku earthquake and tsunami exemplify this, as they caused massive storm damage and flooding, as well as nuclear meltdowns at the Fukushima Daiichi nuclear power plant off Japan's eastern coast.

Similarly, the effects of disasters such as Hurricane Katrina, which struck the Gulf Coast of the United States in 2008, were exacerbated by human factors, such as city planning decisions (Aldrich, 2012). Thus, it is important to keep in mind that the effects and causes of disasters can be quite complex.

The Effects of Disasters on Individuals, Families, and Communities

Because disasters can result in injury and death, they can seriously disrupt short- and long-term family functioning. Recent large-scale disasters such as the Tohoku earthquake and tsunami caused more than 15,000 deaths (Nelson, 2013). The immensely destructive 2010 earthquake in Haiti caused many thousands of deaths and injuries, with conflicting reports putting the number of deaths anywhere from 46,000 to 316,000 (Wells, 2013). Hurricane Katrina took fewer lives than the earthquakes in Japan and Haiti, but left significant damage from which the Gulf Coast is still recovering.

These so-called "mega disasters" can result in staggering death tolls. But even in smaller-scale disasters, where fewer lives are taken, the impact on people's lives can be immense. Beyond the devastation caused by death and injury, people often experience economic losses, financial difficulties, and a range of psychological symptoms, such as post traumatic and acute stress disorders, relational strain, and poor sleep (Watson, 2008). One of the most significant causes of stress for families and communities following disasters is temporary and permanent geographic displacement (Bonanno et al., 2010; Wadworth, Santiago, & Einhorn, 2009). Further complicating recovery is that people often find themselves with limited resources to aid unanticipated transitions. Many people, for instance, have little or no insurance coverage on their losses; even among policy holders, though, misinformation, loopholes, and bureaucratic claim structures can impede recovery (Hollander, 2013).

Coping and Resilience in the Aftermath of Disasters

The negative psychological effects of traumatic events appear most acute in the weeks and months after a disaster. But how do disasters shape people's long-term coping and mental health? It might be surprising to learn that, over time, most people cope effectively with the effects of disasters. In fact, it appears that people are often more resilient to loss than they realize (Hobfoll, 2001). As Shalev and Errera (2008) put it, "good adaptation is the most frequent outcome of adversity" (p. 151). Stanley, Bulecza, and Gopalani (2012) similarly remarked that although "psychological disruption is viewed as normal in immediate aftermath of disaster…mental health wellness will return in time for most" (p. 96). Offering a general estimate of adaption levels, Bonanno et al. (2010) suggested that no more than 30% of people typically experience serious stress symptoms following disasters.

Given people's apparent hardiness and resilience following disasters, many researchers are working to document the specific ways in which people effectively adapt to, and perhaps even grow from, traumatic events (Ai, Cascio, Santangelo, & Evans-Campbell, 2005; Bonanno et al., 2010; Hobfoll, 2001; Vazquez, Cervellion, Perez-Sales, Vidales, & Gaborit, 2005). A critical takeaway point from this research is that people's experiences following disasters can range from temporary distress to chronic mental disorder (Stanley et al., 2012). Layne et al. (2009) captured the range of people's responses to traumatic events with their typology of "adjustment trajectories." The seven adjustment trajectories include positive and negative response patterns. Negative responses to trauma include the trajectories of *severe persisting distress* (i.e., persistent poor functioning), *decline* (i.e., initial stress resistance followed by a downward spiral), and *stable maladaptive functioning* (i.e., problematic pre- and posttraumatic functioning). These trajectories represent high levels of stress and detrimental coping responses. The remaining four trajectories represent more positive responses. These trajectories include *stress resistance* (i.e., stable and adaptive functioning before and after disasters), *protracted recovery* (i.e., a gradual return to normal functioning), *resilience* (i.e., temporary distress followed by full recovery), and *posttraumatic growth* (i.e., improvement and increased resilience after a disaster event).

The last trajectory mentioned—posttraumatic growth—is perhaps the most intriguing, if not controversial. Layne et al. (2009) stated that posttraumatic growth "occurs when a system is able to implement effective adjustment processes that not only restore homeostatic balance...but also increase its level of functioning and associated capacities to levels that are higher than those found prior to trauma exposure" (p. 34). This suggests that disasters can serve as turning points in people's lives that put into perspective the significance of their personal relationships, the ordering of their life priorities, their potential for personal achievement, and their sense of inner strength (Honeycutt & Mapp, 2012; Shalev & Errera, 2008; Tedeschi & Calhoun, 2004). Tedeschi and Calhoun (2004) described this phenomenon as the "transformative power of suffering" (p. 2). Joseph (2011) related posttraumatic growth to a shattered vase. When a vase falls from a table and shatters, it cannot be put back together. Yet beauty and purpose can be restored, not by restoring the shattered pieces to their initial form, but by transforming them into a mosaic. Trauma survivors, like the shattered vase, seem to possess this same capacity for positive transformation.

Disasters and Hope

Another way to consider the effects of disasters is through the prism of hope. Natural disasters can be hope-depleting events: they interfere with people's goals and aspirations, tax their resources, impede their ability to plan for the future, and upset any semblance of normalcy. Although most people have a general sense of what hope is, moving beyond a "general sense" is a bit of a challenge (Folkman, 2010). Fortunately, a rather robust literature on hope exists, the origins of which date back several centuries. Early thinking on hope comes from religious texts and from Greek mythology (Eliott, 2005). Secular and scientific perspectives on hope are more recent, appearing in medicine and the social sciences by the middle of the 20th century (Jacoby, 2003). Social scientific, medical, and evolutionary perspectives converged in a conception of hope as an individual quality that could be cultivated within social systems (Eliott, 2005). Hope was viewed as a strength that helped people manage extraordinarily difficult circumstances in their lives, such as illness and war-related trauma (Eliott, 2005; Jacoby, 2003).

Among the many social scientific perspectives on hope, one of the most impactful and heuristic was developed by the psychologist C. R. Snyder and his colleagues (Snyder, 2000a, 2002). At the core of Snyder's perspective is the belief that hope is a goal-based, cognitive, and motivational construct. Hope involves how people conceptualize, pursue, and feel about the short- and long-term goals that are important to them. This goal-centric perspective grew out of Snyder's own research on excuse making (see Snyder, 2002), as well as earlier goal-based perspectives on hope (e.g., Menninger, 1959; Stotland, 1969).

There are three critical constructs in hope theory: goals, pathways, and agency. Goals are the "cognitive targets" of hope (Snyder, Thompson, Shorey, & Heinze, 2003, p. 58). Pathways are the mental routes people create to achieve their goals. Agency—functioning as the motivational component of the theory—represents the desire and efficacy people have to pursue the mental routes they conjure up in pathways thinking. Snyder et al. (2003) noted that each construct poses a separate but related question: goals pertain to the question *what do I want?*, pathways pertain to the question *how will I get there?*, and agency pertains to the question *how will I get motivated?*

When people possess high levels of hope, hope theory asserts that they have well-articulated routes to achieve what they want, and high motivation to persevere or re-route their goal pursuits when obstacles arise. People with low hope levels have few pathways toward their goals, along with limited agency to overcome goal blockages. Emotions also play a role in hopefulness, such that successful goal pursuits produce positive emotion, whereas unsuccessful goal pursuits produce negative emotion (Snyder, 2002). Over time, people develop cognitive and emotional sets that influence how they view their abilities and their willingness to pursue "stretch goals" that push them beyond their perceived limits (Snyder, 2002, p. 53). As will be discussed, these factors might take on heightened importance following disaster events. Although hope is conceived as disposition, it can also fluctuate over time and vary across contexts (e.g., work, school, and relationships; Snyder, 2002) as people experiences successes and setbacks in the various spheres of their life.

Snyder and colleagues' "elaborated hope model" visually depicts hope's development and its influence on behavior (see Snyder, 2002). Hope theorists believe that dispositional hope begins to form in infancy as babies experience a sense of self and learn to identify things they want (Shorey, Snyder, Yang, & Lewin, 2003). The hope model captures the early stages of hope development (i.e., "learning histories"), the creation of pathways and agency thoughts (i.e., "prevent sequences"), and the specific points of goal attainment/non-attainment (i.e., "event sequences"). The model also includes a series of feedback loops suggesting that positive and negative thoughts and emotions consistently shape and reshape individuals' previously-developed cognitive and emotional sets.

Research shows that hope is a positive force in people's lives. Scores on the Trait Hope Scale have predicted—above and beyond a host of covariates—such outcomes as grade point average and graduation rate among college students (Snyder, Shorey, Cheavens, Pulvers, Adams, & Wiklund, 2002), job performance among executives (Peterson & Byron, 2008), and positive behavioral functioning following trauma in children (Barnum, Snyder, Rapoff, Mani, & Thompson, 1998). Especially germane to this chapter, state and trait measures of hope have been found to be positively correlated to mental health and perceived coping following Hurricane Katrina (Hackbarth, Pavkov, Wetchler, & Flannery, 2012), and the September 11 terrorist attacks (Ai et al., 2005).

The Effects on Disasters on Hope and Hope's Consequences for Disaster Responses

To further integrate hope theory into the study of disaster response and recovery, it is helpful to utilize Snyder's (2002) elaborated hope model. The model includes a component called "surprise events," which are events that knock people off course in the pursuit of goals, primarily by dampening agency thinking. Disasters are quintessential surprise events, even for people residing in disaster-prone regions, because disasters often unexpectedly disrupt people's goal pursuits at varying levels of severity (Boss, 2002). As noted earlier, hope theory asserts that high- and low-hope persons differ in how they respond to barriers that might block their goal pursuits. In general, high hope individuals respond more efficaciously to setbacks that block their goals. Hope should therefore help people respond to crises in ways that help them more quickly regroup and marshal resources in productive ways.

Depending on how devastating the effects of a disaster are, people's goals may need to be quite small at first. Walsh (2007) reflected on this point, quoting a man recovering from the effects of a tornado that destroyed his family's home and business: "At first we were in a state of shock and disoriented, at a total loss about what to do. Then we dusted ourselves off, took stock of our predicament, and took charge to clear out the debris and figure out our options. We just kept hugging each other and taking it step by step" (p. 211). This man's experience demonstrates the reestablishment of obtainable goals via pathways thinking. The positive emotional and motivational feedback that resulted from the family's achievement of small goals likely supported their pursuit of larger goals. Walsh (2007) referred to this process as "mastering the possible." Taylor, Feldman, Saunders, and Ilardi (2000) described a similar phenomenon when discussing a therapeutic approach for helping clients develop workable goal hierarchies. What hope offers people facing trauma and tragedy, in sum, is belief that the future can get better (even if only slowly) through incremental steps.

Messages of Hope

If hopefulness is an asset *following* natural disasters, it is important to promote hope within our communities *before* disasters transpire. Hope, functioning as a "social commerce," must be cultivated before disasters occur to create resilient communities that are prepared to manage traumatic events (Snyder, Cheavens, & Sympson, 1997). Hope can be developed through communication occurring within and between families, communities, and local and national governments (Snyder & Feldman, 2000). To date, though, most research on hope has focused on psychological processes (Snyder, 2002). Scholars working from a communication perspective can contribute to this area by focusing on the communication processes that create and sustain hopefulness (Merolla, in press).

But what does it mean to work from a communication perspective? In the context of social and personal relationships, an especially informative description of a communication perspective was offered by Sillars and Vangelisti (2006). The authors argued that there are least five principles that constitute a communication perspective in the study of relationships: interdependence, reflexivity, complexity, ambiguity, and indeterminancy.

Based on Sillars and Vangelisti's (2006) principles, a communication perspective on hope suggests that (a) hope is constructed in interaction patterns between people, over time (*interdependence*); (b) a high- or low-hope view of the future is partly shaped through routine communication, joint interaction, and storytelling occurring in relational systems, such as families and social organizations (*reflexivity*); (c) hopefulness is personally expressed through, and propagated in others, via diverse verbal and nonverbal codes and cues (*complexity*); (d) past, current, and planned behavior can be interpreted in various ways based on people's unique experiences, suggesting hopefulness can contribute to the ways in which people understand and explain day-to-day events (*ambiguity*); and (e) communication borne (in part) out of hope, or intended to enhance hope in others, will have expected and unexpected consequences based on myriad factors at individual (e.g., personality), relational (e.g., family history), and societal (e.g., culture) levels (*indeterminancy*). To summarize, the communication researcher should study hope by focusing on verbal and nonverbal interaction that supports, and is shaped by, a hopeful mindset. To put these ideas in a single statement, akin to a working hypothesis, it is proposed that hope is created, maintained, enhanced, and dashed across the lifespan in the moment-by-moment interactions and cyclical communication patterns in which people engage.

The Benefits of Hope and Hopeful Communication Surrounding Disaster Events

Hope potentially contributes to coping and resilience in regards to natural disasters in three ways. First, it compensates for or generally mitigates the onslaught of future stressors. Second, it shapes immediate and long-term post-disaster goal pursuits. And, third, it promotes adaptive recollections of past traumatic experiences. Each of these ideas is explored in turn.

Hope Mitigates the Onslaught of Stressors

Recovery from disasters depends in part on how well people are prepared for them. Preparation includes various factors, such as the quality of cities' infrastructure, municipalities' emergency response abilities, citizens' insurance coverage, as well as individuals' psychological preparedness to manage trauma (e.g., based on previous traumatic experiences). People living in tornado-prone areas, for instance, can be more or less prepared by having appropriate underground shelter available. Such shelters must be accessible in homes, community buildings, and schools. Beyond issues such as infrastructure and physical readiness, preparation for disasters involves families' unique instrumental and social resources (Hobfoll, 2001; Hobfoll, Horsey, & Lamoureux, 2009). This suggests that recovery necessitates not only effective first response teams, disaster-proof building designs, and effective warning systems, but also the development of people's social skills and coping abilities. People's well-being prior to the experience of difficult life events indeed shapes how they respond to those events (Joseph, 2011). Thus, long before disasters strike, it is necessary to build up people's pathways and agency thinking (and related communication skills) across life domains. As noted earlier, Snyder's (2002) hope model indicates that the development of positive pathways and agency thinking begins early in life, suggesting disaster preparedness is a long-term and multi-faceted issue.

If we conceptualize hope—and related "dispositional attributes," such as optimism and self-efficacy—as a valuable pre-trauma resource (Berger & Weiss, 2009, p. 66), it would seem that increased hope can protect against or compensate for the impact of the stressors that inevitably result from disasters. As Hobfoll (2001) stated, "those who have built a stronger armamentarium of personal, social, economic, and other sustaining resources will be more well suited to adapt to severe and traumatic stress" (p. 354). Models of resilience suggest hope could operate in various ways following disaster events. Hope could be conceptualized, for instance, as a buffer, compensatory, or inoculator variable (see Zimmerman & Brenner, 2010). These differing conceptualizations demonstrate some of the ways that researchers across the social sciences can further integrate hope into research on disasters and resilience.

The communication that supports hopefulness occurs in families, schools, and communities. Teacher-student interaction, in particular, is crucial, because it is in this context that students learn life skills, learn about discipline, and receive social support (Henderson, 2012). Hope, furthermore, is not just an individual strength. It is also a community one. Hopefulness is linked to empathy and the willingness to engage in pro-social activities in one's community. Snyder and Feldman (2000) argued that the creation and support of hope requires collective and comprehensive action in multiple communication contexts. This includes making our families, schools, and communities less violent; modeling helping behaviors for children; creating workplaces that empower employees and support their self-worth; and supporting strong local governments with policies and programs that enable people to pursue and achieve their personal, familial, and group goals. Wilson and Gettings (2012), in their work on preventing child abuse, called for *asset-building models*, which similar to the ideas presented in this chapter, "recognize the importance of reducing risk factors associated with a host of social problems," while also acknowledging that focusing on risk alone "is insufficient and tends to lead to fragmented community responses" (p. 283). Building social assets, alongside physical and municipal ones, then, can strengthen communities and potentially improve responses to stressful events. And the benefits of social asset development could be experienced intergenerationally, because learning to "think hopefully," noted Snyder and colleagues, promotes gratitude and a desire to pass on life lessons to others (Shorey, Snyder, Rand, Hockemeyer, & Feldman, 2002).

The communication occurring within community relationships is especially critical for shaping the nature of disaster response. According to Bonnano et al. (2010), "it is well documented that disaster survivors chiefly depend on, and are taken care of by, their families, relatives, friends, and neighbors" (p. 25). It is neighbors and community members, in fact, who are often the first responders when disasters occur (Aldrich, 2012). Thus, building trust in communities can be considered an essential form of disaster preparation. Friends and community members, for example, have important information about people in communities who are especially vulnerable, and this knowledge can be used to save lives during recovery efforts. Aldrich (2012) convincingly demonstrates through multiple studies of disasters that social capital is amongst the most important variables predicting disaster recovery. Analyzing the 1995 Kobe earthquake, Aldrich reported that "social capital—more than economic conditions, earthquake damage, population density, inequality, or geography—proved essential over the long term" in explaining recovery (p. 87). Across all the disasters he studied, Aldrich concluded that strong relationships between individual community members, networks across communities, and community members and their political leaders enable more efficient evacuation efforts. These relationships also predict the extent to which people move back and rebuild in disaster-affected locations (Aldrich, 2012).

The social capital that Aldrich (2012) calls for, moreover, arises from the same interpersonal and intergroup communication practices that foster hope. These practices include the neighborly small talk and information sharing that occurs on front porches, in parks, and in community centers. When people decide to rebuild in a community because of the powerful connection they have to it—something Snyder and Feldman (2000) call "anchoring"—we might conceptualize that decision as one of rooted in hope and shared goals for the future (for themselves, their families, and their community). Given the importance of social capital and hope in creating resilience and facilitating coping following disasters, we would be well advised to do all we can in our local communities to formally and informally support connections between citizens. By creating spaces that encourage communication between community members, we can build the trust, social capital, and hope that supports resilience and coping when disaster strikes (Aldrich, 2012; Snyder & Feldman, 2000).

With greater hope, people might be more likely to engage in effective emotional and problem-focused coping (Folkman, 2010). With greater trust, community members might be more willing to heed official warnings in a timely fashion, take part in disaster preparedness training, and donate to recovery efforts (Henstra, 2010; Seo, Sun, Merolla, & Zhang, 2012). And with denser and more actively engaged social networks, preparation and evacuation information can be spread quickly and efficiently, potentially saving lives and expediting recovery (Aldrich, 2012).

Hope Shapes Immediate and Long-Term Post-Disaster Goal Pursuits

One of the most significant forms of communication related to hopefulness is social support (Snyder, 2002). Likewise, supportive communication is among the most vital functions of close relationships for promoting coping and resilience following trauma (Bonnano et al., 2010; Tedeschi & Calhoun, 2004; Walsh, 2007). A rich literature exists on social support involving scholars from across the social sciences. Goldsmith's (2004) communication-centered approach to social support focuses on how people "co-construct" stressors as manageable. When stressful events occur in life, it is beneficial to share our frustrations and uncertainties with confidants, such as spouses, best friends, and co-workers. This form of interaction is known as *troubles talk*. Through troubles talk, people can share their stressors in a way that enables exploration of their goals. They can lament their fears while also fortifying their perseverance to manage stressors (Goldsmith, 2004). Further, by talking about the things that cause distress, people can feel a greater sense of control, which can foster active and constructive coping responses (Stanley et al., 2012). Using a hope theory framework, one could argue that support leads to positive outcomes when it offers useful guidance on how to reestablish one's goals, reconstruct goal pathways, and bolster agency thinking.

Related to troubles talk is a form of communication known as *communal coping* (Afifi, Hutchinson, & Krouse, 2006). Communal coping transpires when groups of people view the problems they are facing as the responsibility of the entire group, rather than the responsibility of individuals (Afifi et al., 2006). Communal coping seems especially important in communities that lack access to resources. Through communal coping, groups of individuals, and perhaps entire communities, work together in ways that enable them to conceptualize problems as "co-owned" and manageable. When individuals are facing significant hardships, they can gain a sense of hope for the future when they feel like they are not alone—that people are available to help them negotiate the new realities they face following a traumatic event. Afifi, Felix, and Afifi (2010) cast light on some of these issues in their study of communal coping among victims of a series of wild fires in Santa Barbara, California. They found that, among evacuees, perceived communal coping moderated the effects of uncertainty on mental health. The authors stated that the benefits of communal coping might be included in public service announcements. "Integrating effective communal coping strategies into disaster prevention and recovery programs," said the authors, "could further improve the health of individuals, families and larger communities" (p. 343).

In addition to supportive communication, several other forms of communication are essential for promoting hope and coping. This interaction transpires between parents and children (Lazarus, Jimerson, & Brock, 2002; Shaw et al., 2012); first responders, volunteers, and psychological first-aid practitioners (Greenstone & Leviton, 2011; Kantor & Beckert, 2011); teachers, school administrators, and students (Jaycox, Morse, Tanielian, & Stein, 2006); disaster relief organizations and donors (Fessler, 2013); users of social media (e.g., Ushahidi; Shirky, 2010); and local governments and citizens (Henstra, 2010; Kusumasari, Alam, & Siddiqui, 2010). Though discussion of these important forms of interaction is beyond the scope of this chapter, they represent key forms of communication that contribute to disaster recovery (and perhaps hope).

Hope Promotes Adaptive Recollections of Traumatic Events

In 1995, following the Oklahoma City bombing, observers throughout the United States were impressed and heartened by the way that Oklahomans came together to help one another. The phrase "Oklahoma Standard" was used to describe this sentiment. The Oklahoma Standard phrase has continued to be used, and was widely referenced by citizens and government officials (including President Barack Obama) in the days after a series of tornadoes affected Oklahoma in the spring of 2013. President Obama, speaking on May 26, 2013 to a crowd in Moore, said, "people here pride themselves on the 'Oklahoma Standard'—what Governor Fallin has called, 'Being able to work through disasters like this, and [to] come out stronger on the other side' And that's what we've been seeing this week" (Mechaber, 2013).

The Oklahoma Standard phrase—as well as similar phrases such as "New Jersey Strong" and "Colorado Tough" that were used following recent disasters in those states (Siegler, 2013)—is symbolic of a sense-making process that occurs after traumatic events. In this process, people recast disasters, through phrases and narratives, as events that reaffirm their values and support resiliency to future setbacks. Beyond any "healing influence" such narratives have for people, Hobfoll (2001) argued that they fulfill a basic human need (p. 344). Hobfoll suggested that the "codification of trauma events into the social history of the tribe has important survival value for the group" (p. 344).

Narrativizing and symbolizing strength and resilience (i.e., in the context of loss) might also be viewed as the discursive construction of hope, optimism, and transformation within individuals and communities. At the community level, we can learn from disasters in ways that reduce susceptibility to future disasters. We can build better buildings, create better warning systems, and develop better response systems. Individuals and families can also learn from disaster experiences in ways that promote hope. Families can collectively create meaning by highlighting the positive aspects of overcoming tragedy (Berger & Weiss, 2009). In the field of communication, this is known as *adaptive joint storytelling* (Trees & Koening Kellas, 2009). Through adaptive joint storytelling and *experience swapping* people can reframe past hardships as indicative of strength (Goldsmith, 2004). Older generations can impart life lessons to younger generations about the possibilities and imperatives of overcoming adversity, thus offering perspective on negotiating dialectical tensions between loss and gain, despair and hope, and harm and resilience. The passed-down, hard-earned wisdom of people who have experienced devastating disasters perhaps contributes to positive change and coping methods that can be tapped in times of struggle.

Denham's (2008) ethnographic research with an American Indian family in Idaho showed how trauma stories about past hardships and repression support the continuity of family culture, provide a means of interpreting current struggles, and ultimately foster hope and resilience. Although such narratives often begin at the dyadic or family level, they can eventually shape society (Tedeschi & Calhoun, 2004). According to Tedeschi and Calhoun, disasters prompt us to ask "who 'we' are in the aftermath of the events, what principles should guide the society, and what meaning the trauma has for the society" (p. 14). Such interaction can be termed *renewal discourse*, which is a future-oriented, hopeful communication that celebrates and memorializes a community's values and wherewithal to overcome tragedy (Veil, Sellnow, & Heald, 2011). Trauma stories, as well as physical spaces, such as memorial sites, commemorate perseverance, honor victims, and celebrate the efforts of first responders in ways that call for a hopeful, peaceful future (Veil et al., 2011). The ways in which we narrativize and memorialize hope following large-scale tragedies also occurs on a much smaller scale within our day-to-day discourse. Marriage and family scholars use the phrase "glorifying the struggle" to describe how relational partners take pride in overcoming difficult periods in their past (Buehlman, Gottman, & Katz, 1992). Glorification of past struggle, whether through public memorials or private conversations, can strengthen people's resolve and promote hope.

There are, of course, many other critical elements of post-disaster communication that contribute to our understanding of resilience and recovery. This includes, for instance, the ethical treatment of victims and survivors (Wadsworth et al., 2009) and the evolving standards for media coverage of disasters (Perkins & Izard, 2010). Examining these types of issues is important because as people reflect on past traumatic events, they can gain new perspective that enables them to better address the challenges that come with future disasters.

Conclusions

This chapter provided an overview of the prevalence, effects, and responses to natural disasters. Based on hope theory (Snyder, 2002), disasters were conceptualized as surprise events that deplete hope by interfering with people's pathways toward important goals in their life. Despite the extreme physical devastation and psychological trauma that disasters cause, most people show rather amazing resolve and resilience (Bonnano et al., 2010). This chapter suggests that dyadic and intergroup communication processes reflect and contribute to the ways in which people effectively cope with, and potentially thrive following, disaster-related loss.

Because hope seems to be a valuable resource for managing disasters, it makes sense that we should cultivate it—as a social commerce (Snyder et al., 1997)—long before disasters strike. This follows Snyder's (2000b) logic that the hope we develop in the good times helps us through the bad times. Or, as Snyder more elegantly stated, "By learning to hope, today's generation is equipped to grapple with tomorrow's adventures" (p. 25).

References

Afifi, T. D., Hutchinson, S., & Krouse, S. (2006). Toward a theoretical model of communal coping in post-divorce families and other naturally occurring groups. *Communication Theory, 16,* 378–409.

Afifi, W. A., Felix, E. D., & Afifi, T. D. (2012). The impact of uncertainty and communal coping on mental health following natural disasters. *Anxiety, Stress, & Coping: An International Journal, 25,* 329-347.

Ai, A. L., Cascio, T., Santangelo, L. K., & Evans-Campbell, T. (2005). Hope, meaning, and growth following the September 11, 2001, terrorist attacks. *Journal of Interpersonal Violence, 20,* 523-548.

Aldrich, D. P. (2012). *Building resilience: Social capital in post-disaster recovery.* Chicago, IL: University of Chicago Press.

Barnum, D. D., Snyder, C. R., Rapoff, M. A., Mani, M. M., & Thompson, R. (1998). Hope and social support in the psychological adjustment of children who have survived burn injuries and their matched controls. *Children's Health Care, 27,* 15-30.

Berger, A., Kousky, C., & Zeckhauser, R. (2008). Obstacles to clear thinking about natural disasters: Five lessons for policy. In J. M. Quigley & L. A. Rosenthal (Eds.), *Risking house and home: Disasters, cities, public policy* (pp. 73-94). Berkeley, CA: Berkeley Public Policy Press.

Berger, R., & Weiss, T. (2009). The posttraumatic growth model: An expansion to the family system. *Traumatology, 15,* 63-74.

Bonanno, G. A., Brewin, C. R., Kaniasty, K., & La Greca, A. M. (2010). Weighing the costs of disaster: Consequences, risks, and resilience in individuals, families, and communities. *Psychological Science in the Public Interest, 11,* 1-49.

Boss, P. (2002). *Family stress management: A contextual approach* (2nd ed.). Thousand Oaks, CA: Sage.

Buehlman, K. T., Gottman, J. M., & Katz, L. F. (1992). How a couple views their past predicts their future: Predicting divorce from an oral history interview. *Journal of Family Psychology, 5,* 295-318.

Cavallo, E., & Noy, I. (2010). *The economics of natural disasters: A survey.* (IDB Working Paper Series No.IDB-WP-124). Retrieved from Inter-American Development Bank website: http://www8.iadb.org/res/publications/pubfiles/pubIDB-WP-124.pdf

Denham, A. R. (2008). Rethinking historical trauma: Narratives of resilience. *Transcultural Psychiatry, 45,* 391-414.

Eliott, J. (2005). What have we done with hope?: A brief history. In J. Eliott (Ed.), *Interdisciplinary perspectives on hope* (pp. 3-45). New York: Nova Science.

Fessler, P. (2013, January 12). The 'second disaster': Making well-intentioned donations useful. *NPR.* Retrieved from http://www.npr.org

Folkman, S. (2010). Stress, coping, and hope. *Psycho-Oncology, 19,* 901-908.

Goldsmith, D. J. (2004). *Communicating social support.* Cambridge, UK: Cambridge University Press.

Greenstone, J. L., & Leviton, S. C. (2011). *Elements of crisis intervention: Crises and how to respond to them.* Belmont, CA: Brooks/Cole.

Guha-Sapir, D., Vos, F., Below, R., & Ponserre, S. (2012). *Annual disaster statistical review 2011: The numbers and trends.* Brussels: Centre for Research on Epidemiology of Disasters.

Gutterman, S. (2013). Magnitude 8.2 earthquake strikes Russian Far East. *Reuters.* Retrieved from http://www.reuters.com

Hackbarth, M., Pavkov, T., Wetchler, J., & Flannery, M. (2012). Natural disasters: An assessment of family resiliency following Hurricane Katrina. *Journal of Marital and Family Therapy, 38,* 340-351.

Henderson, N. (2012). Resilience in schools and curriculum design. In M. Ungar (Ed.), *The social ecology of resilience: A handbook of theory and practice* (pp. 297-306). New York: Springer.

Henstra, D. (2010). Evaluating local government emergency management programs: What framework should public managers adopt? *Public Administration Review, 70,* 236-246.

Hobfoll, S. E. (2001). The influence of culture, community, and the nested-self in the stress process: Advancing conservation of resources theory. *Applied Psychology: An International Review, 50,* 337-421.

Hobfoll, S. E., Horsey, K. J., & Lamoureux, B. E. (2009). Resiliency and resource loss in times of terrorism and disaster: Lessons learned for children and families and those left untaught. In D. Brom, R. Pat-Horenczyk, & J. D. Ford (Eds), *Treating traumatized children: Risk, resilience, and recovery* (pp. 150-163). London, UK: Routledge.

Hollander, S. (2013, March 4). Sandy stirs legal mess: Residents struggle with bureaucracy. *Wall Street Journal.* Retrieved from http://online.wsj.com

Honeycutt, J. M., & Mapp, C. M. (2012). Family communication surrounding emotional trauma: The aftermath of hurricanes. In F. C. Dickson & L. M. Webb (Eds.), *Communication for families in crisis: Theories, research, strategies* (pp. 361-379). New York: Peter Lang.

Jacoby, R. (2003). Between stress and hope: A historical perspective. In R. Jacoby & G. Keinan (Eds.), *Between stress and hope: From a disease-centered to a health-centered perspective* (pp. 3-26). Westport, CT: Praeger.

Jaycox, L. H., Morse, L. K., Tanielian, T., & Stein, B. D. (2006). *How schools can help students recover from traumatic experiences: A toolkit for supporting long-term recovery.* Santa Monica, CA: Rand Corporation.

Joseph, S. (2011). *What doesn't kill us: The new psychology of posttraumatic growth.* New York: Basic.

Kantor, E. M., & Beckert, D. R. (2011). Preparation and systems issues: Integrating into a disaster response. In F. J. Stoddard, Jr., A. Pandya, & C. L. Katz (Eds.), *Disaster psychiatry: Readiness, evaluation, and treatment* (pp. 3-17). Arlington, VA: American Psychiatric Publishing.

Kusumasari, B., Alam, Q., & Siddiqui, K. (2010). Resource capability for local government in managing disaster. *Disaster Prevention and Management, 19,* 438-451.

Layne, C. M., Beck, C. J., Rimmasch, H., Southwick, J. S., Moreno, M. A., & Hobfoll, S. E. (2009). Promoting "resilient" posttraumatic adjustment in childhood and beyond: "Unpacking" life events, adjustment trajectories, resources, and interventions. In D. Brom, R. Pat-Horenczyk, & J. D. Ford (Eds.), *Treating traumatized children: Risk, resilience, and recovery* (pp. 13-47). London, UK: Routledge.

Lazarus, P. J., Jimerson, S. R., & Brock, S. E. (2002). *Helping children after a natural disaster: Information for parents and teachers.* National Association of School Psychologists. Retrieved from National Association of School Psychologists website: http://www.nasponline.org/resources/crisis_safety/naturaldisaster_ho.pdf

Mechaber, E. (2013, May 26). *President Obama Tours Tornado Damage in Moore, Oklahoma: "We've Got Your Back."* Retrieved from The White House Blog: http://www.whitehouse.gov/blog/2013/05/26/president-obama-tours-tornado-damage-moore-oklahoma-weve-got-your-back

Menninger, K. (1959). Hope. *American Journal of Psychiatry, 116*, 481-491.

Merolla, A. J. (in press). The role of hope in conflict management and relational maintenance. *Personal Relationships.*

National Oceanic and Atmospheric Association (2012, December 20). *Preliminary info on 2012 U.S. billion-dollar extreme weather/climate events.* Retrieved from NOAA website: http://www.ncdc.noaa.gov/news/preliminary-info-2012-us-billion-dollar-extreme-weather-climate-events

Nelson, S. (2013, March 11). Japan marks two-year anniversary of earthquake, Fukushima nuclear disaster. *U.S. News & World Report.* Retrieved from http://www.usnews.com

New York Times. (2009, May 6). Sichuan earthquake. Retrieved from http://www.nytimes.com

Perkins, J., & Izard, R. (2010). In the wake of disaster: Lessons learned. In R. Izard & J. Perkins (Eds.), *Covering disaster: Lessons from media coverage of Katrina and Rita* (pp. 1-18). New Brunswick, NJ: Transaction.

Peterson, S. J., & Byron, K. (2008). Exploring the role of hope in job performance: Results from four studies. *Journal of Organizational Behavior, 29*, 785-803.

Seo, M., Sun, S., Merolla, A. J., & Zhang, S. (2012). Willingness to help following the Sichuan earthquake: Modeling the effects of media involvement, stress, trust and relational resources. *Communication Research, 39*, 3-25.

Shalev, A. Y. & Errera, Y. L. E. (2008). Resilience is the default: How not to miss it. In M. Blumenfield & R. J. Ursano (Eds.), *Intervention and resilience after mass trauma* (pp. 149-172). Cambridge, UK: Cambridge University Press.

Shaw, J. A., Espinel, Z., & Shultz, J. M. (2012). *Care for children exposed to the traumatic effects of disaster.* Washington, DC: American Psychiatric Publishing.

Shirky, C. (2011). *Cognitive surplus: How technology makes consumers into collaborators.* New York: Penguin.

Shorey, H. S., Snyder, C. R., Rand, K. L., Hockemeyer, J. R., & Feldman, D. B. (2002). Somewhere over the rainbow: Hope theory weathers its first decade. *Psychological Inquiry, 13*, 322-331.

Shorey, H. S., Snyder, C. R., Yang, X., & Lewin, M. R. (2003). The role of hope as a mediator in recollected parenting, adult attachment, and mental health. *Journal of Social and Clinical Psychology, 22*, 685-715.

Siegler, K. (2013, September 15). *Colorado flooding forces thousands from homes.* NPR. Retrieved from http://www.npr.org

Sillars, A. L., & Vangelisti, A. L. (2006). Communication: Basic properties and their relevance to relationships research. In A. L. Vangelisti & D. Perlman (Eds.), *The Cambridge handbook of personal relationships* (pp. 331-351). Cambridge, UK: Cambridge University Press.

Snyder, C. R. (2000a). Hypothesis: There is hope. In C. R. Snyder (Ed.), *Handbook of hope: Theory, measures, and applications* (pp. 3-21). San Diego, CA: Academic.

Snyder, C. R. (2000b). Genesis: The birth and growth of hope. In C. R. Snyder (Ed.), *Handbook of hope: Theory, measures, and applications* (pp. 25-38). San Diego, CA: Academic.

Snyder, C. R. (2002). Hope theory: Rainbows in the mind. *Psychological Inquiry, 13*, 249-275.

Snyder, C. R., Cheavens, J. S., & Sympson, S. C. (1997). Hope: An individual motive for social commerce. *Group Dynamics: Theory, Research, and Practice, 1*, 107-118.

Snyder, C. R., & Feldman, D. B. (2000). Hope for the many: An empowering social agenda. In C. R. Snyder (Ed.), *Handbook of hope: Theory, measures, and applications* (pp. 389-412). San Diego, CA: Academic.

Snyder, C. R., Shorey, H. S., Cheavens, J., Pulvers, K. M., Adams, V. H., III, & Wiklund, C. (2002). Hope and academic success in college. *Journal of Educational Psychology, 94*, 820-826.

Snyder, C. R., Thompson, L. Y., Shorey, H. S., & Heinze, L. (2003). The hopeful ones: A psychological inquiry into the positive mind and heart. In R. Jacoby & G. Keinan (Eds.), *Between stress and hope: From a disease-centered to a health-centered perspective* (pp. 57-79). Westport, CT: Praeger.

Stanley, S. A. R., Bulecza, S., & Gopalani, S. V. (2012). Psychological impact of disasters on communities. *Annual Review of Nursing Research, 30*, 89-123.

Stotland, E. (1969). *The psychology of hope.* San Francisco, CA: Jossey-Bass.

Taylor, J. D., Feldman, D. B., Saunders, R. S., & Ilardi, S. S. (2000). Hope theory and cognitive-behavioral therapies. In C. R. Snyder (Ed.), *Handbook of hope: Theory, measures, and applications* (pp. 109-122). San Diego, CA: Academic.

Tedeschi, R. G., & Calhoun, L. G. (2004). Posttraumatic growth: Conceptual foundations and empirical evidence. *Psychological Inquiry, 15*, 1-18.

Trees, A. R., & Koenig Kellas, J. (2009). Telling tales: Enacting family relationships in joint storytelling about difficult family experiences. *Western Journal of Communication, 73*, 91-111.

U.S. Geological Survey. (2013). *Earthquake facts and earthquake fantasy.* Retrieved from U.S. Geological Survey website: http://earthquake.usgs.gov/learn/topics/megaqk_facts_fantasy.php

Vasquez, C., Cervellion, P., Perez-Sales, P., Vidales, D., & Gabronit, M. (2005). Positive emotions in earthquake survivors in El Salvador (2001). *Journal of Anxiety Disorders, 19*, 313-328.

Veil, S., R., Sellnow, T. L., & Heald, M. (2011). Memorializing crisis: The Oklahoma City National Memorial as renewal discourse. *Journal of Applied Communication Research, 39*, 164-183.

Wadsworth, M. E., Santiago, C. D., & Einhorn, L. (2009). Coping with displacement from Hurricane Katrina: Predictors of one-year post-traumatic stress and depression symptom trajectories. *Anxiety, Stress, & Coping, 22*, 413-432.

Walsh, F. (2007). Traumatic loss and major disasters: Strengthening family and community resilience. *Family Process, 46*, 207-227.

Watson, P. J. (2008). Psychological first aid. In M. Blumenfield & R. J. Ursano (Eds.), *Intervention and resilience after mass trauma* (pp. 85-106). Cambridge, UK: Cambridge University Press.

Wells, J. (2013, March 11). Researchers dispute Haitian government's death toll from 2010 earthquake. *Toronto Star.* Retrieved from http://www.thestar.com

Wilson, S. R., & Gettings, P. E. (2012). Nurturing children as assets: A positive approach to preventing child maltreatment and promoting healthy youth development. In T. J. Socha & M. J. Pitts (Eds.), *The positive side of interpersonal communication* (pp. 277-295). New York: Peter Lang.

Zimmerman, M. A., & Brenner, A. B. (2010). Resilience in adolescence: Overcoming neighborhood disadvantage. In J. W. Reich, A. J. Zautra, & J. S. Hall (Eds.), *Handbook of adult resilience* (pp. 283-308). New York: Guilford.

• CHAPTER ELEVEN •

The State of Cancer Care Communication Across the Lifespan: The Role of Resilience, Hope, and Decision-making

Lisa Sparks
Chapman University and University of California, Irvine

Veronica Hefner
Amy H. Rogeness
Chapman University

The focus of this chapter is to explore the important roles resilience and hope play in family decision-making in cancer communication contexts. We do this by integrating scholarship from the lifespan communication literature. It is vitally important to unpack the subtle complexities, nuances, and difficulties of health messages that communicate resilience and hope in cancer contexts versus messages that miss the mark in communicating health messages about disease conditions across the lifespan. In order to provide the best care for cancer patients across the lifespan from childhood to adolescence, to early adulthood, middle age, and later life, providers must pay attention to the unique and difficult barriers patients face at different ages and how these barriers can get in the way of patient preferences for and ability to process messages, which could potentially influence decision-making and health outcomes (Sparks, 2008).

Cancer is increasing dramatically as the leading cause of childhood death in the United States (http://abcnews.go.com/Health/conquering-childhood-cancer/story?id=20348929). Recent estimates indicate that nearly 9 million Americans have a history of cancer (http://dccps.nci.nih.gov/ocs/) with cancer remaining second to heart disease as the leading cause of death in the

United States (http://www.cdc.gov/nchs/fastats/lcod.htm). Moreover, the number is expected to increase as the U. S. population ages even with increased improvements in early detection and treatment of cancer (see Sparks & Nussbaum, 2008). The goal of achieving effective evidence-based communication with cancer patients is not a direct or simple path, and must be better understood and realized. The study of communication practices during cancer care for patients at each life stage is critical for improving cancer care as well as to consider the caregivers whose time and care often go unnoticed or under the radar. The unique aspects of communicating delicate aspects of resilience and hope during cancer care at different life stages is crucial to consider in achieving more effective and competent cancer care for both formal and informal providers.

In order for providers to have the proper evidence-based communicative tools to implement in communicative practices involving cancer care across the lifespan, it is also important to understand that individuals of similar chronological age often undergo very different life experiences (Sparks, 2007). These different experiences can influence communication in relationships. One life experience that can differ between individuals of the same chronological age is the presence or absence of a cancer diagnosis (Sparks & Nussbaum, 2008). Prior research indicates that experiencing cancer at different life stages likely generates different responses due to the ways by which providers communicate concepts (Harzold & Sparks, 2008; Sparks & Nussbaum, 2008; Sparks, Villagran, Parker-Raley, & Cunningham, 2007) of resilience and hope as well as how cancer patients take on resilience and hope messages from their providers and their loved ones. Communicating such subtle messages of resilience and hope can likely make a difference in decision-making and health outcomes for patients experiencing cancer depending upon stage of cancer and stage of life.

The impact of such a diagnosis, and subsequent interactions related to the diagnosis, can be overwhelming for patients due to the increased anxiety and emotion that most patients and those caring for them experience when hearing the "c" word for the very first time, especially as patients age (Sparks, 2003; Sparks, 2007; Sparks, O'Hair, & Kreps, 2008; Sparks & Nussbaum, 2008). Although many newly diagnosed patients have known others who have been diagnosed with cancer, more often than not these individuals have little to no experience with the cancer culture and any norms associated with this unknown world (Sparks, 2003). The health messages surrounding each diagnosis and treatment protocol for patients must be tailored to each life stage and family situation, as well as their cultural and health belief systems. Recognizing the complexities of effective cancer care communication with patients and family caregivers across the lifespan is important to consider because the ways we approach cancer care become more complex as we age. Our goal is to design and deliver cancer communication messages to match the communication skills, needs, and pre-dispositions of specific audiences at each stage across the lifespan. Effective health communication can encourage cancer prevention, inform cancer detection and diagnosis, guide cancer treatment, support successful cancer survivorship, and finally to promote the best end-of-life care (Sparks, 2007).

Extending Sparks' (2007) prior research, the purpose of this chapter is to shed light on the powerful potential to strategically use health communication messages to reduce cancer risks, incidence, morbidity, and mortality, while enhancing quality of life across the continuum of cancer care (prevention, detection, diagnosis, treatment, survivorship, and end-of-life care) with particular attention to communicating messages of resilience and hope across the lifespan. Thus, this chapter reviews the unique physical, cognitive, language, and interactive-relationship characteristics of caring for the patients across the lifespan as well as the family members connected to the patient in the complex, confusing, and overwhelming cancer-related health environment with particular foci on communicating delicate messages of hope and resilience. It should be evident that age-related physiological changes, cognitive changes, and life experiences of older individuals tend to complicate the ways health care providers and family members care for the aging patient who has been diagnosed with cancer (see Sparks & Nussbaum, 2008; Sparks & Turner, 2008).

From a perspective grounded in lifespan developmental communication, the notion of understanding conversational barriers that are unique to caring for the patient is first put forth followed by an explanation of how messages of resilience and hope can play out differentially across the lifespan. Once such conversational barriers are addressed and better understood in terms of older adult adaptation to such deficits across the lifespan, researchers, practitioners, and family members involved in caring for patients at each life stage will have more clearly defined ways of constructing messages that patients will likely comprehend and process, which may contribute to better decision-making and health outcomes (Sparks & Turner, 2008). As Sparks & Turner suggested, cancer messages must be designed specifically for targeted groups across the lifespan. Insight into the unique difficulties of all related communication barriers that get in the way of cognitive message processing and information seeking strategies involved in the aging process is emphasized from a lifespan perspective (see also Sparks, 2007). Delicate and emotionally laden cancer messages of resilience and hope to date have not been explored from a lifespan communication perspective. This chapter attempts to answer that call so that more effective and relevant health campaigns can ultimately be launched to reach each patient and each family at each life stage.

Cancer Communication and the Family

The family dynamic changes dramatically when one of its members is diagnosed with cancer (Harzold & Sparks, 2007). For instance, the psychological uncertainty associated with cancer changes traditional family relations sometimes resulting in an increase in topic avoidance behaviors with a patient for fear of saying or doing something inappropriate or wrong (Gotcher, 1993; Bevan & Sparks, 2011; Bevan, Rogers, Andrews, & Sparks, 2011). This avoidance often impacts patient adjustments and adaptations to their illness (Bevan et al., 2011). Interestingly, patients who report the most effective adjustment to the cancer experience also reported the highest quality of patient-family communication (Gotcher, 1993), indicating a strong need for interaction with loving, and caring family members (Harzold & Sparks, 2007). The communicative tactics patients and family members use will characterize these interactions.

In particular, parents who can competently communicate their cancer diagnosis and treatment plans may offer their children a better understanding of the disease. As parent-child relationships change across the lifespan, so do levels of competence in the communicative exchange into adulthood (Duran, 1989). Wiemann (1977) defines communicative competence as "the ability of an interactant to choose among available communicative behaviors in order that he or she may successfully accomplish his or her own interpersonal goals during an encounter while maintaining the face and line of his or her fellow interactants within the constraints of the situation" (p. 198). Wiemann's (1977) conceptualization of competence centers on relational competence where effectiveness and appropriateness are viewed as necessary outcomes of a competent conversation. An effective interaction is one in which both partners of the dyad experience satisfaction. Hence, relational competence is viewed as the successful management of the adult-child-parent relationship as the criterion for effectiveness. Communication competence influences health outcomes (Query & Kreps, 1996). With increased competency, cancer patients enact skills that include empathic listening and verbal and nonverbal messages that are encoded and decoded to manage the situation with sensitivity. As such, relational competence in the parent-child dyad is important for cancer care.

Whether a child feels his or her parent is effectively conveying information and responding appropriately to the child's questions may affect the relational satisfaction of the parent-child dyad. Communication competence is considered an important construct, however, the nature of competence in communicating is not clear and somewhat elusive (Spitzberg & Cupach, 1984, Query & Kreps, 1996). Query and Kreps (1996) discuss a relational model for communication competence, but little research exists on communication competency between the child and parent during the cancer experience (see Harzold & Sparks, 2007). The cancer experience is a complex series of events that can possibly involve screening, diagnosis, treatment, recovery, and end-of-life care. Taking into account the interactant's success at achieving his or her communicative goal, how competently a parent communicates with his or her child during these different situations and throughout the parent's cancer experience, may also greatly impact the nature of the parent-child relationship and perceived communication satisfaction (see Hecht, 1978a/1978b).

Emotional support is another important factor in adjustment to the cancer diagnosis and treatment, and in parent-child relational satisfaction (see e.g. Gotcher, 1993; Harzold & Sparks, 2007) The ability to express emotion and integrate emotions into messages is related to communication competency (Spitzberg & Cupach, 1984). Further, communication competence can be extremely important in the cancer context. Harzold and Sparks' (2007) finding that a parent's withholding of cancer information from an adult child is dissatisfying also implies that communication competence and satisfaction issues often emerge as a problem in the caregiving relationship. In contrast, when a child has been diagnosed with cancer, some of the many responsibilities parents face in their often new role as caregiver include: (1) providing physical assistance and emotional support to the patient; (2) being a liaison between the patient and an interdisciplinary team of providers; (3) handling financial and social affairs for the patient; and (4) monitoring symptoms and communicating them to providers (Wright, Sparks, & O'Hair, 2013). These tasks present numerous communicative challenges for caregivers and patients navigating the cancer care environment. For instance, whereas many parents are doing an adequate job in relating feelings during the cancer experience, many others are not, which may impact relational adjustment and satisfaction for the child or parent (Harzold & Sparks, 2007). Harzold and Sparks (2007) and Hecht's (1978a/1978b) research findings suggest that satisfaction is decided by both interactants, which involves knowing how to interact, referencing actual communication behavior, and taking into account the interactant's success at satisfactorily achieving his or her communicative goals. Thus, just as communicative satisfaction is a two-way street in the cancer environment, it may also be important to consider the ways in which communicating messages of resilience and hope may also play out relationally. The temperament and disposition of each child can greatly vary within the same family. Consequently, the relationship between parents and different siblings is dynamic and unique, with each individual responding to and modifying the behavior of the other (e.g. Dumas & Lafreniere, 1995; Pecchioni, Wright, & Nussbaum, 2005). Family decision-making processes are a two-way street with parents influencing communicative patterns of their children and vice versa. Joint decision-making and autonomy are best achieved through collaborative problem solving, parental modeling, negotiation, and compromise (e.g., allowing the child to decide when to set the table or when to walk the dogs) (Crockenberg, Jackson, & Langrock, 1996; Lamborn, Dornbush, & Steinberg, 1996). When children are given opportunities for decision-making in areas that matter less, they are more likely to conform to parental expectations that matter more. Conflict resolution in collaborative decision-making between parents and children has been found to play out in later childhood in the resolution of peer-group interpersonal issues (e.g. Crockenberg & Lourie, 1996; Kochanska, 1992). Developmental stages and child dispositions are important factors to consider in family decision-making in the early years of family life. As children grow older and more mature, they can be granted more autonomy and play a larger role in individual and family decision-making (Baumrind, 1996a). These developmental characteristics are important for families experiencing cancer and all the various decisions they will face from diagnosis to treatment to adherence through survivorship and possible recurrence and even complicated and delicate health and family issues surrounding the death and dying process (see Sparks & Villagran, 2008/2009).

Understanding the complexities underlying communication with the aging patient diagnosed with cancer can be tricky due to a host of issues unique to aging (Sparks & Nussbaum, 2008). Indeed, communication not only plays a crucial role in assessing a patient's mental and physical health, but, additionally, after patients are diagnosed with an illness such as cancer, the communicative relationships also influence how they will get well (Nussbaum, Pecchioni, Robinson, & Thompson, 2000; Sparks & Nussbaum, 2008; Pecchioni, Ota, & Sparks, 2004). Due to the complexities of the health care provider–older adult patient relationship, barriers that older adults and their partners and caregivers face in conversation and some implications of such barriers must be better understood, as well as the connection to the ways in which older adults adapt to potential cognitive and physical deficits and adaptive communication patterns acquired across the lifespan. As Cohen

(1994) argues, the nature and management of cancer for adults across the lifespan depends upon not only biological processes, but psychological and social processes as well.

Age-related physiological changes, cognitive changes, and life experiences of older individuals tend to complicate the ways health care providers and family members care for the aging patient who has been diagnosed with cancer (Sparks, 2007). Paying attention to potential age-related conversational barriers that are unique to caring for the aging patient is crucial. For instance, Sparks (2007) describes the unique ways in which older cancer patients adjust to their communicative, psychological, affective, and behavioral environment in different ways than their younger counterparts. It is important to first understand that communication barriers in cancer care for the aging patient can be caused by both primary and secondary characteristics of aging (Nussbaum et al., 2000). For instance, primary characteristics of aging may include developmental changes that result solely from the process of aging (i.e. wrinkles), whereas secondary characteristics are typically changes that emerge because of events and choices that take place during the lifespan (e.g., poor diet) (Sparks, 2007). Aging patients often experience age-related developmental changes across the lifespan that contribute to adaptation to cognitive (e.g. memory loss and/or decrease in retrieval; decreases in function and processes), physical (e.g. presbyopia or decrease in elasticity of lenses of the eye; presbycusis or decrease in hearing ability), and relational changes (see Sparks, 2007 for detailed discussion). Additionally, Nussbaum, Baringer, and Kundrat (2003) state that an understanding of successful adaptation and effective management of cancer by older adults cannot be accomplished without the study of the interpersonal communication of older adults. First, the nature and management of cancer for older adults depends upon not only biological processes, but psychological and social processes as well (Cohen, 1994). Socioemotional Selectivity Theory advanced by Carstensen (1992) proposes that older adults reduce their overall social interactions while maintaining those relationships that provide the most emotional support. This can enlighten our understanding of where a diagnosis of cancer will be most disruptive in an aging patient's relational world and also where or with whom hope and resilience promoting communication matters most.

Further, it is worth noting that when the cancer patient is older, it is highly likely that the primary caregiver will be a spouse or a daughter (Bevan & Sparks, 2011; Cicirelli, 1992), which changes the caregiving relationship as compared to younger cancer patients. Caregiver roles are becoming more complex with physical distance becoming more common among families (Bevan & Sparks, 2011), which impacts communication conflict strategies including topic avoidance and negative health perceptions (Bevan, Rogers, Andrews, & Sparks, 2011), as well as information quality, uncertainty, and quality of care (Bevan, Jupin, & Sparks, 2011). Long-distance caregiving (LDC) is a unique family communication situation that can be challenged by shifting familial roles, the decline of care recipients' physical and/or mental abilities, and difficulties in obtaining sufficient, accurate health information, which can all be compounded by physical distance (Bevan & Sparks, 2011). To fulfill their caregiving duties while coping with this vast array of LDC challenges and highlighting positive aspects of the situation, distant family caregivers may employ avoidant and uncertain communication strategies over messages of resilience and hope with their care recipients. However, because topic avoidance is negatively associated with both relational and individual well-being (Bevan, Rogers, Andrews, & Sparks, 2011), it may be important for caregivers and patients to engage in relational, emotional, and uncertain communication territory including delicate messages of resilience and hope. Because of the complexities involved in the emotional, spiritual, and physical demands of caregiving, caregivers may find it difficult but ultimately rewarding to communicate effective and appropriate messages of resilience and hope while helping cancer patients navigate the cancer care journey.

Communicating Resilience

Although cancer is a traumatic event or crisis that takes a toll existentially, psychosocially, and physically, receiving a cancer diagnosis in old age can be especially challenging (Esbensen, Swane, Hallberg, & Thome, 2008). Becoming a cancer patient can suddenly become extremely chaotic, and sometimes these individuals begin to deal with a possibility of death without any helpful strategies (Persson & Hallberg, 2004). Pudrovska (2010) argues that understanding the diverse outcomes of cancer on an individual's psychological well-being is vitally important. Because of the potential for negative effects of cancer, it is important to determine a way that individuals can more effectively and successfully deal with the cancer experience. One such avenue is through resilience. Althought resilience is often viewed as an ongoing process of stressor management, developing resilience can be seen as a positive strategy that can help cancer patients and their families deal with a cancer diagnosis. Resilience patterns likely differ based on stressor experience, activation of previously identified and accumulated assets and resources to manage the experience, and competent communication related to the experience. Resilient individuals are likely most able to utilize various internal and external assets to maintain equilibrium and even possibly produce what could be described as "post-traumatic" growth due to an array of pertinent life experiences aquired across the lifespan.

Resilience is defined as the ability to sustain a stable equilibrium during exposure to a potentially disruptive and isolated event, such as cancer (Bonanno, 2008). Resilient individuals may be able to utilize various internal assets as well as external assets in order to maintain equilibrium and potentially produce post traumatic growth moving forward. Resilience can also be thought of as a process (Buzzanell, 2010), or even a combination of protective or promotive resources specific and appropriate to the context, cast across the ecological model (for a review of various perspectives, see Reich, Zautra, & Hall, 2010). Ability or capacity may be informed by characterizations that go beyond the individual, and are also likely informed by an individual's emotionally close relationships, social network, and extended social circumstances. Further, individuals who can maintain equilibrium during tragic life events are able to remain relatively stable and keep healthy levels of physical and psychological functioning (Bonanno, 2008). Those who have resilience have the ability to overcome a negative event and maintain social competence, functional capacity, and mental health (Wu, Sheen, Shu, Chang, & Hsaio, 2013). Resilient individuals may potentially experience transient distress, but they are able to generally maintain a steady trajectory of healthy functioning (Bonanno, Papa, & O'Neill, 2001). Resilient individuals with cancer, therefore, would be able to maintain healthy functioning while enduring the physical and emotional tolls of a cancer diagnosis. Ho, Ho, Bonanno, Chu, and Chan (2010) found that hereditary colorectal cancer (HCRC) patients who received genetic testing were psychologically resilient. Additionally, the sample showed higher levels of resilience and lower levels of chronic dysfunction. This finding could illustrate the effect that resilience has upon an individual's cancer experience. Genetic testing may or may not be the source of psychological resilience, however, it may be the case that individuals who have more specific health information about their genetic background are better equipped to deal with the uncertainties involved with a cancer diagnosis when it materializes.

Bonanno (2008) argues that paths to resilience are multiple and unexpected, but resilience is not uncommon. Life events will certainly happen, but it is how we respond to traumatic events that distinguish more resilient individuals from less resilient individuals. Resilient individuals sometimes cope with adversity through the use of laughter and positive emotion (Bonanno, Noll, Putnam, O'Neill, & Trickett, 2003; Keltner & Bonanno, 1997). Positive emotions quiet and undo negative emotions, and therefore, can help reduce distress levels (Keltner & Bonanno, 1997). Additionally, positive emotions can increase the contact and support from people in the individual's environment (Bonanno & Keltner, 1997). If positive emotions increase contact and support from those around an individual, it can lead to more emotional and instrumental support, which has been shown to lessen the effect of negative experiences on physical and psychological symptomatology (Wills & Bantum, 2012). This is related to resilience in the fact that individuals with more emotional and instrumental support would be able to maintain a more positive outlook regarding the cancer diagnosis and could therefore remain strong. Finding opportunities for humor, laughter, and positivity during such life-changing events may help promote resilience processes (Beck & Socha, chapter 3).

Due to the fact that the development of resilience feasibly has a positive effect on the experience of cancer, it is important that messages of resilience be used within communication and messages surrounding cancer. Whether the messages are transferred between patient and treatment team or patient and child, messages of resilience are important to include. Messages of resilience among those affected by cancer can positively change the experience into one that may not take a negative toll. For instance, messages of survival often include enduring narratives and stories of individual's own cancer experience across the cancer continuum as they describe their diagnosis, detection, treatment, and survivorship stories to trusted others in how they are coping with the cancer experience (e.g., see literal and figurative "war stories," Beck & Socha, chapter 12). Resilent messages of survivorship can be inspiring to others and may contribute to one's own ability to respond resiliently to cancer and its ongoing phases. Such positive narratives of surviving and thriving may involve content level messages (i.e. instructions for carrying out recommended responses or treatments, etc.) as well as relational level messages and exchanges (i.e. emotional support) of different invested parties. Further, "messages of hope and resilience," both intrapersonally (internally) and interpersonally (externally) via close relationships and their implications for those involved in cancer care are countless and, as such, must be further explored and better understood.

Messages promoting resilence within individuals or in their responses to events likely foster hopeful thinking and planning for the future. While resilience is important to consider when communicating with individuals affected by cancer it is closely connected with the construct of hope, which is another important tool that must be utilized within messages.

Communicating Hope

Hope has long been recognized as an important component of psychological growth and change (Freud (1905/1968). Snyder's (1994) hope theory has drawn considerable theoretical and empirical support as an explanatory model for hope. Similarly, Herth's (2000) conceptualization of hopefulness has greatly influenced the practice of health psychology, nursing, medicine, and related fields. Herth's approach particularly overlaps with Snyder's hope enhancement strategies, as participants are encouraged to share stories about challenges in their lives as well as the lives of family members or friends and to explore how these challenges show courage and optimism. Communicating messages of hope with individuals experiencing cancer and their family and friends must be delicately delivered to match the current emotional needs of those involved while also considering how past experiences may impact such needs and related health decision-making.

Hope is associated with a wide range of psychosocial and physical benefits (Snyder et al., 2011), and appears to be an important component of coping with adversity (Linley & Joseph, 2004) and therapeutic change (Snyder & Lopez, 2009). Snyder's Hope Scale (Snyder et al., 1991; Snyder et al., 1996) and Herth's Hope Index (Herth 2000; 2001), both demonstrate the value of hope as a social psychological construct related to optimal functioning. The hope theories developed by Snyder (2000) and Herth (2001) conceptualize hope as a cognitive construct related to a wide range of social, emotional, and physical benefits. Indeed, these theories have influenced research over the past several decades, demonstrating associations between self-reported hopefulness and academic achievement, athletic performance, physical health and wellness, coping with illness and loss, psychological adjustment, social-emotional problem-solving, and the quality of interpersonal relationships (see also Rand & Cheavens, 2009).

Most studies ($k = 19$; number of studies) have typically measured hope utilizing either the Hope Scale (Snyder et al., 1991; 1996) or Children's Hope Scale (Snyder, Hoza et al., 1997), to assess their intervention's ability to enhance hope in participants. Other studies ($k = 7$) relied on the Herth Hope Scale (Herth, 2000).[1] Both self-report instruments yield an overall score that reflects state hopefulness. The psychometric properties of these instruments indicate adequate internal consistency, content validity, and convergence with theoretically similar constructs, such as optimism and self-efficacy.

Hope has also been defined as a "multidimensional dynamic life force characterized by a confident yet uncertain expectation of achieving future good, which to the hoping person is realistically possible and personally significant" (Dufault & Martocchio, 1985, p. 380). Just as resilience, hope is an important part of the cancer experience that may be of benefit to the patient. Hope has a significant meaning and is thought to be a source of strength for individuals experiencing cancer (Ebsensen, Swane, Hallberg, & Thome, 2008). Siimilar to Snyder's conceptualization of hope, Stanton, Danoff-Burg, and Huggins (2002) found that hope was a significant predictor of psychological well-being among individuals with cancer. Esbensen et al. (2008) found that when cancer was experienced as a life-threating situation, hope was extremely important. Hope was intimately connected to the future and hope was a source of strength for surviving the disease, even though the future seemed unreliable (Esbensen et al., 2008). Finally, hope was also connected to the idea of enjoying life and those around them (Esbensen et al., 2008).

Berendes et al. (2010) found that most of their cancer patients reported reasonably high levels of hope. Further, an association was found between hope and symptoms (pain, cough, fatigue) of lung cancer, meaning that higher levels of hope were highly associated with lower pain. It appears that hope potentially regulates perception of pain and pain management. The researchers also found that higher levels of hope were related to lower levels of fatigue, and higher hope was associated with lower depression (Berendes et al., 2010). Esbensen, Østerlind, Roer, and Hallberg (2004) found that lower quality of life in elderly persons with newly diagnosed cancer was associated with lower levels of hope. These results indicate an important association between hope and the experience of cancer. Pudrovksa (2010) found that older white men who had cancer were more vulnerable to depression. To combat the experience of depression, Pudrovska argues patients should be screened for depression and psychosocial interventions should be utilized. However, one could assume that messages of resilience and hope could also help to combat the depression. As evidenced above, positive messages of hope can combat the negative physical symptoms of cancer, which could also combat the negative psychological symptoms of cancer. Further, hope may serve different goals for the various stages of cancer. For instance, at the stage of entering hospice, hope is still present but serves different goals for patients and family members than in the earlier stages of cancer. If hope can affect the way an individual experiences cancer, this needs to be capitalized upon in treatment and messages surrounding cancer to help foster the development of hopeful thinking and decision-making during the process.

Combined messages of hope and resilience are important to include in messages with cancer patients. While messages promoting resilience may help patients maintain a stable trajectory of life, messages of hope can provide patients, and their loved ones, with confidence about their fight with cancer.

As discussed previously, caregivers and children of cancer patients have an important role within the cancer experience. Just as messages of hope and resilience positively affect the patient, it could be assumed that messages of hope and resilience would encouragingly support the caregivers and children when dealing with a loved one's or parent's cancer. We argue that messages of hope and resilience are positive forces that must be utilized in communication with cancer patients.

Family Decision-making

Communicating effective and appropriate health messages can greatly impact decision-making and health outcomes (Sparks, 2008). In terms of message framing and related decision-making to achieve better health outcomes for cancer patients (see Sparks, 2007; Sparks & Turner, 2008), positively and negatively framed information are equal in terms of content of the factual or numerical health information but it is most often the tone of the information that leads individuals to perceive it differently. Individuals will cognitively process messages differentially based on framing as well as different life experiences across the lifespan. Researchers have long recognized the magnitude of examining cognitive processing as mediating the link between messages and subsequent behavior (e.g. Sparks & Turner, 2008). For instance, Mitchell (2000) and Mitchell et al., (2001) found that overall message quality is the best predictor of attitude change, and that cognitive processing of the message in terms of understanding, interpretation and related decision-making is a key mediator of that relationship. Although messages of resilience and hope have not been adequately studied in the health communication arena, research consistently suggests the need to begin addressing the unique ways by which cancer communication messages are processed and received across the lifespan, and differential ways older adults adapt to such difficult health diagnoses such as cancer and decision-making than their younger counterparts.

Research has demonstrated that serious illness impacts the lives of patients, their families, and loved ones with a number of scholars making the argument that serious illness is indeed a family issue (e.g., Ballard-Reisch, 1996; Harzold & Sparks, 2007; Pecchioni & Sparks, 2007; Sparks, 2003; Sparks, 2008). Serious illnesses such as a cancer diagnosis add demands, strains, and hardships to families who must deal with numerous changes and decisions that impact the entire family. Families are often uniquely qualified in terms of understanding patient attitudes and decision-making strategies and can therefore assist as an important resource in helping the patient to make better decisions about their care (Blustein, 1998).

Prior research indicates a range of factors confront families as they decide about terminal care of a family member (Rothchild, 1994). Many families react to their sense of guilt and hopelessness by pushing for maximal medical intervention until the end of life. This often results in patient failure to resist such pressure and persuasion, consequently accepting treatments that they very likely would not have chosen on their own. Rothchild claims that family decision-making is impacted according to the following variables: 1) patient's role in the family (boss, scapegoat, caregiver); 2) ages of patient and family members; 3) family continuity and cohesion; 4) who is considered to be "family;" 5) how information and decisions are shared within the family; 6) presence of denial, guilt, and anger; 7) communication of treatment wishes to proxies; 8) comfort with sophisticated technology; 9) ethnicity and religion; and 10) economic pressures.

Family decisions are negotiated every day from family decisions in the childhood and adolescent years to middle and later life family decisions, many of which occur in health care environments. Family decision processes in the health care environment are particularly difficult and complex because of the associated uncertainties, emotions, technical language, and subsequent health outcomes (e.g. Harzold & Sparks, 2007; Sparks, 2003). Conflicting information from various sources can be difficult to navigate and process to make the most informed health care decisions. Families make decisions about health issues using information from a variety of sources including insurance provider lists, Internet research, recommendations from primary care physicians and specialists, interpersonal communication with friends and family members, and mediated messages (see Pecchioni & Sparks, 2007). As families are confronted with cancer, messages of resilience and hope with the patient and involved family members will likely impact important decisions that may extend the patient's life. Cancer messages matter across the lifespan as each life stage will likely need unique adaptations of resilient and hopeful messages depending on life stage and family relationships that are based on a history of prior interactions. By paying attention to potential conversational barriers likely to be present at each life stage from younger adults with less life experiences to draw from and with older adult adaptations to increasing deficits across the lifespan, researchers, practitioners, and family members involved in caring for cancer patients will have more clearly defined ways of constructing messages inclusive of appropriate resilience and hope characteristics that patients can more easily digest, comprehend, process, and enact, which may contribute to better decision-making and subsequent health outcomes.

Conclusion

This chapter reviewed the unique physical, cognitive, language, cultural, and interactive-relationship characteristics likely to be involved when communicating messages of resilience and hope with cancer patients across the lifespan as well as the family members connected to the patient in the complex, confusing, and overwhelming cancer-related health environment. By first understanding unique communication barriers patients are likely to experience across the lifespan, researchers, practitioners, and family members can then begin to construct messages in more systematic, informed, and understandable ways. Such tailored research-based messages will have a greater likelihood of reaching and impacting patients diagnosed with cancer at every life stage.

As Sparks and Nussbaum (2008) emphasized the consideration of health literacy in designing health messages targeting the unique characteristics of older adults, it is also important that health communication scholars strive to craft strategic messages and interventions that engage and inspire patients to be active participants in their cancer care at every life stage. Designing and delivering cancer communication messages to match the specific communication skills, needs, and pre-dispositions of the patient population at each life stage is an additional component of health care delivery to consider when communicating messages of resilience and hope.

By understanding how patients' barriers, communicative skills, and relationships change across the lifespan, we can begin to pay closer attention to the designing of relevant and compelling messages that can break down barriers patients and caregivers face to increase health outcomes across the lifespan. Cancer communication messages must be designed and delivered to match the communication skills, needs, and pre-dispositions of such segmented yet complex audiences (Sparks & Turner, 2008). Effective health communication can encourage cancer prevention, inform cancer detection and diagnosis, guide cancer treatment, support successful cancer survivorship, and finally promote the best end-of-life care at each stage of life.

Caring for patients with cancer at each life stage can be quite complex and fraught with misunderstandings that often lead to poor quality care. As such, what can we do to communicate effective messages of resilience and hope for cancer patients across the lifespan?

Construct and tailor health messages in a systematic, understandable way for each patient and his or her unique characteristics across each life stage and across varying types of cancer.

Focus upon both the biological and the psychosocial nature of cancer.

Focus on the communicative abilities of the patient at each life stage as well as formal and informal caregivers caring for patients.

Include the entire social and care network in all decisions.

Understand age-related communication barriers (young and old).

Balance sincere messages of resilience and hope considering each life stage and each cancer stage by teasing out content and relational messages.

Seek opportunities for promotiong hope and resilience by creating a mindful action plan of pre-, during, and post-diagnosis and treatment approaches.

Communicating delicate messages of resilience and hope may be among the most difficult messages to balance in the cancer situation. It is important that formal and informal caregivers include messages of resilience and hope when caring for cancer patients. Resilience messages help patients maintain a stable trajectory of life, while messages of hope often increase patient confidence in their cancer journey and related decision-making. Family decision-making has become increasingly complex as family life has dramatically changed over the last several decades. Changing roles of women becoming more integrated in the labor force, increases in divorce rates, increased mobility, increased longevity, and complex health care environments are just some of the crucial changes that are impacting families and thus, arguably, impacting family decision-making across the life span. A few final thoughts that families should consider when implementing difficult and delicate messages of resilience and hope to family members at every life stage and related decision-making processes: 1) Identify the most important 2-3 issues; 2) Understand all possible alternative strategies and options; 3) Achieve satisfaction in choosing the best strategy for the family; 4) Enact an action plan for implementing the decision; 5) Evaluate the decision and refine as needed. Snyder's hope theory in terms of goals, pathways, and agency certainly supports these suggestions (see e.g. Snyder et al., 2011), while also considering how patients and their familes cope with adversity (Linley & Joseph, 2004) and therapeutic or curative change processes (Snyder & Lopez, 2009).

These are a few simple steps to get families thinking about how to construct the most effective decision-making processes that occur frequently during the cancer experience, however, more evidence from empirically based studies is needed to substantiate ways in which family decision-making processes are impacted by and impact individuals and their families across every life stage.

Tailored research-based messages will have a greater likelihood of reaching and impacting the patients diagnosed with cancer and caregivers who are often frontline communicators and decision-makers. Health communication scholars have various theoretical, methodological, and pragmatic communication-based approaches that provide important contributions to the complexities of caring for cancer patients. Formal and informal providers can team together to tailor messages of resilience and hope to patients dealing with cancer at different life stages.

Messages of resilience and hope can be used to select interventions that mindfully increase social support and tap into more proactive and positive ways of thinking about how to best approach the cancer experience. For instance, motivational interviewing might be effectively used to help patients and family members work with the provider team to set clear, objective, and meaningful goals that can serve as the targets for treatment. Further, cognitive-based message interventions may be particularly useful in helping recognize and challenge negative thoughts that take away the motivation to work toward their goals. Furthermore, health communication based problem-solving and skills training can help individuals obtain proper positive social support to cope with stress and adversity along the cancer journey. Other positive health communication interventions can be useful in increasing resilience and hope as well as positive affect and well-being. Rather than using resilence and hope as a first-order intervention approach, providers and practitioners may potentially utilize messages of resilience and hope as second-order evidence-based as a proactive cognitive approach to communicatively guide their interventions (Wilson & Gettings, 2012). By working closely together, we can effectively communicate such messages across health care settings, across disciplines, across cultures and subcultures throughout the world in an effort to create vast improvements in how we communicate health messages with patients and caregivers undergoing the cancer experience.

References

Ballard-Reisch, D. (1996). Coping with alienation, fear, and isolation: The disenfranchisement of adolescents with cancer and their families. In E. Berlin Ray (Ed.), *Communication and disenfranchisement: Social health issues and implications* (pp. 185–208). Mahwah, NJ: Lawrence Erlbaum Associates.

Baumrind, D. (1996a). A blanket injunction against disciplinary use of spanking is not warranted by the data. *Pediatrics, 98,* 828.

Berendes, D., Keefe, F. J., Somers, T. J., Kothadia, S. M., Porter, L. S., & Cheavens, J. S. (2010). Hope in the context of lung cancer: Relationships of hope to symptoms and psychological distress. *Journal of Pain and Symptom Management, 40*, 174-182.

Bevan, J., Jupin, A., & Sparks, L. (2011). Information quality, uncertainty, and quality of care in long distance caregiving. *Communication Research Reports, 28*, 190-195. doi:10.1080/08824096.2011.566105

Bevan, J., Rogers, K., Andrews, N., & Sparks, L. (2011). Topic avoidance and negative health perceptions in the distant caregiving context. *Journal of Family Communication, 12*, 300-314.

Bevan, J., & Sparks, L. (2011). Communication in the context of long-distance family caregiving. An integrated review and practical applications. *Patient Education and Counseling, 85*, 26-30.

Blustein, J. (1998). The family in medical decision making. In J. F. Monagle & D. C. Thomasma (Eds.), *Health care ethics: Critical issues for the 21st century* (pp. 81-91). Gaithersburg, MD: Aspen Publishers.

Bonanno, G. A. (2008). Loss, trauma, and human resilience: Have we underestimated human capacity to thrive after extremely aversive events? *Psychological Trauma: Theory, Research, Practice, and Policy, S*, 101-113.

Bonanno, G. A., & Keltner, D. (1997). Facial expressions of emotion and the course of conjugal bereavement. *Journal of Abnormal Psychology, 106*, 126-137.

Bonanno, G. A., Noll, J. G., Putnam, F. W., O'Neill, M., & Trickett, P. (2003). Predicting the willingness to disclose childhood sexual abuse from measures of repressive coping and dissociative experiences. *Child Maltreatment, 8*, 1-17.

Bonanno, G. A., Papa, A., & O'Neill, K. (2001). Loss and human resilience. *Applied and Preventive Psychology, 10*, 193-206.

Buzzanell, P. M. (2010). Resilience: Talking, resisting, and imagining new normalcies into being. *Journal of Communication, 60:1*, 1-14.

Carstensen, L. L. (1992). Social and emotional patterns in adulthood: Support for socioemotional selectivity theory. *Psychology and Aging, 7*, 331-338.

Cicirelli, V. G. (1992). *Family caregiving: Autonomous and paternalistic decision making*. Newbury Park, CA: Sage.

Cohen, G. (1994). Age-related problems in the use of proper names in communication. In M. L. Hummert, J. M. Wiemann, & J. F. Nussbaum (Eds.), *Interpersonal communication in older adulthood: Interdisciplinary theory and research* (pp. 40-57). Thousand Oaks, CA: Sage.

Crockenberg, S., Jackson, S., & Langrock, A. M. (1996). Autonomy and goal attainment: Parenting, gender, and children's social competence. *New Directions in Child Development, 73*, 41-55.

Crockenberg, S., & Lourie, A. (1996). Parents' conflict strategies with children and children's conflict strategies with peers. *Merrill-Palmer Quarterly, 42*, 495-518.

Dufault, K., & Martocchio, B. C. (1985). Hope: Its spheres and dimensions. *Nursing Clinics of North America, 20*, 379-391.

Dumas, J. E., & LaFreniere, P. J. (1995). Relationships as context: Supportive and coercive interactions in competent, aggressive, and anxious mother-child dyads. In J. McCord (Ed.), *Coercion and punishment in long-term perspectives* (pp. 9-33). New York: Cambridge University Press.

Duran, R. L. (1989). Social competence in adulthood. In J. F. Nussbaum (Ed.), *Life span communication: Normative processes* (pp. 195-224). Hillsdale, NJ: Lawrence Erlbaum.

Epstein, R. M., & Street, R. L. (2007). *Patient-centered communication in cancer care: Promoting healing and reducing suffering*. (NIH Publication No. 07-6225). Bethesda, MD: National Cancer Institute.

Esbensen, B. A., Østerlind, K., Roer, O., & Hallberg, I. R. (2004). Quality of life of elderly persons with newly diagnosed cancer. *European Journal of Cancer Care, 13*, 443-453.

Esbensen B. A., Swane, C. E., Hallberg, I. R., & Thome, B. (2008). Being given a cancer diagnosis in old age: A phenomenological study. *International Journal of Nursing Studies, 45*, 393-405.

Freud, S. (1905/1968). *The complete psychological works of Sigmund Freud* (pp. 281-302). In J. Strachey (Ed.), *Psychical (or mental) treatment*. London: Hogarth Press.

Gotcher, J. M. (1993). The effects of family communication on psychosocial adjustment of cancer patients. *Journal of Applied Communication Research, 21*, 176-188.

Harwood, J., & Sparks, L. (2003). Social identity and health: An intergroup communication approach to cancer. *Health Communication, 15*, 145-170.

Harzold, E., & Sparks, L. (2007). Adult child perceptions of communication and humor when the parent is diagnosed with cancer: A suggestive perspective from communication theory. *Qualitative Research Reports in Communication, 7*, 67-78.

Hecht, M. L. (1978a). The conceptualization and measurement of interpersonal communication satisfaction. *Human Communication Research, 4*, 253-264.

Hecht, M. L. (1978b). Measures of communication satisfaction. *Human Communication Research, 4*, 350-368.

Herth, K. A. (2000). Enhancing hope in people with a first recurrence of cancer. *Journal of Advanced Nursing, 32*, 1431-1441.

Herth, K. A. (2001). Development and implementation of a hope intervention program. *Oncology Nursing Forum, 28*, 1009-1017.

Ho, S. M. Y., Ho, J. W. C., Bonanno, G. A., Chu, A. T. W., & Chan, E. M. S. (2010). Hopefulness predicts resilience after hereditary colorectal cancer genetic testing: A prospective outcome trajectories study. *BMC Cancer, 10*, 1-10. doi: 10.1186/1471-2407-10-279

Linley, P. A., & Joseph, S. (2004). *Positive psychology in practice*. New York: Wiley.

Keltner, D., & Bonanno, G. A. (1997). A study of laughter and dissociation: Distinct correlates of laughter and smiling during bereavement. *Journal of Personality and Social Psychology, 73*, 687-702.

Kochanska, G. (1992). Children's interpersonal influence with mothers and peers. *Developmental Psychology, 28*, 491-499.

Lamborn, S. D., Dornbusch, S. M., & Steinberg, L. (1996). Ethnicity and community context as moderators of the relations between family decision making and adolescent adjustment. *Child Development, 67*, 283-301.

Mitchell, M. M. (2000). Motivated, but not able? The effects of positive and negative mood on persuasive message processing. *Communication Monographs, 67*, 215-225.

Mitchell, M. M., Brown, K. M., Morris Villagran, M., & Villagran, P. D. (2001). The effects of anger, sadness and happiness on persuasive message processing: A test of the Negative State Relief Model. *Communication Monographs, 68,* 347-359.

Nussbaum, J. F., Baringer, D., & Kundrat, A. (2003). Health, communication, and aging: Cancer and the older adult [Special Issue]. *Health Communication, 15,* 185-194.

Nussbaum, J. F., Pecchioni, L., Robinson, J. D., & Thompson, T. (2000). *Communication and Aging* (2nd ed.). Mahwah, NJ: Lawrence Erlbaum Associates.

O'Hair, D., Kreps, G. L., & Sparks, L. (Eds.) (2007). *Handbook of communication and cancer care.* Cresskill, NJ: Hampton Press.

O'Hair, D., Kreps, G. L., & Sparks, L. (2007). Conceptualizing cancer care and communication. In D. O'Hair, G. L. Kreps, & L. Sparks. (Eds.), *Handbook of communication and cancer care* (pp. 1-11). Cresskill, NJ: Hampton Press.

Pecchioni, L., Ota, H., & Sparks, L. (2004). Cultural issues in communication and aging. In J. F. Nussbaum & J. Coupland (Eds.), *Handbook of communication and aging research* (pp. 167-207). Mahwah, NJ: Erlbaum.

Pecchioni, L., & Sparks, L. (2007). Health information sources of individuals with cancer and their family members. *Health Communication, 21,* 1-9.

Pecchioni, L., Wright, K., & Nussbaum, J. F. (2005). *Life span communication.* Mahwah, NJ: LEA.

Persson, L., Hallberg, I. R. (2004). Lived experience of survivors of leukemia or malignant lymphoma. *Cancer Nursing, 27,* 303-313.

Pudrovska, T. (2010). What makes you stronger: Age and cohort differences in personal growth after cancer. *Journal of Health and Social Behavior, 51,* 260-273.

Query, J. L. Jr. & Kreps, G. L. (1996). Testing a relational model for health communication competence among caregivers for individuals with Alzheimer's disease. *Journal of Health Psychology, 1,* 335-351.

Rand, K. L., & Cheavens, J. S. (2009). Hope theory. In S. J. Lopez & C. R. Snyder (Eds.), *Oxford handbook of positive psychology* (pp. 323-333). New York: Oxford University Press.

Reich, W., Zautra, A. J., & Hall, J. S. (Eds.). (2010). *Handbook of adult resilience.* New York: Guilford.

Rothchild, E. (1994). Family dynamics in end-of-life treatment decisions. *General Hospital Psychiatry, 16,* 251-258.

Snyder, C. R. (1994). *The psychology of hope.* New York: Free Press.

Snyder, C. R. (2000). *Handbook of hope.* San Diego, CA: Academic Press.

Snyder, C. R., Feldman, D. B., Taylor, J. D., Schroeder, L. L., & Adams, V. H. (2000). The roles of hopeful thinking in preventing problems and enhancing strengths. *Applied and Preventative Psychology, 9,* 249-270.

Snyder, C. R., Harris, C., Anderson, J. R., Holleran, S. A., Irving, L. M., & Sigmon, S. T., et al. (1991). The will and the ways: Development and validation of an individual-differences measure of hope. *Journal of Personality and Social Psychology, 60,* 570-858.

Snyder, C. R., Hoza, B., Pelham, W. E., Rapoff, M., Ware, L., & Danovsky, M., et al. (1997). The development and validation of the Children's Hope Scale. *Journal of Pediatric Psychology, 22,* 399-421.

Snyder, C. R., & Lopez, S. J. (2009). *Oxford handbook of positive psychology*. New York: Oxford University Press.

Snyder, C. R., Lopez, S. J., Pedrotti, J. T. (2011). *Positive psychology: The scientific and practical exploration of human strengths*. Thousand Oaks, CA: Sage.

Snyder, C. R., Parenteau, .S. C., Shorey, H. S., Kahle, K. E., & Berg, C. (2002). Hope as the underlying process in the psychotherapeutic change process. *International Gestalt Journal, 25*, 11-29.

Snyder, C. R., Rand, K. L., & Sigmon, D. R. (2002). Hope theory. In C. R. Snyder & S. J. Lopez (Eds.), *Handbook of positive psychology* (pp. 257-276). New York: Oxford University Press.

Snyder, C. R., Sympson, S. C., Michael, S. T., & Cheavens, J. (2001). Optimism and hope constructs: Variants on a positive expectancy theme. In E. C. Chang (Ed.), *Optimism and pessimism: Implications for theory, research, and practice* (pp. 101-125). Washington, DC: American Psychological Association.

Snyder, C. R., Sympson, S. C., Ybasco, F. C., Borders, T. F., Babyak, M. A., & Higgins, R. L. (1996). Development and validation of the state hope scale. *Journal of Personality and Social Psychology, 70*, 321-335.

Snyder, C. R., & Taylor, J. D. (2000). Hope as a common factor across psychotherapy approaches: A lesson from the dodo's verdict. In C. R. Snyder (Ed.), *Handbook of hope* (pp. 89-107). San Diego, CA: Academic Press.

Sparks, L. (Ed.). (2003). An introduction to cancer communication and aging: Theoretical and research insights. [Special Issue]. *Health Communication, 15*, 123-131.

Sparks, L. (2007). Cancer care and the aging patient: Complexities of age-related communication barriers. In H. D. O'Hair, G. L. Kreps, & L. Sparks (Eds.), *Handbook of communication and cancer care* (pp. 233-249). Cresskill, NJ: Hampton Press.

Sparks, L. (2008). Family decision-making. In W. Donsbach (Ed.), *The International Encyclopedia of Communication*, 4, (pp. 1729-1733). Oxford, UK and Malden, MA: Wiley-Blackwell.

Sparks, L., & Nussbaum, J. F. (2008). Health literacy and cancer communication with older adults. *Patient Education and Counseling, 71*, 345-350.

Sparks, L., O'Hair, H. D., & Kreps, G. L. (Eds.) (2008). *Cancer, communication and aging*. Cresskill, NJ: Hampton Press.

Sparks, L., & Turner, M. M. (2008). Cognitive and emotional processing of cancer messages and information seeking with older adults. In L. Sparks, H. D. O'Hair, & G. L. Kreps, (Eds.), *Cancer, communication and aging* (pp. 17-45). Cresskill, NJ: Hampton Press.

Sparks, L., & Villagran, M. (2008). *La Comunicación en el Cancer: Comunicación y apoyo emocional en el laberinto del cancer*. [English translation: Communication and emotional support in the cancer maze.] Madrid, Spain: Aresta.

Sparks, L., & Villagran, M. (2009). Talking Cancer. www.editorialaresta.com

Spitzberg, B. H. & Cupach, W. R. (1989). *Handbook of interpersonal competence research*. New York: Springer-Verlag.

Stanton, A. L., Danoff-Burg, S., & Huggins, M. E. (2002). The first year after breast cancer diagnosis: Hope and coping strategies as predictors of adjustment. *Psycho-Oncology, 11*, 93-102.

Wiemann, J. M. (1977). Explication and test of a model of communicative competence. *Human Communication Research*, 3, 195-213.

Wills, T. A., & Bantum, E. O. (2012). Social support, self-regulation, and resilience in two populations: General-population adolescents and adult cancer survivors. *Journal of Social and Clinical Psychology*, 31, 568-592.

Wilson, S. R., & Gettings, P. E. (2012). Nuturing Children as Assets: A Positive Approach to Preventing Maltreatment and Promoting Healthy Youth Development. In T. J. Socha & M. J. Pitts (Eds.) *The Positive Side of Interpersonal Communication* (pp 277-295). New York: Peter Lang.

Wright, K. B., Sparks, L., & O'Hair, H. D. (2013). *Health communication in the 21st century* (2nd ed.). Oxford, UK: Blackwell.

Wu, L., Sheen, J., Shu, H., Chang, S., & Hsaio, C. (2013). Predictors of anxiety and resilience in adolescents undergoing cancer treatment. *Journal of Advanced Nursing*, 69, 158-166. doi: 10.1111/j.1365-2648.2012.06003

Section Three
Imparting Hope and Resilience

• CHAPTER TWELVE •

Life's "War Stories": Accounts of Resilience and Hope

Thomas J. Socha
Alfredo Torres
Old Dominion University

"A true war story, if truly told, makes the stomach believe."
—O'Brien (1990, p. 1)

Among life's ordeals examined throughout this volume "war" per se is certainly among the most significant. By definition, war per se is "any kind of active hostility or contention between living beings" (*Oxford English Dictionary Online*, 2014) where the lives of enemy combatants can be placed at risk. Besides war per se, there are "wars broadly put," or "conflicts between opposing forces or principles" (*Oxford English Dictonary Online*, 2014). Wars broadly put are typically described using the language of war per se, and similar to war per se, can place lives at varying degrees of risk. For example, fire fighters "battle" blazes. Law-enforcement officers "fight" crime. DEA agents "fight" the "war on drugs." Medical doctors and researchers "wage war" on cancer. Rescue workers literally risk their lives "battling" the elements. Astronauts "brave" new "fronts" to boldly go where no one has gone before. These individuals and many similar others place their lives in varying degrees of risk as they perform their duties involving crime, natural disasters, disease, and many similar ordeals on behalf of others. On the dark side too, bank robbers, crime bosses, drug dealers, and evil despots "clash" with the good guys and "fight" on their sides of what they might perceive as "war" per se, risking their lives for their causes.

On yet other war "fronts" where death is also faced, patients "battle" fatal illnesses (see Sparks et al., chapter 11, this volume). We read, for example, stories about the recent death of comedian Robin Williams that report about his "battle" with depression. Commuters "dodge bullets" (sometimes real, sometimes metaphoric) that can include near-fatal accidents as they "fight" traffic. And, those living on coasts, in mountains, and on plains face all sorts of natural disasters—the "wrath of mother nature"—including earthquakes, floods, hurricanes, tornados, and so on, as they sometimes must "fight" to stay alive (see Merolla, chapter 10, this volume). Of course not all wars per se endanger human life. Some roles in wars per se are removed from the fields of battle (e.g., supply and medical personnel, pilots of drones, etc.) and battles on some fronts may pose little, if any, imminent risk to losing life in the short run, but may carry increasing risk over time, as in "fighting" the modern "battle of the bulge" ("war" on obesity).

Those who return from wars per se and wars generally put, that is, "veterans" (e.g., of law enforcement, the militaty, etc.) and "survivors" (of abuse, cancer, concentration camps, etc.) may (or may not) want to communicate about their experiences of war by telling what is commonly referred to as a "war story." Veterans and survivors themselves can of course tell their own war stories. Alternatively, war stories can also be told on behalf of veterans and survivors as well as those who have died. Those who tell the war stories of others also may (or may not) have participated in war per se or war broadly put including fellow veterans, medical personnel, journalists, filmmakers, historians, and more.

Veterans' and survivors' reasons to tell (or not tell) war stories undoutedly vary. Some may be motivated to share life lessons with, and/or warn, future generations, highlight the work of heroes; pay tribute to the fallen; and/or to remember the lost. Some may want to tell their personal war stories to mental health professionals and religious/spiritual counselors in hopes of somehow benefitting themselves (and possibly others) therapeutically, emotionally, and/or spiritually. Some may want to tell their personal war stories to others for relational purposes such as initiating or refreshing friendship bonds forged in battle during reunions, as among cancer survivors sharing war stories during annual Relay for Life fundraising events, or veterans of war per se, swapping war stories in VFW or American Legion halls, or during reunions on Veteran's Day. And finally, some may want to tell war stories as a means of persuasion. The first author, for example, recalls when he was a child, his mother, a nurse, would sometimes share personal war stories about injured children from her job working in the "trenches" of a children's hospital as a way to warn him and his brothers about the ills that can befall children who do not listen to their mother.

Similar to the first author's mother's job as a nurse and role as a parent, there are a wide array of occupations and roles that not only tell war stories per se and broadly put, but also warn of dangerous, impending "fronts." On the war per se front, journalists and broadcasters report war stories of active conflicts, but also tell war stories to persuade the citizenry and government to support those in war. On the human-risk front, statisticians and actuaries working in insurance companies issue reports and develop policies that read like "battle plans" to insure against a legion of risks facing human life and property. On the health-care front, epidemiologists, CDC workers, and health reporters issue warnings about pandemics and plagues. On the crime front, law enforcement personnel, crime reporters, and similar roles all warn about dangerous neighborhoods and crime zones. And, of course on the weather front, meteorologists stand at the ready to report about storm fronts. The primary job of these and other similar occupations and societal roles is to track and tell stories of approaching fronts (of crime, health, weather, world conflicts, etc.). Related to resilience, these individuals and groups (a) warn us about all sorts of potential dangers, (b) persuade us to go about daily living more safely in order to avoid and minimize future dangers, (c) teach us how to cope with the tasks of surviving post-war or post-storm, and in general, (d) add to our storehouses of information in service of preventing, managing, and/or bouncing back from struggles or battles.

In war per se and war broadly put, as well as post-war, we also find artists singing and performing war stories. For example, shortly after Hurricane Katrina—a circumstance similar to war per se that left residents of New Orleans homeless, hungry, and without schools and places of work and worship—an inspirational song written by singer/song writer Jimmy Buffet offered a message to those when all is lost "...breathe in, breathe out, move on." There are also websites devoted to music that tell war stories (e.g., see http://ultimateclassicrock.com/songs-about-war/) and, of course, Edwin Starr (1970) asked in his song "War? What is it good for?"

This chapter seeks to help advance the theme of the volume on hope and resilience by offering a conceputalization of war stories told about wars per se, wars broadly put, and related kinds of discourse as communicative accounts of resilience that have the potential to facilitate hope and increase resilience. That is, war stories of wars per se and wars broadly put communicate about human resilience and survival in the face of life/death ordeals and/or significant struggles, and, depending on a variety of factors that we will explore later in the chapter, war stories may also help to strengthen and empower hearers so they too might survive and cope with post-war struggles, avoid pitfalls, or in other words, enhance resilience. And, drawing on hope theory (Snyder, 2000), hearing stories of veterans and survivors may also help facilitate pathways thinking (ways around obstacles) as well as promote agentic thinking (I am worthy of survival), both of which are key factors of facilitating hope.

The chapter also seeks to further expand our conceptual understanding of war stories for use in future communication research. First, although the conventions used to label an event as war per se may generally be understood (although the Vietnam War/Conflict may be an exception) the process of labeling an event as war broadly put may not be straightforward. For example, should photocopy repair technicians who share their "battles" with particular machines with fellow technicians count as telling war stories broadly put (Orr, 1996)? Or, when we read a newsletter headline, "Tales From the Trenches: A Call for Stories From the Front Lines," although it may sound like it refers to a war story per se, does it? This particular headline refers to a form of war broadly put where the author is "...seeking written perspectives from front line child-support professionals who describe their success stories and experiences" (National Child Support Enforcement Association, 2014). If this particular kind of discourse is to be considered a war story broadly put, it is assumed that there is a war front of some kind being fought on behalf of children, and those battling at the front are somehow regarded as warriors for kids. This former example may also qualify as a war story broadly put if repairing machines is somehow perceived as a battle and their subsequent talk about machines as war stories. If there are winners and losers, that is, machines winning battles over people, or people winning battles over machines then such tales might be classified as stories of "war."

Second, wars per se, as well as wars broadly put, are, sadly, also a lifespan phenomenon. In the U.S., experiences of war per se primarily occur among those in early-adulthood to early-middle adulthood (ages 18–30) who chose to volunteer for military service. However, sadly, around the world, children (from infants to age 17) are experiencing war per se (Daiute & Turniski, 2005; Green, chapter 9, this volume). And, although in general those in later life may not face war per se as enemy combatants, they can face war per se as victims and refugees, and can also face war broadly put on many fronts that include healthcare, mobility, and more.

Third, we must remember that experiencing war per se and war broadly put and their accompanying war stories are situated in historical times and places. Thus, although war stories might share basic structural and content elements, it would seem that the war stories of WWII veterans, for example, would be qualitatively different from the war stories of veterans from Vietnam, or Afghanistan, and even within a particular war per se, war stories would be different depending on the particular front on which one battled (in WWII in Europe or the Pacific).

Finally, among the possible outcomes of individuals experiencing wars per se and wars broadly put, and about which veterans and survivors can communicate, include: survival-unharmed, survival-injured (suffering short-term and/or long-term damage), survival-strengthened, or of course death (literally or metaphorically). Related to the theme of this volume, the ability to survive and return home from war per se as well as war broadly put (whether unharmed, harmed, or strengthened) speaks to the essence of the concept of resilience, "the quality or fact of being able to recover quickly or easily from, or resist being affected by, a misfortune, shock, illness, etc.; robustness; adaptability" (*Oxford English Dictionary Online*, 2014). Further, war stories as accounts of human resilience, can, in some circumstances, function as a communicative means of facilitating hope. Following hope theory (Snyder, 2000), sharing war stories per se and broadly put can be conceptualized as one means among many to promote pathways thinking, that is, offering insights into how we might manage obstacles, as well as how we might avoid pitfalls. Thus, war stories (per se and broadly put) as accounts of human resilience are one means that can potentially facilitate hope and can be included among the many forms of positive interpersonal communication (Socha & Pitts, 2012).

In the remaining pages, we will take a closer look at the concept of war story as an account of human resilience potentially facilitating hope as follows. First, we will review previous literature about the "war story." Second, drawing on the review, we will illustrate the theoretical utility of Burke's (1969) dramatistic pentad as well as Positioning Theory (Davies & Harre, 1990) to better understand what factors might influence the effective communication of war stories as accounts of resilience facilitative of hope. Finally, following these reviews, we will conclude that effectively communicating war stories (per se as well as broadly put) in order to facilitate resilience and hope is a vital but complex form of lifespan communication that is worthy of future study. Effectively communicating war stories involves striking a balance between and among the content of the war story, the circumstances of its telling, qualities of tellers, manner of telling, and reasons for its telling. Let's turn next to a review of the literature of "war stories."

Studies of War Stories Per Se

Veterans of war per se (and war broadly put) are subjected to events that are stored as both personal memories and collective memories. Lomsky-Feder (2004) argued, in an analysis of wars per se, that as social constructions wars per se focus attention on the agent and forces constraining the agent in recounting the memory. That is, what is the agent free to recall and free to disclose? Lomsky-Feder finds patterns in war pe se recollections. One pattern finds "war as foreign to the course of normal life, perceiving it as a difficult and stressful experience with far-reaching and transformative repercussions"

(p. 83): an autobiographical memory of war per se. Another pattern finds war as "national [collective] memory" that is negotiated "...among different groups and interests" (p. 84). This latter pattern focuses on the "strategic use and liberating potential" of war remembrances and retellings as they are regulated and constrained by social and cultural forces. "As such, personal narratives of war veterans should be read as a cultural text that interweaves the private experience with collective representations that constitute the memory field of war" (p. 85). Thus, each war story (per se and broadly put) is a contextualized representation of both private and public memories.

Sim and Alspaugh (2011) conceptualized war stories (per se and broadly put) as a genre. "A war story is a narrative that presents a non-routine and difficult event for the purpose of explicating a more general piece of knowledge" (p. 463). War stories as a genre share common elements. Sim and Alspaugh's content analysis of elicited war stories (broadly put) asked participants to recall a "highly memorable occasion when adversity was overcome with great effort" (p. 460). They offered five key features of war stories broadly put that could easily apply to war per se. First, war stories are about exceptional circumstances. For example, telling a story about commuting safely to work would not be considered a war story unless commuting meant overcoming some adversity with great effort like traversing minefields, being shot at, changing a flat on the side of a busy interstate, and so on.

Second, war stories are diverse and resistant to be combined into a single "grand" narrative. Each war story is a personal account, and although a particular adversity may be experienced by lots of people, each person's war story is unique. This is illustrated by the work of the Shoah Foundation (USC Shoah Foundation, 2014), where they have collected over 53,000 testimonies of survivors of the Holocaust. There are also many Internet sites such as HolocaustSurvivors.org that feature many survivor stories and photos where each survivor shares his/her own unique account. Among such stories is that of Isak Borenstein (2014):

> I was arrested in the forest and taken to a prison in Dnepropetrovsk. In jail somebody told them I looked like a Jew. They brought me down into the death chamber of the jail. There in the basement of the jail was a dark room. It was maybe 6 feet wide and 25 feet long. Just one brick was taken out for air. They kept me down there for ten days.... In the death chamber I was tortured. I was given cold showers. I was beaten with leather straps until my skin turned the color of wood...I was put into a labor camp near Dnepropetrovsk...It was pure luck that I survived.... They came to get us to go defuse this bomb. There was no way we could unscrew the fuse. So I asked them to bring me a metal chisel and a hammer. I sat down on the bomb and tried to knock it loose. I kept hammering until the fuse broke off. At this everybody started running

away. I just got up and looked at it, like it was nothing. Dead today or dead tomorrow. I don't know if I was so stupid. I did not care if I was alive. I was so lucky.

Another Holocaust survivor, Eva Galler (2014), recalls:

> They took us to a cattle train. People started to run away from the train, but they were shot. Once on the train we had to stand because there was no room to sit down. A boy tore the barbed wires from the train window. The young people started to jump out of the window. Many jumped. The SS on the rooftop of the train shot at them with rifles. My father told us, the oldest three, "Run, run—maybe you will stay alive. We will stay here with the small children because even if they get out, they will not be able to survive." To me he said, "You run, I know you will stay alive. You have the Belzer Rebbe's blessing." He was very religious and he believed this. My brother Berele jumped out, then my sister Hannah, and then I jumped out. The SS men shot at us. I landed in a snowbank. The bullets did not hit me. When I did not hear anything anymore, I went back to find my brother and my sister. I found them dead. My brother Berele was 15. My sister Hannah was 16. I was 17.

Although these two stories are part of larger WWII and Holocaust narratives and share common elements of those surviving unimaginable adversities faced in war, they are also each unique and highly personal accounts of human resilience.

Third, war stores as text can be analyzed using the any and all of the theories concepts from the humanities. There are many sides of war stories as post-modern constructions where meanings in war stories are social constructions open to many interpretations that are, in part, dependent on the positions of the tellers and hearers (Davies & Harre, 1990). This point provides a warrant to consider the utility of Positioning Theory (Davies & Harre, 1990) in future analyses of war stories (something we will take up later in the chapter).

Fourth, war stories are not just texts; they are performances. "Participants carefully select and self-edit the stories they tell to emphasize points that are relevant to the situation or to help them achieve a goal" (Sim & Alspaugh, 2011, p. 461). As with all stories, the performance element is of course significant to the effectiveness of telling war stories. An essay by O'Brien (1990), for example, noticed the sunlight on the face of a fellow Vietnam combatant and friend standing next to him just before his friend stepped on a booby trap and was blown to bits. He also recalls another fellow combatant and friend singing the song, "Lemon Tree," as together they scraped what was left of his friend's body from the tree. This finding of war stories as performance provides a clear theoretical warrant for the utility of Dramatistic Analysis (Burke, 1969) as a means to more closely understand and interpret war stories.

And fifth, war stories are instructive and historical. They serve multiple purposes for multiple audiences. Rizzuti (2011), in "War Stories for Beer," tells his Vietnam war story as a means to help psychologists better understand PTSD. In his essay he mentions a variety of audiences for war stories including "families of combat veterans, readers of literature, academic types interested in teaching/studying Vietnam War or the effects of combat...readers of novels and Professors of Literature and History...Professors of behavioral sciences [in psychology and Sociology], and history professors" (p. 73). This point too adds an additional warrant for the use of Dramatistic analysis in future studies of war stories as the audiences for such stories is quite diverse and assumed to have varying agenda as they listen to, or read, war stories.

The literature on war stories also features articles and books on war stories conveyed in film. For example, some film scholars have focused on the way music is used in war movies as Pieslak (2007) did in his analysis about music and films about the war in Iraq. Pieslak argues that music was used to "inspire combat, as a psychological tactic, and as a form of soldiers' expression" (p. 123). Other film scholars examine the tellers of war stories. Braudy (2007), for example, examined director Clint Eastwood's telling of war stories in the films *Flags of our Fathers* and *Letters from Iwo Jima*. He noticed that the late careers of directors can be their best. "I have called *Letters* Clint Eastwood's Iliad, but it is not an Iliad of grand single combats between heroic warriors so much as one of hierarchy and subordination and submission to rigid ideals that leave little room for individual nature" (Braudy, 2007, p. 23). Although the telling of war stories has been understudied in interpersonal communication the scholarly literature about war movies is large and rich and further emphasizes the performative sides of war stories.

Another aspect of war stories examined in the scholarly literature pertains to family discourse. Seaton's (2006) article, "Do you really want to know what your uncle did? Coming to terms with relatives' war actions in Japan" focuses on war stories as family oral histories. Seaton also examines problems Japanese families face in managing public-familial conflicts pertaining to war stories. Interviews with Japanese war per se veterans and their families finds that Japanese families (and school children) do not want to talk about issues of war responsibility. "The Japanese are frequently accused of failing to address the past or denial, ignorance, or amnesia concerning the war. ...the reality is...that debate over war responsibilty issues has ensured that war history remains highly contested in Japan..." (p. 54). Underlying motivations to face the past in Japanese families are highly complex. Seaton was distressed, for example, about revealing the stories gathered for the study to the families as they would cause undue family stress by revealing face-threating actions. In Japanese families, it would seem that the content of war stories told by family members, if told at all, would be heavily shaped by cultural norms. Such stories may not (or may) be viewed as sources of pride for Japanese families, and are perhaps less useful in facilitating resilience and hope. Indeed, for some families telling war stories in this particular cultural context may disempower and diminsh hope. But, is the situation of telling or avoiding telling face threatening war stories in Japan different than Vietnam veterans telling war stories that involved committing war crimes? Some stories from Vietnam, for example, are featured on the Library of Congress website, "Experiencing the Vietnam War: Stories from the Veterans' History (*Experiencing the Vietnam War*, 2014). This site offers edited versions of numerous personal experience war stories that emphasize the heroic sides of war. Alternatively, there are also thousands of other websites that tell darker war stories of witnessing the killing of civillians, needless deaths of friends, followed by decades of failed attempts at therapy, and more. One website that is representative of dark Vietnam war stories is "Hell of a War, The Story of a Vietnam Veteran" (Hell of a War, 2014), where the Vet tells his story of being drafted, not wanting to kill cilivians (but being forced to), having little food (feeling he was being left to die), and thirty plus years of weekly failed therapy attempts most of which took place during a time when the term *post-traumatic stress disorder* (PTSD) had yet to be coined.

Today, with respect to the telling of war stories for therapeutic reasons, the topic of PTSD figures large. According to the Mayo Clinic website (Mayo Clinic, 2014):

> Post-traumatic stress disorder (PTSD) is a mental health condition that's triggered by a terrifying event—either experiencing it or witnessing it. Symptoms may include flashbacks, nightmares and severe anxiety, as well as uncontrollable thoughts about the event. Many people who go through traumatic events have difficulty adjusting and coping for a while, but they don't have PTSD—with time and good self-care, they usually get better. But if the symptoms get worse or last for months or even years and interfere with your functioning, you may have PTSD.

PTSD symptoms are "generally grouped into four types: intrusive memories, avoidance, negative changes in thinking and mood, or changes in emotional reactions" (Mayo Clinic, 2014) and should these occur for more than a month, or are severe, medical attention is needed.

Psychiatric and medical communities are increasingly sensitive to the uniquely contextualized war stories that returning war per se veterans tell. Russell (2013), for example, reflected on the vastly different kinds of homecomings of returning veterans of WWI and WWII compared with Vietnam, and those of Iran, Iraq, and Afghanistan, and the therapeutic and medical implications of these varied experiences on veterans' tellings of their war stories as a part of PTSD therapy. Some veterans (WWII) returned to tell their war stores amid public celebrations as heroes, while others returned to a world that not only did not want to hear their war stories, but to one where they were spit on and publically ridiculed.

A U.S. government website, the National Center for PTSD (2014) of the Department of Veterans Affairs, features the latest information about the treatment of PTSD for professionals, researchers, families, and veterans. The site reports "Cognitive behavioral treatments typically include a number of components, including psychoeducation, anxiety management, exposure, and cognitive restructuring. Exposure and cognitive restructuring are thought to be the most effective components" (PTSD Professional, 2014). These therapeutic approaches share a common assumption that repeated tellings of a traumatic war story (exposure) is an effective therapeutic means to re-experience the trauma in order to diminish its negative effects as well as move the veteran or survivor to a place where deeper insights might be gained. Experimental research has found that such an approach is effective in reducing PTSD symptons (PTSD Professional, 2014). Thus, there is empircal evidence that the telling of war stories for those experiencing PTSD can have psychological benefits for the teller. The benefits of retelling war stories for those veterans without PTSD is not known and awaits future research.

A final thread of research about war stories can be found in the literature of organizational communication. Wines and Hamilton (2008), for example, argue that when needing to change organizational culture, "One component of a less costly approach is to tell new and different stories within the corporation because stories establish the DNA that gives organizations, families, and individuals their identities" (p. 433). Among the stories that organizational participants tell, similar to military organizations, pertain to battles on a variety of fronts that include heroes fighting the forces of evil, winning battles, and more. In fact within military organizations war stories are used to create and teach organizational culture. Kaurin (2007), for example, showcased war stories as a primary means to teach warrior identity, ethics, and more. However, today's military traning includes not only traditional aspects of battle preparation but also training for *military operations other than war* (MOOTW). Although combat and MOOTW training may require different skill sets, both are still a part of the overall military culture that is created, shared, and perpetuated by means of stories. "Telling, retelling and discussing war stories is something that is done as an integral part of military life" (p. 12).

Summary

War stories can be regarded as a genre of narrative where personal and collective memories of overcoming signficant (sometimes life-threatening) ordeals are shared (or not) by veterans and survivors themselves as well as others for a variety of reasons within the contexts of relationships, families, organizations, and mass-media culture. War stories as expressions of personal and collective identity matter in the management of personal and social relationships as well as within societal groups and organizations. The literature of war stories also documents therapeutic benefits for those who tell war stories as well as organizational benefits for using war stories in changing organizational cuture. Past literature also suggests the utility of considering Dramatistic Analysis (Burke, 1969) and Positoning Theory (Davies & Harre, 1990) in future studies of war stories. We turn next to a brief explication of these theories to argue for their utility.

Dramatistic Analysis and Positioning Theory

As highlighted in the previous section, war stories per se and broadly put are performed. They are told at home while gathered around dinner tables, shared at bars, posted on the Internet, filmed for televison or the big screen, sung about, and more. As war stories are perfomed, participants are postioned; an "assigment of parts or roles to speakers in the discursive construction of personal stories" (Langenhove & Harre, 1993, p. 83) which matters in ascertaining whether the war story will have its desired effects.

Kenneth Burke's Dramatistic Pentad (Burke, 1969) represents a potentially heuristically rich analytical scheme for use in the analysis of war stories as accounts of resilience that have the potential to facilitate resilience and hope. For Burke, effective communication in the form of identification relied on a balance of five elements of his Pentad. We will introduce these elements and briefly consider their implications for communicating war stories.

Acts

For Burke, the act of telling a war story focuses on what happened. What is the action? What is going on? From past studies we learn that war stories per se and broadly put communicate a "narrative" of a "memory" (personal and/or shared) about a "significant ordeal" that is "overcome" to some extent where the "language of war per se" is used to tell the story (e.g., terms like "battle," "fight," etc.). By defintition, war stories are accounts of resilience, of bouncing back, of survival in the face of war per se and/or war broadly put.

Studies of the content of war stories show that they are, on the one hand, highly unique expressions of individuals' personal memories and identities and as such are impossible to summarize in an overarching narrative. Thus, although the experience may be of the same "ordeal" (e.g., Vietnam War) there are potentially an endless number of war stories to be told about it. Yet, on the other hand, war stories are also expressions of shared memories and identities that are open to the vicissitudes of culture, negotiation, and political process. Thus, on the other hand we also have, to some extent, a standarization of the elements of the war story such that a plotline can become recognizable and war stories emerge as a genre of discourse.

A key element of the content of the effective war story refers to the "significance" of the ordeal. Hearing a war story about "hanging on the ledge," "seconds away from death," for example, would be likely perceived as "signficant" by most hearers. Further, to count as a war story there needs to be an opposing force (human or natural), that serves as an enemy of some kind with which to engage in battle. Thus, in making choices about the content of a war story veterans and survivors must consider what will a particular listener want to hear?

Scenes

The element of scene for Burke asks where is the war story being told? What is the background situation? Does the content fit the scene? Theoretically, war stories can be told in any context, but they also seem to "fit" some scenes "better" than others. As war stories focus on overcoming ordeals, we would expect to find them in scenes where lamenting and forgetting might typically happen such as bars, therapists' offices, confessionals, family dinners, VFW halls, American Legion halls, corporate offices, and the Internet. Each of these scenes places different kinds of performance expectations on the teller. That is, telling a war story among veterans on a Friday night at the American Legion hall is different than telling the same war story at home during a holiday dinner. Each of these rhetorical situations calls forth different kinds of expectancies that must be considered if the narrative is to increase identification.

Agents

Who is involved in the telling and hearing war stories? What are their roles? To effectively tell war stories this element is of particular significance. Reading and listening to the first person narratives of Holocaust survivors (two were included earlier) is different than hearing a historian tell the stories about their ordeals. Hearing stories from war-veteran uncles who might have committed war crimes, for example, also changes the hearer's perceptions of the teller. Also, we must ask about the rules of war story telling, such as who is "allowed" to tell a particular war story? For example, among military veterans, unless the teller was under fire and/or somehow injured in the line of duty, they are occupying a role of diminished legitimacy in telling a given war story to other vets. However, it might be OK if they told the same story to a neice or nephew. Further, theoretically, the pool of the tellers of war stories (broadly put) is large as it would include anyone who has overcome a significant obstacle. The pool of hearers of war stories broadly put is again theoretically large, but pragmatically, however, would likely be limited to roles such as mental health professionals, bar tenders, academics, families, and so on.

In war stories, agents can cast themselves (or be cast by others) as heroes, victims, bystanders, or villians. How a teller of a war story positions himself or herself is also dependent in part on the roles of the hearers. That is, if the hearers of a war story are, for example, sympathetic family members, the teller might be more willing to adopt a heroic role, whereas the same teller might be just another soldier doing his/her job when telling the story to a fellow veteran. For those fighting cancer, for example, telling their war story might change not only as a function of the qualities of the hearer, but also change over the course of the treatment as the roles of family members might change as a function of repeated tellings.

Positioning theory (Davies & Harre, 1990) would predict that the same war story will have different interpretations dependent on the relative position of the teller in relation to the hearer, that is, if the teller of a war story is a teacher, and the hearer is a student, the interpretation would be different if the hearer was a fellow vet. One can position oneself in a war story as a first-person actor or commentator, or can let the hearer position the teller.

Agency

How do the agents act when telling war stories? By what means do they act? A member of the first author's extended family used to voluntarily tell a few war stories from his experiences in WWII in the Pacific to his nephew and first author in animated verbal stories, but only after family dinners had ended, and only after the women had left the room. He would not share war stories with his female relatives. In the *Hell of a War* (2014) video the teller shares his story via a video uploaded to YouTube as a part of a university course focusing on the Vietnam War, where the professor is also a veteran telling his story. Some may tell their war stories in writing, while others may tell their story via a screenplay shown on the silver screen. Some tell the war story in angry tones.

For example, some Vietnam veterans tell their war stories in angry protest of their mistreatment that includes returning their war medals (e.g., see *Why Vietnam Veterans Threw Back Their Medals*, 2014; *Vietnam Veterans' Treatment Coming Home*, 2014).

Purpose

Why do the agents tell war stories? What do they want? This final componenet of Burke's Pentad highlights the motivations for telling war stories. Thus far, we see that motivations to tell war stories (per se and broadly put) can vary from gaining personal therapeutic benefit, to forming relational bonds, to protesting, to gaining attention, and more. It is also likely that there are many motives that combine to motivate someone to tell the war story. However, a hearer's perceptions of a teller's motives will affect a hearer's interpretations; that is, if a person is perceived to be telling a war story for the purpose of self-promotion, a hearer might view the story as less interesting, lowering identification.

Conclusions and Implications for Future Inquiry

The "war story" is a communicative means to express resilience where its effectiveness as a force for increasing resilience would seem to depend on striking a balance between and among the act, scene, agent, agency, and purpose as well as the relative position of the teller and hearer. This essay raises many questions for future research on war stories as accounts of resilience facilitative of hope. For example, how should a person returning home with a diagnosis of cancer go about telling his/her cancer war story to faciliate resilience within his/her family? And, as the days pass, should a cancer patient alter the ongoing story? How? And, when should a cancer patient begin to hear the war stories of other cancer survivors? It would seem that timing (an element of scene and purpose) is important in shaping when and if the war story can serve as a source facilitative of resilience and hope. There would seem to be benefits for the tellers of war stories (although we need to see if there are others), but are there benefits for hearers? As couples experience wars, if, how, and for what purpose do they share their war stories with each other? How do family members of different generations tell war stories at home? What is the effect of communicating war stories (per se and broadly put) on the quality of family relationships? These and many other questions about war stories remain for future inquiry, but also suport this essay's primary contention: war stories can serve as a communicative archetype of human resilience potentially faciliative of hope—a form of positive communication.

References

Borenstein, I. (2014). Survivor stories. Retrieved from http://www.holocaustsurvivors.org/data.show.php?di=record&da=survivors&ke=1

Braudy, L. (2007). Flags of our fathers/Letters from Iwo Jima. *Film Quarterly, 60*, 16-23.

Burke, K. (1969). *A grammar of motives.* Los Angeles: University of California Press.

Daiute, C., & Turniski, M. (2007). Young people's stories of conflict and development in post war Croatia. *Narrative Inquiry, 15*(2), 217-240.

Davies, B., & Harre, R. (1990). Positioning: The discursive production of selves. *Journal of the Theory of Social Behavior, 20*, 43-63.

Elliott Sim, S., & Alspaugh, T. A. (2011). Getting the whole story: An experience report on analyzing data elicited using the war stories procedure. *Empirical Software Engineering, 16*, 460-486.

Experiencing the Vietnam War. (2014). Retrieved from http://www.loc.gov/vets/stories/

Galler, E. (2014). *Survivor stories.* Retrieved from http://www.holocaustsurvivors.org/data.show.php?di=record&da=survivors&ke=6

Hell of a war. (2014). Retrieved from https://www.youtube.com/watch?v=D-t__6RzIJ4/.

Kaurin, P. M. (2007, January). War stories: Narrative, identity, and reacasting military ethics pedagogy. A paper presented at the annual meeting of the International Society for Military Ethics, Springfield, VA. Retrieved from http:isme.tamu.edu/ISME07/Kaurin07.html

Langenhove, L .V., & Harre, R. (1993). Positioning and autobiography: Telling your life. In N. Coupland & J. F. Nussbaum (Eds.), *Discourse and lifespan identity* (pp. 81-99). Newbury Park, CA: Sage.

Lomsky-Feder, E. (2004). Life stories, war and veterans; On the social distribution of memories. *Ethos, 32*, 82-109.

Lutters, G. L., & Seaman, C. B. (2007). Revealing actual documentation usage in software maintenance through war stories. *Information and Software Technology, 49*(6), 576-587.

Mayo Clinic. (2014). Post traumatic stress disorder. Retrieved from http://www.mayoclinic.org/diseases-conditions/post-traumatic-stress-disorder/basics/definition/con-20022540

National Center for PTSD. (2014). Retrieved from http://www.ptsd.va.gov/professional/index.asp.

National Child Support Enforcement Association. (2014). Retrieved from http://www.ncsea.org/

O'Brien, T. (1990). How to tell a true war story. In T. O'Brien (Ed.), *The things they carried* (pp. 64-81). New York: Houghton Mifflin.

Orr, J. E., (1996). *Talking about machines: An ethnography of a modern job.* Ithaca, NY: Cornell University Press.

Oxford English Dictionary Online. (2014). Retrieved from www.oed.com.

Pieslak, J. R. (2007). Sound targets: Music and the war in Iraq. *Journal of Musicological Research, 26*, 123-129.

Rizzutti, T. P. (2011). War stories for beer. *Literature in the Arts: An International Journal of the Humanities, 23*, 72-78.

Russell, S. S. (2013). Veterans' stories: What they may have to tell is—A personal reflection. *Urologic Nursing, 33,* 92-96.

Seaton, P. (2006). Do you really want to know what your uncle did? Coming to terms with relatives' war actions in Japan. *Oral History, 34,* 53-60.

Sim, S. E., & Alspaugh, T. A. (2011). Getting the whole story: An experience report on analyzing data elicited using the war stories procedure. *Empirical Software Engineering, 16,* 460-486.

Snyder, C. R. (Ed.). (2000). *Handbook of hope: Theories, measures, applications.* San Diego, CA: Academic Press.

Socha, T. J., & Pitts, M. J. (Eds.). (2012). *The positive side of interpersonal communication.* New York: Peter Lang.

Starr, E. (1970). Edwin Starr website. Retrieved from http://www.edwinstarr.info/

USC Shoah Foundation. (2014). Retrieved from http://sfi.usc.edu/

Vietnam veteran's treatment coming home. (2014). Retrieved from https://www.youtube.com/watch?v=WbynlYWYC5U.

Why Vietnam veterans threw back their medals. (2014). Retrieved from https://www.youtube.com/watch?v=_kiJnQxnnNc.

Wines, W. A., & Hamilton, J. B. (2008). On changing organizational cultures in injecting new ideologies: The power of stories. *Journal of Business Ethics, 89,* 433-447.

• CHAPTER THIRTEEN •

Fostering Civic Resilience and Hope Through Communication Activism Education

David L. Palmer
University of Northern Colorado

Lawrence R. Frey
University of Colorado Boulder

> Let us think of education as the means of developing our greatest abilities, because in each of us is a private hope and dream which, fulfilled, can be translated into benefit for everyone.
>
> —U.S. President John F. Kennedy (1961, para. 7)

Education, inherently, is bound to hope and resilience; by its very nature, teaching seeks to instill in students both the hope for a better future and the capacity to overcome obstacles to its realization, with research demonstrating the potential of education to develop students' resilience and hope (see, e.g., Bernat, 2009; Brooks, 2006; J. H. Brown, D'Emidio-Caston, & Benard, 2001; Esquivel, Doll, & Oades-Sese, 2011; Knight, 2007). Nowhere is that bond among education, resilience, and hope more evident than in *civic education*, which, as part of the larger landscape of democratic education (with its roots in Dewey, 1916), teaches students to be engaged community members, with research showing that civic education positively affects students' resilience and hope regarding participation in community life (see, e.g., Allen, 2011; Niemi & Junn, 1998).

One pedagogy employed in civic education to make students more resilient and hopeful community members is embodied educational experiences in community contexts, such as internships and service-learning. Research has revealed many valuable personal, social, and civic outcomes of experiential education (see, e.g., meta-analyses of service-learning by Celio,

Durlak, & Dymnicki, 2011; Conway, Amel, & Gerwien, 2009; Novak, Markey, & Allen, 2007; Yorio & Ye, 2012), including positive effects on students' civic resilience and hope, typically viewed in that literature as increased citizenship knowledge, beliefs, attitudes, values, intentions, responsibilities, and behaviors (see e.g., Battistoni, 2013; Billig, 2002; Kraft & Wheeler, 2003). Some research also has demonstrated positive effects of civic-based experiential education on community organizations with which students participate (see, e.g., Edwards, Mooney, & Heald, 2001; Grey, Ondaatje, Fickler, & Geschwind, 2000), although those effects have received little attention compared to student learning (see Stoecker & Tryon, 2009).

The effects of civic experiential pedagogy on communities with which students interact, via their participation with community groups and organizations, however, has received virtually no attention (see Cruz & Giles, 2000; Geller, Zuckerman, & Seidel, 2014; Stoecker & Tryon, 2009). Moreover, that pedagogy most often has employed a charity model that views those educational experiences as student volunteers engaging in civic action to "help" communities and their members to adapt to and recover from adverse conditions (see, e.g., Artz, 2001; Britt, 2012, 2014; Morton, 1995; Verjee, 2010). For example, traditional civic instruction teaches students that poverty is a natural outcome of an economic system that privileges the class of hard-working, entrepreneurial individuals and that does not reward those who lack the motivation and discipline to attain higher class status; moreover, traditional poverty solution models stress civic volunteerism in the form of feeding, clothing, and sheltering "the poor" (using "disability language" rather than "person-first language") to have them adapt to and reintegrate into the existing system. That charity approach is in line with an "adaptation and recovery" perspective of resilience as stressed systems "bouncing back" from adversity (Coutu, 2002) and achieving "reintegration" (Richardson, 2002), a standard view that is reflected in Gunderson's (2000) depiction of resilience research as the study of how strained systems "return to equilibrium or a steady-state following a perturbation" (p. 426). Employing that perspective, civic resilience educators have instructed students and communities with which they are engaged how to, for instance, prepare for and recover from natural disasters (e.g., Cutter et al., 2008).

The charity view of civic experiential education has been challenged by scholars who adopt a social justice activism pedagogical perspective (for an overview of social justice education, see, e.g., Ayers, Quinn, & Stovall, 2009) to promote educational experiences that challenge and change systemic conditions that produce injustice (with respect to social justice activism service-learning, see, e.g., Artz, 2001; Bickford & Reynolds, 2002; Britt, 2012, 2014;

Cipolle, 2010; DePaola, 2014; Kahne & Westheimer, 1996; Marullo & Edwards, 2000; Maybach, 1996; Mitchell, 2014; Rosner-Salazar, 2007; Sternhouse & Jarrett, 2012; Wade, 2000; Wang, 2013; Warren, 1998; Westheimer & Kahne, 2007). Those scholars recognize that, with regard to poverty, liberal capitalism, by definition, is a stratified economic system that demands a poor class, one that is required to serve the production and privileged lifestyle requirements of the elite class, and that the system's organizational structures, which include education, inherently are designed to maintain that stratified system of power (see, e.g., McLaren, 2005). That system explains why, despite a host of poverty-based civic and education initiatives across the last three decades, poverty levels in the United States have continued to rise (see, e.g., Gould, Mishel, & Shierholz, 2013). From a social justice perspective, the solution is not to accept (or merely adapt to) poverty as an unfortunate social outcome and to volunteer time to "help" those who are poor but, instead, to expose, resist, and transform systems of power that create poverty in the first place. This difference in social change strategies often is referred to as "first-order" vs. "second-order" change (see Watzlawick, Weakland, & Fisch, 1974), in which the former "wants to help marginalized, community-based groups become part of the mainstream...[whereas the latter] does not just move the players into new positions on the board, it changes the board itself" (Pearce, 1998, p. 275). First-order change aids individuals after they have experienced, in this case, social justice problems, whereas second-order change prevents social justice problems from occurring by changing macrolevel systems and structures that create those problems (see, e.g., Wilson & Gettings, 2012).

Social justice activism teaching, thus, pushes students beyond the role of volunteer to that of social advocate, or, more aptly, community activist, who works with, for, and on behalf of communities that are struggling to enact second-order change of systems and structures that produce lived conditions of social injustice. To the extent that goal is accomplished, social justice activism teaching, potentially, nurtures in students and in community members, groups, and organizations the resilience and hope that is needed to continue the struggle against oppression, marginalization, and injustice. Hence, although resilience scholarship has begun to uncover how civic education can play a role in assisting communities to prepare for, adapt to, and recover from adversity, that scholarship has not addressed adequately how aiding marginalized communities to recover from social injustice adversity may entrain them back into webs of oppression and subjugation that caused, and will continue to cause, that adversity. Thus, attention needs to focus on how social justice activism teaching can promote civic resilience and hope to sustain participants' efforts to enact systemic change.

Communication scholarship, unfortunately, also has demonstrated a lack of attention to social justice activism teaching, in general, and to how it can promote participants' civic resilience and hope. Although communication scholars have been interested in a communication approach to social justice for some time (see, e.g., Frey, Pearce, Pollock, Artz, & Murphy, 1996; Swartz, 2006; for a historical overview, see Hartnett, 2010), with Frey and Carragee (2007a, 2007b, 2012) articulating and offering empirical examples of communication activism for social justice research, only a few communication scholars have applied a social justice perspective to communication education (see, e.g., Darling & Leckie, 2008; Flores, 2013; Frey et al., 1996; Lee, 2006; Makau, 1996; Pearce, 2006), and to civic experiential communication education, more specifically (with regard to service-learning, see, e.g., Artz, 2001, Crabtree, 1998; Fixmer-Oraiz & Murray, 2009; Ransom, 2009). Recently, however, Frey and Palmer (2014a) proposed and offered empirical examples of *communication activism pedagogy*, which "teaches students how to use their communication knowledge and resources (e.g., theories, research methods, pedagogies, and other practices) to work together with community members to intervene into and reconstruct unjust discourses in more just ways" (Frey & Palmer, 2014b, p. 8). Frey and Palmer (2014b) argued that communication activism pedagogy is a unique and significant form of civic experiential education because "activism, fundamentally, is an accomplishment of (constituted in), and is accomplished through, communication" (p. 24).

This chapter examines the nature and potential of communication activism pedagogy to develop in students and community members the resilience and hope that are needed to create and sustain social change, in general, and social justice, in particular. We first explicate communication activism pedagogy and then explain its connections to important processes associated with fostering resilience and hope. We then explore effects of communication activism pedagogy on students', community members', and teachers' resilience and hope. We conclude by arguing that communication activism pedagogy aligns with expanded conceptions of resilience and hope that move away from adaptation and equilibrium models; in this case, by promoting civic resilience and hope that challenges and changes unjust systemic conditions.

Communication Activism Pedagogy

Although communication activism pedagogy (CAP) projects are diverse in scope and technique, they take as their prime goal the creation of teaching spaces and practices that highlight, challenge, and attempt to change the lived realities of social injustice, such as poverty, homelessness, racial discrimination, gender violence, and economic inequality, to name but a few. CAP educators, thus, believe that it is their ethical duty, and the moral duty of students they teach, to do something about significant social injustices that characterize contemporary life (see Jovanovic, 2014). That stance stands in sharp contrast to the dominant educational position that has been designed, chiefly, to prepare students for life in the for-profit corporate sector and, in line with corporate values, teaches them that individual advancement is more important than collective good, and that not attaining the "American dream" is a result of individuals' characteristics (e.g., lack of motivation and effort) and has nothing to do with systemic factors (e.g., government and corporate economic policies; see Palmer, 2014).

To accomplish CAP's goals of promoting social justice, students first must become aware of social injustices; consequently, CAP is grounded in pedagogical philosophies, theories, and practices that develop students' critical consciousness of injustice. Foremost among those approaches is *critical pedagogy*, which, grounded in Brazilian educator Paulo Freire's (1970) work, represents an "educational movement, guided by passion and principle, to help students develop consciousness of freedom, recognize authoritarian tendencies, and connect knowledge to power and the ability to take constructive action" (Giroux, 2010, para. 1). Critical pedagogy, as Simpson (2014) explained, is comprised of three components "(a) an analysis of knowledge and power, (b) the necessity of a democratic imagination and of hope, and (c) education as an opportunity for agency and social change" (p. 85).

From a CAP perspective, however, developing students' critical consciousness is a necessary but not sufficient condition for eliminating social injustices; students also need to be taught, and provided with opportunities, to intervene into unjust situations and systems to make them more just. As Bell (2007) explained:

> The goal of social justice education is to enable people to develop the critical analytical tools necessary to understand oppression and their own socialization within oppressive systems, and to develop a sense of agency and capacity to interrupt and change oppressive patterns and behaviors in themselves and in the institutions and communities of which they are a part. (p. 2)

The centerpiece of CAP, consequently, is *intervention*, in which students work directly with community members affected by injustice and with groups and organizations fighting injustice to change systemic conditions that create and sustain injustice. CAP, thus, prepares students for, guides them through, and helps them to reflect on their interventions to understand and experience how social injustice can be directly challenged and changed through communication activism. The intervention, then, is the teaching practice that exposes students to conditions of lived oppression and to community resistance and change tactics in action, and that provides direct assistance to communities struggling against significant adversity (see, e.g., Templeton, 2010).

Communication educators are ideally positioned to provide instruction in social justice intervention because they teach communicative practices—from how to communicate collaboratively in groups, to how to present persuasive public speeches and performances, to how to create and disseminate media products, such as video documentaries (see Frey & SunWolf, 2009)—that can be employed to intervene into unjust discourses and to reconstruct them in more just ways. For example, to promote awareness of and to encourage action to end the genocide that was occurring at the time in South Sudan, Welker (2012) had students in her communication course interact with and interview Sudanese refugees in the United States about their experiences with violence in South Sudan and then taught those students how to publicly present those narratives in a community-based theater/performance piece titled *A Prayer for Sudan*. As another example, to confront rampant anti-immigration rhetoric and violence being directed toward Latino/a migrant workers laboring in the Vidalia onion fields in Lyons, Georgia, Kennerly (2014) had students in her intercultural communication course work alongside those migrant workers, with students in a colleague's advanced video production course using their production skills to visually document those interactions; expose connections among ethnicity, structural poverty, and migrant labor; and advocate for immigration reform policies, with the video documentary widely disseminated, including showing it on local television. Both of those CAP projects also involved collaborations between members of different generations (and other identity differences, such as class and ethnicity).

Teaching communication students how to be critically conscious of social injustice and systemic conditions that produce and maintain it, and how to use their communication knowledge and skills to intervene into unjust discourses to attempt to produce more just outcomes, is a form of social justice experiential education that stands in sharp contrast to the charity-oriented approach that characterizes most civic experiential education. The next section explicates key CAP processes that promote resilience and hope.

Communication Activism Pedagogy Processes to Promote Resilience and Hope

Activist educators promote resilience and hope in students and in community members, groups, and organizations by providing instruction that offers assistance and care to those who are struggling with adversity. As the material in this section demonstrates, CAP promotes resilience and hope by (a) creating shared community, (b) mobilizing social support to meet community needs, and (c) assisting stressed communities as they make decisions to manage problems.

Communication Activism Pedagogy and Creating Shared Community

Resilient groups require, first and foremost, a sense of community—a collective "us" in which members are ready to act on behalf of each other's shared interests. Shared crises instinctually draw people together, be it a sinking ship or the struggle for civil rights; membership in a community that shares the same dilemma is the social stage on which collective adversity management can occur.

CAP reflects the assumption in scholarship on resilience that people are sturdier and more proficient the more that they act together against adversity (see, e.g., Norris, Stevens, Pfefferbaum, Wyche, & Pfefferbaum, 2008). To clarify this idea, consider its opposite: that people struggling through hardships without community, essentially, are an aggregate of disenfranchised and isolated individuals whose division makes them more prone to resilience failure—the state in which affected individuals are divorced from assets and resources that aid them in their struggles with adversity, and, as a consequence, cannot recover individually and cannot work collectively to confront systemtic causes of adversity. Victims of sexual abuse, for example, often isolate themselves (see, e.g., Futa, Nash, Hansen, & Garbin, 2003; McKillop, Smallbone, Wortley, & Andijc, 2012), and, consequently, they are divorced from collective solutions both to their case and to the wider social problem of systemic sexual violence. Reinforcing the idea that people who experience significant crises belong to a vibrant community of others who share their plight is a vital step in creating conditions for collective resilience, and that is particularly the case for people who are members of oppressed, marginalized, and underresourced groups (see, e.g., Bottrell, 2009; Hernández, 2002; Tummala-Narra, 2007). CAP, thus, reflects Sonn and Fisher's (2009) premise that collective resilience is predicated on group boundary formation, a discursive "us" whose members share adversity narratives, common values and goals, and adversity management resources.

Squires and Creager (2014), for example, connected their CAP to an economically challenged community in St. Paul, Minnesota, to resist a public transit project that could fracture and dismantle that and other neighborhoods. In a joint venture between the University of Minnesota and Gordon Parks High School, an alternative high school named after the African American photographer, Gordon Parks, students gathered historical narratives of the neighborhood from residents (especially from elders) and wove those stories into digital slideshows that were presented in a variety of public venues. Community members responded with a reinvigorated sense of history, involvement, and cooperative mindset that, united (including the university and the high school), they could alter the transit project in ways that maintained their community. In this sense, CAP promotes Goodman et al.'s (1998) view of resilience as a "sense of community, characterized by high concern for community issues, respect for and service to others, sense of connection, and needs fulfillment" (p. 261).

Moreover, by linking students with those who are marginalized, oppressed, and underresourced, CAP builds community between members of traditionally disparate groups. Squires and Creager's (2014) work, for instance, connected high school students with local elders who had historical insight about the community, providing opportunities for community elders to pass onto future generations lessons that they had learned about community life (both in general and with respect to that neighborhood). Squires and Creager, thus, demonstrated how CAP interventions can promote dialogue that spans generational differences, a process and outcome that run counter to standard (nontraditional) teaching paradigms.

As another example, to confront common public stereotypes and misconceptions about those serving time in prison (e.g., as uneducated people who are immoral and drug dependent), Deal (2014) guided students' collaboration with prison inmates to produce *Committed*, a theater of testimony performance—a type of performance that "explores social injustices by challenging socially constructed stereotypes of race, class, gender, sexual orientation, disability, and other forms of difference" (p. 438)—that had students and prisoners interact and learn about and then perform the other. The performance, held in Farmville, Virginia's Robert R. Moton Museum—the site of a historic 1951 walkout by Black students to protest substandard facilities at their all-Black school—led students, inmates, and local audiences to rethink their mutual misconceptions about each other, a social process that functioned as a bridge across cultural divides that had separated them.

Additionally, as Hartnett (1998) showed in a similar CAP project in which prisoners in a communication course that he taught in a maximum security prison reenacted the Lincoln-Douglas debates about slavery, attending guards and community members came to understand how many of the tropes of racism that characterized those debates in the mid-19th century carried through to today, a realization that resulted in community members viewing this physically separated and segregated population of prisoners as fellow human beings rather than "caged animals," and that led to more humane daily treatment of them by guards within that prison system.

Communication Activism Pedagogy and Mobilizing Social Support

Social support, the perception and actuality that people are cared for and have assistance, especially in times of distress, is crucial for fostering both individual and community resilience and hope (see, e.g., Norris et al., 2008; Ozbay, Fitterling, Charney, & Southwick, 2008). Although social support, typically, is conceived at the individual level (the extent to which a person has it), it also applies at a collective level, such that resilient communities "develop effective ways of coping with the challenges of living...[and] have the capacity and resourcefulness to cope positively with adversity" (Sonn & Fisher, 1998, p. 459). Social support, cast across a community, thus, is the web of resilience-supportive interactions that aids individuals and groups as they adapt to and overcome adversity, fostering resilience patterns to adversity.

Social support takes multiple forms, including informational, instrumental, and emotional, the right combination of which can produce *social capital* in the form of resources for communities to coalesce around and mutually confront social problems. Cuny, Thompson, and Naidu (2014), for instance, mobilized students working at the University of North Carolina Greensboro's Speaking Center, to encourage and equip members of local underrepresented groups to present oral arguments at local school board meetings recommending educational policies to confront the academic achievement gap that exists between White students and Black and Latino/a students. Cuny et al. and their students provided those community members with social support and social capital in the form of a training space (instrumental support), public speaking pedagogical workshops (informational support), and consistent affective support throughout the public speaking preparation and presentation phases (emotional support). The combination of these social support forms not only brought community members together but it also offered communication resources that were needed to impel this social justice community advocacy initiative.

Communication Activism Pedagogy and Making Decisions to Manage Problems

In addition to creating a shared sense of community and acquiring social support, or, perhaps, because of those processes, members of resilient communities are adept at making decisions together and then acting on those decisions (see, e.g., Bryan, 2005). To overcome adversity, groups must be proficient at defining problems that affect them, identifying solutions to those problems, and enacting those solutions—group characteristics that often are characterized as "community competence." Cottrell (1976), for example, defined a *competent community* as one whose members

> (1) are able to collaborate effectively in identifying the problems and needs of the community; (2) can achieve a working consensus on goals and priorities; (3) can agree on ways and means to implement the agreed upon goals; and (4) can collaborate effectively in the required actions. (p. 197)

Collaborative problem solving is central to participatory civic education. Democracies privilege deliberative problem solving and employ corresponding decision-making methods (e.g., majority rule and consensus). Decision-making in democratic systems has been the focus of a large body of research, both in institutional and community settings, and, as a field of study, it has been tied to social activism since the early 1960s (see, e.g., Clark & Teachout, 2012; Gastil, 1993; Polletta, 2004). Activist groups, typically, seek to optimize consensus building and they envision their decision-making processes and practices as an embodiment of their political values, although they often do not live up to those values and need aid doing so. Palmer (2007), for example, conducted communication activism research with an antiglobalization affinity group of which he was a member that was having difficulty enacting consensus. He instituted an original consensus-building program, in line with group communication diagnostic and intervention models (see, e.g., Shultz, 1999; Sunwolf & Seibold, 1999), that taught the group's members how to better employ consensus decision-making practices.

CAP educators often seek such creative and innovative ways to aid oppressed communities' decision-making and problem solving. Osnes and Bisping (2014), for example, worked with indigenous, energy-oppressed Mayan communities in Guatemala to eliminate their burning of open fires in the home, which cause widespread health problems and countless premature deaths, and contribute substantially to climate change (see Lumoa, 2010). One simple modern solution is a clean-burning stove that the community (in particular, the women, who oversee fire-related activity) can use with a modicum of instruction. To engage community members in decision-making about this technology, Osnes and Bisping used Boal's (1985) theater of the oppressed to teach them about toxic effects of open fires and health benefits of clean-burning stoves. University students worked with local village children to create and perform theater productions that illustrated the ideas of their energy justice project, followed by forums in which community members discussed those ideas and that highlighted women's voices (which, typically, are suppressed in that culture) about their role in community sustainability.

Effects of Communication Activism Pedagogy on Resilience and Hope

When the CAP processes examined above are enacted successful, they have the power to create and sustain participants' hope and resilience. More specifically, CAP, potentially, engenders resilience and hope in students, community members, and instructors, alike.

First, CAP represents a unique form of social justice resilience education that creates hope in a class of student political advocates who are equipped to do the hard work of confronting and changing systemic conditions that create and sustain social injustice. "Hope," in this context, represents a combination of cognitive, affective, and behavioral characteristics. From a cognitive perspective, building on Stotland's (1969) work that hope reflects the expectation of goal achievement, Synder and colleagues (for an overview, see Snyder, 1994) identified two interrelated cognitive components of hope: *pathways*, perceived capability to generate successful means to accomplish desired goals, and *agency*, perceived motivation to use those means to accomplish desired goals. From an affective perspective, Averill, Caitlin, and Chon (1990) viewed hope as an emotion, with Bruininks and Malle's (2005) survey finding that people commonly "conceptualize hope as an emotion that serves the function of keeping a person focused on the desired outcome" (p. 352), especially for important but less likely outcomes over which people do not have much personal control, which characterize social justice endeavors.

CAP promotes cognitive and affective characteristics of hope by exposing students to people's lived experiences of oppression and marginalization, which leads students to understand more fully those lived experiences and to become motivated to change those unjust conditions. A student who participated in Hart and Walker's (2014) social justice activism health-care service-learning project in Belize noted that she "learned how things work, benefitting some people and hurting some. I won't be able to ignore that now" (p. 312). Another student from that course said:

> I knew about and had experienced prejudice in my life, and I'd seen others discriminated against, but this experience showed me more about the level and depth of these problems. By working together, I believe that we can change things. The community showed me that and made me believe. (Hart & Walker, p. 306)

Such experiences develop in students significant "identity anchors" that they rely on "when explaining who they are for themselves and in relation to each other" (Buzzanell, 2010, p. 4). Indeed, as Carey (2014) showed, students who completed his environmental advocacy communication course, in which they worked with an environmental group to prevent timber sales in the Pacific Northwest United States, developed a sense of an "activist self" that became an important and explicitly stated identity anchor. As a student in Enck's (2014) CAP course, titled "Gender and Violence: Dominance, Resistance, and the Cultural Production of Meaning," which had students work with organizations that actively challenge gender violence, stated at the end of the course:

> Coming into this class, I would have never described myself as a "feminist" or an "activist." After this class, now I see myself in these ways and am proud to call myself both of these. I will strive to make the world better by initiating conversation with others as often as possible. (p. 214)

The development of an activist self leads students to express hope and confidence that they can make a difference regarding social justice issues. As a student in Enck's (2014) CAP course explained:

> This class never ceased to amaze me. There was a focus on problems, but there was also a focus on being more hopeful. I know I can make the world better if I take these lessons out into the world. (p. 214)

Such comments from students who have participated in CAP endeavors could be critiqued for reflecting merely Pollyannish *optimism*, a stable tendency to "believe that good rather than bad things will happen" (Scheier & Carver, 1985, p. 219), or *wishing* for things that are not expected to occur, which is engaged in to "generate positive affect and occasionally even to escape reality by fantasizing about the future" (Bruininks & Malle, 2005, p. 338), were it not for the guided social justice interventions that are the hallmark of CAP education. By engaging in concrete actions to do something about social injustice (e.g., stop destruction of national forests and prevent violence against people on the basis of their gender, race, and other identity markers), CAP not only promotes students' cognitive and affective hope but it integrates action as a fundamental component of hope (regarding the importance of the relationship between hope and action in education, see Generett & Hicks, 2004; Hicks, Berger, & Generett, 2005). That combination is what led a student at the end of Gilbert's (2014) performance advocacy course, which focused on preventing genocide, to claim, "I will keep on advocating, especially now that I know what to do."

Moreover, students in CAP courses become more hopeful and resilient social justice advocates, in part, because they understand crucial differences between social justice and charity approaches. As a student in Murray and Fixmer-Oraiz's (2014) course, in which students worked with a variety of social justice organizations in North Carolina, explained:

> Before this class, I had done some community service [charity]. I was even a part of an organization...[that] uses some of the media techniques we learned about in class to advocate for the homeless in Chapel Hill. However, I had not been asked to examine and distinguish the difference between community service and activism, and I did not feel strongly that I could do a tremendous amount to help resolve social injustices. Learning to distinguish (although I realize we never actually defined the difference between the two) activism from community service helped me to locate exactly what kind of change I wanted my actions as an advocate for social justice to have. Not to discredit or devalue the actions of those who do community service but I do not want to be part of a band-aid solution. I want my work and my efforts as an advocate for social change to help stimulate long-term, institutional social change. This class helped me to learn the difference between the two, and to find ways to help work towards systemic social change.... Most important, my experience with service-learning helped me to realize how passionately I want to make activism a way of life. (p. 185)

In addition to its effects on students, CAP leads members of marginalized communities and groups and organizations supporting those communities to view the educational system as reaching out to them, caring about them, and wanting to work with them (and, thereby, deconstructing the all-too-common "town–gown" divide between local communities and colleges). For example, according to Kennerly (2014), Andrea Hinojosa, the cofounder and executive director of the Southeast Georgia Communities Project (SGCP), the social justice organization that Kennerly collaborated with to create the video documentary about Latino/a migrant workers (described earlier), said "that showing the video at local community meetings has introduced SEGCP as a caring community-based organization, and demonstrated that issues facing Lyons's Latino/as are important to GSU [Georgia State University]" (p. 346).

Community members also see the benefits of CAP for changing their lived struggles for the better. As an example, in Deal's (2014) CAP theater of testimony performance that involved students and prisoners exchanging roles, "prisoner-actors Tim and Robert both shared that in the days following the performance, several officers at the jail had spoken to them for the first time, and that such acknowledgment was welcomed" (p. 452). In the case of Osnes and Bisping's (2014) theater for energy justice, a staff member with the local nongovernmental organization with which these scholars worked remarked after the public performance, "I saw that people were paying a lot of attention, especially during the part that smoke affects children. People were saying, 'We need to pay attention to this because our children are there in the house with us'" (p. 477). Influencing parents (and other adult community members) via children's theatrical performance has been documented in other research that shows the power of such intergenerational persuasion (see, e.g., Conquergood, 1988; Sithamparanathan, 2003; Sun, 2009). Moreover, the young children who performed the theater skits in Osnes and Bisping's CAP, being the generation most likely to make the change from burning open fires to using fuel-efficient cook stoves, certainly saw the intended outcome; as one of those students shared, "I don't like the house because there is a lot of smoke and danger from the fire. All of those things are real, and they don't have to happen. We could use the stoves" (p. 477).

Finally, CAP offers teachers the resilience and hope that they need to continue employing this important form of teaching. Carey (2014), in describing lessons learned from teaching his environmental advocacy course (described earlier), noted that not only did students come to identify themselves as activists but that he renewed his view of himself as an activist:

> This project reminded me of what it means to be a lifelong academic activist, as communication activism requires commitment to embodied social justice that does not end after class sessions are over. Such activism transcends the confining categories and disciplines of academia via a commitment to promoting social justice through teaching, research, and service, creating, in the case of teaching, opportunities for students to learn to be activists. (p. 281)

Sustaining resilience is especially important for CAP educators because of the significant time and energy that CAP demands, and maintaining hope is crucial because of frustration that teachers (and students and community members) can experience from not being able to systemically change significant social justice problems. As Hart and Walker (2014), reflecting on their international health CAP, stated:

> Although social justice activism service-learning endeavors require far more time and work than teaching traditional courses (including those that employ other forms of service-learning), they also, simultaneously, rejuvenate and fill us with hope for the possibilities of academic instruction changing the world. (p. 317)

Conclusion: Communication Activism Pedagogy and the Promotion of Adaptive and Transformative Social Justice Resilience and Hope

Contemporary education, in general, concentrates, primarily, on student professional training for the corporate sector (see Palmer, 2014), with only a small portion of it focusing on social problems and an even smaller portion examining social justice problems. Some educators have employed experiential pedagogy (e.g., service-learning) to offer students civic educational opportunities, but most of that civic experiential education is conducted from a charity perspective that (albeit, often unintentionally) promotes first-order change that reproduces systemic conditions that are sources of problems being confronted. Colby, Ehrlich, Beaumont, and Stephens (2003) provided a humorous but compelling example of the effects of that approach, noting:

> A faculty member at one campus we visited told of a student volunteering at a soup kitchen who very much enjoyed the experience and felt that it had made him a better person. Without thinking through the implications of his statement, he said, "I hope it is still around when my children are in college." (p. 71)

Both corporate and charity-oriented civic education, certainly, can cultivate resilience and hope in students (and, in the case of civic education, in community members and organizations interacting with those students), but they do so from a perspective that is predicated on perpetuating the status quo, which means preserving systemic features that create and maintain injustice. Those educational approaches, thus, envision resilience and hope, in line with traditional definitions, as adversity adaptation and system reintegration (see, e.g., Luthar, Cicchetti, & Becker, 2007; Richardson, 2002).

Scholars, however, have recognized the limitations of that view, for, as Norris et al. (2007) maintained, "in some circumstances, stability (or failure to change) could point to a lack of resilience" (p. 130); indeed, in circumstances where change is needed, "resilience discourse" that promotes adaptation "as another means of preserving the status quo... may be simply another mode of oppression" (McMahon, 2006, p. 50). In such cases, it is better for unjust systems to fail than to adapt successfully and continue their unjust practices.

There is, however, another alternative, as scholars have conceived of resilience not only as adaptation and system reintegration but also as transformation of systems (see, e.g., McMahon, 2006). As D. D. Brown and Kulig (1996–1997) argued:

> The concept of resiliency in the context of communities needs to be grounded in a notion of human agency, understood in the sense of the capacity for meaningful, intentional action.... Individuals and collectives are resilient in the first sense insofar as they act in such a way as to recover from what they define as negative physical or social events. Individuals and collectives are resilient in a second sense insofar as they act to transform their physical and social environments to mitigate against such events in the future. (p. 30)

This view of resilience as transformation and social change, demanding critique (McMahon, 2006, p. 55), resistance (see, e.g., Bottrell, 2007), and intervention (see, e.g., D. D. Brown & Kulig, 1996-1997), is in line with a social justice approach (see Morrow, 2008), which would argue that adaptability is a necessary condition in the struggle against injustice (for, clearly, the failure of systems to adapt to conditions threaten their existence, ultimately leading to their extinction), but it is not a sufficient condition; that struggle must be tied to social resistance that transforms systemic conditions of social injustice. As D. D. Brown and Kulig (1996-1997) maintained, "People might not only cope with a specific crisis, they might also take actions to eventually mitigate or remove the structural basis for such crises, e.g., poverty" (p. 42). The difference between system adaptability and transformation, thus, mirrors the difference between first-order and second-order change, with, in the context of social justice, adaptability referring to practices that communities can employ to adjust to unjust social conditions, and transformation referring to practices that communities can employ both to change localized conditions of oppression and to support the broader project of refashioning social systems and structures that produce injustice in the first place.

This view of resilience and hope as transformative social change to create just systems has important implications for civic, democratic education. As McMahon (2006) argued:

> Education within a democratic society and for democratic participation goes beyond preparing students to be passive, job-ready citizens. For active citizenship in a democratic society, resilience for all students must be seen as being "able to participate in society so as to transform inequities that impeded full participation in democratic life" (Simon 2001, 12).... A resiliency concept based on an ideology of emancipation (Freire 1998) or education for democratic transformation (Portelli and Solomon 2001), rather than reinforcing existing hegemonic structures, has the potential to be meaningful, empowering, and transforming. (pp. 54, 50)

By teaching students how to use their communication resources to intervene with, for, and on behalf of marginalized communities to change systemic conditions that create injustice, communication activism pedagogy seeks not only to aid affected communities to adapt to and recover from adversity but also to challenge and transform homeostatic sociostructural conditions that are the genesis of social injustices. Britt (2012) aptly described communication activism pedagogy as a form of teaching in which

> students are encouraged to see themselves as potential change agents who, supported by a critical pedagogical structure, begin to uncover systemic causes and pressures that lead to disparities in resources, rights, and dignity.... The best outcomes are achieved when students both recognize systemic influences on important social issues and have some success intervening to change the dominant system. (p. 85)

Communication activism pedagogy, thus, promotes both the adaptive resilience and hope that are needed to weather and challenge social injustice, and the transformative resilience and hope that are needed to strive toward and achieve systemic social change. In the final analysis, adaptive resilience and hope without long-term systemic social justice is a recipe for lifetimes of misery, but transformative resilience and hope without weathering injustices means never achieving the life that all people deserve.

References

Allen, J. K. (2011). Teaching for civic engagement: Lesson learned from integrating positive psychology and future studies. *Journal of University Teaching & Learning Practice*, 8(3). Retrieved from http://ro.uow.edu.au/jutlp

Artz, L. (2001). Critical ethnography for communication studies: Dialogue and social justice in service-learning. *Southern Communication Journal*, 66, 239–250. doi:10.1080/10417940109373202

Averill, J. R., Caitlin, G., & Chon, K. K. (1990). *Rules of hope*. New York: Springer-Verlag.

Ayres, W., Quinn, T., & Stovall, D. (Eds.). (2009). *Handbook of social justice in education*. New York: Routledge.

Battistoni, R. M. (2013). Civic learning through service learning: Conceptual frameworks and research. In R. G. Bringle, P. H. Clayton, & J. A. Hatcher (Eds.), *Research on service learning: Conceptual frameworks and assessment: Vol. 2A: Sudents and faculty* (pp. 111–132). Sterling, VA: Stylus.

Bell, L. A. (2007). Theoretical foundations for social justice education. In M. Adams, L. A. Bell, & P. Griffin (Eds.), *Teaching for diversity and social justice* (2nd ed., pp. 1–14). New York: Routledge.

Bernat, F. P. (2009). Youth resilience: Can schools enhance youth factors for hope, optimism, and success? *Women & Criminal Justice*, 19, 251–66. doi:10.1080/08974450903001610

Bickford, D. M., & Reynolds, N. (2002). Activism and service-learning: Reframing volunteerism as acts of dissent. *Pedagogy*, 2, 229–252. doi:10.1215/15314200-2-2-229

Billig, S. H. (2002). Support for K–12 service-learning practice: A brief review of the research. *Educational Horizons*, 80, 184–189.

Boal, A. (1985). *Theatre of the oppressed* (C. A. McBride & M.-O. L. McBride, Trans.). New York: Theatre Communications Group.

Bottrell, D. (2007). Resistance, resilience and social identities: Reframing "problem youth" and the problem of schooling. *Journal of Youth Studies, 10*, 597-616. doi:10.1080/13676260701602662

Britt, L. L. (2012). Why we use service learning: A report outlining a typology of three approaches to this form of communication pedagogy. *Communication Education, 61*, 80-88. doi:10.1080/03634523.2011.632017

Britt, L. L. (2014). Service-learning in the service of social justice: Situating communication activism pedagogy within a typology of service-learning approaches. In L. R. Frey & D. L. Palmer (Eds.), *Teaching communication activism: Communication education for social justice* (pp. 139-166). New York: Hampton Press.

Brooks, J. E. (2006). Strengthening resilience in children and youths: Maximizing opportunities through the schools. *Children & Schools, 28*(2), 69-76. doi:10.1093/cs/28.2.69

Brown, D. D., & Kulig, J. C. (1996-1997). The concept of resiliency: Theoretical lessons from community research. *Health and Canadian Society, 4*, 29-52.

Brown, J. H., D'Emidio-Caston, M., & Benard, B. (2001). *Resilience education*. Thousand Oaks, CA: Corwin Press.

Bruininks, P., & Malle, B. F. (2005). Distinguishing hope from optimism and related affective states. *Motivation and Emotion, 29*, 327-355. doi:10.1007/s11031-006-9010-4

Bryan, J. (2005). Fostering educational resilience and achievement in urban schools through school-family-community partnerships. *Professional School Counseling, 8*, 229-227.

Buzzanell, P. M. (2010). Resilience: Talking, resisting, and imagining new normalcies into being. *Journal of Communication, 60*, 1-14. doi:10.1111/j.1460-2466.2009.01469x

Carey, C. (2014). Ground-truthing a timber sale: Teaching environmental communication in the Mt. Hood National Forest. In L. R. Frey & D. L. Palmer (Eds.), *Teaching communication activism: Communication education for social justice* (pp. 261-290). New York: Hampton Press.

Celio, C. I., Durlak, J., & Dymnicki, A. (2011). A meta-analysis of the impact of service-learning on students. *Journal of Experiential Education, 34*, 164-181. doi:10.1177/105381591103400205

Cipolle, S. B. (2010). *Service-learning and social justice: Engaging students in social change*. Lanham, MD: Rowman & Littlefield.

Clark, S., & Teachout, W. (2012). *Slow democracy: Rediscovering community, bringing decision making back home*. White River Junction, VT: Chelsea Green.

Colby, A., Ehrlich, T., Beaumont, E., & Stephens, J. (2003). *Educating citizens: Preparing America's undergraduates for lives of moral and civic responsibility*. San Francisco, CA: Jossey-Bass.

Conquergood, D. (1988). Health theatre in a Hmong refugee camp: Performance, communication, and culture. *TDR, 32*, 174-208. doi:10.2307/1145914

Conway, J. M., Amel, E. L., & Gerwien, D. P. (2009). Teaching and learning in the social context: A meta-analysis of service learning's effects on academic, personal, social, and citizenship outcomes. *Teaching of Psychology, 36*, 233-245. doi:10.1080/00986280903172969

Cottrell, L., Jr. (1976). The competent community. In B. Kaplan, R. Wilson, & A. Leighton (Eds.), *Further explorations in social psychiatry* (pp. 195-209). New York: Basic Books.

Coutu, D. L. (2002, May). How resilience works. *Harvard Business Review*, pp. 46-55.

Crabtree, R. D. (1998). Mutual empowerment in cross-cultural participatory development and service learning: Lessons in communication and social justice from projects in El Salvador and Nicaragua. *Journal of Applied Communication Research, 26*, 182-209. doi:10.1080/00909889809365501

Cruz, N. I., & Giles D. E., Jr. (2000). Where's the community in service-learning research? *Michigan Journal of Community Service Learning*, Special Issue, 28-34. Retrieved from http://ginsberg.umich.edu/mjcsl

Cuny, K. M., Thompson, M., & Naidu, H. P. (2014). Speaking for a change: Using speaking centers to amplify marginalized voices in building sustained community movements for social justice. In L. R. Frey & D. L. Palmer (Eds.), *Teaching communication activism: Communication education for social justice* (pp. 381-410). New York: Hampton Press.

Cutter, S. L., Barnes, L., Berry, M., Burton, C., Evans, E., Tate, E., & Webb, J. (2008). A place-based model for understanding community resilience to natural disasters. *Global Environmental Change, 18*, 598-606. doi:10.1016/j.gloenvcha.2008.07.013

Darling, A. L., & Leckie, L. (2009). Applied communication research in educational contexts. In L. R. Frey & K. N. Cissna (Eds.), *Routledge handbook of applied communication research* (pp. 481-505). New York: Routledge.

Deal, C. E. (2014). Acting for social justice: Students, prisoners, and theatre of testimony performance. In L. R. Frey & D. L. Palmer (Eds.), *Teaching communication activism: Communication education for social justice* (pp. 435-460). New York: Hampton Press.

DePaola, T. (2014). Collaborating for social justice through service learning. *New Directions for Community Colleges, 165*, 37-47. doi:10.1002/cc.20089

Dewey, J. (1916). *Democracy and education: An introduction to the philosophy of education*. New York: McMillan.

Edwards, B., Mooney, L., & Heald, C. (2001). Who is being served? The impact of student volunteering on local community organizations. *Nonprofit and Voluntary Sector Quarterly, 30*, 444-461. doi:10.1177/0899764001303003

Enck, S. (2014). Feminist communication activism pedagogy—"Gender and violence: Dominance, resistance, and the cultural production of meaning." In L. R. Frey & D. L. Palmer (Eds.), *Teaching communication activism: Communication education for social justice* (pp. 199-230). New York: Hampton Press.

Esquivel, G. B., Doll, B., & Oades-Sese, G. V. (Eds.). (2011). Resilience in schools [Special issue]. *Psychology in the Schools, 48*(7), 649-651.

Fixmer-Oraiz, N., & Murray, B. (2009). Challenging pedagogy: Reflections on communication activism and service-learning. *Rocky Mountain Communication Review, 6*(2), 52-55.

Flores, L. A. (2013). Striving for social justice—The excellence of inclusion in education. *Western Journal of Communication, 77*, 645-650. doi:10.1080/10570314.2013.823514

Freire, P. (1970). *Pedagogy of the oppressed* (M. B. Ramos, Trans.). New York: Herder and Herder.

Frey, L. R., & Carragee, K. M. (Eds.). (2007a). *Communication activism: Vol. 1. Communication for social change*. Cresskill, NJ: Hampton Press.

Frey, L. R., & Carragee, K. M. (Eds.). (2007b). *Communication activism: Vol. 2. Media and performance activism.* Cresskill, NJ: Hampton Press.

Frey, L. R., & Carragee, K. M. (Eds.). (2012). *Communication activism: Vol. 3. Struggling for social justice amidst difference.* New York: Hampton Press.

Frey, L. R., & Palmer, D. L. (Eds.). (2014a). *Teaching communication activism: Communication education for social justice.* New York: Hampton Press.

Frey, L. R., & Palmer, D. L. (2014b). Introduction: Teaching communication activism. In L. R. Frey & D. L. Palmer (Eds.), *Teaching communication activism: Communication education for social justice* (pp. 1-42). New York: Hampton Press.

Frey, L. R., Pearce, W. B., Pollock, M. A., Artz, L., & Murphy, B. A. O. (1996). Looking for justice in all the wrong places: On a communication approach to social justice. *Communication Studies, 47,* 110-127. doi:10.1080/10510979609368467

Frey, L. R., & SunWolf. (2009). Across applied divides: Great debates of applied communication scholarship. In L. R. Frey & K. N. Cissna (Eds.), *Routledge handbook of applied communication research* (pp. 26-54). New York: Routledge.

Futa, K. T., Nash, C. L., Hansen, D. J., & Garbin, C. P. (2003). Adult survivors of childhood abuse: An analysis of coping mechanisms used for stressful childhood memories and current stressors. *Journal of Family Violence, 18,* 227-239. doi:10.1023/A:1024068314963

Gastil, J. (1993). *Democracy in small groups: Participation, decision making and communication.* Philadelphia, PA: New Society.

Geller, J. D., Zuckerman, N., & Seidel, A. (2014). Service-learning as a catalyst for community development: How do community partners benefit from service-learning? *Education and Urban Society.* Advance online publication. doi:10.1177/0013124513514773

Generett, G. G., & Hicks, M. A. (2004). Beyond reflective competency: Teaching for audacious hope-in-action. *Journal of Transformative Education, 2,* 187-203. doi:10.1177/1541344604265169

Gilbert, J. (2014). Performing advocacy: Staging marginalized voices. In L. R. Frey & D. L. Palmer (Eds.), *Teaching communication activism: Communication education for social justice* (pp. 231-259). New York: Hampton Press.

Giroux, H. (2010, October 17). Lessons from Paulo Freire. *Chronicle of Higher Education.* Retrieved from http://chronicle.com

Goodman, R. M., Speers, M. A., McLeroy, K., Fawcett, S., Kegler, M., Parker, E.,... Wallerstein, N. (1998). Identifying and defining the dimensions of community capacity to provide a basis for measurement. *Health Education & Behavior, 25,* 258-278. doi:10.1177/109019819802500303

Gould, E., Mishel, L., & Shierholz, H. (2013, September 18). *Already more than a lost decade: Income and poverty trends continue to paint a bleak picture.* Retrieved from Economic Policy Institute website: http://www.epi.org/publication/lost-decade-income-poverty-trends-continue

Grey, M. J., Ondaatje, E. H., Fickler, R. D., Jr., & Geschwind, S. A. (2000). Assessing service-learning: Results from a survey of "Learn and Serve America, Higher Education." *Change, 32*(2), 30-39. doi:10.1080/00091380009601721

Gunderson, L. H. (2000). Ecological resilience—In theory and application. *Annual Review of Ecology and Systematics, 31,* 425-439. doi:10.1146/annurev.ecolsys.31.1.425

Hart, J. L., & Walker, K. L. (2014). International health activism: A service-learning pedagogy to promote global responsibility. In L. R. Frey & D. L. Palmer (Eds.), *Teaching communication activism: Communication education for social justice* (pp. 293-320). New York: Hampton Press.

Hartnett, S. J. (1998). Lincoln and Douglas meet the abolitionist David Walker as prisoners debate slavery: Empowering education, applied communication, and social justice. *Journal of Applied Communication Research, 26*, 232-253. doi:10.1080/00909889809365503

Hartnett, S. J. (2010). Communication, social justice, and joyful commitment. *Western Journal of Communication, 74*, 63-93. doi:10.1080/10570310903463778

Hernández, P. (2002). Resilience in families and communities: Latin American contributions from the psychology of liberation. *Family Journal, 10*, 334-343. doi:10.1177/1068807020100030111

Hicks, M. A., Berger, J. G., & Generett, G. G. (2005). From hope to action: Creating spaces to sustain transformative habits of mind and heart. *Journal of Transformative Education, 3*, 57-75. doi:10.1177/1541344604270924

Jovanovic, S. (2014). The ethics of teaching communication activism. In L. R. Frey & D. L. Palmer (Eds.), *Teaching communication activism: Communication education for social justice* (pp. 105-138). New York: Hampton Press.

Kahne, J., & Westheimer, J. (1996). In the service of what? The politics of service learning. *Phi Delta Kappan, 77*, 593-599.

Kennedy, J. F. (1961, July 25). *Proclamation 3422–American education week, 1961*. Retrieved from The American Presidency Project website: http://www.presidency.ucsb.edu/ws/?pid=24146

Kennerly, R. M. (with Davis, T.). (2014). Service-learning, intercultural communication, and video production praxis: Developing a sustainable program of community activism with/in a Latino/a migrant community. In L. R. Frey & D. L. Palmer (Eds.), *Teaching communication activism: Communication education for social justice* (pp. 321-352). New York: Hampton Press.

Knight, C. (2007). A resilience framework: Perspectives for educators. *Health Education, 107*, 543-555. doi:10.1108/09654280710827939

Kraft, N., & Wheeler, J. (2003). Service learning and resilience in disaffected youth: A research study. In J. Eyler & S. H. Billig (Eds.), *Deconstructing service learning: Research exploring context, participation, and impacts* (pp. 213-238). Greenwich, CT: Information Age.

Lee, W. (2006). The desire to know and to love is never too small: My musings on teaching and social justice. In O. Swartz (Ed.), *Social justice and communication scholarship* (pp. 193-214). Mahwah, NJ: Lawrence Erlbaum.

Lumoa, J. R. (2010, March 8). *World's pall of black carbon can be eased with new stoves*. Retrieved from Yale University Environment 360 website: http://e360.yale.edu/feature/worlds_pall_of_black_carbon_can_be_eased_with_new_stoves/2250

Luthar, S. S., Cicchetti, D., & Becker, B. (2000). The construct of resilience: A critical evaluation and guidelines for future work. *Child Development, 71*, 543-562. doi:10.1111/1467-8624.00164

Makau, J. M. (1996). Notes on communication education and social justice. *Communication Studies, 47*, 135-141. doi:10.1080/10510979609368469

Marullo, S., & Edwards, B. (2000). From charity to social justice: The potential of university-community collaboration for social change. *American Behavioral Scientist, 43*, 895-912. doi: 10.1177/00027640021955540

Maybach, C. W. (1996). Investigating urban community needs: Service learning from a social justice perspective. *Education & Urban Society, 28*, 224-236. doi:10.1177/0013124596028002007

McKillop, N., Smallbone, S., Wortley, R., & Andijc, I. (2012). Offenders' attachment and sexual abuse onset: A test of theoretical propositions. *Sex Abuse, 24*, 591-610. doi:10.1177/1079063212445571

McLaren, P. (2005). *Capitalists and conquerors: A critical pedagogy against empire*. Lanham, MD: Rowman & Littlefield.

McMahon, B. J. (2006). Conceptions of resilience: Compliance or transformation? *Journal of Educational Reform, 71*, 49-58, doi:10.1080/00131720608984567

Mitchell, T. D. (2014). How service-learning enacts social justice sensemaking. *Journal of Critical Thought and Praxis, 2*(2), Article 6. Retrieved from http://lib.dr.iastate.edu/jctp

Morrow, B. H. (2008, September). *Community resilience: A social justice perspective*. Oak Ridge, TN: Community and Regional Resilience Initiative. Retrieved from http://www.resilientus.org/wp-content/uploads/2013/03/FINAL_MORROW_9-25-08_1223482348.pdf

Morton, K. (1995). The irony of service: Charity, project and social change in service-learning. *Michigan Journal of Community Service-Learning, 2*, 19-25. Retrieved from http://ginsberg.umich.edu/mjcsl

Murray, B., & Fixmer-Oraiz, N. (2014). From community service to democratic education: Making (class)room for communication activism. In L. R. Frey & D. L. Palmer (Eds.), *Teaching communication activism: Communication education for social justice* (pp. 169-198). New York, NY: Hampton Press.

Niemi, R. G., & Junn, J. (1998). *Civic education: What makes students learn*. New Haven, CT: Yale University Press.

Norris, F. H., Stevens, S. P., Pfefferbaum, B., Wyche, K. F., & Pfefferbaum, R. L. (2008). Community resilience as a metaphor, theory, set of capacities, and strategy for disaster readiness. *American Journal of Community Psychology, 41*, 127-150. doi:10.1007/s10464-007-9156-6

Novak, J. M., Markey, V., & Allen, M. (2007). Evaluating cognitive outcomes of service learning in higher education: A meta-analysis. *Communication Research Reports, 24*, 149-157. doi:10.1080/08824090701304881

Osnes, B., & Bisping, J. (2014). Theatre for energy justice. In L. R. Frey & D. L. Palmer (Eds.), *Teaching communication activism: Communication education for social justice* (pp. 461-484). New York: Hampton Press.

Ozbay, F., Fitterling, H., Charney, D., & Southwick, S. (2008). Social support and resilience to stress across the life span: A neurobiological framework. *Current Psychiatry Reports, 10*, 204-310. doi:10.1007/s11920-008-0049-7

Palmer, D. L. (2007). Facilitating consensus in an antiglobalization affinity group. In L. R. Frey & K. M. Carragee (Eds.), *Communication activism: Vol. 1. Communication and social change* (pp. 325-353). Cresskill, NJ: Hampton Press.

Palmer, D. L. (2014). Communication education as vocational training and the marginalization of activist pedagogies. In L. R. Frey & D. L. Palmer (Eds.), *Teaching communication activism: Communication education for social justice* (pp. 45–76). New York: Hampton Press.

Pearce, W. B. (1998). On putting social justice in the discipline of communication and putting enriched concepts of communication in social justice research and practice. *Journal of Applied Communication Research, 26,* 272–278. doi:10.1080/00909889809365505

Pearce, W. B. (2006). Reflections on a project to promote social justice in communication education and research. In O. Swartz (Ed.), *Social justice and communication scholarship* (pp. 216–238). Mahwah, NJ: Lawrence Erlbaum.

Polletta, F. (2004). *Freedom is an endless meeting: Democracy in American social movements.* Chicago, IL: University of Chicago Press.

Ransom, L. S. (2009). Sowing the seeds of citizenship and social justice: Service-learning in a public speaking course. *Education, Citizenship and Social Justice, 4,* 211–224. doi:10.1177/1746197909340871

Richardson, G. E. (2002). The metatheory of resilience and resiliency. *Journal of Clinical Psychology, 58,* 307–321. doi:10.1002/jclp.10020

Rosner-Salazar, T. A. (2003). Multicultural service-learning and community-based research as a model approach to promote social justice. *Social Justice, 30*(4), 64–76.

Schier, M. F., & Carver, C. S. (1985). Optimism, coping, and health: Assessment and implications of generalized outcome expectancies. *Health Psychology, 4,* 219–247. doi:10.1037/0278-6133.4.3.219

Schultz, B. G. (1999). Improving group communication performance: An overview of diagnosis and intervention. In L. R. Frey (Ed.), D. S. Gouran, & M. S. Poole (Assoc. Eds.), *The handbook of group communication theory and research* (pp. 371–394). Thousand Oaks, CA: Sage.

Simpson, J. S. (2014). Communication activism pedagogy: Theoretical frameworks, central concepts, and challenges. In L. R. Frey & D. L. Palmer (Eds.), *Teaching communication activism: Communication education for social justice* (pp. 77–103). New York: Hampton Press.

Sithamparanathan, K. (2003). Interventions and methods of the theatre action group. *Intervention, 1,* 44–47. Retrieved from http://www.interventionjournal.com

Snyder, C. R. (1994). Hope and optimism. In V. S. Ramachandran (Ed.), *Encylcopedia of human behavior* (Vol. 2, pp. 535–542). New York: Academic Press.

Sonn, C. C., & Fisher, A. T. (1998). Sense of community: Community resilient responses to oppression and change. *Journal of Community Psychology, 26,* 457–472. doi:10.1002/(SICI)1520-6629(199809)26:5<457::AID-JCOP3>3.0.CO;2-O

Squires, C. R., & Creager, P. W. (2014). Alternative high school students and digital storytelling: A collaborative university–high school social justice project. In L. R. Frey & D. L. Palmer (Eds.), *Teaching communication activism: Communication education for social justice* (pp. 411–433). New York: Hampton Press.

Sternhouse, V. L., & Jarrett, O S. (2012). In the service of learning and activism: Service learning, critical pedagogy, and the Problem Solution Project. *Teacher Education Quarterly, 39,* 51–76. Retrieved from ERIC database. (EJ977356)

Stoecker, R., & Tryon, E. A. (Eds.). (2009). *The unheard voices: Community organizations and service learning.* Philadelphia, PA: Temple University Press.

Stotland, E. (1969). *The psychology of hope*. San Francisco, CA: Jossey-Bass.

Sun, A. (2009). *Promoting breast cancer screening among Chinese American women through young children's theatrical performance* [Doctoral dissertation]. Available from Proquest Dissertations and Theses database. (UMI No. 3366987)

Sunwolf, & Seibold, D. R. (1999). The impact of formal procedures on group processes, members, and task outcomes. In L. R. Frey (Ed.), D. S. Gouran, & M. S. Poole (Assoc. Eds.), *The handbook of group communication theory and research* (pp. 395-431). Thousand Oaks, CA: Sage.

Swartz, O. (Ed.). (2006). *Social justice and communication scholarship*. Mahwah, NJ: Lawrence Erlbaum.

Templeton, R. (2010). Activist interventions: Community organizing against "zero tolerance" policies. In J. A. Sandlin, B. D. Schultz, & J. Burdick (Eds.), *Handbook of public pedagogy: Education and learning beyond schooling* (pp. 420-433). New York: Routledge.

Tummala-Narra, P. (2007). Conceptualizing trauma and resilience across diverse contexts: A multicultural perspective. *Journal of Aggression, Maltreatment & Trauma, 14*, 33-53. doi:10.1300/J146v14n01_03

Verjee, B. (2010). Service-learning: Charity-based or transformative? *Transformative Dialogues, 4*(2), Article 2. Retrieved from http://www.kpu.ca/td

Wade, R. C. (2000). Beyond charity: Service learning for social justice. *Social Studies & the Young Learner, 12*(4), 6-9.

Wang, Y. (2013). Impact of service-learning courses with a social justice curriculum on development of social responsibility among college students. *Journal of Community Engagement and Higher Education, 5*(2), Article 4.

Warren, K. (1998). Educating students for social justice in service learning. *Journal of Experiential Education, 21*, 134-139. doi:10.1177/105382599802100305

Watzlawick, P., Weakland, J., & Fisch, R. (1974). *Change: Principles of problem formation and problem resolution*. New York: W. W. Norton.

Welker, L. (2007). Staging Sudanese refugee narratives and the legacy of genocide. In L. R. Frey & K. M. Carragee (Eds.), *Communication activism: Vol. 3: Struggling for social justice amidst difference* (pp. 139-178). New York: Hampton Press.

Westheimer, J., & Kahne, J. (2007). Introduction. *Equity & Excellence in Education, 40:2*, 97-100.

Wilson, S. R., & Gettings, P. E. (2012). Nurturing children as assets: A positive approach to preventing child maltreatment and promoting healthy youth development. In T. J. Socha & M. J. Pitts (Eds.), *The positive side of interpersonal communication* (pp. 278-295). New York: Peter Lang.

Yorio, P. L., & Ye, F. (2012). A meta-analysis on the effects of service-learning on the social, personal, and cognitive outcomes of learning. *Academy of Management Learning & Education, 11*, 9-27. doi:10.5465/amle.2010.0072

About the Editors and Contributors

Editors

Gary A. Beck, Ph.D., Assistant Professor of Communication, Old Dominion University, Norfolk, Virginia

Thomas J. Socha, Ph.D., Professor of Communication, University Professor, and Graduate Program Director, Old Dominion University, Norfolk, Virginia

Contributors

Bryan Asbury, M.S., Doctoral student, University of Iowa, Iowa City, Iowa

Patrice Buzzanell, Ph.D., Professor of Communication, Purdue University, West Lafayette, Indiana

Rachel DiCioccio, Ph.D., Associate Professor of Communication, and Director of Graduate Studies, University of Rhode Island, Kingston, Rhode Island

Lawrence (Larry) R. Frey, Ph.D., Professor of Communication, University of Colorado Boulder, Boulder, Colorado

Erik Green, Ph.D., Assistant Professor of Communication, Concordia University Texas, Austin, Texas

Jacquelyn Harvey-Knowles, M.A., Doctoral student, University of Washington, Seattle, Washington

Veronica Hefner, Ph.D., Assistant Professor of Communication Studies, Chapman University, Orange, California

Valerie Manosov, Ph.D., Professor of Communication, University of Washington, Seattle, Washington

Tim P. McKenna-Buchanan, Ph.D., Assistant Professor of Communication Studies, Manchester University, North Manchester, Indiana

Rachel M. McLaren, Ph.D., Assistant Professor of Communication Studies, University of Iowa, Iowa City, Iowa

Andy J. Merolla, Ph.D., Associate Professor of Communication, Baldwin Wallace University, Berea, Ohio

Sandra Metts, Ph.D., Professor of Communication, Illinois State University, Normal, Illinois

David L. Palmer, Ph.D., Associate Professor of Communication, University of Northern Colorado, Greeley, Colorado

Joshua Pederson, Ph.D., Assistant Professor of Communication Studies, University of Alabama, Tuscaloosa, Alabama

Brittany L. Peterson, Ph.D., Assistant Professor of Communication Studies, Ohio University, Athens, Ohio

Lisa M. Ponche, B.A., Master's Degree Student, Old Dominion University, Norfolk, Virginia

Ashley M. Poole, M.A., Adjunct Faculty Member, Old Dominion University, Norfolk, Virginia

Amy H. Rogeness, M.S., Adjunct Professor, Chapman University, Orange, California

Suchitra Shenoy-Packer, Ph.D., Assistant Professor of Communication, DePaul University, Chicago, Illinois

Lisa Sparks, Ph.D., Foster and Mary McGaw Endowed Professor in Behavioral Sciences, Head/Director of the Master of Science graduate program in Health and Strategic Communication in the Schmid College of Science and Technology, Chapman University, Orange, California

Alfredo Torres, M.A., Adjunct Faculty Member, Old Dominion University, Norfolk, Virginia

Anita L. Vangelisti, Ph.D., Jesse H. Jones Centennial Professor of Communication, University of Texas at Austin, Austin, Texas

Author Index

• A •

Abbey, S., 32
Adams, V., 134, 181, 193, 214, 251
Aden, R. 147, 151
Afifi, T., 146, 148-151, 154, 179, 181, 186-187, 189-190
Afifi, W., 82, 90
Alam, Q., 187, 191
Aldrich, D., 178, 185-186, 190
Alexander, A., 74
Allemand, M., 82, 86, 90
Allen, J., 235-236, 251, 256
Allen, M., 256
Allen, T. 21, 23, 29-30,
Al-Mabuk, R., 85, 90
Alspaugh, T., 224, 225, 233-234
Alvesson, M., 138, 146, 151, 153
Amel, E., 236, 252
Ames, C., 19, 26, 30
Amnesty International, 158, 161, 173
Amundson, N., 126, 134
Anderson, J., 11, 99, 118, 157, 169, 174, 214
Anderson, N., 30, 32.
Andijc, I., 241, 256
Andrews, N., 198, 202, 212
Angucia, M. 161, 173
Annan, J., 158, 163, 173
Ansell, E., 53, 71, 92
Arnau, R., 44, 52
Arnett, J., 123-124, 134, 136-137
Artz, L., 236, 238, 251, 254
Aryemo, F., 158, 163, 173

Asbury, B., xv, 4, 75, 93, 259
Ashcraft, K., 138, 151
Astin, J., 29, 33
Atchley, R., 134
Averill, J., 245, 251
Avolio, B., 131-132, 134
Ayres, W. 251

• B •

Babyak, M., 11, 215
Bachman, G., 64-65, 69, 87, 91
Baer, R., 17, 23-24, 30-31
Bakhtin, M., 168, 172-173
Ballard-Reisch, D., 207, 211
Bantum, E., 204, 216
Barber, B., 136
Bardacke, N., 27, 31
Baringer, D., 201, 214
Barker, E., 128, 135
Bares, L., 253
Barnes, S., 20, 22, 30
Barnes-Farrell, J., 134
Barnum, 181, 190
Barrett, G., 50, 131-132, 134
Baucom, D., 27, 30, 79, 91
Baum, C., 23, 30
Baumeister, R., 53, 63, 69, 73, 74, 86-88, 91, 94
Baumrind, D., 200, 211
Baxter, L., 160, 168, 173
Beach, S., 3, 83, 91
Beaumont, E., 249, 252

Beavin, J. 162, 175
Beck, C. J., 191
Beck, C. S., 153
Beck, G. A., xiii, xiv, xvii, 1, 4, 54, 64, 78, 116, 119, 204, 259
Becker, B., 89, 92, 249, 255
Beckert, D., 187, 191
Belew, B., 2, 51
Bell, E., 142-142, 151
Bell, L., 239, 251
Bellah, C., 86, 92
Bellavia, G., 57, 73
Below, R., 101, 177, 190
Benard, D., 235, 252
Bender, K., 129-130, 134
Bennett, K., 78, 93
Berendes, D., 206, 212
Berg, C., 215
Bergan, J., 32
Berger, A., 177, 184, 188, 190
Berger, J., 247, 255
Berger, R., 184, 188, 190
Berk, L. 44, 49
Berlyne, D., 37, 49
Bernat, F., 235, 251
Berry, J., 81, 83, 92, 93, 253
Bevan, J., 198, 201, 202, 212
Bickford, D., 236, 251
Billig, S., 236, 251, 255
Bippus, A., 35, 54, 58, 59, 74
Bishop, S., 16, 30, 32
Bisping, J., 244-245, 248, 256
Bissett, S., 32
Bittman, B., 44, 49
Black, K., 138, 141, 142, 151
Blissett, S., 45, 51
Block, J., 7, 11
Blustein, D., 123, 125, 128, 136, 207, 212
Boal, A., 245, 252
Bochantin, J., 47, 51
Boden, J., 63, 69
Boehm, S., 131, 135
Bogels, S., 25, 31
Bohanek, J., 141, 150, 154

Bohlig, A, 123, 125, 128, 136
Bohlmeijer, E., 25, 30
Bohus, M., 30
Bolles, R., 128, 134
Bonanno, G., xii, xvii, 7, 40, 43, 49, 151, 177-179, 190, 203-204, 212-213
Bond, J., 28, 31-32
Bonner, G., 19, 33
Bono, G., 64, 69, 83, 87, 93
Bono, J. 31
Boon, S., 77, 91
Booth-Butterfield, M., 36, 46, 50-51
Booth-Butterfield, S., 36, 46-47, 50
Borders, T., 11, 23, 33, 173, 215
Borenstein, I., 224, 233
Borgen, W., 126, 134
Boss, P., 181, 190
Bottrell, D., 241, 250, 252
Bourhis, A. 132, 136
Bowers, V., 142, 152
Bowes, L., 141, 145, 151
Brady, L., 28, 30
Branigan, C., 88-89, 91
Braudy, L., 226, 233
Brenner, 184, 194
Brewin, C., 177, 190
Brier, M., 158, 163, 173
Britt, L., 236, 251, 252
Brock, S., 187, 191
Brogan, S., 143, 154
Broniarczyk, K., 147, 155
Brooks, G., 37, 50
Brooks, J., 63, 69, 235, 252
Brooks, R., xviii
Brotto, L., 19, 30
Brown, B., 15, 18-19, 30-31
Brown, D. 249-250, 252
Brown, J., 235, 249-250
Brown, K., M., 126, 214,
Brown, K. W., 20, 22, 29-31, 33
Brown, P. 58-59, 69
Bruch, H., 131, 135
Bruininks, P., 245-246, 252
Brummans, B., 138, 151

Bryan, J., 75, 244, 252, 259
Bryant, C., 67, 69, 124, 128, 136
Buber, M., 170, 173
Buchheld, N., 23, 30, 33
Buehlman, K. 189, 190
Buis, T., 32
Bulecza, S., 178, 193
Bull, R., 132, 136
Burke, K. 98, 114, 116, 223, 225, 229-230, 232-233
Burleson, B., 67, 69
Burt, K., 124, 136
Burton, C., 141, 151, 253
Buss, D., 78, 93
Buttenmuller, V., 33
Buzzanell, xv, xvi, 5, 7, 100, 107, 116, 131, 133-134, 138-154, 158, 163, 165, 172-173, 203, 212, 246, 252, 259

• C •

Cairns, D., 25, 31
Caitlin, G., 245, 251
Calhoun, L. 179, 186, 188, 193
Campana, K., 82, 93
Campbell, W., 20, 30, 35, 92, 179, 190
Campion, M., 132, 136
Canary, H., 141, 149-150, 152
Cann, A., 35, 45, 50, 79, 91
Cantú, E., 141, 152
Carey, C., 77, 93, 246, 248, 252
Carlson, L., 18, 30, 32
Carmody, J., 30, 32
Carpenter, C., 74, 79, 91
Carragee, K., 238, 253-254, 256, 258
Carson, C., 59. 70
Carson, E., 98. 116
Carson, J., 27, 30
Carson, K., 27, 30
Carstensen, L., 56, 69, 71, 201, 212
Carver, C., 246, 257
Cascio, T..179, 190

Cassidy, J., 56, 73
Caughlin, J., 68, 69
Cavallo, E., 177, 190
Cazona, M., 145, 155
Celio, C., 235, 252
Cervellion, P. 179, 193
Chadwick, P., 24, 30
Chan, E., 203, 213
Chang, S., 203, 215-216
Chapman-Waldrop, 32
Charney, D., 243, 256
Cheavens, J., 181-182, 193, 205, 212, 214-215
Checton, M., 55, 73
Chen, Y., 132-133, 135
Cheney, K., 156, 160-161, 163-164, 169, 171, 173
Chernichky, S., 147, 155
Chon, K., 245, 251
Christie, N., 97-99, 112, 116
Chu, A., 203, 213
Chung, S., 33
Cicchetti, D., 40, 51, 89, 92, 249, 255
Cicirelli, V., 201, 212
Ciesla, J. , 17, 30
Cipolle, S., 237, 252
Clark, G., 74
Clark, S., 244, 252
Clarkberg, M., 135
Cloven, D., 66, 69
Coatsworth, J., 29-30, 157, 174
Cobb, R., 88, 91
Cohen, G., 200-202
Cohen, E., 152
Cohen, S., 66, 69
Cohn, M., 41, 50
Colby, A., 249, 252
Coleman, S., 81, 92
Comtois, K., 27, 32
Concato, J., 157, 174
Conger, R., 67, 69
Conn, C., 142, 152
Conquergood, D., 248, 252
Conroy, S., 133, 135

Conway, J., 236, 252
Cooren, F., 138, 151
Cordova, J. 20-21, 33
Cottrell, L., 244, 253
Coutu, D., 236, 253
Crabtree, R., 238, 253
Creager, P., 242, 257
Creswell, J., 18, 31
Crockenberg, S., 200, 212
Crowley, J., 20-21, 31
Crumley, L., 54-55, 57, 66, 74
Cruz, N., 236, 253
CSUCS, 158, 174
Cuny, K., 243, 253
Cupach, W., 59, 64, 70, 72-73, 77, 82, 93, 199, 215
Cutter, S., 236, 253

• D •

D'Abate, C., 127, 135
D'Emidio-Caston, M., 235, 252
D'Enbeau, S., 142, 152
Dagnan, D., 24, 30
Daiute, C., 222, 233
Dal Grande, E., 130, 137
Danoff-Burg, S., 206, 215
Danovsky, M., 214
Darling, S., 21, 31, 238, 253
Davidov, M., 60, 71
Davies, B., 223, 225, 229, 231, 233
Davila, J., 81, 88, 92
Davis, D., 82, 93
Davis, H., 35, 50
Davis, K., 21, 25, 29, 31
Davis, P., 33
Davis, T., 255
Dawson, D., 135
de Bruin, E., 25, 31
de Jong, G., 160, 174
Deal, C., 242, 247, 253
Dean, R., 48, 50, 56, 71

Dekeyser, M., 21, 24, 31
Delfabbro, P. 157, 174
Denham, A., 188, 190
Denhart, C., 122, 137
DePaola, T., 237, 253
Devins, G., 32
DeVoe, M., 56, 71
DeWall, C., 91
Dewey, J., 235, 253
Dewulf, D., 21, 31
DiCioccio, R., 5, 7, 34-36, 38, 50-51, 259
Dickson, K., 17, 30, 134, 152, 191
Dodge, C., 165, 174
Doll, B., 235, 253
Donovan-Kicken, E., 58, 70
Dornbusch, S., 213
Douglas, K. 60, 70-71, 73-74, 243, 255
Dowling, J., 46-47, 50
Downs, W., 85, 90
Duckworth, J., 142, 152
Dufault, K., 205, 212
Duffy, M., 31
Dula, C., 81, 92
Dumas, J., 200, 212
Duncan, L, 27, 29, 30-31, 103-104
Duran, R., 198, 213
Durlak, J., 236, 252
Dyer, J., 8, 12, 40, 50, 89, 91
Dykstra, T., 32
Dymnicki, A., 236, 252

• E •

Earley, P., 61, 70
Earlywine, M., 23, 33
Earvolino-Ramirez, M., 42, 50
Eaton, J., 66, 70
Ebberwein, C., 125, 135
Eccles, J., 136
Edman, J., 33
Edwards, B., 236-237, 253, 256
Egan, L., 64, 70

Egbert, N., 137
Eggert, L., 67, 73
Ehrlich, T., 249, 252
Eifert, G., 32
Einhorn, L., 178, 193
Eisenberger, N., 18, 31
Eisenbraun, A., 44, 52
Ellen, J., 33
Elliott, S., 233
Emanuel, A., 17, 30
Emerson, C., 173
Enck, S., 246, 253
Enright, R., 64, 70, 84, 92
Epstein, R.. 126, 135, 213
Erickson, S., 46, 50
Eriksen, E., 98, 117
Errera, Y., 176, 178-179, 192
Esbensen, B., 202, 206, 213
Espinel, Z., 177, 192
Esquivel, G., 35, 253
Etzel, K., 45, 50
Evans, E., 253
Evans, K., 53, 71, 92,
Evans-Campbell, T., 179, 190
Exline, J., 64, 74, 86-88, 91, 94
Experiencing the Vietnam War, 227, 233
Extremera, N., 135

• F •

Falato, W., 82, 90
Farb, N., 29, 32
Faris, J., 148, 152
Farrell, H., 53, 72
Fawcett, S., 254
Feeley, T., 132-133, 135
Feeney, J., 55, 57, 65, 66, 70
Feist, H., 130, 137
Feldman, D., 150, 154, 182, 184-186, 192-193, 214
Feldman, G. 24, 31
Feldstein, S., 46, 50

Felix, E., 190
Felmlee, D., 66-67, 70, 73
Felton, D., 44, 49
Fessler, P., 187, 190
Fickler, R., 236, 254
Fincham, F., 57, 70, 78, 81, 83-84, 87-88, 91-92
Finkel, E., 86, 93
Finnstrom, S., 161, 174
Fisch, R., 8, 12, 121, 137, 237, 258
Fisher, A., 241, 243, 257
Fitterling, H., 243, 256
Fivush, R. 141, 151, 154
Fixmer-Oraiz, N., 238, 247, 253, 256
Flanagan, K., 64, 70
Flannery, M., 181, 191
Fledderus, M., 30
Fletcher, K., 19, 32, 53, 71
Flores, L., 238, 253
Flynn, M., 129, 131, 136
Folkman, S., 180, 186, 190
Forsyth, J., 32, 118, 174
Franenfield, P., 50
Fredrickson, B., 41-42, 50, 52-53, 70, 88-89, 91
Freire, A., 239, 250, 253-254
Freud, S., 205, 213
Frey, L. 6- 7, 12, 235, 238, 240, 252-259
Friedberg, J., 88, 91
Frohne, N., 82, 93
Frymier, A., 48, 52
Futa, K., 241, 254

• G •

Gabor, E., 143, 152
Gabronit, M., 193
Galambos, N., 128, 135
Galante, J.. 26, 31
Galler, E., 225, 233
Gambrel, L., 16, 18-20, 31
Garbin, C. 241, 254

Garland, E., 29, 32
Garmezy, N., 7, 11
Gartner, A., 82, 93
Gastil, J., 44, 254
Gehart, D., 21, 31
Geisler, C., 44, 153
Geller, J., 236, 254
Generett, G., 247, 254-255
Gergen, K., 162, 173-174
Gerwien, D., 236, 252
Geschwind, S., 236, 254
Gettings, P. 8, 12, 184, 194, 211, 216, 237, 258
Giddens, A., 172, 174
Gil, K., 27, 30
Gilbert, J., 247, 254
Giles, D., 236, 253
Gill, T., 157, 174
Giroux, H., 239, 254
Glaze, L., 98, 116
Glomb, T., 31
Goffman, E. 58, 70, 112-114, 116, 160, 162, 170-171, 174
Golden, A., 139, 144, 153
Goldsmith, D., 66-67, 69-71, 186, 188, 190
Golinelli, D., 98, 116
Gonzalez Herero, V., 135
Goodall, K., 21, 31
Goodey, E., 18, 30
Goodman, R., 242, 254
Gopalani, S., 178, 193
Gotcher, J., 198-199, 213
Gottlieb, B., 66, 71
Gottman, J., 56, 65, 69, 71, 83, 189, 190
Gould, E., 237, 254
Graham, E.,. 36, 37, 50, 51
Grant, D., 107, 109, 115, 116
Graves, N., 126, 135
Gray, J., 51
Greco, C., 17, 19, 25, 31-32
Green, A., 141, 145, 153
Green, E., xvi, 4, 156, 222, 259
Greene, C., 154

Greenberg, M., 29-30
Greenstone, J., 187, 190
Greeson, J., 18, 24, 31, 33
Gregory, D., 46, 48, 50
Grewal, P., 39, 51
Grey, M., 38, 236, 254
Griffin, D., 57, 73, 251
Grossman, P., 23, 30-31
Grusec, J., 60, 71
Guerrero, L., 64-65, 69, 87, 91
Guha-Sapir, D., 177, 190
Gunderson, L., 236, 254
Gunnestad, A., 98, 117
Gupta, S., 99, 118
Gutterman, S., 177, 190

• H •

Hackbarth, M., 181, 191
Haefner, J., 132, 135
Hall, J. H., 78, 83, 87, 91,
Hall, J. S., 7, 12, 121, 136, 194, 203, 214
Hallberg, I. 202, 206, 213-214
Hamilton, J., 228, 234
Hammoud, A., 145-146, 153
Hampel, A., 54-55, 74
Han, M., 147, 151
Hannon, P., 86, 93
Hansen, D., 241, 254
Hansson, R., 71
Hardy, S., 157, 174
Hargrave, T., 75, 91
Harre, R., 223, 225, 229, 231, 233
Harris, C., 9, 11, 214
Harris, P., 87, 93
Harrison, E., 141, 153
Hart, J., 245-246, 248, 255
Hartnett, S., 152, 238, 243, 255
Harvey, J., 5, 7, 15, 20-21, 31, 157, 174, 259
Harwood, J., 213
Harzold, E., 196, 198-199, 207-208, 213

Havighurst, R., 135
Hayashi, K. 44, 51
Hayes, A., 24, 28, 31-32
Heald, C., 188, 193, 236, 253
Hecht, M., 199, 213
Hefner, V., xvi, 195, 259
Heidenreich, T., 30
Heiman, J., 19, 30
Heinze, L., 180, 193
Hell of a war, 233
Helmer, I., 88, 93
Hember, M., 24, 30
Henderson, N., 184, 191
Hendrick, C., 79, 91
Hendrick, S., 79, 91
Henkens, K., 137
Henstra, D., 186, 187, 191
Herberman, E., 98, 116
Hernández, P., 241, 255
Herth, K., 205, 213
Hess, J., 124, 135
Hicks, M., 134-135, 247, 254-255
Higgins, R., 11, 215
Hill, P., 82, 86, 90-91, 154, 247
Hixenbaugh, M., 3, 11
Ho, J., 136, 203, 213
Hobfoll, S., 178-179, 184, 188, 191
Hockemeyer, J., 150, 154, 185, 192
Hockenberry, M., 46, 50
Holden, G., 81, 92
Hollander, S., 178, 191
Holleran, S., 11, 214
Holling, C., 7, 11
Holquist, M., 173
Holter, A., 84, 92
Honeycutt, J., 179, 191
Hook, J., 82, 93
Hopkins, J., 23-24, 30
Horan, S., 47, 51
Hornsey, K., 60, 70-71, 73- 74
Horsey, K., 184, 191
Hoyt, W., 81, 92
Hoza, B., 205, 214
Hsaio, C., 203, 216

Huggins, M., 206, 215
Hugo, G., 130, 137
Huston, D., 18, 29, 32
Hutchinson, S., 186, 189
Hyatt, J., 129, 135

• I •

Ilardi, S., 182, 193
Iribarren, S., 26, 31
Irving, L., 11, 99, 118, 157, 169, 174, 214
Isaksson, K., 130, 135
Ishii, H., 44, 51
Iwanaga, S., 44, 51
Izard, R., 189, 192

• J •

Jackson, S., 162, 175, 200, 212
Jacobs, F., 3, 11
Jacobs, J., 136
Jacoby, R., 180, 191, 193
Jaffee, S., 141, 145, 151
Jarrett, O., 237, 257
Jasser, S., 33
Jaycox, L., 187, 191
Jennings, S., 20, 29, 32
Jimerson, S., 187, 191
Johansson, G., 130, 135
Johnson, J., 33, 51, 86, 92
Jones, K., 21, 32
Jones, S., 67, 71
Jones, W. 50, 53, 71
Jordans, M., 160, 174
Jorgenson, J., 139, 153
Joseph, S., 159, 176, 179, 184, 191, 205, 210, 213
Jovanovic, S., 239, 255
Joy, S., 33
Junn, J. 235, 256
Jupin, A., 202, 212

• K •

Kabat-Zinn, J., 15-16, 18-19, 25-27, 32
Kachadourian, L., 88, 92
Kahle, K., 215
Kahne, J., 237, 255, 258
Kaniasty, K., 177, 190
Kantor, E., 187, 191
Karekla, M., 32
Kärreman, D., 138, 146, 151, 153
Karremans, J., 64, 71
Kashy, D., xii, xviii
Katz, L., 189-190, 191
Kaurin, P., 228, 233
Kawai, K., 44, 51
Keefe, F., 212
Keeling, M., 16, 18-20, 31
Kegler, M. 254
Keith, S., 146, 148, 150-151
Kelley, D., 64, 74, 84, 92
Keltner, D., 43, 49, 203-204, 212-213
Kendig, H., 129, 136
Kennedy, J., 235, 255
Kennerly, R., 240, 247, 255
Kerssen-Griep, J. 124, 135
Kessler, J., 53, 73
Khatiwada, I., 137
Kiburz, K., 21, 29
Kiefer, R., 81, 92
Kilpatrick, S., 86, 92
Kim, S., 117
Kimata, H., 44, 51
King, S., 137
Kirby, E., 139-140, 142, 146, 153
Kleban, M., 56, 71
Klein, R., 66, 71
Kleinknecht, N., 23, 33
Kliewer, W., 81, 92
Knight, C., 235, 255
Knobloch, L., 55, 73, 84, 92
Kobasa, S., 32
Kochanska, G., 200, 213
Koenig Kellas, J., 193

Komproe, I., 60, 174
Koschmann, M., 100, 114, 117
Kothadia, S., 212
Kousky, C., 177, 190
Kowalski, R., 71, 72
Kraft, N., 236, 255
Krahn, H., 128, 135
Kreps, G., 196, 198-199, 214- 215
Krietemeyer, J., 30
Kriminalomsorgen, 97, 99, 101, 115, 117
Krone, K., 146, 153
Krouse, S., 186, 189
Krusemark, E., 20, 30
Kuhn, C., 42-43, 51, 138, 151
Kulig, J., 249-250, 252
Kumar, S., 24, 31
Kumpfer, K., 43, 51
Kundrat, A., 201, 214
Kunze, F., 131, 135
Kusumasari, B., 187, 191
Kuyken, W., 30
Kwon, P., 143, 153

• L •

LaBelle, S., 47, 51
Labouvie-Vief, G., 56, 71
LaFreniere, P., 212
LaGreca, A., 177, 190
Lambert, N., 91
Lamborn, S., 200, 213
Lamoureux, B., 184, 191
Lancioni, G., 33
Langenhove, L., 229, 233
Langrock, A., 200, 212
Larkin, G..41, 50
Larsen, G., 38, 51
Lasch, C., 76, 92
Lavy, S., 56, 73
Lawton, M., 56, 71
Layne, C., 179, 191

Lazarus, P., 67, 71, 89, 92, 99, 117, 187, 191
Leary, M., 53-54, 57, 62, 65, 70-71, 92, 133, 135
Leckie, L., 238, 253
Ledford, C., 145, 155
Lee, T. 113, 117
Lee, W., 238, 255
Lefcourt, H., 43, 51
Leigh, E., 19, 30
Leijssen, M., 21, 31
Lerner, R., 3, 11
Levenson, R., 56, 58, 65, 69, 71
Levinson, S., 58-59, 69
Leviton, S., 187, 190
Lewin, M., 181, 192
Lewis, M., 50, 97, 117
Leysen, S., 21, 31
Liapunov, V., 173
Lieberman, M., 18, 31
Lilley, B., 24, 30
Lillis, J., 28, 31
Lim, S., 143-144, 153
Lindenboim, N., 27, 32
Lindlof, T., 101, 116-117
Linehan, M., 19, 27, 32
Lira, C., 134
Liu, M., 142, 146, 152
Lobo, M. 138, 141-142, 151
Loewenstein, G., 53, 70
Lomsky-Feder, E., 223, 233
Lopez, N., 81, 92
Lopez, S., 135, 205, 210, 214-215
Lourie, A., 200, 212
Lucas, K., 138, 145, 147, 150, 152, 154
Lumoa, J., 244, 255
Luna, L., 83, 93
Luoma, J., 28, 31
Luthar, S., 7, 40, 51, 89, 92, 249, 255
Lutters, G., 233
Lyall, S., 97, 117

• M •

Ma, S., 26, 32
MacDermid Wadsworth, S., 147, 155
MacDonald, G., 54, 65, 71
MacTavish, K., 141, 154
Maddi, S., 15, 18, 28, 32
Magaletta, P., 92
Magnuson, C., 84, 92
Magsamen-Conrad, K., 55, 73
Maguire, K., 74
Maietta, H., 127, 136
Maio, G., 81, 92
Makau, J., 238, 255
Malle, B., 245, 246, 252
Mani, M., 181, 190
Manusov, V., 5, 7, 15, 20-21, 31, 259
Mapp, C., 179, 191
Marin, K., 141, 150, 154
Markey, V., 236, 256
Martin, A., 8, 11, 121, 124, 136
Martin, R. 35-39, 43-45, 49-51,
Martocchio, B., 205, 212
Marullo, S., 237, 256
Mascaro, N., 44, 52
Masten, A., 5-6, 11, 63, 72, 100, 117, 124, 136, 157, 174
Masuda, A., 28, 31
Maybach, C., 237, 256
Mayo Clinic, 227, 233
McAtee, J., 125, 126, 136
McBee, L., 27, 32
McBride, M., 139, 153, 252
McClanahan, A., 143, 154
McCollum, E., 21, 31
McCubbin, H. 12, 141, 142, 154
McCubbin, M.,141, 142, 154
McCullough, M., 64, 69, 72, 81, 83-84, 86-87, 91-93
McCurry, S., 32
McDaniel, M., 86, 93
McGhee, P., 41-42, 51
McGuinness, T., 90- 91

McHugh, L., 22, 32, 137
McKenna-Buchanan, T., xv, 97, 259
McKillop, N., 241, 256
McLaren, P., 256
McLaren, R. xiv, 4, 53-55, 57, 60, 65-66, 68, 72-73, 237, 259
McLeroy, K., 254
McMahon, B., 249-250, 256
McMearty, K., 33
Mead, S., 24, 30
Mechaber, E., 187, 192
Medved, C., 139, 142-144, 153-154
Meisenbach, R., 142, 152, 154
Menninger, K., 180, 192
Merolla, A., 4, 8, 11, 82-83, 92, 176, 182, 186, 192, 220, 260
Metts, S., 4, 64, 72, 75, 77, 82, 84, 86, 90, 92-93, 260
Meyer, J., 37, 51
Michael, S., 61, 72, 215
Michalak, J., 30
Mikulincer, M. 56, 72-73
Milardo, R., 66, 71
Miller, A., 82, 83, 86, 93
Miller, C., 65, 66, 72, 73
Miller, J., 19, 32
Miller, L. E., 68, 69
Miller, L. M., 83, 93
Miller, R., 53, 72, 73
Miller, T., 51
Mills, R., 53, 72
Mishel, L., 237, 254
Mitchell, T., 207, 213-214, 237, 256
Moen, P. 135, 136
Mooney, L., 236, 253
Moreno, M., 191
Morgeson, F., 132, 136
Morone, N., 19, 32
Morris, J., 143, 154, 214
Morris Villagran, M., 214
Morrow, B., 250, 256
Morse, C., 86, 93, 187, 191
Morton, K., 236, 256
Moscovitch, M., 135

Moss, A., 175
Mullet, E., 86, 93
Mumby, D., 140, 151, 153-154
Murakami, K., 44, 51
Murphy, A., xvi, 1, 2-3, 12,
Murphy, B., 238, 254
Murphy, K., 88, 93, 123, 128, 136
Murray, S., 7, 12, 57, 73, 238, 247, 253, 256
Myers, B., 81, 92

• N •

Naidu, H., 243, 253
Nash, C., 241, 254
National Center for PTSD, 228, 233
National Child Support Enforcement Association, 222, 233
Nazar, J., 53, 72
Negel, L., 53, 71, 92
Nelson, S., 137, 178, 192
Neto, F., 86, 93
Newman, B., 136
Nezu, A., 45, 51
Nezu, C. 45, 51
Nichols, M., 42, 51, 127
Nicotera, A., 139, 154
Niemi, R., 235, 256
Nix, R., 29- 30
Nkomo, S., 142-143, 151
Noll, J., 203, 212
Noone, J., 129, 136
Norander, S., 147, 151
Norris, F., 241, 243, 249, 256
Norwood, K., 3, 142, 155
Notter, M., 141, 154
Novak, J., 236, 256
Noy, I., 177, 190
Nussbaum, J., 56, 73, 196-197, 200- 201, 209, 212-215, 233

• O •

O'Brien, T., 152, 219, 225, 233
O'Callaghan, P., 161, 172, 174
O'Donovan, A., 21, 33
O'Hair, H., 196, 199, 214- 216
O'Leary, K., 57, 70
O'Loughlin, K., 129, 136
O'Neill, K., 203, 212
Oades-Sese, G. 235, 253
Obradovic, J., 124, 136
Ojambo, F., 159, 174
Oliver, J., 21, 32, 89, 92
Oloya, O., 161, 174
Ondaatje, E., 236, 254
Orr, J., 222, 233
Osgood, D., 124, 136
Osnes, B., 244-245, 248, 256
Østerlind, K., 206, 213
Ota, H., 200, 214
Owen, L., 119, 129, 131, 136
Oxford English Dictionary Online, 223, 233
Ozbay, F., 243, 256

• P •

Paleari, F., 84, 91
Palma, S., 137
Palmer, D., 6-7, 92, 212, 235, 238-239, 244, 249, 252-257, 260
Papa, A., 37, 50, 203, 212
Parenteau, S., 215
Parker, E., 136, 196, 254
Parks, M., 66, 67, 71, 73, 242
Patel, K., 18, 30
Pavkov, T., 181, 191
Payne, S., 19, 30
Pearce, P., 26, 31, 173-174, 237- 238, 254, 257
Pecchioni, L., 56, 73, 200, 207-208, 214
Pederson, J., 4, 53, 60, 68, 72-73, 260

Pedrotti, J., 215
Pelham, W., 214
Penman, D., 17, 29, 33
Pennebaker, J., 172, 174
Pepping, C., 21, 33
Perez-Sales, P., 179, 193
Perkins, J., 137, 189, 192
Perry, E., 33, 132, 136
Persson, L., 202, 214
Peterson, B., xv, 97. 100, 114, 117, 260
Peterson, S., 181, 192
Pfahl, M., 147, 151
Pfefferbaum, B., 241, 256
Pfefferbaum, R. 241, 256
Pham, P., 175
Pieslak, J., 226, 233
Pilkington, R., 130, 137
Pistorello, J. 32
Pitts, M., 12, 92, 194, 216, 223, 234, 258
Platt, M.,123, 125, 128, 136
Ploeger-Bernard, D., 137
Pollock, M., 147, 151, 238, 254
Polusny, M., 32
Ponche, L., 4, 119, 260
Ponserre, S., 177, 190
Poole, A., 4, 119, 260
Poole, M., 257-258
Porter, J., 39, 51, 212
Pratt, J., 97-98, 112, 117
Priem, J., 54-55, 66, 72, 73
ProCon.org, 113, 117
Proulx, K.. 19, 33
Pudrovska, T., 202, 206, 214
Puhlik-Doris, P., 51
Pulvers, K., 181, 193
Putnam, L., 139-140, 151, 153-154, 162, 203, 212

• Q •

Query, J., 198-199, 214
Quinn, T., 236, 251

• R •

Rabinow, P., 162, 174
Rachal, K., 64, 72
Raes, F., 21, 31
Rafferty, H., 174
Rajagopal, D., 56, 71
Ramirez, J., 7, 12
Rancer, A., 36-37, 51
Rand, K., 8, 11, 121, 124, 136, 154, 185, 191-192, 205, 214- 215
Ransom, L., 238, 257
Ranter, J., 64, 70
Rapoff, M. 181, 190, 214
Raundalen, M., 165, 174
Rawlins, W., 142, 154
Reed, P., 22, 32
Regalia, C., 84, 91
Reibel, D., 33
Reich, W., 64, 70, 121, 136, 194, 203, 214
Reider, M., 132, 136
Reilly, L. 17, 30
Remke, R., 138, 142, 152
Reuter, J., 126, 134
Reynolds, N., 236, 251
Richardson, G. 19, 30, 42, 51, 100, 110, 117, 158, 174, 236, 249, 257
Rimes, K., 26, 33
Rimmasch, H. 191
Rivera, K., 150, 155
Riviere, S., 86, 93
Rizzutti, T., 233
Robe, J., 122, 137
Robichaud, D., 138, 151
Robinson, J., 200, 214
Robinson, S., 59, 73
Roer, O., 206, 213
Rogeness, A., 195, 260
Rogers, K. 198, 202, 212
Rogge, R., 20, 30
Roloff, M., 65-66, 69, 72, 77, 93
Root, L., 64, 69, 87
Rose, P. ,57, 73

Rosen, D., 44, 52
Rosenberg, J. 137
Rosenzweig, S., 19, 33
Rosner-Salazar, T., 237, 257
Ross, M. 137
Rothchild, E., 208, 214
Roughgarden, J., 11
Rubin, E., 161, 164, 173-174
Rusbult, C., 65, 86, 93
Russell, S., 70, 227, 234
Ruth, G., 136
Rutter, M., 39, 42, 51
Ryan, R., 18-19, 22, 30

• S •

Sabaawi, M., 33
Sanders, C., 66, 70
Santangelo, L. 179, 190
Santiago, C., 78, 193
Saunders, R., 182, 193
Sayare, S., 97, 117
Scherer, M., 82, 93
Schier, M., 257
Schmidt, K., 23, 33, 81, 92
Schmitt, S., 99, 118
Schneider, H., 92
Schrodt, P., 149, 151, 154
Schroeder, L., 214
Schultz, B., 257, 258
Schwartz, G., 19, 33
Scott, A., 68, 69
Scott, C., 112, 118
Seaman, C., 233
Seaton, P., 226, 234
Segal, Z., 26, 32, 33
Segrin, C., 138, 154
Segrist, K., 137
Seibold, D., 244, 258
Seidel, A., 236, 254
Seligman, M., 3, 11
Sellnow, T., 188, 193

Seo, M., 186, 192
Shackelford, T., 78, 93
Shalev, A., 176, 178-179, 192
Shamah, D., 141, 154
Shapiro, J. 19, 21, 29-30, 32- 33, 53, 73
Shaver, P. 24, 56-57, 72-73
Shaw, J., 177, 187, 192
Shea, A., 8, 11, 121, 124, 136
Sheen, J., 203, 216
Shenoy, S., 5, 131, 138, 150, 152, 154, 260
Shepherd, G., 143, 154
Shi, J., 129, 137
Shierholz, H., 237, 254
Shirky, C., 187, 192
Shoji, S., 44, 51
Shorey, H., 150, 154, 180-181, 185, 192-193, 215
Shu, H., 203, 216
Shultz, J., 177, 192, 244
Sibinga, E., 20, 33
Siddiqui, K., 187, 191
Siegler, K., 188, 192
Sigmon, D., 11, 214, 215
Sillars, A., 60, 72, 182-183, 192
Sim, S., 224-225, 233- 234
Simpson, A., 22, 32
Simpson, J. 72, 92, 239, 257
Singh, N., 29, 33
Sithamparanathan, K., 248, 257
Smallbone, S., 241, 256
Smart, L., 63, 69
Smith, C. 87, 93
Smith, G., 17, 23, 24, 30, 31
Smith, M. 33,
Snyder, 4, 6, 8-9, 11, 39- 40, 44, 48, 52, 61, 72-73, 84, 93, 99-100, 106, 118, 121, 124, 134, 137, 149, 150, 154, 157, 165, 168-169, 174, 180-182, 184-186, 189-190, 192-193, 205-206, 210, 214-215, 221, 223-234, 245, 257
Socha, T., 1, 4, 9, 12, 54, 64, 78, 92, 194, 204, 216, 219, 223, 234, 258, 259

Solomon, D., 54, 55, 57, 66, 72, 73, 250
Somers, T., 212
Sommer, K., 86, 91
Sonn, C. 241, 243, 257
Soule, K., 77, 93
Southwick, J., 191, 243, 256
Spark, N., 1, 12
Sparks, L. 4, 48, 52, 195- 202, 207- 209, 212- 216, 219, 260
Speca, M., 18, 30
Speers, M., 254
Springer, C?. 51, 53, 71, 92, 134, 191, 215, 251
Squires, C., 242, 257
Srinivas, V., 88, 91
Stafford, L., 57, 74
Stan, C., 67, 73
Stanley, S., 16, 29, 33, 178-179, 186, 193
Stanton, A., 206, 215
Starr, E., 221, 234
Stavrou, A., 163, 175
Steil, R., 30
Stein, B., 187, 191
Steinberg, L., 200, 213
Steiner, M., 82, 90
Stephens, J., 249, 252
Sternhouse, V., 237, 257
Steuber, K., 65, 66, 72
Stevens, S., 241, 256
Stewart, S., 32
Stocker, S., 86, 93
Stoecker, R., 236, 257
Stone, C., 122, 137, 150, 155
Storey, L., 174
Stotland, E., 180, 193, 245, 258
Stovall, D., 236, 251
Stover, E., 175
Street, R., 191, 213
Strosahl, K., 28, 31, 32
Suchday, S., 88, 91
Sullivan, W., 162, 174
Sulsky, L., 77, 91
Sum, A., 122, 137
Sun, S., 86, 192, 248, 258

Sunwolf, 244, 258
Sutton, R., 60, 71, 73-74
Swane, C., 202, 206, 213
Swartz, O., 238, 255, 257, 258
Sympson, S., 11, 182, 193, 215

• T •

Tabak, B., 83, 93
Tajfel, H., 137
Tan, S., 44, 49
Tanielian, T., 187, 191
Tanner, J., 23, 136, 137
Tate, E., 253
Taylor, A., 130, 137
Taylor, B. 101, 116, 117
Taylor, J., 138, 151, 182, 193, 214, 215
Teachout, W., 244, 252
Teasdale, J., 26, 32-33
Tedeschi, R., 179, 186, 188, 193
Tell, B., 137
Templeton, R., 91, 240, 258
ten Klooster, P., 30
Terry, M., 62, 71
Teuscher, U., 137
The PEW Center on the States, 99, 117
The World Fact Book, 99, 118
Theiss, J., 55, 65, 73
Theron, L., 143, 155
Thoburn, J., 21, 32
Thome, B., 202, 206, 213
Thompson, A., 12
Thompson, E., 12
Thompson, L. 180, 193
Thompson, M., 243, 253
Thomson, R., 180, 181, 190
Thompson, T., 200, 214
Tindle, H., 19, 32
Toarmino, D., 32
Todorov, N., 64, 70
Tol, W., 160, 174
Toney, L., 23, 24, 30

Toosi, M., 129, 137
Torres, A., 4, 9, 219, 260
Tracy, S., 59, 73, 112, 118, 150, 155
Trees, A., 124, 135, 188, 193
Trejnowska, A., 21, 31
Trickett, P., 203, 212
Trubskyy, M., 137
Tryon, E., 236, 257
Tugade, M., 41, 42, 50, 52
Tummala-Narra, P. 241, 258
Turkle, S., 2, 12
Turner, J., 137
Turner, L. 133-134, 140-143, 146, 148, 150-152
Turner, M., 197, 207, 209, 215
Turner, P., 142,155
Turniski, M., 222, 233

• U •

U.S. Geological Survey, 177, 193
Updegraff, 17, 30
USC Shoah Foundation, 224, 234

• V •

Van Dam, N., 23, 33
Van Dusen, D., 59, 73
Van Horn, C., 122, 137
Van Kessel, 93
Van Lange, P., 64, 71
Van Solinge, H., 137
Vanden Hoek, K.. 64, 70
Vangelisti, A., 53-57, 66, 69-71, 73-74, 78, 93, 182-183, 192, 260
Vasquez, C., 193
Veale, A., 163, 175
Vedder, R., 122, 137
Veehof, M., 30
Veil, S., 188, 189, 193
Verjee, B., 236, 258

Vidales, D., 179, 193
Vilaythong, A., 44, 52
Villagran, M., 145, 147, 155, 196, 200, 214-215
Vinck, P., 159, 160, 175
Vos, F., 177, 190

• W •

Wachs, K., 20, 21, 33
Wade, N., 85, 94, 237, 258
Wadsworth, M., 189, 193
Wahler, R., 33
Walach, H., 23, 30, 33
Waldron, V., 64, 74
Walker, K., 7, 11, 245-246, 248, 255
Wallace, H., 64, 74, 88, 94, 176, 260
Walsh, F., 144, 151, 182, 186, 193
Wang, M., 129, 137, 237, 258
Wanzer, M., 46, 48, 50, 52
Ware, L., 214
Warren, K., 237, 258
Washienko, K. 8, 12
Watson, P. 178, 193
Watzlawick, P. 12, 121, 137, 162, 175, 237, 258
Waugh, C., 41, 50
Way, B., 18, 31
Weakland, J., 8, 12, 121, 137, 237, 258
Webb, J., 134, 152, 191, 253
Weber, K., 47, 51
Weiner, D., 19, 32, 82, 90
Weir, J.. 38, 51
Weiss, R., 35, 83, 94, 184, 188, 190
Welker, L., 240, 258
Wells, J., 178, 193
Welton, S., 21, 32
Wenzel, K., 87, 94, 127, 135
Wertlieb, D., 3, 11
West, R., 149, 146, 151, 155
West, S. 82, 93
Westburg, N., 48, 52

Westgard, J., 49
Westheimer, J., 237, 255, 258
Wetchler, J., 181, 191
Wheeler, J., 236, 255
Whitman, S., 28, 30
Wieland, S., 139, 153
Wiemann, J., 198, 212, 216
Wierda, M., 175
Wieselquist, J., 64, 74
Wiklund, C., 181, 193
Wilkins, J., 44, 52
Wilkum, K. 147, 155
Williams, J. xiii, xviii
Williams, J. C., 29, 33
Williams, J. M. 26, 33
Williams, M., 17, 18, 33
Williams, T., 173
Wills, T., 66, 69, 204, 216
Wilson, K., 28, 31, 32
Wilson, S., 8, 12, 119, 147, 155, 184, 194, 211, 216, 237, 253, 258
Wines, W., 228, 234
Wingrove, J., 26, 33
Winocur, G., 135
Winton, A., 33
Wirtz, J. 67, 71
Wohl, M., 88, 94
Woodyatt, L., 87, 94
Worden, S., 159, 175
World Economic Forum, 137
Worthington, E., 64, 72, 81-83, 85-86, 91-94
Wortley, R., 241, 256
Wright, K., 56, 73, 124, 137, 199-200, 214, 216
Wu, L., 203, 216
Wyche, K. 241, 256

• Y •

Yang, T., 31, 181, 192
Ybasco, F., 11, 215

Ye, F., 236, 258
Yorio, P., 236, 258
Youndt, M. 127, 135
Young, S., 53- 55, 58-59, 74, 78, 93-94, 120, 147, 151, 233, 258

• Z •

Zamperini, L., 2
Zapata, C., 35, 50
Zautra, A., 7, 12, 121, 136, 194, 203, 214
Zeckhauser, R., 177, 190
Zeelen, J., 173
Zhang, S., 57, 74, 82, 83, 92, 186, 192
Zijlstra, B., 25, 31
Zimmerman, M., 7, 12, 184, 194
Zuckerman, N., 236, 254
Zukin, C., 122, 137
Zvolensky, M., 32
Zylowska, L., 18, 29, 33

Subject Index

• A •

abuse, xiii, 9, 80
    See child
    human rights, 159
    sexual, 241
    See survivor
    verbal, 82
    victimization, 88
acceptance, 2, 16, 20, 23, 28-30
    following transgression, 87
    and hope, 164-166
acknowledgement, 83
activism, 236-240, 244-245, 247-248, 250-251
adaptable/adaptation, 7, 25, 63, 100, 130, 141, 147, 157, 178, 197, 201, 236, 238, 249
advice,
    advice-seeking, 134
    career, 127
    community, 128
    and coping, 142-143
    perceived, 66
affection, 79, 83, 85
affirmation, 167
agency, 6, 8, 9, 39-40, 45, 48, 61, 84, 89, 165, 130, 250
    actor, 113
    agents, 158
    and critical pedagogy, 239
    See Dramatistic Pentad
    and Hope, 84, 89, 100, 106, 115, 121, 149-150, 157-158, 168-169, 180-181, 184, 186, 210, 245-246,
    See resilience
    self-agency, 148
age-related, 131, 197, 201, 210, 215
aggression, 20, 29, 34, 37, 54, 63, 80-81
    aggressive communication, 37
aging, 22, 134, 197, 200-201
ambivalence, 163
anger, 21, 56, 64, 65, 78-79, 82, 84, 85, 106, 208
apology, 64-65, 69, 82, 83, 86-88
appreciation, 2, 10, 149
argument, 49, 78, 128, 207
assessments, 17, 83
assets, 6-8, 63, 121, 125, 133, 141, 185, 202-203, 241
    See hope
    See resilience
attachment, 21, 25, 192
attitudes, 104, 126, 131, 143, 207, 236
audience, 5, 113, 162

• B •

balance, , 21, 29, 128, 139, 179,
    content-relational messages, 210
    constructing war stories, 223
    homeostatic, 7, 142, 179
    work-family, 5, 139
    work-life, 21, 128
    See Dramastic Pentad
battle(s),
    See war
bravery, 134
broaden-and-build theory, 41-42
buffer, 66-68, 184

See Resilience
bullying, 9, 46

• C •

cancer, 4, 19, 46, 47, 129, 195-211, 219, 220, 231-232
caregiver/caregivers, 29, 32, 48, 49, 112, 140, 143, 155, 196-197, 199-202, 207-211, 214
children, xvi, 87, 90, 100, 107-108, 143, 146-149, 156-161, 163-166, 168-169, 171-173, 181, 184, 187, 198, 207, 212
   See assets
   and autism, 29
   Childen's Hope Scale, 205
   and discipline, 81-82
   education, 10, 53, 62, 247-249
   and family decision-making, 200, 220
   See family
   health conversations, 187, 198, 207
   human development, 3
   See humor
   See mindfulness
   modeling hope, 184
   See parent-child
   See resilience
   socialization, 60-62
   See Uganda
   See war
citizenship, 236, 250
close relationships, 45, 76-77, 86, 90, 186, 203-204
closeness, 27, 35, 45
cognition, 11, 40, 41, 44, 126
collaboration/ collaborative, 200, 242
comfort, 59, 66, 68, 120, 157, 208
commitment, 20, 28, 31, 75, 80, 88, 91, 94, 125, 133, 248
communication activism pedagogy, xvii, 233-234, 238-240, 243-244, 246, 248, 250-251
communication barriers, 132, 157-158, 169, 172, 195, 197, 200-201, 209-210
communication competence, 44, 76, 126, 198-199, 202

communication effectiveness, 20, 27, 59, 198-199, 225, 229, 232
communication interventions, 26-29, 209-211, 240, 246
communication networks, 100, 148, 158
communication patterns, 183, 200
communication practices, 27, 196
communication process, 189
communication skills, 184, 197, 209, 240
constructive communication, 75
community, 2, 6, 7, 10, 69, 104-105, 128, 138, 141-144, 148, 159-161, 166-171, 183-186, 188, 235-238, 240-249
compassion, 21, 149
compensate, 83, 86, 121, 184
competence, 17, 19, 35, 44, 59, 122, 154, 157-158, 198-199, 203, 244
conflict, 11, 20, 35, 39, 47, 56, 60-61, 65-66, 80-81, 83, 139, 149, 156, 158-160, 173
   Gottman's cascade model of marital conflict, 83,
   strategies, 201
coping, 9, 18, 27, 40, 41, 42, 43, 44, 45, 46, 47, 48, 49, 64, 68, 76, 89, 90, 176, 178, 179, 181, 183, 184, 185, 186, 187, 188, 189, 202, 204, 205, 215, 227, 243
courage, 15, 30, 32, 143, 205
creative/creativity, 41-42, 43, 244
critical, 33, 49, 59, 63, 84, 89, 133, 141, 160, 179, 180, 185, 189, 196, 239, 251
culture, 98, 100, 140, 143, 147, 153, 161-162, 168, 172, 174, 183, 188, 191, 196, 228-230, 245
curiosity, 16, 25, 162

• D •

dark side, 69, 70, 72, 73, 93, 219
death, 9, 39, 99, 103, 145, 150, 159, 168-169, 171, 178, 193, 195, 200, 202, 219, 221, 223, 224, 230
deception, 54, 77-80, 90, 92

decision-making, 48, 105, 123, 134, 136, 161, 195, 197, 200, 205-208, 210, 215, 244-245
depression, 19, 20, 30, 32-33, 45, 46, 137, 193, 206, 219
destructive communication, 65
diagnosis, 6, 196-199, 200-204, 207, 209-210, 213, 215, 232
dialectics/dialectical, 4
    Dialectical Behavior Therapy, 27-28
    tensions, 188
dialogue, 4, 6, 10, 69, 156, 168, 170, 242
disappointment, 89, 93, 126, 150
disasters, xvi, 182-185, 189
    natural, 2, 4, 9, 138, 176-180, 187-189, 219-220, 236
    technological, 177
    as turning points, 179
disclosure, 55, 174
diversity, 135, 172, 251
divorce, 9, 64, 67, 76, 148-150, 189-190, 210
dramatism, 113-114
dramturigical perspective, 113, 114, 162
Dramatistic Pentad, 223, 225-226, 229
dying, 200

• E •

education, 29, 31, 33, 109, 110, 123-126, 129, 132, 135, 146, 152, 169, 235-240, 244-247, 249-252
efficacy, 45, 46, 48, 52, 92, 180, 184, 205,
emerging adulthood,
    See lifespan
emotion, 21, 27, 28, 31, 33, 35, 36, 39, 40, 41, 42, 43, 44, 49, 50, 53, 54, 56, 66, 67, 69, 71, 84, 85, 86, 88, 92, 102, 117, 180, 181, 196, 199, 203, 212, 245
emotional intelligence, 124
emotional support, 45, 90, 199, 201, 204, 215, 243
empathy, 21, 24, 36, 75, 82-84, 91, 94, 184
employment, 39, 119-127, 131-134, 136
empower, 184, 221

empowerment, 127, 153, 253
encouragement, 134
end-of-life, 49, 197, 199, 209, 214
engagement, 2, 16, 17, 22, 251
esteem, 17, 19, 35, 53, 55, 57, 63, 67, 69, 112, 123, 128, 135, 271, 276
ethics, 212, 228, 233
everyday, 5, 8, 16, 22, 31-32, 38, 45, 48, 50, 98, 114, 116, 138, 140, 142, 145, 146, 149, 153, 154, 174
equilibrium, 202-203, 236, 238
expectation, 89, 110, 127, 205, 245, 271
external assets, 202-203
    See resilience

• F •

face-saving, 160
face-threatening, 226-227
failure, 4, 40, 125, 171, 208, 241, 249-250
family, xii, 2, 5, 7, 10, 12, 27, 29, 31, 34, 38, 40, 46, 51, 54, 66, 74-76, 81-83, 88, 90-92, 94, 98, 104, 106-107, 114-115, 125, 128-129, 133-134, 138-155, 157, 164-165, 169, 171, 178, 182-183, 188-191, 193, 195-198, 200-202, 205-214, 226-227, 230, 231, 232, 252
    See patient-family communication
fear, 15, 57, 72, 78-79, 85, 102, 149, 157, 174, 198, 211
first-order change vs. second order change, 8, 66-67, 121-122, 105-106, 182-183
flexible, 98, 124, 125
flexibility, 41-43, 125, 131, 135
flourish, 3, 126
forgiveness, xv, 21, 31, 63-65, 70, 72-76, 79-94, 159-160, 170-171
friendship, 34, 41, 43, 83, 93, 220

• G •

goal/goals, 6, 8-10, 36, 39-40, 45, 59, 61-64, 66, 73, 76-78, 84, 89, 99-

100, 106, 115-116, 121, 125-126, 132-134, 149-150, 157, 163, 169, 176, 180-186, 189, 196-199, 206, 210-212, 239, 242, 244, 245
gratitude, 172-173, 185
group(s), xii, 17, 20, 22, 27, 109, 122, 129, 141, 156, 158, 166, 184, 186, 188, 200, 241, 244, 246
grudge theory, 86

• H •

habits, 98
happiness, 11, 42, 45, 63, 84-85, 89, 121
happy, 39, 130, 148, 169
hardiness,
    See resilience theory
harmony, 68, 160
healing, 42, 85, 188
health, xiii, 9-10, 16-19, 21, 28-29, 39, 40-42, 44, 84, 88, 121, 129-130, 141, 146, 150, 178, 181, 187, 195-198, 200, 201-203, 205, 207-211, 220-221, 227, 244
health communication, 196-197, 211
    cancer communication, 207
health outcomes, 18, 28, 195-198, 207-209
healthcare, xiii, 30, 222
hope, xi-xvii, 9, 10, 84, 88-90, 133-134, 176, 187
    See acceptance
    across the lifespan, 2
    See activism
    anchoring, 165, 185
    and apologies, 64
    and children, 160
    and communal coping, 186-187
    and community, 170, 235, 242-243
    and coping, 185-186
    critical pedagogy, 239, 245
    and disabilities, 149
    and disasters, 180, 183-184
    and education, 124, 235, 238, 245-250
    building, 3
    See family

false hope, 63
and forgiveness, 75
and healthcare, 195-196, 201-202, 206, 208
Herth's Hope Index, 205
hopeful communication, 188
    and humor, 35-37, 42, 46, 48-49
    and hurtful experiences, 54, 56-57
    and hurtful feedback, 61-63, 66
See interpretive social science, 162
origins, 180
and mindfulness, 25
messages of, 182-183, 195-196, 197, 206-210, 223
and parent-child communication, 199-200
pathways/pathways thinking, 5-6, 8-9, 39-40, 48, 61-64, 66, 68, 84, 99-100, 106, 115, 121, 123-126, 134, 149-150, 157, 169, 180-182, 184, 186, 189, 210, 221, 223, 245
See politeness theory
and prisons, 98-99, 102-104, 107-108, 110-111, 113-115.
and reducing face threat, 58
and rituals, 168, 171
Snyder's Elaborated Hope Model, 181-182
Snyder's Hope Theory, xi, 4-6, 8-9, 39-40, 44-45, 99-100, 106, 121, 134, 149-150, 157-158, 169, 180, 190, 205, 210
See social justice
and social networks, 68
sources, 125, 127
and stories, 163-166, 172-173, 188-189, 220-221, 223, 229, 232
and tough love, 76
thinking hopefully, 185
trait hope scale, 181
and unemployment, 120-121, 123, 125
and wellbeing, 206, 211
and work, 139

humor, xiv, 5, 7, 34-39, 42-52, 59, 73, 80, 85, 204, 213, 249
    arousal/relief/release theory, 37
    Incongruity theory, 37
    superiority/disparagement theories, 37
Hurricane Katrina, 178, 181, 191, 193, 221
hurt/hurtful, xiv-xv, 4
    experience of, 53-75, 84-86, 166
    of humor, 34-35,
    interpersonal, 39, 48
    preventing, 56-58
    messages, 54-55, 78-79, 80, 81-82

• I •

identity
    anchors, 158-160, 166-167, 172
    community, 143, 159
    construction, 146, 149-150
    exploration, 122-123, 133
    loss of, 9, 160
    professional, 122, 125-126, 128, 132-133
    See resilience
    social, 4, 139, 164
    secure, 57
    stigmatized, 112
    228-229, 240, 246
incarceration, 97-99, 102, 107, 109, 114-115
incongruity theory, 37
independence, 60
instrumental support, 204, 243
intelligence, 7
interdisciplinary, 199
intergenerational, 127, 161, 248
interpersonal communication, 38, 47, 72, 128, 156-157, 170, 182-183, 196, 205, 208, 223, 226
interpersonal transgressions,
    See transgressions
interpretive social science, 162
interventions, 26-29, 206, 209, 211, 240, 242, 246
intimacy, 45, 107

• J •

jealous/jealousy, 78, 79
job loss, xiii, 6, 9, 141, 143, 148, 150
job search, 127, 132
joke/joking, 34-35, 37, 41
joy, 41-42, 105
justice, 86, 115, 159
    See social justice

• K •

kinship, 34

• L •

laughter, 10, 36, 42, 44, 48-49, 108, 203-204
learning, 2, 6-8, 10, 19, 166
    See education
    environments, 124-126
    the "hard way," 62-63
    histories, 181
    to "live again," 148
    perspective-taking, 144
    to "think hopefully," 185, 189
    service-learning, 235-236, 238, 245, 247-249, 251
    and uncertainty, 123-124
life skills, 184
lifespan, xiii, 2, 17, 22, 25, 27-29, 39, 53, 68-69, 90, 100, 119, 121, 137-140, 196-197, 209-210, 222
    baby boomer generation, 129
    See children
    communication patterns, 187, 201, 223
    and development, 161, 197, 201
    early adulthood, 195, 222
    early childhood, 89
    emerging adults/adulthood, 122-126, 128, 135, 136, 137
    and feedback, 60
    See forgiveness
    hope across the lifespan, 183, 197

See health
See humor
See inmates
intergenerational, 127, 141, 161, 248
lifespan perspective, 57
middle age/adulthood, 195, 222
older adults, 15, 19, 48, 53, 82, 86, 90, 121, 128-129, 131-134, 200-201, 207, 209
See parent(s)
physical/mental changes, 200-201
and resilience process, 16, 147, 150, 196-197
See stories
See work-family
listen, 1, 63, 172, 220, 226
listening, 29, 198, 230
loneliness, 132-133
Lord's Resistance Army/LRA, 156- 160, 162-165, 167-169, 171
loss, 2, 6, 9, 39, 78, 116, 123, 178, 205
ambiguous, 148-149
cognitive, 201
of employment/job, 39, 130, 141-143, 147-148
See identity
See natural disasters
of property, 158, 177-178, 189
of relational qualities, 78, 141
of social ties, 133, 161
as part of the resilience process, 145-146, 188-189
and uncertainty, 182
love, 10, 42, 59, 67, 76, 105, 149-150

• M •

marriage, 2, 67, 83-84
marital conflict, 83
marital dissatisfaction, 35
mediate, 21
mentor, 62
military, 120, 147, 155, 222, 228, 231, 233
mindful, 5, 9, 15-18, 21-29, 133, 147, 210
mindfulness, xiv, 7, 15-33, 147

morality, 164
motivation, 6, 7, 8, 40, 59, 84, 120, 128, 134, 157, 166, 180, 211, 236, 239, 245

• N •

narrative, 75, 126, 134-135, 146-147, 160-162, 172, 188, 204, 224-225, 229-230, 240, 242
as method, 100-101
prison stories, 101, 105-107, 109, 113-114
natural disasters,
See disasters
negative affect, 19, 56
negative emotions, 41, 43, 54, 56, 78, 84-85, 88-89, 147, 203
nonverbal, 36, 55, 59, 85, 111, 163, 183, 198
nursing, 27, 46-47, 49, 205

• O •

older adults,
See lifespan
open-mindedness, 43-44
openness, 16, 23, 41, 77
optimism, 27, 41-42, 45, 58, 84, 127, 184, 188, 205, 246, 251
online communication, 139, 143, 156, 176
ePortfolios, 126-127
for family narrative construction, 147
optimistic, 45, 127
organizational, 98, 139, 140-141, 144, 150
communication, 228-229, 237

• P •

pain, 2, 17, 18, 19, 42, 53-54, 68, 75, 106, 206
parent(s), xiii, 15, 22, 27, 29, 55, 60-63, 76, 81-82, 84, 89-90, 100, 104, 106,

SUBJECT INDEX

133, 144, 148-149, 160-161, 165, 169, 187, 198-200, 207, 220, 248
  See family
  See mindfulness
  See parent-child communication
parent-child communication, 41, 61, 68, 198-199
passion, 239
patient-family communication, 198
pedagogy, 235-236, 238-239, 249-251
personal control, 45, 245
personal growth, 3, 56, 68, 176
physical, 28, 37, 41, 147, 188-189
  See abuse
  being, 173
  benefits, 19, 199
  complaints, 17
  conflict, 28, 80, 108
  events, 250
  health, 38, 44, 88, 131, 164, 200, 206
  pain, 54
  See readiness
  See resources
  structure, 110
  symptoms, 206
pleasure, 36-37
politeness theory, 58-59, 70
positive affect, xiv, 19, 27, 35-36, 42, 211, 247
positive communication/messages, xiii, 38, 206, 233
positivity, 10, 36, 149, 204
prison, 97-102, 104, 106-115, 148, 170, 224, 242-243
  See inmates
privacy, 80
psychology/psychological, 38-39, 62, 108, 201, 207, 226
  adjustment, 28, 47, 205
  benefits, 18-19, 37. 64, 160, 228
  conditions, 19
  distress, 66, 178
  harm, 160
  and health, 19, 39, 41, 85
  See hope
  See humor
  See resilience
  See resilience theory
  See resources
  symptomatology, 204, 206
  See trauma
  See uncertainty
  well-being, 35, 39-40, 42, 49, 87, 202, 206

• Q •

quality, 1, 223
  See Resilience
  of communication, 20, 83, 198, 202, 207
  of family relationships, 232
  of health, 29, 209
  See hope
  See humor
  of life, 17, 19-21, 25, 29, 49, 131, 197, 207
  of municipalities, 183
  relational, 20, 57, 88, 205
  See resilience
  of sexuality, 19
  of support, 67

• R •

rapport, 40
readiness, 176, 183
reconciliation, 64-65, 75-76, 78, 83, 159,
recover/recovery, 7, 63, 68, 110, 157, 176, 178-179, 181-187, 189, 199, 223, 236-237, 241, 250-251
  economic, 120, 133
  recovery process, 109, 160
  See resilience
  See resilience theory
reframing, 8, 44
relationships, xi, 128, 134, 138, 140, 142-143
  See close relationships
  See interpersonal relationships
  See family
  See lifepan
  See social networks
  See work

religious, 180, 220, 225
resilience/resiliency, xi–xvii, 10, 11, 15, 18, 19, 43, 45, 49, 51, 85, 104, 117, 151, 174, 191, 205, 225, 227
  and anticipatory messages/scripts, 75-76
  as coping process, 40, 65, 67, 84, 89, 109, 186
  as "magic," 3, 5-6, 10, 168
  buffer/buffering
  building, 39-40, 63, 66, 68
  "collective" resilience, 241-242
  and community, 110, 164-173, 240-244
  communication's role, 2, 4-6, 101, 104, 109, 115, 123, 127, 139, 141, 142, 144-147, 149, 157-158, 164, 176, 183-184, 188-189, 196, 204, 221-223, 229
  and Dramaturgical perspective
  as educational/learning process, 63, 68, 75-76, 110, 124, 127, 149, 235-236-246, 248
  etymology, 100, 223
  equilibrium, 202-203, 236, 238
  external resources, 7, 9, 40-41
  See hardiness
  See hope
  See humor
  See family
  internal assets, 7, 16-17, 21, 35
  and the lifespan, 7, 29, 36, 42, 48, 56, 100, 139, 143, 145-147, 197-198, 203, 223
  memorable messages/moments, 105-106, 224
  messages of, 5, 75-76, 195-197, 200-201, 204, 206-211
  mindsets, 104, 126, 134
  organizational, 109, 127
  performing, 75-76, 111, 113-114, 149-150, 230-233
  as positive communication, 223
  and power, 146-147
  protective factors, 40
  and reappraisal, 67
  See resilience theory
  as ritual, 133, 141, 150, 160, 161, 164, 165-166, 168-170
  See social justice
  See social support
  spirituality/religiosity, 105, 220
  See stress
  See stressors
  See survival
  as transformation, 250-251
resilience theory, 36, 124
  adaptation, 7, 63, 100, 130, 141, 147, 157, 178, 197-198, 201, 208, 236, 249
  adjustment trajectories, xi, 145, 179, 186
  See broaden-and-build theory
  Buzzanell's process theory, 7, 100, 138-150, 158, 163, 166, 202-203
  developmental perspectives, 7, 100, 109, 121, 157, 197
  ecological, 7, 9, 40-41, 68, 68-69, 89-90, 98-99, 100, 113, 121, 123, 127, 138, 144, 185-186, 201, 238, 249
  See first order change vs. second order change
  hardiness, xii, 15, 28, 179
  outcome-oriented, 7, 88, 104
  patterns, 6, 202,243
  posttraumatic growth, 76, 179, 189, 203
  psychological, 40, 104, 121, 126, 134, 138, 202-203, 208
  resilience-promoting communication/RPC, xiii, 4, 46
  risk and resilience/resiliency, 7
  trait perspectives, 7, 41, 89, 163
resilient, 15, 18, 22, 39, 42, 43, 44, 49, 66, 75, 89, 100, 104, 106, 109, 110, 171, 178, 182, 203, 208, 235, 243, 244, 247, 250
resistance, 146, 179, 240, 250
resources, 2, 4, 6-10, 18, 40-43, 45, 56, 68, 78, 84, 89-90, 98, 121, 130, 133, 141, 143-146, 178, 180, 182, 184, 186, 202-203, 238, 241-243, 250

respect, 10, 78, 105, 161, 164, 171, 227, 236, 242
responsibility, 1, 64, 68, 82, 83, 87, 186, 226
responsiveness, 51
restraint, 58
roles, 4, 76, 86, 112, 123-124, 140-142, 172, 195, 201-202, 210, 220-221, 229-231, 247
romantic relationship(s), 35, 47, 76, 78, 83, 143

• S •

sacrifice, 170
satisfaction, 19, 20-22, 27, 29, 35, 46-48, 64, 67, 88-89, 125, 128, 198-199, 210
Sentiment override hypothesis, 83
sexual abuse, 241
sexuality, 19
social interaction, xvii, xv, xvii, 47, 201
social justice, 236-240, 243, 245-250
social networks, 66, 90, 114, 186
social support, xiii, 7, 41, 45, 66-68, 115, 121, 124, 125, 127-128, 133, 147, 160, 184, 186, 211, 241, 243-244
socioemotional selectivity theory, 201
soldiers, 2, 157-160, 162-167, 169-172
  See war
stability, 39, 45, 70, 78, 88, 120, 126, 249
story/stories, 1, 9, 16, 18, 60, 101-103, 106, 108-111, 113, 116, 141-143, 147, 149-150, 157-166, 169, 171-173, 188, 195, 204, 205, 219-232, 242
stress, xii, 9, 16-18, 20-21, 38-49, 73, 86, 89, 129, 145, 160, 178-179, 184, 211, 226-227, 236
stressors, 7-9, 39, 45-48, 66-67, 100, 121, 124, 128, 141, 176, 183-184, 186
support network, 45, 128, 136, 137
supportive communication, 67, 186-187
survival/survivors, xiii, 2, 5, 134, 164, 171, 188, 204, 221, 223, 229
system(s), 180, 209, 238-239, 240-241, 249
 balance, 7
 belief, 196
 change, 7, 238, 240, 245, 247-251
 economic, 236-237
 ecosystem, 7
 See family
 See first order change vs. second order change
 homeostatic balance, 179
 immune, 18
 political, 244
 power, 239
 See prison
 relational, 180, 183
 support, 43, 67
 and structures, 237
 warning and response, 184, 188

• T •

therapy, 19, 28, 90, 227-228
thinking, 2, 3, 5, 6, 8-9, 42, 45, 61, 67, 90, 98, 100, 106, 115, 122, 134, 145, 149, 150, 157, 165, 168-169, 173, 180-182, 184, 186, 204, 206, 210-223, 227, 249
thriving, 204
training, 2, 17-22, 26-29, 81, 112, 120, 122, 124, 131-132, 157, 169, 186, 211, 228, 243, 249
training programs, 81
transgression(s), xv, 21, 47, 63-64, 75-79, 81-90
trauma, xiii, 9, 39, 42, 46, 49, 141, 147, 150, 161, 176, 179-184, 186, 188-189, 228
trust, 61, 64, 75, 78, 82-83, 87, 156, 161, 185-186
truth, 77-78, 160, 167
turning points, 3, 179

• U •

Uganda, xvi, 10, 156-163, 168, 170, 172-173

uncertainty, 123-124, 130, 144, 161, 164, 187, 198, 202
understanding, 1, 2, 8, 10, 42-44, 46, 75, 89-90, 98, 100, 101, 111, 113, 128, 156, 158, 162-163, 172-173, 189, 197-198, 201-202, 207, 209, 222
unemployment, 4, 120, 121, 122, 134, 147, 150

• V •

values, 2, 10, 55, 188, 236, 239, 242, 244
verbal, 20, 36, 59, 67, 78, 80, 82, 163, 183, 198, 231
victim, 55, 64, 65, 66, 67, 68, 76, 78, 82, 83, 84, 85, 86, 87, 88, 89, 161
violence, 63, 69, 156, 161, 162, 164, 169, 170, 239, 240, 241, 246

• W •

war, xvi, 1, 2, 4, 9-10, 160-161, 169, 171-173, 177, 180, 204, 219-232
well-being, 17, 19, 27, 29, 35, 38-39, 40, 42, 81, 87, 128, 130, 132-134, 138, 141, 154, 170, 184, 202, 206, 211
wellness, 178, 205
wisdom, 188
work, 1, 2, 5, 16, 18-19, 21, 29, 34, 43, 47, 49, 58, 62-63, 67-68, 70, 71, 75, 109, 112, 120, 123-128, 130-131, 133-134, 138-148, 150, 158, 160, 162, 164-168, 170, 172, 181-182, 184, 186-187, 211, 220-221, 224, 238-242, 245-248
work-family, 139-150
work and personal life theory, 139
workload, 131
workplace, 126-127, 131-132, 140

LIFESPAN COMMUNICATION
Children, Families, and Aging

Thomas J. Socha, *General Editor*

From first words to final conversations, communication plays an integral and significant role in all aspects of human development and everyday living. The Lifespan Communication: Children, Families, and Aging series seeks to publish authored and edited scholarly volumes that focus on relational and group communication as they develop over the lifespan (infancy through later life). The series will include volumes on the communication development of children and adolescents, family communication, peer-group communication (among age cohorts), intergenerational communication, and later-life communication, as well as longitudinal studies of lifespan communication development, communication during lifespan transitions, and lifespan communication research methods. The series includes college textbooks as well as books for use in upper-level undergraduate and graduate courses.

Thomas J. Socha, Series Editor | *tsocha@odu.edu*
Mary Savigar, Acquisitions Editor | *mary.savigar@plang.com*

To order other books in this series, please contact our Customer Service Department at:

        (800) 770-LANG (within the U.S.)
        (212) 647-7706 (outside the U.S.)
        (212) 647-7707 FAX

Or browse online by series at www.peterlang.com

www.ingramcontent.com/pod-product-compliance
Ingram Content Group UK Ltd.
Pitfield, Milton Keynes, MK11 3LW, UK
UKHW022238230426
12048UKWH00018BA/1327